You and Your Future

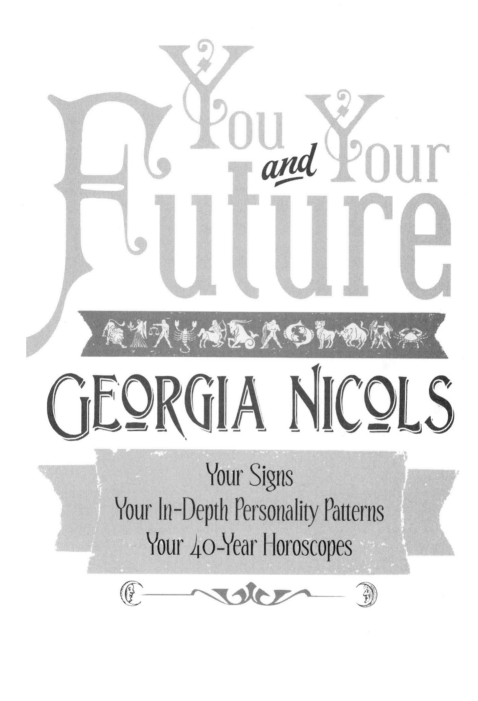

You and Your Future

GEORGIA NICOLS

Your Signs
Your In-Depth Personality Patterns
Your 40-Year Horoscopes

ANANSI

This edition published in 2011 by
House of Anansi Press Inc.
110 Spadina Avenue, Suite 801
Toronto, ON, M5V 2K4
Tel. 416-363-4343
Fax 416-363-1017
www.anansi.ca

Distributed in Canada by
HarperCollins Canada Ltd.
1995 Markham Road
Scarborough, ON, M1B 5M8
Toll free tel. 1-800-387-0117

15 14 13 12 11   1 2 3 4 5

Library and Archives Canada Cataloguing in Publication

Nicols, Georgia
You and your future / written by Georgia Nicols.

ISBN 978-0-88784-237-5

1. Astrology. 2. Horoscopes. I. Title.

BF1708.1.N53 2010   133.5   C2010-902473-7

JACKET DESIGN: Daniel Cullen
TEXT DESIGN: Daniel Cullen

 Canada Council Conseil des Arts
for the Arts du Canada

 ONTARIO ARTS COUNCIL
CONSEIL DES ARTS DE L'ONTARIO

We acknowledge for their financial support of our publishing program the Canada Council for the Arts, the Ontario Arts Council, and the Government of Canada through the Canada Book Fund.

Printed and bound in Canada

With gratitude to Pat for his loving
support and encouragement every step of the way.

With grateful thanks to my friend Margaret Atwood
for sharing with me her knowledge of publishing ways.

And to the memory of my wonderful
father, John, and my brother, Fred.

CONTENTS

"Naming your myth is the first step in having power over it."
RICHARD IDEMON

PREFACE

Ever since I discovered horoscope columns in newspapers when I was twelve years old, I've been intrigued by astrology. It seemed to me to be a fascinating, esoteric source of knowledge. I never heard about it at school, or from my parents, or at church. In the small town where I grew up, nobody talked about it. And yet, there it was in the newspaper for everyone to see!

Once I started to develop crushes on boys and fall madly in love, I avidly read my sign and my boyfriend's sign, looking for help about LIFE! My parents dismissed these columns, and no one else I knew seemed interested in them.

Nevertheless, I would lie on the floor in the living room with the newspaper, studying the horoscope columns, learning about the signs of my family and friends. I never really questioned how it worked, but I think I vaguely believed some kind of subtle vibration from the heavens affected us, and that this was the basis of astrology. I think a lot of people think that the movement of the stars affects us.

The truth is I don't know why astrology works but I don't think the movements of the planets and stars affect us at all. How could they? They're so far away!

Of course, the Moon affects us. It is much, much closer to the Earth, and science has established that the Moon has a gravitational pull on bodies of water, thereby causing the ocean tides. And we are bodies of water (no matter how much beer we drink). And there's no doubt that a Full Moon is reflected in police reports and records at emergency wards in hospitals. (Oh yeah!) And, of course, the word "lunatic" has its origin in the word "lunar" (meaning related to the Moon).

But the planets and stars? That seems far-fetched.

Nevertheless, I don't worry about why astrology works because I know that it does. When forced to come up with an explanation, I say something like this:

Nothing in life exists in and of itself. Everything exists in relationship to something else. The concept of dark would not exist without the concept of light. The notion of up implies the notion of down. There is no in if there is no out. Everything is related.

For example, I am holding a pen in my hand. There are many definitions for this pen: it is a writing tool; it's made of metal and oil by-products; it's a possession of mine; it's a product made by Sanford Corporation. I could go on with different definitions. However, one definition of this pen in my hand is that it is *not anything else in the universe*. It's not the table or the piano or the lamp, or anything else in this room. It's not even another identical pen. It's just this *particular* pen.

In the same way, when a baby is born, at the moment it draws its first breath, giving it independence from its mother, it exists. And this existence is in juxtaposition to everything else in the universe.

This ever-present juxtaposition of everything means there is a *relationship between everything*. And if there is a relationship between everything, there is a *correlation*.

Astrology is based on this correlation. It reflects the correlation of the movement of the planets in the sky with people and events on planet Earth. Because these planets move in predictable cycles, we can predict similar cycles reflected in our own lives.

As above, so below.

The fact that everything is interconnected is, for me, why astrology works. Astrology is just a patterning of knowledge. It is a soft science about how our lives unfold.

You can approach this book like you would approach a buffet. Pick and choose what you want. Many people will read the sections on How to Be a Happier Aries, Taurus, etc. for all twelve signs. I think this is a great idea because in truth — *we all have all twelve signs in our makeup*. The time of our birth simply creates a different combination or "weighting" of these signs. You might say everyone has all the food groups in them — but some people are more meat and potatoes while some people are more salad. It's portion control!

As my hero Julia Child (Leo with Gemini Rising) would say, *"Bon appetit!"*

Georgia Nicols
Vancouver, B.C.
June 14, 2010

CHAPTER ONE

WHY ASTROLOGY?
WHY NOT?

For more than ten thousand years, astrologers were among the finest minds — mathematicians, scientists, doctors, and philosophers. Today, astrology still has an educated following. Every country in the world embraces its own form of astrology.

What I am suggesting is: why wouldn't you use this ancient system of wisdom to help you?

Astrology is not about vibes and crystal balls. Astrology is based on mathematics; specifically, the cycles of the Sun, the Moon, and the planets in our solar system.

I hope this book can help you learn more about yourself, help you to better plan your future, and help you to get a better handle on your life.

I use astrology in many ways, but here is one way it helped me:

> For thirteen years, I rented a townhouse on King's Road in Vancouver near the University of British Columbia. I loved living there. It was a close-knit neighbourhood, only one block long, and full of friendly, interesting people. (There were a few duds.)
>
> However, all the time I lived there, I also owned a piece of land on a nearby island. One day, to everyone's horror, we were all given eviction notices because our townhouses were to be torn down. We were being forced to move!
>
> Everyone began looking for places to rent or buy. I, however, simply moved into a new house on my island property, which I had built in the year prior to getting evicted.

Did I see the eviction coming? Of course not. Astrology is not a crystal ball. However, according to my own chart, I saw that I would be moving in the next year. Since this was inevitable, I started to build the house I had always dreamed of building.

This is just one way that looking at my chart has helped me. Being able to see a particular cycle in the future can be a godsend! It allows you to prepare yourself — psychologically, emotionally, and practically for whatever lies ahead.

Our lives are a series of cycles within cycles. Daily cycles, weekly cycles, monthly cycles, annual cycles, and the cycles of the changing seasons. Astrology is based on the mathematical cycles of the planets moving through the signs. A good astrologer can interpret data from these cycles and correlate them to the cycles of your chart and predict the future with reasonable accuracy.

And hey — of course you're concerned about the future. This is where you're going to spend the rest of your life!

CHAPTER TWO

YOU ARE MORE
THAN YOUR SIGN!

When you read your horoscope every day, most of you read one sign —
the sign that lines up with your birthday.[1] Many people do not know that your sign
("I'm a Leo!") is actually the sign where the Sun was when you were born. So, to
be more correct, your "sign" is your Sun Sign.

Confused?

Each of us has an astrological chart showing where all the planets are. That's how
astrology works. It shows the sign that your Sun is in and the sign that your Moon
is in and the sign that Mercury, Venus, Mars, and the rest of the planets are in. So
your "Sun Sign" is just one part of you.

You also have a Rising Sign. (This is sometimes called the Ascendant.) The Rising
Sign is très important! In fact, it is the biggest reason people of the same sign appear
to be so different.

What Is the Rising Sign?

Your birthday tells you what your Sun Sign is because your Sun Sign is based on
the *day of the year* you were born. The Rising Sign is based on the *time of day* you
were born, as well as the day of the year. This is more specific.

Your Rising Sign is your mask or your *persona*. It's how you project yourself
outwardly to the world. It has a lot to do with your appearance, your personality,
and your outward packaging. In truth, your Rising Sign is the *modus operandi* that
you adopted as a child to survive in your family. It's your game face.

Your Rising Sign indicates how you make things happen in your life, or how you
will attain your future. It's the style you use to get what you want. To put it another

---

1. If you are born at the beginning or at the end of your sign, you're born on the cusp. This means you probably
have the qualities of both signs. However, here is something important to know: the dates in newspapers or magazines are average dates for each sign. In truth, each sign can begin or end on a different date, depending on the
year. If you were born on the cusp, and aren't sure what sign you are, you have to check with an astrologer about
the particular year you were born. This is why some columns have different dates from others. I chose the same
dates as Sydney Omarr's because I admired him (no doubt because we have very similar charts).

way, if I have to describe someone, and if I could know only *one* thing about them
— I want to know their Rising Sign.

Consider this example:

Let's take a look at the birth of baby Johnny. No matter what month of the year
Johnny is born (this means he could be any sign), he is the fourth child in a family
who already have three rambunctious boys under the age of eleven. You get the
picture. "Don't run with scissors!"

Common sense says that little Johnny will assume a certain game face to survive
in that family. If he is a scrapper, defending himself right from the moment he arrives
— he might be Aries Rising. (A warrior!) Or, if Mom or Dad is powerful, he might
be Scorpio Rising: strong, tough, and able to stand up for himself, but also a child
with an extremely strong role model for a parent. Or he might be Libra Rising if he
assumes the role of the peacemaker among his squabbling sibblings.

Your Rising Sign shows how you chose to survive in your family. It also shows
how you might have imitated a particular parent or taken on a certain style, which,
of course, is your signature for the rest of your life.

It is because of the Rising Sign that all Aries, or all Capricorns, or all of any sign,
are not the same and, in fact, are amazingly different!

Therefore, if you know what your Rising Sign is, all the information about it will
apply to you equally as much as the information about your Sun Sign. And hey —
when I say equally, I mean it will apply equally in terms of *describing* you and it
will apply just as equally in terms of *predicting* your future.

This is why, if you know your Rising Sign, you will have TWO signs to read every
day, every week, and in every annual forecast — and certainly in this book. Bonus!

And now the painful caveat. It's best to ask an astrologer or to get a computer
program to compute your Rising Sign. Or you can Google Rising Sign Calculator
and a "calculator" will come up.

No simple table can be fully accurate. The table on page 5 will only put you in the
ballpark of your Rising Sign. But if you have nothing else, this table will narrow it
down to one of three signs for you. This means you might have to read the description for three signs to figure out which Rising Sign you have. (Not as bad as having
to butter your toast with hard butter.)

Find your sign in the horizontal shaded bar and follow the column downwards to
line up with the time of day you were born. Your Rising Sign will be either the sign
you "land" on — or the sign on either side. Good luck!

To know your Rising Sign as well as your Sun Sign is more than satisfying idle
curiosity. It will help you make pivotal decisions in the future. Since important decisions are often tough to make, why not use everything at your disposal to help?[2]

---

2. That famous Leo Arnold Schwarzenegger said running for governor of California was the second hardest
decision he had ever made in his life. His toughest decision was in 1978, when he decided to get a bikini wax.

How to Find Your Rising Sign

Choose the time in the left column to match your birth time (a.m. or p.m.) to your sign. Example: If you are a Virgo who is born at 10:23 a.m. you are Sagittarius Rising.

SIGN	Aries	Taurus	Gemini	Cancer	Leo	Virgo
12am-2am	Aquarius	Picsces	Aries	Taurus	Gemini	Cancer
2am-4am	Pisces	Aries	Taurus	Gemini	Cancer	Leo
4am-6am	Aries	Taurus	Gemini	Cancer	Leo	Virgo
6am-8am	Taurus	Gemini	Cancer	Leo	Virgo	Libra
8am-10am	Gemini	Cancer	Leo	Virgo	Libra	Scorpio
10am-Noon	Cancer	Leo	Virgo	Libra	Scorpio	Sagittarius
Noon-2pm	Leo	Virgo	Libra	Scorpio	Sagittarius	Capricorn
2pm-4pm	Virgo	Libra	Scorpio	Sagittarius	Capricorn	Aquarius
4pm-6pm	Libra	Scorpio	Sagittarius	Capricorn	Aquarius	Pisces
6pm-8pm	Scorpio	Sagittarius	Capricorn	Aquarius	Pisces	Aries
8pm-10pm	Sagittarius	Capricorn	Aquarius	Pisces	Aries	Taurus
10pm-12am	Capricorn	Aquarius	Pisces	Aries	Taurus	Gemini

SIGN	Libra	Scorpio	Sagittarius	Capricorn	Aquarius	Pisces
12am-2am	Leo	Virgo	Libra	Scorpio	Sagittarius	Capricorn
2am-4am	Virgo	Libra	Scorpio	Sagittarius	Capricorn	Aquarius
4am-6am	Libra	Scorpio	Sagittarius	Capricorn	Aquarius	Pisces
6am-8am	Scorpio	Sagittarius	Capricorn	Aquarius	Pisces	Aries
8am-10am	Sagittarius	Capricorn	Aquarius	Pisces	Aries	Taurus
10am-Noon	Capricorn	Aquarius	Pisces	Aries	Taurus	Gemini
Noon-2pm	Aquarius	Pisces	Aries	Taurus	Gemini	Cancer
2pm-4pm	Pisces	Aries	Taurus	Gemini	Cancer	Leo
4pm-6pm	Aries	Taurus	Gemini	Cancer	Leo	Virgo
6pm-8pm	Taurus	Gemini	Cancer	Leo	Virgo	Libra
8pm-10pm	Gemini	Cancer	Leo	Virgo	Libra	Scorpio
10pm-12am	Cancer	Leo	Virgo	Libra	Scorpio	Sagittarius

ARIES

MARCH 21 – APRIL 19

ARIES THE RAM
(MARCH 21 – APRIL 19)

"I AM."

"Every morning in Africa, a gazelle wakes up. It knows it must outrun the fastest lion or it will be killed. Every morning in Africa, a lion wakes up. It knows it must run faster than the slowest gazelle, or it will starve. It doesn't matter whether you're a lion or a gazelle — when the sun comes up, you'd better be running."

ROGER BANNISTER
British Neurologist
First Athlete to Break the Four-Minute Mile
(B. MARCH 23, 1929)

"Racing is life. Anything before or after is just waiting."

STEVE MCQUEEN
American Actor Who Raced Motorcycles and Cars
The Magnificent Seven, Bullitt, The Great Escape,
and *The Thomas Crown Affair*
(MARCH 24, 1930–NOVEMBER 7, 1980)

Element: Fire
Ruling Planet: Mars
Quality: Cardinal
Opposite Sign: Libra
Symbol: The Ram
Glyph: Curved Horns Suggesting Pronounced Eyebrows
Lucky Gems: Diamond and Red Carnelian[1]
Flower: Buttercup
Colours: Red and Orange
Part of the Body: Head

You Like: Winning, being first, sports cars, thrilling competitions, and arts and crafts. You're a daredevil in life. You're not an ambulance chaser. *Au contraire!* You're probably the reason the ambulance is racing somewhere. You'll try anything once.

You Don't Like: Losing, mundane details, pessimism, and slowpokes.

Where You Shine: Courageous, enthusiastic, exciting, straightforward, energetic, honest, and downright friendly.

So Who's Perfect? Hot-tempered, reckless, tactless, bossy, impatient, and overbearing. ("Moi?" Yes, you.)

---

1. Here are a few facts for the trivia buffs. Some are rock-solid — like the fact that Mars is the ruler of Aries or the fact that Aries rules the head. However, lucky gem? Flower? Colour? These can vary according to different sources. Just so you know.

What Is Aries-ness?²

The fastest way to get a quick hit of any sign is to understand the ruling planet of that sign and what it means in astrology. The ruling planet of Aries is Mars, which was named after the Roman god of war. Mars rules aggression, conflict, emotional passion, assertiveness, and the ego. It also rules our muscles and adrenal glands. (Starting to get the picture?)

This is why you rise to every challenge! This is why you can't resist a dare. (It's also why you chase fire trucks. Well, not literally. The truth is, half the people on fire trucks are Aries because you're all closet arsonists.)

You love jazzy sports cars and competitive racing, and you sometimes dress like an extra from *Raiders of the Lost Ark.*

"My goal is not to be a race-car driver. The reason I'm racing is because
I enjoy being in the car and being on the edge."
JACQUES VILLENEUVE
Canadian Champion Race Car Driver
(B. APRIL 9, 1971)

You were the kid in elementary school who raced to be first in line at the drinking fountain because you had to win. (Lord knows you hate to lose.) Your eager competitiveness makes you want to be the first on the scene to get the scoop. You want to be the firstest with the mostest and the biggest!

"I want to top expectations. I want to blow you away."
QUENTIN TARANTINO
American Film Director, Actor, and Screenwriter
Reservoir Dogs, Pulp Fiction, and *Kill Bill*
(B. MARCH 27, 1963)

Please understand: every person has Mars somewhere in their chart, showing where they express their aggression and encounter conflicts. However, only the sign of Aries is *ruled* by Mars. *Capisce?*

---

2. No one is just one sign because everyone's chart is made up of different planets. Therefore, this section captures the Aries archetype — the qualities of "Aries-ness." Many other signs will have Aries characteristics as well. Therefore, the discussion of one sign is not an exact description of that person; rather it is a description of the qualities of that sign.

Heads Up!

Aries rules the head, which is why you plunge through life head first. It is also why many Aries people have a scar on their head or their face. You love hats. You also like cool shades, earrings, visors, caps, and anything that calls attention to your head. Many of you walk slightly stooped with your head forward.

My Uncle Jack was an Aries and he had more than a hundred hats.[3] He was a Mountie in the RCMP before joining the navy as a sailor during the Second World War. He served on the *Wetaskiwin*. (They called it the "wet-assed Queen.") After the war, he worked as a policeman for the Canadian Pacific Railway.

One hundred hats? A Mountie? A scrappy sailor? A policeman? An Aries! What was your first clue?

Aries people often have a reddish tinge to their hair or their beard. Think Vincent van Gogh (March 30, 1853–July 29, 1890). Many Aries people have freckles. They frequently have strong eyebrows or a pronounced brow. In fact, I often mutter "Aries eyebrows" if I spot someone who looks like an Aries (however, some Scorpios also have this same look).[4] Prominent eyebrows or a hooded look are a giveaway for Aries. Check out actors Jack Black, Marlon Brando, Matthew Broderick, Ali MacGraw, Gregory Peck, and Omar Sharif; also check out founder of *Playboy* magazine Hugh Hefner, composer Andrew Lloyd Webber, environmental activist David Suzuki, Scottish singing sensation Susan Boyle, and NHL goaltender Roberto Luongo. Can you see the look?

Because Mars rules the blood and the muscles, Aries is a hot-blooded sign — quick to anger, but just as quick to subside and forgive. You don't hold a grudge. When you blow up, you're a firecracker. POW! Then it's over.

> "Get mad, then get over it."
> COLIN POWELL
> American Four-Star General and Former Secretary of State
> (B. APRIL 5, 1937)

Moi, Moi, Moi!

You are the first sign, which is why you're sometimes called the baby of the zodiac. Your sign starts on the spring equinox, when plants are budding and everything is coming alive. Hey, this is you! Fresh and bursting with life! (The bud thang.) This symbolizes who you are — spontaneous, eager, and full of zing! (Lose the zebra pants.)

This reference to being the baby of the zodiac is not casual. You love beginnings, especially darling little infants, adorable puppies, and tiny kittens. Baby "anything" never fails to elicit soft cooing sounds from you regardless of your age or gender.[5]

---

3. Jack Adlard (1920–2008) married my mother's sister Betty.
4. This is not surprising, because until the discovery of Pluto in 1930, Mars ruled both Aries and Scorpio.
5. Aries women whisper "I want to have your baby" or scream "I want to bear his children!" (You know who you are.)

Aries is associated with beginnings and births of people, animals, ideas, events, and even nations.

Not only do Aries love baby animals, they love *all* animals. Naturally, all signs might love animals, but two signs are noted for this trait — Aries and Sagittarius. This is why many Aries people are wranglers, animal trainers, or animal rights activists.

"I've always loved animals and I always thought that they were, if not better, then the absolute equal of any two-legged creature that God ever created."

ALI MACGRAW
American Actress and Animal Activist
Love Story and *The Getaway*
(B. APRIL 1, 1938)

We've Got Your Number

Number One is you. You are the first sign. You want to be first in any competition. You want to be the first to discover anything. You want to be the first to create something. You appreciate life in its first coochy-coo stages. No sign more than you is associated with beginnings or being Number One.

This is why you're an initiator. You like to start things. You create the prototype. You tackle anything just to see if you can do it. You want to puncture the mystique of something to discover how it works. ("Hmmm, so that's how they do it. I thought so. Very clever.")

Aries will try anything once — anything!

Ram Wasn't Built in a Day

Not for nothing are you Aries the Ram. But it is the relationship of your ruling planet to your muscles which is why you're so athletic and physically competitive.[6] Mars is the ruler of the ego. This is why you're quick to defend any attack. It's also why you naturally take the lead if you're in a group. And if you're ever in a group and find yourself wrestling for this leadership, you're probably dealing with another Aries!

Aries energy is expressed not only by having your Sun in Aries but also by being Aries Rising or having your Moon in Aries. You know when you're talking to an Aries because their conversation is often brief, staccato-like, and full of authority.[7] Aries people are comfortable with brief, to-the-point exchanges. (Which is not to say that Aries cannot be chatty, soft and cuddly, and touchy-feely, because they can. But not if they're busy!)

---

6. French psychologist and statistician Michel Gauquelin devoted much of his life to trying to determine whether astrology had scientific validity or not. He discovered that a greater-than-average number of Olympic champions had Mars prominent in their charts in one of two places that traditionally demonstrate either personal grit and competitiveness or a very strong ambition to succeed. In 1955 Gauquelin published these findings in *L'influence des astres*. This is generally referred to as "the Mars effect."
7. I have my Mars in Aries. I used to call my Aries friend Ahna Marcantognini on the phone. We had telegram conversations that made those who didn't have Aries in them accuse me of being rude. "Hi, I'm late. Be there in an hour. Bye." Five seconds. Done. (Easy peasy.)

Three Roles That Aries Embraces

To help you better grasp your sign, in addition to understanding the influence of fiery Mars, here are three broad ways to view Aries:

1. The Warrior
2. The Artisan
3. The Pioneer/Hero

The Warrior

Your ruler, Mars, is the god of war, which makes you a warrior. Naturally, a warrior is performance-ready to meet life's vicissitudes head-on. The warrior's only option is winning. Victory is what you seek.

Many of you are drawn to organizations that have a military structure. Obviously, the military is one example; however, others will join firefighting, police work, the Coast Guard, and other organizations with clear lines of authority. Many also go into investigative journalism.

You're always poised and ready for attack. This doesn't mean you're aggressive in a negative way — far from it. Aries is a wonderful, friendly, open, generous sign! But you never back down from a fight. You have the first word and the last.

Consciously or unconsciously, you take this military stance into every walk of life. In other words, you are quick to engage! If challenged, you respond. You don't necessarily throw out the first barb, but you won't back down from a fight. It's almost a matter of principle with you. You don't like bullies and you don't like anybody messing around with you. You'll be polite to a point, but you have your limits. And just as the soldier can fight on an empty stomach and no sleep, you can undergo gruelling conditions to achieve what you want. You're no wuss!

You are, however, seduced by a challenge! We see a classic example of this in the movie *The Godfather*, where James Caan (b. March 26, 1940) plays the role of Sonny Corleone ("Badabing bada boom!"). Sonny's fatal flaw in the movie is his hot-headed temper. Upon hearing that his sister has been beaten by her husband, he jumps in his car, alone and unprotected (a very bad move), and drives off, only to be ambushed and shot down by those who predicted this very behaviour. Who better to play this hot-tempered role than an Aries actor? I rest my handbag.

Even your clothes (no matter what your job) often have a hint of a military motif — perhaps epaulets on the shoulders of your blouse or your shirt, or shirts with little button tabs to hold your rolled-up sleeves in place. (Cool!) You might choose jackets with pronounced rows of buttons, and, of course, you might even be so bohemian as to wear military jackets or khaki fatigues.[8]

You're the boldest and bravest of all the twelve signs (and, at times, the most foolhardy). Others admire your fearlessness and courage. ("I'm astride my white stallion. Is that Lawrence of Arabia ahead? No! It's Rommel — the Desert Fox! *Gasp*. I knew this moment would come. I have a date with destiny!"[9])

The Artisan

"Painting is not for me either decorative amusement or the plastic invention of felt reality; it must be every time: invention, discovery, revelation."

MAX ERNST
German Surrealist Painter, Sculptor, and Poet
(APRIL 2, 1891–APRIL 1, 1976)

Aries people love to work with their hands. You will attempt anything because you confidently tell yourself, "Hey, they've got two hands, I've got two hands. I mean, how tough can this be?"

This is why, unlike Geminis, who also like to work with their hands (but prefer training), you don't wait to be shown how. You plunge right in!

"I want do a Mandarin-language movie.
It'll probably be the next movie I do after the one I do next."

QUENTIN TARANTINO
American Film Director, Actor, and Screenwriter
Reservoir Dogs, Pulp Fiction, and *Kill Bill*
(B. MARCH 27, 1963)

My Aries friend Ahna was always painting and trying new techniques with water-colours and pens; yet, somehow, she was also constantly writing short stories and novels. These activities took place when she wasn't playing backgammon far into the night with me. (I think the writing and painting came *after* the photography.)

I never met an Aries who didn't have a darkroom of sorts. Then there's sewing, knitting, weaving, carving, metalwork, painting, drawing, glassblowing, leather-work, beadwork, sign painting, pottery, soap- and candle-making, model-building, carpentry, cabinet-making, and scrapbooking, to say nothing of the performing arts. *You're fascinated by the process of creation!*

---

8. I recall when my daughter Kelly was in Grade 6 and it was Parents' Day at her school. As she went out the door that morning, she turned to me and said, "Puh-leeze don't wear your army pants!"
9. These are my Walter Mitty words. However it's interesting to note that author and cartoonist James Thurber (1894–1961), who wrote *The Secret Life of Walter Mitty,* had both Moon in Aries and Mars in Aries. *Quelle surprise.*

Secretly, you want to know how it's done. Once you discover you can do something — and believe me, you can do anything — you generally lose interest. You're ready for something new.

> "The worst thing you can do is censor yourself as the pencil hits the paper. You must not edit until you get it all on paper. If you can put everything down, stream-of-consciousness, you'll do yourself a service."
> STEPHEN SONDHEIM
> Award-Winning American Composer and Lyricist
> *A Funny Thing Happened on the Way to the Forum* and *Sweeney Todd*
> (B. MARCH 22, 1930)

But here is where the embarrassing part comes: soon, you don't need that darkroom, or that big loom, or that kiln, or all that gorgeous fabric. (Aaaggh.) You're bored! You've figured it out. You've conquered this little challenge. But now you're stuck with all of this leftover stuff, which becomes juicy ammo for those who accuse you of not being able to finish anything! (The injustice of it all!)

Awright awreddy. You lose interest in something once it starts to feel like drudgery or work. So what? I say tell your detractors these are "ongoing projects." You will always pursue whatever is new and fresh because you're an Aries! (So many worlds to conquer, so little time!)

The Pioneer/Hero

The archetype of "the hero" is pure Aries. You view life as a quest, as a struggle for something you want, and in order to achieve this you must be victorious. And, if you are truly victorious, what you achieve will benefit those around you.

Joseph Campbell, in his book *The Hero with a Thousand Faces*, describes this journey in terms of seventeen stages. These are generally reduced to eight levels, beginning with the Call to Adventure and ending with The Master of Two Worlds.[10] (Let's face it — just the phrase "Call to Adventure" stirs your blood! You want every day to be an adventure!)[11]

Small wonder Aries is the sign of the pioneer. Think of an arrowhead: you are the tip of that arrowhead. You're the vanguard in society. If you're not literally pioneering places on planet Earth, then you're pioneering new ideas and fresh activities in the world around you.

Your desire for adventure makes you less concerned with security. You just want to have enough money to pull off your next caper or buy the equipment for your next hands-on project or stunt. You need liquid cash!

---

10. *The Hero's Journey: Joseph Campbell on his Life and Work*, ed. Phil Cousineau (New York: Harper and Row, 1990).
11. I know an Aries named Alan Mills who always says, "What can we do to make this day spectacular?" He loves hats, music, and vigorous debates. He played the lead role in a local production of *Godspell*, and is self-employed in computer technology. Classic Aries.

"We live at the edge of the world, so we live on the edge. Kiwis will always sacrifice money and security for adventure and challenge."

LUCY LAWLESS
Actress and Singer
Xena: Warrior Princess
(B. MARCH 29, 1968)

Many Aries are slightly loath to own their own home. They see it as something that ties them down and hinders their freedom to go exploring whenever and wherever they want to go.

WHAT'S WITH THOSE DIRTY PICTURES?[12]

Most signs have curious contradictions and you are no exception. After decades of observing Aries clients, I have come to the following conclusion, and frankly it surprised me. Despite the fact that you are bold and fearless, and despite the fact that you have a constant desire to explore new territory — the truth is you *do* need security!

Ponder, if you will, the classic warrior/adventurer mentality. The warrior is brave, fearless, ready for adventure, and happy to claim new territory and win victories and spoils for the emperor or king. But who is feeding this soldier? The king!

In order to be constantly on the move, ready to fight in any arena, the soldier must be fed, clothed, and housed by his commander.

The first time I noticed this, I was living in London in a flat in SW Kensington with three other roommates. Occasionally, these two impossibly good-looking Irish brothers would crash on our living-room floor. They were both Aries and both in the navy. We had fun pubbing together, but they constantly bemoaned their regimented existence and told us how they lived for shore leave and how they could hardly wait for their enlisted time to be over.

Imagine my surprise to discover that when their time was up, they re-enlisted! One of my flatmates, also Irish but ten years older, said, "Of course they're back in the navy! They don't want to worry about washing their socks, or doing their laundry, or getting their meals. They want to be taken care of!"

Hmmmm. My Aries uncle Jack, who was a Mountie, a feisty sailor, an artist, and a cabinetmaker, worked as a policeman for the CPR for *thirty years*. Hmmm. My Aries proofreader Renee Doruyter is a fabulous jazz singer with several CDs. She is also a painter, a fabulous seamstress, a jewellery maker, and, in truth, much more; however, she was employed at her newspaper for thirty years in a department with four other Aries. (I couldn't make this up.)

---

12. The Rorschach ink blot test is a method used for psychological evaluation. The subject's comments on various ink blots are supposed to reveal personality characteristics. The old joke is that a shrink is showing a patient these ink blots and the patient consistently responds with answers like "That's a pelvis" or "Those are someone's genitals." Finally, the psychiatrist says, "You seem to have a fascination with sex." The patient replies, "Whaddya mean? You're the one with the dirty pictures!"

This means that even though you seek the freedom of action to be constantly competitive and explore new projects, at heart you want the security that is provided by a benefactor — your government or your employer.

Heroic contradictions! Perhaps it all comes down to how one defines security. The movie *The Hurt Locker* is about a man who exchanges one kind of security (home and family) for another (the army) because he's hooked on the rush of defusing bombs.

This is why so many Aries remain in the military or remain as long-term employees (always complaining about their chains). They want their adventure, but part of them does not want the insecurity of dealing with life in addition to dealing with all the other exciting challenges they seek. No wonder my Aries friend Al always says, "I live for my weekends!"

WE LOVE HEROES!

Not only does Aries often live a life that follows the hero's journey, Aries people also love heroes! Aries children and teenagers have pictures on their bedroom walls of their heroes. And, in a curious 180-degree flip-flop, Aries people are often viewed as heroes by others.

People like Steve McQueen, William Shatner (Captain Kirk), Leonard Nimoy (Spock), Bob Woodward (reporter who broke the Watergate scandal), Lucy Lawless (Xena), Alec Guinness (Obi Wan Kenobi), Jack Webb (*Dragnet*'s Sergeant Joe Friday), Marlon Brando, Gus Grissom (astronaut), Alec Baldwin, Robert Downey, Jr. (Iron Man), Roberto Luongo, Heath Ledger, Spencer Tracy, Gregory Peck, Francis Ford Coppola, Jackie Chan, Russell Crowe, Dennis Quaid, Omar Sharif, Steven Seagal, Trevor Linden, Andy Garcia, Charlie Chaplin, and William Holden have been perceived in heroic terms at one time or another in their lives.

This means Aries people are both perceived as heroes by those around them and, in turn, they themselves love their own heroes! It's a two-way street, but, no matter how you cut it — it's a hero thang.

"A lot of times when you go through a very traumatic situation
and it's emotionally difficult to deal with you come back spiritually stronger.
It changes you in a way."
ELVIS STOJKO
Canadian Figure Skating Champion
(B. MARCH 22, 1972)

Aries in Love

In the movie *The King and I*, actor Yul Brynner (who was a Cancer) perfectly describes the Aries approach to love when he sings, "A man must be like honeybee, and gather all he can. To fly from blossom to blossom, a honeybee must be free."

The curious thing about Aries and romance is this: in one way, it is their nature to be bold and make the first move. And they often do! Yet (who knew?) Aries can be incredibly shy. They fear being rebuffed. Too painful for their ego! Plus they know that their heroic, swashbuckling style is not necessarily going to do the trick when it comes to hearts and flowers. This is why the classic hero in Hollywood movies is depicted as suddenly becoming John Wayne gosh-golly-gee-thank-you-ma'am tongue-tied in the presence of a purty lady.

But one thing is certain: to seduce Aries you have to make them laugh.

"There is nothing wrong with going to bed with someone of your own sex.
People should be very free with sex; they should draw the line at goats."
ELTON HERCULES JOHN
British Singer, Songwriter, Composer, and Pianist
"Rocket Man," "Candle in the Wind," and "Don't Let the Sun Go Down on Me"
(B. MARCH 25, 1947)

Once Aries overcome their initial shyness, they move fast! Remember, this is a sign who knows what they want. When someone is in their sights — they go after them! Naturally, to overcome their shyness, Aries of both sexes wear a tough mask they sometimes hide behind. You're bold, flirtatious, cavalier, and like to pretend that whatever happens is really no big deal — but inside your heart is thumping wildly!

Your impetuous nature makes you fall in love very fast and marry young. This is because you like adventure, and first love is such a wild ride! Plus you're always looking for something to make life exciting, and what beats falling in love and suddenly getting married? Of course, you also wake up fairly quickly, and many of you split from this starter marriage. (There's no dust on your shoulders!) But if children are involved, you might stay. You are loyal to children.

Sexually, you guys are noisy! We're talking screaming, yelling, scratching, and fighting. (The neighbours love you.) Because you like a daring element in anything that you do, many of you toy with (and carry out) public sex.[13] It brings out the

---

13. Friends don't let friends drive naked.

competitive spirit in you. I'm sure it was an Aries who started the Mile-High Club. After all, Aries are risk takers. You like doing something outrageous, even if it's just for your own personal satisfaction. It lets you chortle with pleasure and makes you feel cocky and full of derring-do!

Aries lovers like to play with fur, leather, silk, and certainly toys. Hey, you're imaginative. Plus, sex is basically another expression of the artisan in you coming out. Another obvious reason you use these accoutrements is because you've got all this *stuff* at your fingertips! (Who else has fourteen projects on the go?)

Aries lovers are bossy, competitive, daring, and passionate! But after the dust settles they are surprisingly loyal, especially if family is involved.

Nevertheless, variety in the bedroom is a must. Routine bores you! (I have an Aries friend in Chicago named Ruth who broke her arm falling out of bed while she was having sex. She was soooo proud of this.)

The Aries Boss

"There was often antagonism and chair throwing and stamping of feet, which is kind of a healthy thing to do when you're arguing about what's funny. That healthy tension was something that held the group together."

ERIC IDLE

British Actor, Singer, and Songwriter

One of the Members of the British Comedy Group Monty Python

(B. MARCH 29, 1943)

Aries are bold and fearless. The brave sergeant who leads his men to battle is an Aries. (I chose sergeant because Aries is a very hands-on kind of leader. Aries gets right in the mud and mixes with the troops, squatting on the ground to look at a map or play dice. Aries knows how to be "one of the guys.") Nevertheless, Aries can be a general, a colonel, or a CEO, because essentially Aries has the natural qualities of leadership. Aries is decisive, quick to act, confident, and energetic. Aries people have an authoritative style in the way they move and speak, which makes others invariably respond and obey. (You're bossy. But nice bossy.)

You want leadership? Think of these Aries natives: American statesman and four-star general Colin Powell, *Playboy* magazine founder Hugh Hefner, and actors Alec Baldwin, Jack Black, Marlon Brando, Steve McQueen, and Gregory Peck. Although many signs are powerful, Aries people are natural leaders because they move quickly, they move first, they're competitive, and they don't want to take orders from anyone. However, the Aries boss is not a prima donna! No task is too menial. Your Aries boss will roll up their sleeves and jump right into the mess so that the job gets done. Aries people are hard workers, and this is why they are so inspirational to those who follow them.

Of course, the Aries boss initiates things. They love to begin all kinds of projects! (But they're not great on closing, which is where they need support). They're full of bright ideas, ahead of the pack in discovering new territory, new products, and new ways of doing things. Ideally, someone is running behind them picking up the pieces and pulling it all together in a practical way.

Aries dreams up the concept and designs the prototype. Aries is the pioneer who introduces a new product, or introduces an existing product into an entirely new area. Aries people work best in short bursts or doing special projects. After six months, they want to do something else.

Never keep your Aries boss waiting. Never. Never.

The Aries Employee

The Aries employee is highly resourceful, because here is a person who is willing to try anything. They're not that worried about getting training. They know they can figure things out on their own. In fact, they love winging it. (What this employee wants to hear is, "No one has ever learned this so fast!" Or, "You are the first person who has ever figured out how this thing really works!")

Aries are hard-working by nature, but they hate to be bored. They love a challenge, and they respond well to competition. They're willing to work under surprisingly difficult conditions as long as people notice their productivity and acknowledge their excellent input.

The downside is that your Aries employee can upset fellow employees by being too bossy or too bold, or by getting into a dust-up with someone. Furthermore, if you have to call this person on the carpet, they might just get up, walk out, and slam the door! Money never holds them to a job. If they get angry, they express themselves very clearly (there will be no doubt in anyone's mind) and then they leave — wham! In fact, the Aries exit is something truly amazing to behold. It is always dramatic. It starts with loud words and colourful phrases, and, if possible, there is always a wonderful slamming of the door for final punctuation. They love the satisfaction of the slammed door!

One expects this behaviour when hiring Aries people in their twenties. However, older Aries tend to mellow. They specialize in the slammed cupboard. It is still effective, but they've learned that at least they're not suddenly outdoors without their purse or out in the cold without their coat.[14] (You know who you are.)

---

14. This is so baaaaad because after a perfect, fiery exit you have to slink back in to get your wallet or keys. It really takes the edge off it all, doesn't it? I hate it. In fact, impulses like this cured me of indulging in this kind of dramatic bravado. Now, I plan ahead.

The Aries Parent

"What in heaven's name is strange about a grandmother dancing nude?
I'll bet lots of grandmothers do it."
SALLY RAND
Burlesque Dancer and Actress
(APRIL 3, 1904–AUGUST 31, 1979)

Aries people make excellent parents. For starters, you adore babies and little children. You're naturally protective and nurturing. All those crazy YouTube home videos of babies doing cute and adorable things are made by amateur Aries wannabe filmmakers. It's an irresistible combo: making a new movie with your new camera of your new baby! (Invariably, a kitten and a very large dog are involved.)

Naturally, the Aries parent is bossy and firm. However, the children in this family know the rules and how everything works. Aries parents are straightforward and clear about what they expect. But they're also very loving and fair, and certainly protective of their kids! (Imagine an Aries hockey dad. Need I say more?)

One of the delightful things that Aries parents will do is introduce their children to all kinds of handicrafts and doing wonderful things with their hands. Aries parents dip Easter eggs, decorate gingerbread houses, create incredible cookies, and bake cakes for any season — Christmas trees with jellybeans and shortbread "human" fingers at Halloween. Imagine an Aries having a chance to decorate a birthday cake! (Say no more!)

The Aries parent will happily play outside with their kids. They're also very active with sports. They want their children to be passionate about something. They're also generous and even indulgent to their brood. Their kids soon learn how to handle their parent's temper, and know to steer clear of doing anything that is bound to wake the sleeping giant. ("Oops! Run!")

"I know that I'm getting the real deal with my mom. I know that
she's telling it like it is. She's proud of me when I've earned it and
she's disappointed in me when I've earned that. She's really my
spectrum on where I am as a person."
LARA FLYNN BOYLE
American Actress
Twin Peaks
(B. MARCH 24, 1970)

The Aries Child

"It has been my observation that parents kill more dreams than anybody."
SPIKE LEE
American Film Director, Producer, Screenwriter, and Actor
Do the Right Thing, Mo' Better Blues, and *Malcolm X*
(B. MARCH 20, 1957)

Here is a highly creative, highly energetic child! It's important to recognize that the Aries child is eager to explore everything. Of course, this eagerness has a natural impatience to it. This is a child who is chomping at the bit to do something or go somewhere. They like to be the first out the door, the first in the car, the first in line, the first to do anything.

This energetic quality will serve them well as an adult; therefore, do not be too ready to curb this trait. Instead, channel this energy through sports, dance, and other kinds of creative activity. These children are seeking ways to express themselves!

Animals are important to Aries people, and this child will truly love a pet. Hey — a pal to explore with! Outdoor activities feed the enthusiasm of these children. However, they also adore all kinds of crafts, games, and special things they can do with their hands. Aries children are extremely creative!

The Aries child has a direct, forthright speaking style. (That's just who they are.) They're honest, to the point, and disarmingly frank. ("Granny, how come you have a moustache?") This is also a child who needs to be treated with respect and fairness. If you use your adult intelligence or clout to "outsmart" this child or show them up in any way — they will be dashed and crestfallen. ("That's not fair!")

The heart that beats inside every little Aries child is the heart of a hero or heroine. They believe that good triumphs over bad. It's very important to be the kind of parent or teacher that they can respect. You have a tall order to live up to!

Their temper tantrums are brief. They can be taught that although it's okay to express how you feel, having a big meltdown doesn't accomplish much.

It's important for the Aries child to fit in at school. This means that an element of competitiveness will be involved. Naturally, these children want to wear what others are wearing so that they look like they're "with it."

When Aries children are upset or angry, they can be calmed by playing or working with or handling metal. For example, putting the cutlery away in a drawer is something they will like to do. If they are learning to knit, give them metal needles.

Likewise, metal cars and trucks will be more satisfying for them to play with than plastic.

Always supervise these children near fire. They are intrigued and fascinated by fire and firecrackers. (This bears repeating: all Aries are closet arsonists.)

Little Aries girls are often tomboys (but not always), and both sexes of children are inclined to hide their sensitivity behind a cocky game face. Even at a young age, they know that true heroes never show they're frightened.

"Childbirth is more admirable than conquest, more amazing
than self-defence, and as courageous as either one."
GLORIA STEINEM
American Feminist, Journalist, Social and Political Activist,
Co-founder of *Ms. Magazine*
(B. MARCH 25, 1934)

How to Be a Happier Aries

"Bitterness is like cancer. It eats upon the host. But anger is like fire.
It burns it all clean."
MAYA ANGELOU
Award-Winning American Poet and Writer
I Know Why the Caged Bird Sings
(B. APRIL 4, 1928)

Your Achilles heel is your Aries temper. You know it and I know it. Because you have a fiery temperament, and you're passionate and hot-blooded, and you're entirely spontaneous — you have a short fuse! You are impatient with others, as well as yourself. Defiant by nature, poised for any challenge, with a warrior mentality — of course, you are easily angered!

"All hockey players are bilingual. They know English and profanity."
GORDIE HOWE
Legendary NHL Hockey Player, Six-Time Winner of the Hart Trophy,
and Six-Time Winner of the Art Ross Trophy. Known as "Mr. Hockey"
(B. MARCH 31, 1928)

The bummer thing about anger is that it destroys your peace of mind, makes you miserable, and makes everyone else around you miserable as well. In fact, if you really think about it, *anger serves no purpose other than to make everyone miserable!*

Even if you have been horribly wronged and must now plan the greatest revenge of your life, you need a calm, clear mind to do this. Right? If your mind is clouded with angry thoughts, your thinking won't be clear, and thus your plan for revenge will be faulty. Ditto for planning a battle. There is *no situation* where anger brings any benefit to you.

Nevertheless, you still get angry. Angry people are not beautiful people. In fact, when we are angry, grouchy, and in a bad mood, we become very unattractive. On top of that, blind rage can make us say or do things we later regret. It's a bummer scene.

So what can we do?

Let's look at anger. Basically, anger is a response to unhappiness. You don't like how things are. You don't like what that person said. You don't like what somebody did to you or someone else. You have to endure something you don't like. Essentially, anger is a response to negativity.

Negativity is wanting things to be different from the way they are.

Meanwhile, the purpose of life is to be happy. So how can we be happy if we're experiencing negativity? Obviously, we have only two options. We can either change the situation or we can suck it up and accept it. The Serenity Prayer is wise:

God, grant me the serenity
To accept the things I cannot change;
The courage to change the things that I can;
And the wisdom to know the difference.

Aries certainly have the courage to change whatever they possibly can, but to do so they need to be clear-headed and not clouded with anger.

Think back to a happy time in your life, perhaps when you were madly in love with someone. You're at a party. You're feeling hot and sexy. You like what you're wearing, you dance well, and your jokes are witty. Then, it happens. You have someone in your arms and you feel like you've met the love of your life. You leave the party, go off to a club or a restaurant for that deep, meaningful discussion filled with laughter and discovery. Elated with the newness of this mutual attraction, you walk out of the restaurant to your car and see that the sun is rising. Impulsively, you both decide to drive to the park and swing on the swings, the way you did as children. You're in love and you're a kid again! It's that thrilling first flowering of romance! Later, arm in arm, you walk back to your car, only to discover that someone has sideswiped your passenger-side mirror. Bummer! Do you get angry? No. You quickly accept the situation and shrug it off. "Hey, caca happens."

Why is it so easy to accept this negative situation? Because you're happy! Anger does not arise in a happy mind. Anger is only a response to negativity. If you encounter a negative situation and do not have a negative response, anger will not arise. "Verrrry interrresting." (Thanks, Arte.)

Let's put it another way. If you go to a party and you hate how you look, and you don't talk to anybody and nobody talks to you, you feel increasingly lonely and sorry for yourself. You leave early and drive straight home. You arrive to discover a voicemail message inviting you to a party in the apartment above, with an added apology for any late-night noise. Are wyou happy to get this invitation? No! You're not in the mood to see anyone, and now you have to listen to that damned racket! And if their noise goes past 1 a.m., you're sure as hell calling the police!

What a difference! In the first scenario, you encounter vandalism to your car but you're not upset because you're in love and so happy. In the second scenario, you encounter an invitation to a party but you're upset because you're unhappy. Furthermore, you're looking for ways to make yourself and others even more miserable!

Isn't this how anger works? The root of anger is an unhappy frame of mind. Okay, you accept this. But, like, duh? How are you going to suddenly become happy in the next ten seconds? Pixie dust?

Ah ha! Here is the secret. You do not have to become "happy." You just have to address your "unhappy" state of mind. There is a *difference*.

Years ago, I had the good fortune to attend a seminar with the brilliant Aries Frederick Hertzberg (April 17, 1923–January 19, 2000), an American psychologist who developed motivation theories for business management. He walked up to the blackboard and wrote down the word "unhappy." He then asked the audience, "What is the opposite of unhappy?"

Naturally, we all answered, "Happy."

"No," he said, "The opposite to unhappy is not unhappy." Then he gave an illustration. If you have a toothache, and someone gives you a pill so you no longer suffer from the pain of the toothache, you are no longer unhappy with the toothache, but you are not necessarily happy. Being happy is something else altogether.

Wow! To me, Hertzberg pointed out an important distinction. We can be unhappy; we can be neutral; and we can be happy.

You don't have to come up with the big secret to happiness. (Sheesh! That's a relief.) All you have to do is get to neutral. (Big difference!) Furthermore, *this is doable*. The reason it is doable is that *patience* is the antidote to anger.

Imagine the very core of your being as sort of like a big egg, maybe somewhere near your heart. Inside this core is unhappiness. Therefore, the lining around this "egg" is a surface that is filled with a lack of ease. We might call it dis-ease. (Which is why chronic unhappiness and stress produce disease.)

So here you have this fragile egg in the core of your being encased by a thin membrane of dis-ease. Without question, the first irritable thing that parachutes in to puncture that tenuous membrane is going to produce anger! That's because the lining of this egg is unstable and "impatient." This is also why *patience is the antidote to anger.*

There is a famous story about a great Indian teacher named Atisha (982–1054). He travelled about the countryside teaching his disciples, and wherever he went he travelled with his cook, who was dirty, unkempt, rude, vulgar — and, on top of all this, he couldn't cook!

Confused and amazed, the students of Atisha said to him, "Master! Why do you travel with this terrible cook? Why don't you get rid of this horrible man?"

Atisha answered, "My cook? I would never abandon my cook. He is my most valued treasure. He gives me the opportunity to practise patience — daily."

When we experience suffering or hardship or disappointment, or when we feel that we are harmed by others, we have a choice of response. We can retaliate with anger and bitterness, or we can see this as an opportunity to practise patience.

There are two kinds of patience: the patience of accepting a bummer situation we can't change, and there is also the patience of not retaliating.

You might think that, by not retaliating, you are being asked to give a lot. (Actually, in a way you are.) But the person you're giving to is *you*! After all, every emotion you ever have first passes through you before it gets to somebody else. *You* feel every bit of *your* anger. You feel every bit of your bitterness. You feel every bit of your judgement or criticism of others. All your negative feelings first pass through *you*. (This is why we are all responsible for our own face by the time we are fifty.)

Therefore, if you can practise the patience of non-retaliation or the patience of acceptance, the big winner is you! And, of course, those around you will likewise be grateful. (Ya think?)

> "I shall allow no man to belittle my soul by making me hate him."
> BOOKER T. WASHINGTON
> American Author, Educator, and Civil Rights Activist
> (APRIL 5, 1856–NOVEMBER 14, 1915)

ARIES
YOUR 40-YEAR HOROSCOPE
1985-2025

Why Go into the Past?

I want you to have faith in your predictions. The only way you can believe what I say is to test these predictions for yourself. This is why I start with brief highlights from the past twenty-five years. If anything in these past twenty-five years resonates with you, then what I say about the next fifteen years will have the same validity. It is all one long timeline — your life.

The past predictions generally apply once you have left home or are "running your life" and making your own decisions. Prior to that, the major events in your life were dictated to you by other people, likely your parents.

1985 – 1990

In the early 1980s, many of you left partnerships or committed relationships. This is why you were forced to rely on your own resources by the mid-1980s. You were standing on your own two feet, which, by the way, you do very well. By 1985, you were popular! In fact, in March 1987, when lucky moneybags Jupiter entered your sign, things were looking great! You knew how to parlay your good fortune into something better so that by 1988–89, money was flowing. Your earnings looked better, and many of you enjoyed praise, a raise, a promotion, or considerable success at that time. ("Yay! Look at me!")

The latter half of the 1980s, especially toward the end, was a time of major changes. If you look back now, you see you were looking for a way to more completely define your individuality. Quite likely, you broke free from anything that was restricting you, especially professionally. Some of you might have become self-employed. Those of you who were working in fields of technology or science, or in (admittedly) fuzzy areas like astrology, might have felt you had new opportunities.

At this time, the bottom line was that you were going to demand work that was more rewarding. (No more salt mines.) Some of you experienced sudden changes with respect to parents at this time as well.

Fortunately, the year 1990 (or one year either side) was a lovely year for home, family, and real estate. Those of you who fixed up your home, or bought real estate for speculation, or purchased a home, have never regretted it.

This was also a time when many of you expanded your family through birth, adoption, or marriage. Family relations were more joyful. People were generous to each other. (Gosh.)

1991 – 1996

By now, you were having fun! This was a great time for love affairs, romance, and vacations, as well as your ability to express your creativity. Artists flourished! Many of you took a lovely trip at this time. Around 1991, in particular, was another classic time to expand your family. Certainly, children were a source of joy.

By 1992–93, many of you managed to improve your job, or get a better job, or get rid of your evil boss. There were many employment opportunities, as well as a chance for you to look at your work from a different point of view to make it more fulfilling.

Soon partnerships became more rewarding. In fact, 1993–94 was an excellent time to enter into partnerships, both professional and intimate. Meanwhile, in another part of the forest, you entered a two- to three-year window where you decided it was time to begin to dismantle much of what you had created since 1980–81. You were streamlining, downsizing, and letting go of people, places, and things. (When you decide to do this — you *really* do it!)

Fortunately, by around 1996, two things were happening. On one hand, lovely opportunities to boost your reputation in the world and make a name for yourself, or get a promotion, or a raise, or recognition, existed for you. ("Look, Ma, no hands!") And yet, at the same time, this was the year when you entered a whole new world, which was, in fact, the beginning of a process that was going to reinvent the new you.

Was this exciting or what?

1997 – 2000

As you entered this new mode of being, which might even have necessitated a different daily wardrobe, you enjoyed more popularity! Something about your new circumstances allowed you to meet new people, especially in groups, or classes, or meetings. Your confidence was strong then, even though you were on relatively new turf.

Sure enough, in February 1999, lucky Jupiter entered your sign for the first time since 1987, boosting your confidence and increasing your poise. You were popular and you felt in touch with your muse. It was easier to get others to appreciate you. For most, this led to increased earnings in 1999–2000, which, incidentally, came at a good time, because your cupboard was getting bare. (And Mother Hubbard was no picnic, lemme tell ya.)

2001 – 2005

Despite giving up jobs, relationships, friendships, belongings, and maybe even residences and countries between 1994 and 1997, here you were again, around 2001, looking at residential moves and job changes! (Whaaat?) This period of instability lasted for about three years. And some of you even made two moves!

At the beginning of the millennium, you changed your job, or your residence, or both, because you were putting the finishing touches on the new you. (This process began, consciously or unconsciously, in 1996.) These finishing touches were meant to refine or hone your thinking process and how you communicate to others. This is why some of you might have moved to a place where there was a different language. ("I thought they spoke English in Boston?")

Nevertheless, the reason some of you had two moves was because around 2003 to 2006 your primary focus was different from a few years earlier. This time you wanted to put down roots and create a solid home base. Therefore, some of you moved yet again because you bought something or chose something better. Those of you who didn't move a second time did renovations, repairs, and improvements to where you already lived.

And what a great time to do this! In 2002–3, family relations were lovely and warm. You might have expanded your family through birth, adoption, or marriage. There was a sense of largesse and increase at home. You might have bought things that made you feel richer at home as well (like butter and vodka). This was the best time in twelve years to buy, sell, or improve where you lived.

By 2003–4, you had lovely opportunities for vacations or family reunions, or in the arts, show business, the entertainment world, or anything to do with the hospitality industry. These areas were particularly fortunate for you. Artists were productive. Not only that, some of you met the love of your life at this time. Romance easily captured your heart!

Perhaps this is why many committed partnerships flourished beautifully by 2005–6.

Meanwhile, you were able to get a better job and improve your health, as well as your employment scene.

Not too shabby.

2006 – 2010

By 2006–7, many of you benefitted indirectly through partners or by receiving inheritances, perks, favours, gifts, payouts, and assistance from others. (In some ways, it felt like the universe owed you a favour.) Meanwhile, this was also a time when children became an increased responsibility, and issues related to children, sports, the arts, the entertainment world, and the hospitality industry were serious and full of responsibilities.

Privately, many of you were asking yourself what you really wanted to be when you grew up. It didn't matter how old you were — that wasn't the point. You were trying to define what your quest was. What exactly was it that you were meant to achieve? Travel and higher education looked very good in 2007–8. This was also an excellent time to explore opportunities in publishing, the media, the law, and anything related to medicine.

On the heels of this, you experienced wonderful chances to boost your name and your reputation. Perhaps because you were working so hard and busting your buns, you got promotions, praise, and acknowledgement for your efforts. Naturally, this paid off with increased responsibility and involvement with groups by 2009–10.

But oy! This was a time of hard work. No question about it. Nevertheless, people could see you were giving it all you had. What else can anyone do?

2011 – 2012

For the first time in your adult life, wild, wacky Uranus is in your sign. Omigawd! (It peeked in briefly last year.) Uranus is the planet of unpredictability, impulsiveness, rebellion, and explosions. (Yikes!) The last time it was in your sign was 1929–34. So here it is, and it's going to stay until 2019. Almost a decade. What will this mean?

For starters, this is going to radically redefine your relationships with partners and close friends. (Yes, this could blow some of them out of the water.) This is why a three-year window from about 2010 to 2013 (maybe longer for some) is a highly contentious time for committed partnerships. ("Go, and never darken my towels again!"[15]) When Uranus is in your sign, it's an indication that you're letting go of old habit patterns and ways of doing things. But, in truth, you're not just letting go — you're breaking free! Wherever you feel stymied, or stultified, or squished by others is exactly where you are going to make tracks for the door! ("So long, and thanks for all the fish!"[16])

This break with the past is definitely happening for many of you because more than one astrological influence indicates that this is in the cards for you. Naturally, not all relationships and partnerships will go by the wayside, but all of them will change! During the next nine years, as Uranus comes near the degree of your Sun in Aries (depending on the day you were born), your need to break free will feel the strongest. Fear not. Basically, Uranus only jiggles what you really should get rid of or become free from. If you are already living your life according to your own wants and dictates, these changes will be much less, if at all.

Good news! You will feel *younger* after this Uranus experience. You'll feel freer. You'll have a whole new outlook and become more aware of things you used to think were a tad *outré*. In fact, many of you will explore astrology, yoga, human consciousness

---

15. Ya gotta love Groucho Marx.
16. This is the title of the fourth book in Douglas Adams's Hitchhiker's Guide to the Galaxy series (London: Pan Books, 1984).

studies, or mind-expanding techniques. It will definitely catapult you out of stagnant or negative situations that you should have left long ago. (You know who you are.) During this time (2011–12) Aries people born prior to March 26 will feel this influence the most.

Fortunately, while all these wild and crazy things are going on, 2011–12 will be a time when you will boost your income! It generally doesn't happen by magic. You do have to do something (like get out of bed).

Incidentally, everything I say can have an umbrella of a year on either side of the date I give, depending on your particular birthday. But the trend and the direction will be there. No question. You might already have noticed this if you were reading about your past. Perhaps many of these things seem relevant but they are all two years off! (That's just your particular timeline.)

At this same time in your life, possibly as early as 2008 or as late as 2014, depending on the day you were born, a powerful force might cause you to change your life direction. Big time! This same force might also trigger a change in your legal status in the world through marriage, divorce, or having a child. It's as if your reputation is going to be transformed and, indeed, it will.

2013 – 2015

In this window of time, people born from March 26 to April 6 will feel the most dramatic changes going on in their life, especially in terms of relationships and partnerships. This is the group that will be stretching their wings to go for the gold! It's important to remember that the influence of Uranus does not take away what you really need. It is simply trying to remove whatever it is that is holding you back from fulfilling your potential. This is why I think Aries people can handle this transit with much more enthusiasm and skillful means. By nature, you are eager to explore new territory! You want to shake off your shackles!

The years 2013–14 are certainly optimistic and happier. Relations with siblings and daily contacts will improve. By 2014, you are feeling very good about where you live, family relationships, and anything to do with your home. This is a wonderful year for real-estate deals. Whether you buy property for speculation or for your own use, it will prove to be a profitable move in the future. Others will buy beautiful things for where they live, so that they feel richer in their humble abode. ("Welcome to my little castle.")

Take note: in this window of time, you might have to get along with less because the resources of others will be cut off to you. Actually, this is not too surprising, because some of you will have split from relationships and are probably getting less practical help from a partner. Alternatively, your partner might lose their job, or go into business for themselves, or do something that diminishes their contribution. ("I think Hawaii is out of the question this year, don't you?" "Hawaii? We can't even afford parking downtown!")

Nevertheless, whatever cutbacks you experience can't be too bad because this is also a time when you like where you live better. You might move to bigger digs. You might buy something bigger. The bottom line is you feel more expansive and more thrilled with where you're living. Similarly, you might "expand" your home scene through an addition to the family — by birth, adoption, or marriage. (But not your deadbeat, sofa-surfing brother-in-law.)

By 2015–16, plans for a vacation look great! (Hawaii is back in the picture.) This is also a marvellous time for romance, love affairs, and anything to do with sports, the arts, the entertainment world, show business, and the hospitality industry. At this time in your life, children will become a source of joy. You feel creative. You're in love. Life is good! ("Mmm, delicious! Is this Grey Goose?")

2016 ~ 2017

I have been discussing the explosive influence of Uranus in your sign. Although this could trigger sudden changes for any of you at any time, in this two-year window the people who will feel this the most will likely be those who were born between April 6 and April 14. (Wear water wings and stay out of the deep end.)

The good news is the loss of income or practical support from others that you might have felt in the past few years is now no longer a problem. (Whew!) If your partner was out of work, they are employed again, or something else has happened to compensate. Perhaps your scholarship or bursary ended but now you have graduated and you're earning money. Whatever the reason, you feel you have *survived*!

This stage in your life is very much a time of preparation, because you're beginning to see your real goals ahead. The year 2016 is a wonderful time to improve your job by getting a better job or better duties, or perhaps your evil boss retires and moves to Hoboken, New Jersey. Something is definitely better in terms of how you earn your money this year!

Your employment scene is not the only thing that is looking up. You feel invigorated and more enthusiastic about life. This could be because by 2017 committed partnerships are looking very sweet indeed. In fact, for some, this is a time when wedding bells are ringing. For certain, all partnerships, both professional and intimate, will be a source of joy and positive support for you.

2018 – 2019

How sweet it is! This marks the beginning of a five-year run that is definitely a time of harvest for your sign. This means that now is the time when your cherished dreams can come true. Depending on your age and where you are in your career path, it might mean a graduation, a great first job, or a serious promotion! Artists might achieve recognition, possibly even major kudos. This is definitely a time when whatever seeds you have planted in the past will come to fruition. For some, this is your ultimate career pinnacle in life.[17]

Of course, the catch is that harvest time is also when you see which seeds didn't grow. (Groan.) For a few of you, it could be a time of disappointment. Get over it.

Don't dwell on what is not working. Instead, focus on what *is* working. (There's no time like the pleasant.)

In this two-year window, wild, wacky Uranus will most likely trigger major changes in the lives of those who were born from April 15 to April 19. Don't worry about the coming changes. Generally, the changes that Uranus brings are liberating! Uranus wants to free you from whatever has been holding you back, or holding you down, or making you not believe in yourself. ("I was lost, but now am found; Was blind, but now I see.")[18]

The particularly lovely thing about this time of harvest for you is that not only are you personally successful, you're also raking it in! You are definitely on the receiving end of the wealth of others. This is a classic time for receiving inheritances, getting money back from the government, a boost from your partner's income that indirectly blesses you, favourable settlements in insurance — something that says you're on the gravy train! Yay!

---

17. Always keep in mind that astrology makes a distinguishing difference between job and career. Your job is what you do to pay the bills. Your career is your "life path" — you may or may not get paid for it. For example, Vincent van Gogh's career was being a painter, but he never sold a painting in his life. Your career might be being a parent.
18. These lyrics are from "Amazing Grace." The song was written by John Newton (1725–1807), who was once a slave-ship captain and who later became a clergyman. The story of his life is poignant and fascinating. It's worth a Google.

Your sexual energy is also hot! Not only are you turned on by life, it looks like you're turned on by someone very appealing within arm's reach. (Oh yeah.) Mind you, who's surprised? When you're hot — you're *hot*! (The combination of money and success is a powerful aphrodisiac.)

2020 – 2022

Things just keep getting better, but that is often how it works when you're on a roll. (Unfortunately, it often works the other way, too, doesn't it? I think that's because life has a way of compounding whatever is happening.)

During 2020–21, lucky moneybags Jupiter is travelling across the very top of your chart, attracting all kinds of opportunities to you (as if everyone wasn't already eating out of the palm of your hand). In down-home terms, you could say this is like putting a good saddle on a good horse. *Make the most of this!* Whenever astrological events indicate that it is a time of success for you, it's important to remember that astrology is not *causing* anything. Astrology is just a language that I'm "reading" to see what's actually happening in your life. I think the Moon is the only thing that can "cause" anything because it's so close to us. Hey — we have actually gone to the Moon! (The lineups at the border were terrible.)

Therefore, when I point out to you that this is an extremely successful time in your life, specifically, it is a time when important people notice you. Not only that, it's a time when all kinds of opportunities are available to you, very likely through these important people. Take advantage of this! It doesn't just flow in through a window like pollen and settle all over you. This is why I use the term "harvest." Whatever you've been doing since 2003, and especially whatever you've been doing since 2010–11 — *this* is what makes a huge difference in 2020!

By 2021, everyone wants to see your face. You're wonderfully popular. This is a great time to join groups, clubs, and professional associations. Your schmooze factor will not only be a source of pleasure for you but it will also put you in contact with people who can make a positive difference in your life. This is also a time when you can begin a lovely friendship that will grow.

Sheesh! I told you it only gets better. In May 2022, lucky Jupiter enters your sign for the first time since 2011 (before that, it entered your sign in 1987 and 1999). However, this time its benefit will be far better than the previous times, because now it is your time of harvest! (Dontcha love it?)

To put it another way, let's say you are a budding actor. The first time Jupiter enters your sign, you might get your first big role where people really notice you. But later, when you are in your time of harvest and Jupiter enters your sign, this could mean you win an Oscar! Do you see the difference?

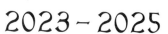

2023 ~ 2025

After that run of terrific luck (your bathroom mirror is covered in kisses), you're making more money! Ya think? It's a given. The window of 2023–24 will definitely boost your earnings, or bring new money streams into your life, or allow you to earn money on the side.

Because there is a more active cash flow in your life during this window of time, you are spending more as well and buying goodies for yourself. (If you get a little ragtop, get spoke wheels.)

However, all good things must come to an end. (And this has nothing to do with the fact that, coincidentally, this is the end of your Aries predictions.) Around 2023, you will find yourself going through garages, attics, and storage lockers, to say nothing of drawers, cupboards, and closets, so you can get rid of what you no longer need. Out it goes! This is a wonderful opportunity to sell what you don't want, or give it away, or recycle it. Let go of all that fabric! And what about that darkroom equipment? All this activity is because you are beginning a two- to three-year journey when you will start to dismantle much of what you have created since 2011. It was a good run, but it's time to move on.

One reason you'll know this is a period of transition is because when you go to places, or see people, or hang out with pals doing familiar activities, somehow, you won't get the same rush or the same pleasure that you used to. In fact, it will feel pretty vacant. ("What's it all about, Alfie?")

This is a sure sign you are changing. A lot of the things that you liked to do before are no longer your first choice or your priority. Ditto for some of the people you used to hang out with. Now they seem a bit boring or juvenile. That's okay — what's happening is you are gearing up for a time in 2025 (or 2026 for some of you) when you're going to enter a whole new sandbox!

This is why you have to lighten your load. You're getting rid of what is no longer relevant in your life in order to sail into something entirely new. Incidentally, the last time you did this was around 1996–97.

A little tip: this new sandbox that you are about to move into will be so different that you might actually change your daily wardrobe. ("Should I pack tropical?") This could be an excuse for new shades, new hats, and, possibly, stylish khakis. Something with panache — but practical.

New is always so exciting, isn't it?

"I wanted to be president of the United States. I really did. The older I get, the less preposterous the idea seems."

ALEC BALDWIN

American Film and Television Actor

The Hunt for Red October and TV's *30 Rock*

(B. APRIL 3, 1958)

Famous Aries Personalities

B. F. Skinner	March 20, 1904–1990
Carl Reiner	March 20, 1922
Fred Rogers	March 20, 1928–2003
Hal Linden	March 20, 1931
Bobby Orr	March 20, 1948
William Hurt	March 20, 1950
Spike Lee	March 20, 1957
Holly Hunter	March 20, 1958
Johann Sebastian Bach	March 21, 1685–1750
Timothy Dalton	March 21, 1946
Gary Oldman	March 21, 1958
Matthew Broderick	March 21, 1962
Rosie O'Donnell	March 21, 1962
Ronaldinho Gaúcho	March 21, 1980
Marcel Marceau	March 22, 1923–2007
William Shatner	March 22, 1931
Andrew Lloyd Webber	March 22, 1948
Elvis Stojko	March 22, 1972
Reese Witherspoon	March 22, 1976
Akira Kurosawa	March 23, 1910–1998
Wernher von Braun	March 23, 1912–1977
Roger Bannister	March 23, 1929
Hope Davis	March 23, 1964
Princess Eugenie of York	March 23, 1990
William Morris	March 24, 1834–1896
Joseph Barbera	March 24, 1911–2006
Lawrence Ferlinghetti	March 24, 1919
Steve McQueen	March 24, 1930–1980
David Suzuki	March 24, 1936
Bob Mackie	March 24, 1940
Tommy Hilfiger	March 24, 1951
Alyson Hannigan	March 24, 1974
Gloria Steinem	March 25, 1934

Aretha Franklin	March 25, 1942
Elton John	March 25, 1947
Sarah Jessica Parker	March 25, 1965
Jeff Healey	March 25, 1966–2008
Robert Frost	March 26, 1874–1963
Leonard Nimoy	March 26, 1931
Alan Arkin	March 26, 1934
James Caan	March 26, 1940
Nancy Pelosi	March 26, 1940
Erica Jong	March 26, 1942
Bob Woodward	March 26, 1943
Diana Ross	March 26, 1944
Martin Short	March 26, 1950
Kenny Chesney	March 26, 1968
Keira Knightley	March 26, 1985
Sarah Vaughan	March 27, 1924–1990
Michael York	March 27, 1942
Jann Arden	March 27, 1962
Quentin Tarantino	March 27, 1963
Mariah Carey	March 27, 1970
Stacy "Fergie" Ferguson	March 27, 1975
Dianne Wiest	March 28, 1948
Karen Kain	March 28, 1951
Reba McEntire	March 28, 1955
Vince Vaughn	March 28, 1970
Julia Stiles	March 28, 1981
Pearl Bailey	March 29, 1918–1990
Eric Idle	March 29, 1943
Marina Sirtis	March 29, 1955
Christopher Lambert	March 29, 1957
Elle Macpherson	March 29, 1963
Lucy Lawless	March 29, 1968
Vincent van Gogh	March 30, 1853–1890
Warren Beatty	March 30, 1937
Eric Clapton	March 30, 1945
Tracy Chapman	March 30, 1964
Céline Dion	March 30, 1968
Norah Jones	March 30, 1979
César Chávez	March 31, 1927–1993
Gordie Howe	March 31, 1928
Liz Claiborne	March 31, 1929–2007

Richard Chamberlain	March 31, 1934
Shirley Jones	March 31, 1934
Christopher Walken	March 31, 1943
Gabe Kaplan	March 31, 1945
Al Gore	March 31, 1948
Rhea Perlman	March 31, 1948
Ewan McGregor	March 31, 1971
Lon Chaney	April 1, 1883–1930
Anne McCaffrey	April 1, 1926
Ali MacGraw	April 1, 1938
Wangari Maathai	April 1, 1940
Annette O'Toole	April 1, 1952
Susan Boyle	April 1, 1961
Rachel Maddow	April 1, 1973
Hans Christian Andersen	April 2, 1805–1875
Max Ernst	April 2, 1891–1976
Buddy Ebsen	April 2, 1908–2003
Alec Guinness	April 2, 1914–2000
Hiroyuki Sakai	April 2, 1942
Linda Hunt	April 2, 1945
Emmylou Harris	April 2, 1948
Christopher Meloni	April 2, 1961
Sally Rand	April 3, 1904–1979
Doris Day	April 3, 1922
Marlon Brando	April 3, 1924–2004
Gus Grissom	April 3, 1926–1967
Wayne Newton	April 3, 1942
Tony Orlando	April 3, 1944
Alec Baldwin	April 3, 1958
David Hyde Pierce	April 3, 1959
Eddie Murphy	April 3, 1961
Maya Angelou	April 4, 1928
Anthony Perkins	April 4, 1932–1992
Craig T. Nelson	April 4, 1944
Evelyn Hart	April 4, 1956
Robert Downey, Jr.	April 4, 1965
Jill Scott	April 4, 1972
Heath Ledger	April 4, 1979–2008
Roberto Luongo	April 4, 1979
Amanda Righetti	April 4, 1983
Spencer Tracy	April 5, 1900–1967

Bette Davis	April 5, 1908–1989
Gregory Peck	April 5, 1916–2003
Arthur Hailey	April 5, 1920–2004
Agnetha Fältskog	April 5, 1950
André Previn	April 6, 1929
Ram Dass	April 6, 1931
Merle Haggard	April 6, 1937
Billy Dee Williams	April 6, 1937
Gheorghe Zamfir	April 6, 1941
Paul Rudd	April 6, 1969
Zach Braff	April 6, 1975
Billie Holiday	April 7, 1915–1959
Ravi Shankar	April 7, 1920
Francis Ford Coppola	April 7, 1939
David Frost	April 7, 1939
Jackie Chan	April 7, 1954
Russell Crowe	April 7, 1964
Mary Pickford	April 8, 1892–1979
Vivienne Westwood	April 8, 1941
Barbara Kingsolver	April 8, 1955
Patricia Arquette	April 8, 1968
Hugh Hefner	April 9, 1926
Michael Learned	April 9, 1939
Dennis Quaid	April 9, 1954
Marc Jacobs	April 9, 1963
Cynthia Nixon	April 9, 1966
Joseph Pulitzer	April 10, 1847–1911
Omar Sharif	April 10, 1932
Steven Seagal	April 10, 1952
Mandy Moore	April 10, 1984
Oleg Cassini	April 11, 1913–2006
Danny Gallivan	April 11, 1917–1993
Joel Grey	April 11, 1932
Peter Riegert	April 11, 1947
Trevor Linden	April 11, 1970
Joss Stone	April 11, 1987
David Letterman	April 12, 1947
Scott Turow	April 12, 1949
David Cassidy	April 12, 1950
Vince Gill	April 12, 1957
Claire Danes	April 12, 1979

Thomas Jefferson	April 13, 1743–1826
Paul Sorvino	April 13, 1939
Peabo Bryson	April 13, 1951
Garry Kasparov	April 13, 1963
Loretta Lynn	April 14, 1934
Julie Christie	April 14, 1941
Pete Rose	April 14, 1941
Robert Carlyle	April 14, 1961
Adrien Brody	April 14, 1973
Sarah Michelle Gellar	April 14, 1977
Leonardo da Vinci	April 15, 1452–1519
Henry James	April 15, 1843–1916
Elizabeth Montgomery	April 15, 1933–1995
Emma Thompson	April 15, 1959
Seth Rogen	April 15, 1982
Emma Watson	April 15, 1990
Charlie Chaplin	April 16, 1889–1977
Peter Ustinov	April 16, 1921–2004
Henry Mancini	April 16, 1924–1994
Pope Benedict XVI	April 16, 1927
Bobby Vinton	April 16, 1935
Dusty Springfield	April 16, 1939–1999
Kareem Abdul-Jabbar	April 16, 1947
Martin Lawrence	April 16, 1965
William Holden	April 17, 1918
Olivia Hussey	April 17, 1951
Sean Bean	April 17, 1959
Jennifer Garner	April 17, 1972
Victoria Beckham	April 17, 1974
Clarence Darrow	April 18, 1857–1938
Hayley Mills	April 18, 1946
James Woods	April 18, 1947
Eric McCormack	April 18, 1963
Conan O'Brien	April 18, 1963
America Ferrera	April 18, 1984
Jayne Mansfield	April 19, 1933–1967
Dudley Moore	April 19, 1935–2002
Al Unser, Jr.	April 19, 1962
Ashley Judd	April 19, 1968
Kate Hudson	April 19, 1979
Hayden Christensen	April 19, 1981

TAURUS

APRIL 20 – MAY 20

TAURUS THE BULL
(APRIL 20 – MAY 20)

"I HAVE."

"A mind all logic is like a knife all blade.
It makes the hand bleed that uses it."
RABINDRANATH TAGORE
Indian Poet, Novelist, Musician, and Playwright
(MAY 7, 1862–AUGUST 7, 1941)

"Ask not what you can do for your country.
Ask what's for lunch."
ORSON WELLES
American Film Director, Writer, Actor, and Producer
Best Known for *Citizen Kane*
(MAY 6, 1915–OCTOBER 10, 1985)

Element: Earth
Ruling Planet: Venus
Quality: Fixed
Opposite Sign: Scorpio
Symbol: The Bull
Glyph: Head of the Bull
Lucky Gems: Emerald, Blue Sapphire, and Jade[1]
Flowers: Daisy and Cowslip
Colours: Greens and Browns
Parts of the Body: Throat and Neck

You Like: The good things in life, the beauty of nature, antiques, music, affluence, and money in the bank. (A mortgage-free home goes without saying — but I just did.)

You Don't Like: Ugly objects, debt, arguments, and bossy people.

Where You Shine: Patient, affectionate, persevering, constructive, practical, kind-hearted, and steadfast.

So Who's Perfect? Materialistic, self-indulgent, unimaginative, inflexible, and lazy.

---

1. Different texts will name different gems and different flowers for different signs. Ditto for the colours (although you are definitely partial to earthy tones). To my way of thinking, the so-called flowers and gems for each sign are fuzzy.

What Is Taurus-ness?[2]

The easiest way to quickly grasp the essence of your sign is to understand what your ruling planet means in astrology. Your ruling planet is fair Venus, the goddess of beauty and love. (The Greeks called this goddess Aphrodite, and she also held domain over vegetation and gardens.)

So right off the bat we see that the essence of Taurus is tied in with beauty, love, fields of tulips, and rose gardens.

Sounds good so far!

To expand a bit more — in astrology, the Moon represents *feelings*. And although the Moon can be in any one of the twelve signs, the very *best* place for the Moon — in anyone's chart — is in Taurus. (Mom always liked you best.) So ah ha! There is this lovely connection between Taurus and *good feelings*.

Sounds even better!

Meanwhile, behind the azalea bush, according to astrology the best sign for your ruler, Venus, to be in is Pisces (whaaat?), because Venus is about beauty and Pisces is about seeking the *ideal* — the perfect rose, the perfect painting, the perfect symphony, the perfect love.

"If we could but paint with the hand what we see with the eye."
HONORÉ DE BALZAC
French Novelist and Playwright
(MAY 20, 1799–AUGUST 18, 1850)

What a winning combo you are! You have an amazing affinity for the perfection of beauty, and, at the same time, you're extremely warm and caring. You are born into a beautiful sign! (Can I go home with you?)

All Things Beautiful

Taurus appreciates all things beautiful. No matter what it is — if it's beautiful, you admire it. You especially appreciate the beauty of nature. You love verdant parks and fragrant gardens with a dizzying array of blooms. It doesn't matter if the flowers

2. No one is just one sign because everyone's chart is made up of different planets. Therefore, this section captures the Taurus archetype — the qualities of "Taurus-ness." Many other signs will have Taurus characteristics as well. Therefore, the discussion of one sign is not an exact description of that person; rather, it is a description of the qualities of that sign.

are planted in a formal English garden or if they're scattered wildflowers growing in a meadow — you love them all.

My mother is a Taurus, and she likes to visit parks and gardens. She often went with her mother, and I tagged along as a little girl. Years later, I drove her (my mother never got her driver's licence) to different parks, especially in Victoria.[3]

Whether as a child or as an adult, whenever I accompanied my mother on her walks through parks I thought it was the polite thing to do. I figured this was what people did on Sunday afternoons if they didn't have something better to do. It was a gentle, civilized time-filler for people who didn't go to movies.

It never occurred to me how much my mother actually loved parks! Now, as an astrologer with a better grasp of what Taurus is all about, I see this Taurus trait so much more clearly! (And sheepishly, I might add.)

In the movie *Howard's End*, a Merchant Ivory Production,[4] the character Leonard Best walks at night through a field of blue flowers that shimmer faintly in the moonlight. It's visually breathtaking! I think that image captures the Taurus appreciation for beauty in the world. (Of course, there are countless beautiful scenes in film, paintings, photography, and real life, but that scene sprang to my mind now, even though I saw the film seventeen years ago.)

---

3. Victoria, B.C. (Canada), has wonderful balmy weather. It is known for being a place where old people go to be with their parents.
4. Merchant Ivory Productions is a film company founded by James Ivory and Ismail Merchant. Their films were, for the most part, directed by the former, produced by the latter, and scripted by Ruth Prawer Jhabvala. James Ivory has Jupiter in Taurus, Ruth Prawer Jhabvala is a Taurus, and Ismail Merchant had Moon in Taurus, which, to me, hugely explains the beautiful look of their films.

Because you adore beauty, you love antiques, paintings, magnificent architecture, fine furniture, classic cars, gorgeous musical instruments, beautifully bound books, elegant candelabras, fine china and glassware, brocade fabric, cashmere sweaters, well-tailored clothing made from lovely fabric, and wood carvings. The list is endless. Small wonder so many of you are in the antiques business or own second-hand stores.

Naturally, your physical appearance reflects your love of beauty as well. Your clothing is not necessarily haute couture or current in a stylish way, but it is always attractive. Taurus people are partial to pastel colours, especially all shades of green. Not only does your appearance reflect your love of beauty, but everything around you echoes your taste for elegance, harmony, and quality.

Nice Guys Finish Happily

"Always be a little kinder than necessary."
J. M. BARRIE
Scottish Author and Dramatist; Creator of *Peter Pan*
(MAY 9, 1860–JUNE 19, 1937)

You people are the nice guys of the zodiac. (You really are!) You're caring, patient, gentle-hearted, and very mellow. You're also practical, conservative in some ways (not in everything), and full of common sense. You have a lovely sense of propriety and make excellent company for anyone. You are reliable, honest, and stable. Without question, you are the warmest of all the Earth signs. Your friendly, mellow quality is even reflected in your appearance, which is often bovine-like.[5]

Your opposite sign, Scorpio (Scorpio and Taurus are two ends of the same plank), is intensely passionate, obsessive, and given to extremes. You are not. However, when your sign goes off the tracks, it has given the world some of its most notorious, frightening individuals! (I won't mention who, because I'm discussing what is nice about Taurus, of caurus.)

You are cooperative and patient. In fact it is this gentle nature, combined with the receptive quality of Venus, that is the reason you are so easily swayed (because you are a suggestible sign). For starters, you're inclined to believe everything you read, because *it's in print*.

Your suggestibility might also explain your love of history — that malleable subject, written by the victors.[6] To be sure, Taurus people often major in history at university or teach history. This is also why you are inveterate newspaper readers.

---

5. This bovine quality is demonstrated in the "cow-like" expression of your eyes. There is also often a strong preference for porterhouse over sirloin.
6. I went to universities in both Canada and the United States. It amazed me how differently the two countries discussed the War of 1812–14. In the United States, it was an American victory. In Canada, it was a Canadian victory, which, of course, it truly was. (Naturally, I will reverse this for the American edition.)

After all, newspapers are simply *current* history. (My Taurus mother will never throw a paper out until she has read it cover to cover, including the obituaries.) And yes — Taurus homes have piles of newspapers.[7]

To be sure, all is not sweetness and light. Your easygoing, gentle manner is partly due to the fact that you are always holding in something of yourself. You're emotionally careful. The reason for this is because somewhere along the way you discovered you were capable of the most destructive, furious rage! Taurus anger eclipses that of all other signs. It is total devastation, the worst in the zodiac. ("Now we see the violence inherent in the system.")[8]

Fortunately, you are slow to anger. The average Taurus person might get angry only once or twice in their life, if that. You're very careful. You don't shoot from the hip or blurt out whatever springs to mind, like many other signs. Oh no! You choose your time carefully. You're uncanny about waiting for the right moment to speak, or ask a question, or bring up a particular subject. Whenever I hear "Let's sleep on it. Give the matter a sober second thought," I think "Hmmm — Taurus."

> "Cheerfulness, it would appear, is a matter which depends fully
> as much on the state of things within, as on the state of things
> without and around us."
>
> CHARLOTTE BRONTË
> British Novelist and Poet
> *Jane Eyre*
> (APRIL 21, 1816–MARCH 31, 1855)

---

7. Newspaper magnate William Randolph Hearst (April 29, 1863–August 14, 1951) was a Taurus.
8. This quote is from the 1975 film *Monty Python and the Holy Grail*.

Four Taurus Qualities

To better understand Taurus, in addition to the description of how Venus makes you appreciate beauty, vegetation, and gentle manners, here are four more ways to think about your sign:

1. Tactile Approach to Life
2. The Country Squire
3. The Midas Touch
4. I Sing!

Tactile Approach to Life

You are the most tactile sign in the zodiac. You discover your world through your fingertips. No matter what you're looking at, you will reach out to touch it. Even if you are buying blank writing paper, you want to feel its texture and thickness. (You're thinking, "Hello? Of course!")[9]

How your clothing *feels* is as important to you as how it looks. You cannot tolerate a scratchy label or coarse wool on your skin. I know a Taurus man who searches for second-hand vicuña shirts because they are softer and already "broken in."

You are the only Earth sign that is ruled by Venus, the goddess of beauty. This is why you love good woods (no *plástico* please), pewter, gold, silver — the real deal. You appreciate touch and texture. You enjoy good soaps, thick towels, high-quality cotton sheets on your bed. More than any other sign, you should have silk underwear. Whatever touches your skin should be the best you can afford.

Of course, your strong tactile senses go beyond the fingertips. You love good food and good drink!

---

9. I am sure many Tauruses bemoan the current practice of encasing products in sealed clear plastic, making it impossible to finger or touch what you are buying. I, too, deplore this. It's also bulkier to steal.

I recall years ago talking to a client who wasn't sure of the exact time of day he was born. Because of this uncertainty, I knew he was either Aries Rising or Taurus Rising. Thinking he might be Aries Rising, I said, "When you were a little boy, did you get into fights easily? Did you have to be the first in line? Were you a scrappy little kid? You might have had freckles?"

He hesitated, then said slowly, "Not particularly."

Deciding he must therefore be Taurus Rising, I said, "Do you like good food, good wine, good sex, and a nice place to live?"

Astonished, he said, "Doesn't everybody?"

I know this boggles your mind, but, no, these are not top priorities for everyone. All you have to do is look around you. Observe other people's choices: what they eat, what they drink, how they live their lives, and what their homes look like. (Gasp!)

I rest my handbag.

Taurus people love their creature comforts! In the perfect world, you awaken on your soft down pillow under organic cotton sheets (maybe Egyptian). You swing your feet out of bed to land on a plush carpet or a heated floor. Your bathroom is beautiful to look at and pleasing to enter. Male or female, you have wonderful fragrances to choose from. And when you wander into the kitchen for coffee, you will grind top-quality fair-trade beans for your espresso machine. (But not all Tauruses are alike. My Taurus mother in her beautifully furnished home drinks instant coffee every morning. She is ninety-three years old, healthy and happy! Instant coffee — what can I say?)

In fact, your tastes are so discerning, you disdain one-stop shopping. You have your favourite haunts for particular products. You know the best bakery for your bread and where to get your coffee, and you know exactly where to go for your fish, or your meat, or your produce. You have a culinary trapline because you are a gourmand!

Once again, how you view yourself is relative. Although my mother undoubtedly loves to decorate a room, enjoys beautiful china and glassware, and faithfully watches *Antiques Roadshow*, she does not consider herself a gourmand. Nevertheless, whenever she visits me, either my daughter or I make a point of getting a loaf of a particular round cornmeal bread with raisins in it that my mother loves to have for her morning toast — and instant coffee. It's an unwritten family law.

Despite your love of good food, you're not a food snob. You know the best apple pie is at a truck stop just outside of Calgary. You know where to go for dim sum in Chinatown and you know the best clam chowder in New York is at The Oyster Bar in Grand Central Station. You want the best food you can find, whether it's at a roadside café or a posh restaurant. (You believe one should practise safe eating and always use condiments.)

"Good bread is the most fundamentally satisfying of all foods;
and good bread with fresh butter, the greatest of feasts."
JAMES BEARD
American Chef and Food Writer
(MAY 5, 1903–JANUARY 21, 1985)

The sign Libra is also ruled by Venus, and Librans, too, adore beauty — but more from a visual point of view. The beauty you desire not only has to look lovely, it has to *feel* sumptuous as well, because what you seek is relaxing, sink-into-the-sofa comfort.

Publications such as *Wine Spectator* and *Cigar Aficionado* are classic Taurus magazines. Many of you sighed wistfully when *Gourmet* folded in 2009.

The Country Squire

"I wouldn't want to move to a smaller house."
BONO
Irish Musician, Activist, and Lead Singer of U2
(B. MAY 10, 1960)

Home is hugely important to Taurus. Everything revolves around the home. Your job is a means to ensure the security of your home and to give you the most beautiful home you could possibly have. Family is the social justification for your home. Family legitimizes your desire to focus on a mansion (if you can afford it) with bedrooms, bathrooms, a swimming pool, and tennis courts.

Your home is your open canvas to express your love of beauty and your knowledge of beautiful things (because you are knowledgeable). People admire your choice of paintings, furniture, and draperies; those handmade tiles you chose; the hues and shades of colours; the broadloom and carpets. All are tastefully exquisite selections!

The masterpiece you create is the identity card that you present to the world. But the person who is most pleased is *you*! You luxuriate in your own wonderful, comfy digs. And the day your mortgage is paid off calls for champagne!

A Taurus woman might create a bedroom worthy of Scheherazade. If possible, it will be her personal boudoir with heated towel rails, piped-in music, a steam shower, a Jacuzzi tub, fine cabinetry, and perhaps a chaise longue.

Naturally, if you can swing it, you'll have a wine cellar. You'll want the most gorgeous home you can buy, preferably on a big tract of land or, better yet, in the country. It might even be a house with a name. (Perfect!)

Of course, you will create your own garden paradise! Imagine a country cottage (larger than the average city home) with sheep grazing nearby. You have your own vegetable garden, as well as an array of sumptuous flowers and a gardener to help, because Taurus, after all, is a gentleman farmer.

> "I never lose sight of the fact that just being is fun."
> KATHARINE HEPBURN
> American Actress
> *The African Queen*, *The Lion in Winter*,
> and *Guess Who's Coming to Dinner*
> (MAY 12, 1907–JUNE 29, 2003)

Taurus newspaper magnate William Randolph Hearst (April 29, 1863–August 14, 1951) started out building a mere bungalow on land he inherited from his mother. Very soon, his ideas grew and grew and finally manifested as a home with fifty-six bedrooms and sixty-one bathrooms on 127 acres. In addition to tennis courts, outdoor swimming pools, extensive gardens, and a movie theatre, the estate also had an airstrip and the world's largest private zoo.

Farther south in Los Angeles, another Taurus, TV producer Aaron Spelling (April 22, 1923–June 23, 2006), built a home that is larger than the White House. He built it on land that was previously owned by yet another Taurus, singer Bing Crosby (May 3, 1903–October 14, 1977). The Spelling home is more than 56,000 square feet with 123 rooms, including twenty-seven bathrooms and five kitchens. It parks one hundred cars and is called "The Manor."

Well, not everyone wants to clean five kitchens and twenty-seven bathrooms. This is just a description of what you might do if you had the money. But one thing is certain: you will always create the most beautiful, comfortable home you can. People will enjoy visiting your home because you have an unerring instinct for creating comfort and leisure. You really know how to live!

"It is a comfortable feeling to know that you stand on your own ground.
Land is about the only thing that can't fly away."
ANTHONY TROLLOPE
British Novelist
Author of "The Chronicles of Barsetshire"
(APRIL 24, 1815–DECEMBER 6, 1882)

The Midas Touch

Taurus is *the* financial wizard of the zodiac. (No question!) You love money and you know it. Having lots of it helps you sleep at night.

"I don't like money, actually, but it quiets my nerves."
JOE LOUIS
World Heavyweight Champion, 1937–1949
(MAY 13, 1914–APRIL 12, 1981)

You want money in the bank and you want to own land. You like having property and a good portfolio. Taurus knows how to take a small amount of money and parlay it into thousands of dollars. Many Taurus people work in banks because they enjoy the clink of coins and the rustle of cash. (Money! Money! Money!)

Once you own something, you will do everything in your power to hold on to it. You fiercely defend your turf and your possessions. Although you like to buy the best and you like a comfortable home, ironically, you're not a spendthrift. You know how to spend your money, and you know how to save it as well.

"I've lost money and made money, but I know
my way around financially."
JACK NICHOLSON
American Actor
One Flew over the Cuckoo's Nest, Chinatown, The Shining, and *A Few Good Men*
(B. APRIL 22, 1937)

Furthermore, you are a collector. Some of you might collect stamps or coins, but, in reality, you'll collect anything. Many of you become serious art collectors, like actor Dennis Hopper (May 17, 1936–May 29, 2010) or businessman Alan Bond (b. April 22, 1938).[10] Often your collections become quite valuable. (*Quelle surprise.*)

---

10. I suspect many great art collectors, regardless of their sign, are Taurus Rising, or they might have Moon in Taurus.

Taurus people can do many kinds of jobs, but they gravitate toward big business. They want to earn lots of money to build a home they love, to buy beautiful things, and to feel secure. They're less concerned about impressing others, although they're pleased when people enjoy experiencing the magic of the beauty and comfort they create.

Taurus is the best sign in the zodiac for making money, handling money, and knowing how to create and build wealth.

> "I'm kidding about having only a few dollars.
> I might have a few dollars more."
>
> JAMES BROWN
> American Singer and Entertainer, "The Godfather of Soul"
> (MAY 3, 1933–DECEMBER 25, 2006)

I Sing!

Actually, not all Tauruses sing. I simply wanted to call attention to the fact that the sign of Taurus rules the throat, and almost all Taurus people have beautiful speaking voices.

Think of the mellifluous voice of George Clooney or the deep, booming tones of Bea Arthur. Or the distinctive voices of Glenn Ford, Glenda Jackson, Katharine Hepburn, James Mason, Henry Fonda, Candice Bergen, George Takei, Jack Nicholson, and James Stewart.

The throat is both your strength and your weakness. Your throat is the first warning sign that a flu or cold is coming. In fact, gargling salt water is a good thing for Taurus (in my opinion).

Whenever I meet a Taurus who doesn't know that their sign rules their throat, I am secretly shocked (although I know most people don't know what part of the body their sign rules). But Taurus people have such distinctive voices! Therefore, to help this forever resonate with you, I compiled this list of great singers, because Taurus is — without question — "The Voice!"

Lionel Hampton, April 20, 1908–August 31, 2002

Luther Vandross, April 20, 1951–July 1, 2005

Carmen Electra, April 20, 1972

Iggy Pop, April 21, 1947

Patti LuPone, April 21, 1949

Kathleen Ferrier, April 22, 1912–October 8, 1953

Peter Frampton, April 22, 1950

Roy Orbison, April 23, 1936–December 6, 1988

Barbra Streisand, April 24, 1942

Kelly Clarkson, April 24, 1982

Ella Fitzgerald, April 25, 1917–June 15, 1996

Albert King, April 25, 1923–December 1, 1992

Ma Rainey, April 26, 1886–December 22, 1939

Johnny Shines, April 26, 1915–April 20, 1992

Bobby Rydell, April 26, 1942

Coretta Scott King, April 27, 1927–January 30, 2006

Sheena Easton, April 27, 1959

Blossom Dearie, April 28, 1924–February 7, 2009

Ginette Reno, April 28, 1946

Willie Colón, April 28, 1950

Tammi Terrell, April 29, 1945–March 16, 1970

Carnie Wilson, April 29, 1968

Willie Nelson, April 30, 1933

Bobby Vee, April 30, 1943

Kate Smith, May 1, 1907–June 17, 1986

Sonny James, May 1, 1929

Shirley Horn, May 1, 1934–October 20, 2005

Judy Collins, May 1, 1939

Rita Coolidge, May 1, 1945

Ray Parker, Jr., May 1, 1954

Tim McGraw, May 1, 1967

Engelbert Humperdinck, May 2, 1936

Lesley Gore, May 2, 1946

Bing Crosby, May 3, 1903–October 14, 1977

Pete Seeger, May 3, 1919

James Brown, May 3, 1933–December 25, 2006

Frankie Valli, May 3, 1934

Randy Travis, May 4, 1959

Lance Bass, May 4, 1979

Blind Willie McTell, May 5, 1898–August 19, 1959

Tammy Wynette, May 5, 1942–April 6, 1998

Ian McCulloch, May 5, 1959

Jimmy Ruffin, May 7, 1939

Ricky Nelson, May 8, 1940–December 31, 1985

Billy Joel, May 9, 1949

Fred Astaire, May 10, 1899–June 22, 1987

Donovan, May 10, 1946

Sid Vicious, May 10, 1957–February 2, 1979

Bono, May 10, 1960

Irving Berlin, May 11, 1888–September 22, 1989

Eric Burdon, May 11, 1941

Steve Winwood, May 12, 1948

Ritchie Valens, May 13, 1941–February 3, 1959

Stevie Wonder, May 13, 1950

Norman Luboff, May 14, 1917–September 22, 1987

Bobby Darin, May 14, 1936–December 20, 1973

David Byrne, May 14, 1952

Eddy Arnold, May 15, 1918–May 8, 2008

Janet Jackson, May 16, 1966

Woody Herman, May 16, 1913–October 29, 1987

Liberace, May 16, 1919–February 4, 1987

Betty Carter, May 16, 1929–September 6, 1998

Taj Mahal, May 17, 1942

Jesse Winchester, May 17, 1944

Enya, May 17, 1961

Meredith Wilson, May 18, 1902–June 15, 1984

Big Joe Turner, May 18, 1911–November 24, 1985

Perry Como, May 18, 1912–May 12, 2001

Charles Trénet, May 18, 1913–February 19, 2001

George Strait, May 18, 1952

Nellie Melba, May 19, 1861–February 23, 1931

Peter Townshend, May 19, 1945

Grace Jones, May 19, 1948

Joey Ramone, May 19, 1951–April 15, 2001

Joe Cocker, May 20, 1944

Cher, May 20, 1946

"I may be a living legend, but that sure don't help
when I've got to change a flat tire."

ROY ORBISON

American Singer, Songwriter, and Musician
"Only the Lonely," "Crying," and "Oh, Pretty Woman"
(APRIL 23, 1936–DECEMBER 6, 1988)

Taurus in Love

"I don't need a man. But I'm happier with one.
I like to have someone I can touch and squeeze and kiss."
CHER
Stage Name of Cherilyn Sarkisian
American Singer, Songwriter, and Actress
Best Known for Sonny and Cher, "I Got You Babe,"
and Roles in *Mask* and *Moonstruck*
(B. MAY 20, 1946)

Guess who is the most tactile sign in the zodiac? It's you. You are the ultimate sensualist! You practically live for pleasure. But despite your love of your creature comforts, I would not dismiss you as a hedonist, because once you set your mind to something, you work hard! But ah, when it comes to the pleasures of love, you're deliciously sensuous and earthy! This is why I often refer to Taurus as a ripe, juicy peach. This is also why I say you've never really slept with somebody until you've slept with a Taurus.

"There is nothing more important in life than love."
BARBRA STREISAND
American Actress, Singer, Songwriter, Director
Funny Girl, Hello Dolly, and *Yentl*
(B. APRIL 24, 1942)

Because you are so tactile and sensuous, you adore being petted and stroked and loved to the max! You can easily spend all day in bed with your lover, getting up only for food — if necessary. Speaking of which, because you love good food and good wine, you enjoy nothing more than cooking a sumptuous meal with your loved one. The act of cooking and then sharing food is actually foreplay for you. That funny scene with Charlie Sheen and Valeria Golino in *Hot Shots! Part Deux*, where he fries bacon and eggs on her stomach, is a spoof of Taurus lovemaking. ("Hmmm, where is that whipped cream?")

Although you might have many affairs before you settle down, when you do settle down, marriage for you is for keeps. This is because you are a sign who seeks security in life. Obviously, you want financial security, job security, and a secure home, so it follows naturally that you want a secure relationship!

"If I get married, I want to be very married."
AUDREY HEPBURN
British Actress and Humanitarian
Charade, Sabrina, and *Breakfast at Tiffany's*
(MAY 4, 1929–JANUARY 20, 1993)

Your emphasis on security is why you are so very loyal once you finally find your true love. Needless to say, you demand 100 percent loyalty in return! You are a very jealous lover because by nature you are territorial about what you own. ("Don't touch! That's mine.")

No matter what your sex or inclination, you will always be drawn to the archetype of your opposite. In other words, if you are looking for a female partner, you want a very *feminine* woman. If you are looking for a male partner, you want a handsome, *masculine* hunk.

Massages, hugs, and constant touching are essential to your lovemaking. You don't need all the words, notes, and little messages that Geminis do. You just want a body you can nudge in the night!

Although you can be generous and occasionally even slavish in your devotion to your lover, you won't marry for money. But you'll be delighted if your lover happens to have a fat bank account and mortgage-free property. Bonus!

"Love or hatred must constantly increase between two persons
who are always together; every moment fresh reasons are found for
loving or hating better."
HONORÉ DE BALZAC
French Novelist and Playwright
La Comédie humaine
(MAY 20, 1799–AUGUST 18, 1850)

The Taurus Boss

"Always be sincere, even if you don't mean it."
HARRY S. TRUMAN
Thirty-third President of the United States, 1945–1953
(MAY 8, 1884–DECEMBER 26, 1972)

The Taurus boss is no slouch and can be demanding at times. They see what needs to be done and they expect their people to execute every task successfully.

Never rush your Taurus boss. This person likes to think things through carefully and clearly before making important decisions or taking action. Others might find this quality infuriating. ("The sky is falling!") However, once the decision has been made, you can have faith that it will be rock-solid.

Your Taurus boss also insists you play by the rules and respect how everything is done. No shortcuts. Taurus applauds a job well and properly done.

Your Taurus boss will want a workplace that is as comfortable as possible, preferably with an office sofa or an overstuffed chair. (A tiny fridge or mini-bar would be nice.) Potted ferns and lush plants are *de rigueur*. Many Taurus bosses raise their own orchids.

You can easily please your Taurus boss with edible gifts — yummy! Your choices are endless, but a few obvious picks are fresh croissants from the best bakery in town for their morning coffee, or wonderful dark chocolate, or perhaps a great bottle of wine. In fact, it's not hard to please the Taurus boss. However, the fastest way to *displease* this boss is to ask for a raise. (Especially if they're the owner.)

You can also impress your Taurus boss by doing your homework and being up on current events, especially if current events are pertinent to your job. You don't have to be clever and witty, but ignorance appalls Taurus. (These guys read newspapers and watch the news, remember?) If you are politically apathetic, hide this fact. Memorize the name of the leader of your country.

"I declare before you all that my whole life, whether it be long or short,
shall be devoted to your service and the service of our great imperial family
to which we all belong."
QUEEN ELIZABETH II
Reigning British Monarch of the Commonwealth of Nations since 1952
(B. APRIL 21, 1926)

The Taurus Employee

"We don't wake up for less than ten thousand dollars a day."
LINDA EVANGELISTA
Canadian Supermodel
(B. MAY 10, 1965)

The Taurus employee is almost an ideal employee. This is a person who likes to fit in and is willing to work hard. The Taurus employee has a great respect for rules and regulations, as well as for the *tradition* of doing things the way they've always been done.

Furthermore, no one more than this employee will respect the machinery, furniture, and surroundings related to the job. The Taurus employee might even polish a brass railing or the boardroom table! (Remember, this person sees the value of antiques and wonderful collector's items that others might completely overlook.)

Taurus employees are reliable and conscientious. However, it's important to know that the reason a Taurus is working is for their own security. Therefore, you have to pay them a decent wage and give them regular praise and raises so they feel rewarded for their hard work. Taurus doesn't like to work on commission. Taurus people like to know exactly what to count on, because this is a sign that budgets. (How else could they splurge on that antique Chippendale four-poster bed?)

This employee is also the perfect person to leave behind "minding the store." Taurus has a lot of moxie and money savvy. They're very good at making financial decisions. Not only are they reliable and conscientious, they are honest. They can run things in your absence, which — admit it — is invaluable!

Nota bene: Never cheat a Taurus. Once they lose respect for you, it's game over. They like to work for people they can respect and, furthermore, they like to sell or create a product they value.

This is one sign that gets rewarding satisfaction from doing a fine job.

The Taurus Parent

"Before I had my child, I thought I knew all the boundaries of myself,
that I understood the limits of my heart. It's extraordinary to have all those
limits thrown out, to realize your love is inexhaustible."

UMA THURMAN

American Actress

Pulp Fiction and *Kill Bill*

(B. APRIL 29, 1970)

It certainly does look like your sign is getting the Nice Guy Award. What
can I say? It's all the truth!

Astrology texts claim the sign of Taurus makes the best parent. Does this mean
you are the most playful parent? Or the most educationally stimulating? Or the
most loving? While you might be any or all of those things, the reason astrology
views Taurus as the best sign for parenting is simple. You are a practical sign who
knows that children need three square meals a day, clean pyjamas, and a warm bed
to sleep in at night. It's that simple.

"Minor things can become moments of great
revelation when encountered for the first time."

DAME MARGOT FONTEYN

British Ballerina

(MAY 18, 1919–FEBRUARY 21, 1991)

It doesn't matter how esoteric some people are in their approach to child-rearing, you
can't ignore the basics. Children need to be fed and clothed and housed. Every Taurus
parent knows this is paramount. Furthermore, this approach to rearing children makes
the children of Taurus parents feel secure in their world (and secure in your arms).

"For me, nothing has ever taken precedence over being
a mother and having a family and a home."

JESSICA LANGE

American Actress (and Avid Gardener)

Frances, *Tootsie*, and *Grey Gardens*

(B. APRIL 20, 1949)

Little indulgences, especially edible sweets and treats, are common with the Taurus parent. A walk along the street to look at neighbourhood gardens will end with an ice cream cone — surely! (My Taurus mother served two desserts a day — lunch and dinner.)

Furthermore, the Taurus parent encourages enterprising money-making adventures in their children. They will help their children set up a lemonade stand or encourage them to take a paper route, babysit, or mow lawns. The Taurus parent is ever mindful of teaching respect for money — how to earn it and certainly how to save it.

Because Taurus people are great traditionalists, much will be made of religious holidays and events that are occasions for family to gather together. Taurus parents are often great cooks, so these get-togethers are always rewarded with wonderful food and drink!

Taurus values family and home and always stays in warm contact with their offspring.

> "I remember being in tears at the hospital after Chloe was born,
> at the thought that someday she would have to leave home."
>
> CANDICE BERGEN
> American Actress
> *Murphy Brown*
> (B. MAY 9, 1946)

Above all — the wise Taurus knows the most important thing a parent can do for their kids is to remain solvent!

The Taurus Child

"Minds ripen at very different ages."
STEVIE WONDER
American Singer, Songwriter, and Activist
"Superstition" and "I Wish"
(B. MAY 13, 1950)

All you have to do is recall how tactile the sign of Taurus is to realize Taurus children need lots of hugging, petting, and cuddling. These children approach their world and their physical environment in an earthy, tangible way.

Taurus children love their food, although possibly, like many young children, they will go through their picky stages. But, generally, Taurus kids will eat practically anything because Taurus people love to eat!

However, this child will not *wear* practically anything. *Au contraire!* The clothing must be comfortable. It is very common for Taurus children to take off clothes they don't find comfortable or demand to wear something else. They like fabric that feels nice to their skin. In fact, the adult Taurus will often remember particular items of childhood clothing with fondness.

Taurus children learn about their world through touching, tasting, and experiencing through first-hand interaction. This is why, very often, Taurus children do not do particularly well in grade school, because this style of teaching isn't how Taurus children like their information to flow to them. Rather than show them pictures and tell them the names of the trees, take these children out into the forest and point out and name the trees, and they will grasp this immediately!

Taurus children feel gratified to help in the kitchen, or to help outside in the yard by raking leaves, or, better yet, to be involved in planting a flower or vegetable garden. They also love to build forts! Not only will they build forts outside, they will be constantly building indoor forts with chairs and blankets and tables. They're trying to build a house! (They know what they want.)

This is not a rebellious child. You can reason with Taurus, but you must be clear in your communications. Once they understand what the situation is, they're very co-operative and happy to oblige. They're also very eager to be young adults. They want to be treated with respect, but, at the same time, they always need lots of hugging! (So important to remember.)

Never hesitate to express your affection and love to a Taurus child. Always respect their toys and possessions. Do not punish them by taking things they own away from them. It's just not fair. And what does this teach? Only that punishment is a consequence of poor choices. Always remember that this a reasonable child who values safety and security and who is capable of long-range thinking, despite the immediate gratification most children crave. This is a wise child in a down-to-earth way.

Above all, Taurus children want a world worthy of respect. They want to respect their elders, their friends, their community, their government, and their country. It does not surprise me that A. A. Milne, the creator of *Winnie the Pooh*, had four planets in Taurus — Jupiter, Saturn, Neptune, and Pluto. According to Winnie the Pooh, "It is more fun to talk with someone who doesn't use long, difficult words but rather short, easy words like, 'What about lunch?'"

> "I was born with an enormous need for affection,
> and a terrible need to give it."
> AUDREY HEPBURN
> British Actress and Humanitarian
> *Charade, Sabrina,* and *Breakfast at Tiffany's*
> (MAY 4, 1929–JANUARY 20, 1993)

How to Be a Happier Taurus

It bears repeating that you are the nice guys of the zodiac. Basically, you are inclined to be middle-of-the-road and reasonable, not falling into extremes.

Earlier, I made reference to the fact that the best sign for anyone's Moon to be in is Taurus. A person with Moon in Taurus is basically sane. They will never have a nervous breakdown. (If they do, they just want attention.) Taurus is one of the most emotionally grounded placements for your Moon, which is your emotional barometer. (This is an indicator of what a warm, grounded sign you are.)

So, how can you promote your happiness? You're decent and kind, and you make the best parents. You enjoy the good things in life, and you also have lots of common sense. What's not to like? Nevertheless, I don't think you're necessarily happier than any other sign, although you might have fewer qualities that drive you to despair.

Anyone will agree that anger, jealousy, fear, and hatred are obvious qualities that lead to unhappiness. But your love of creature comforts and good food and sex doesn't seem to be such a bad thing, does it? So what's the problem?

While it's true that there is nothing wrong with enjoying good food, good wine, lovely furniture, a beautiful home, and great sex, you might become so focused on these things that they come to define you. Material things offer a transitory pleasure. If they really produced happiness, then all rich people would be happy (especially really rich people like Elvis Presley and Howard Hughes).

The fact is, your new car is just a pile of rust waiting to happen. Furthermore, the more you have, the more you have to maintain and keep cleaned, oiled, watered, polished, or whatever. Possessions require *work*! And they take up *space*! And then you have to worry about these items breaking down or being stolen or abused. (Sheesh!) Of course, some objects become obsolete as well. (Oh dear.) Your goodies are not going to last, but, more importantly, your appreciation of them will wane. But you know this. Down deep, you know this.

The real problem with being focused on acquiring beautiful things and wealth is simply that *that is* your focus. There's nothing wrong with any of this stuff, but if that is what your focus in life is . . . you might be shortchanging yourself. (Ya think?)

There's an Eastern saying:

> *Craving for small pleasures*
> *Cannot achieve great pleasure.*

Pleasure! This we like. But what is the "great pleasure"?[11]

I think "great pleasure" alludes to the fact that there are greater rewards in life than just owning things that give you temporary pleasure.

Imagine a baby in a playpen. The baby wants to be well fed, comfortable, and entertained. However, soon the baby will be bored with the toys in the playpen and want new ones. The baby will certainly be upset if the toys break or someone takes them away. When you simplify life to a playpen analogy, you can see the obvious limitations. You see that it's impossible to find true peace of mind if your primary motivation is simply your own comfort and pleasure. "I want my toys forever!" (Voice from the mountaintop: "It ain't going to happen.")

Could it be there's a confusion between pleasure and happiness? You know what gives you pleasure, but what will bring you happiness? You might get pleasure from a fantastic meal, but if you had that same meal every day for five years, would it still give you pleasure? Pleasure can wear itself out. Pleasure has a temporary quality, perhaps because it often involves the senses.

Happiness, however, is a feeling we get from something no matter how many times it occurs. And it doesn't involve the senses — it's internal — like the happiness we feel from helping a loved one.

Years ago, I had the good fortune of hearing R. D. Laing speak at the Hotel Vancouver.[12] As I recall, he was explaining how the meanings of the words in the Bible had changed over the past two thousand years. He said the words Christ spoke at that time meant something different from what we think today.

For example, two thousand years ago, the word "sin" simply meant "to miss a bull's eye." He said the term was in use before archery was created, and probably referred to throwing a knife or a spear at a target. If you missed the target, you had sinned. Feelings of guilt weren't connected with the word. You'd simply missed the target.

He also said that the word "repent" meant to swing 180 degrees on a two-dimensional plane. In other words, if you put a pencil on a table and then you swung it 180 degrees, the eraser would point in the other direction. Once again, the original meaning of the word "repent" was not associated with guilt or remorse in any way.

Therefore, Laing concluded that when Christ said, "Sinners repent," what He was really saying was, "If you think you're missing the mark, try going in the opposite direction."

Now that's interesting!

If you do not feel as fulfilled and enriched as you would like to be, perhaps you might want to "repent" and swing in the opposite direction? This would mean your focus would have to shift from acquiring beautiful things to giving them away! (Wow.)

---

11. (Beyond the G spot.)
12. R. D. Laing (October 7, 1927–August 23, 1989) was a controversial Scottish psychiatrist and author.

This does not mean you would necessarily give your own things away, but you might do some fundraising or lend your efforts to a cause to help those in need. This might be a rewarding experience. The joy of giving is gratifying — and the key to remember is this:

True generosity is giving what is needed.

The interesting thing about the joy of giving is that it is a pleasure that nobody can ever take away from you. It doesn't rust, it doesn't diminish, it doesn't decay, it can't be stolen from you. It's yours for as long as you live. It's a forever thing.

This joy never tarnishes or breaks or wilts. Quite the opposite. It generally leads to greater joy from even more giving. This eventually leads to the sure knowledge that the greatest happiness comes from benefitting others. There is little dispute about this. Over the centuries the finest minds in every discipline have agreed on this.

I remember reading something years ago. (This is from my faulty memory.) It was when Mother Teresa won the Nobel Peace Prize in 1979. She had to fly to Sweden to pick up the money she was awarded as part of this august prize. She refused the grand banquet that is normally a part of this event and asked instead that the money ($192,000) be donated to the poor in India. (She had more than six hundred missions, including hospices for the elderly and those dying from AIDS, leprosy, and tuberculosis.) Incidentally, according to Gallup polls, this woman consistently rated as the most admired person in the twentieth century. Well, when this tiny woman was getting off the plane in Sweden, bare feet in sandals on cold snow, reporters swarmed her and asked her how she could live such a life of sacrifice. "Sacrifice?" she said. "I don't live a life of sacrifice. But coming here today — *this* was a sacrifice."

The pleasure and joy of giving exceed and outweigh the pleasure and joy of getting. Giving allows you to derive satisfaction from knowing you are living a life that has greater meaning and one that will leave a shining legacy after you have gone.

"In all affairs, it's a healthy thing now and then to hang a question mark on the things you have long taken for granted."
BERTRAND RUSSELL
British Philosopher, Mathematician, Hisorian, Pacifist, and Social Critic
(MAY 18, 1872–FEBRUARY 2, 1970)

TAURUS
YOUR 40-YEAR HOROSCOPE
1985 ~ 2025

Why Go into the Past?

I want you to have faith in your predictions. The only way you can believe what I say is to test it for yourself. This is why I start with brief highlights from the past twenty-five years. If anything in the past twenty-five years resonates with you, then what I say about your future will have the same validity. It is all one long timeline — your life.

The past predictions generally apply once you have left home or are "running your life" and making your own decisions. Prior to that, the major events in your life were dictated to you by other people, likely your parents.

1985 – 1990

For some of you, we have to peek back a bit farther, because since 1983–84, you had been undergoing big changes. For many, major partnerships were falling apart. Fortunately, by 1985–86, things started to look better. Something happened around this time to boost your reputation in the eyes of others. In fact, you were looking swell! You might have had a promotion, a raise, or some acknowledgement that made you feel proud. Others took advantage of this positive influence to change their job to a new field, perhaps in healing, medicine, the law, or something travel-related or connected with higher education.

Around 1986, you were enjoying greater popularity. The only downside was that around 1987–89, many of you lost the practical, financial, and emotional support you had from others. Obviously, this change threw you back on your own resources.

In March 1988, lucky Jupiter entered your sign, where it stayed until March 1989. This definitely brought good things your way! It increased your opportunities to explore new areas, both in terms of work and in terms of relating to others. In fact, education and travel soon broadened your world. (The collectors among you surely made excellent purchases, for which you are still grateful.)

By 1989–90, most of you were able to boost your earnings because cash was flowing. (You love your money!) Naturally, this increased cash flow made you spend money as well, which is why you were generous to loved ones as well as to yourself by purchasing goodies for your home. (You love your home!)

Around 1985 (perhaps a year in either direction), a huge event took place that you had never before experienced. Pluto entered Scorpio, which is directly opposite your sign. Since Pluto takes about 250 years to travel through all twelve signs, you had never experienced this influence before in your life. In particular, at this time, Pluto most strongly affected those of you who were born between April 20 and May 7.

This influence of Pluto forced many of you out of relationships because they were just not working. You had no choice. It's a curious fact that one of the many things Pluto rules is garbage. This explains why Pluto rules anything that is extraneous or no longer needed in our lives. Therefore, when Pluto was directly opposite your sign, not only did it thrust you into major power struggles with others, it heralded a stage in your life when you had to give up things that had outlived their usefulness. If you saw this, letting go of these things was not too difficult. If you failed to see this, letting go was painful.

Hidden intentions now came out. Certain relationships that were in a comfortable routine, but not entirely honest, suddenly had to face harsh truths. People you encountered at this time were literally life-changing. ("Dad, I want you to meet Darth.")

However, Pluto also aroused your ambition and gave you tremendous energy to go after whatever you wanted! This time period was by no means a complete loss. It was just a huge shift in how things were in your life, in particular, with respect to whatever was no longer relevant.

1991 – 1996

For those who were born between May 7 and May 20, this was the time when you most strongly felt Pluto forcing major changes in your life by way of power struggles, encountering very powerful people, ending relationships, and removing people and events from your life in ways that were quite shocking.

Pluto is associated with death and destruction; nevertheless, Pluto always wants a superior result. The classic example is surgery. Pluto will cut through your body (which is certainly trauma to your flesh and blood) in order to remove an offending organ or tumour so that ultimately you are healthier. But it ain't fun getting there!

Love, romance, vacations, and good times were a blessing in 1992–93. Many of you also expanded your family through birth, adoption, or marriage. Some of you met your true love! ("Black Magic Woman!")

Soon you beautifully improved your job by getting a better job, better duties, a better boss, or better working conditions. By 1995, partnerships and relationships were extremely supportive. In fact, in 1996–97, some of you received inheritances, gifts, and goodies, or benefitted indirectly through partners or the wealth of others.

However, at the same time (around 1996) you began to let go of a lot. This heralded a two- to three-year window when you were letting go of people, places, and possessions. Some of you moved. Some of you left jobs. Some left relationships. All of this was a buildup to something new a few years down the road.

Meanwhile, anything to do with travel, higher education, publishing, the media, medicine, and the law flourished beautifully in 1996–97. Many of you took a memorable trip, or cut a book deal, or went back to school. Some encountered exciting new partners from other cultures and different backgrounds. ("Chez moi ou chez toi?")

1997 ~ 2000

By 1997, you were on a roll because lucky Jupiter was travelling across the top of your chart. This two-year window offered you many chances to boost your good name among your peers. Perhaps you got a promotion, or a raise, or recognition for what you did. Something happened that catapulted you favourably in the eyes of others. ("My name is up in lights!") Who is surprised that by 1998–99 you were more popular! (Everyone loves a winner.)

During this time, huge changes took place because the latter part of the 1990s was a time when you were letting go of whatever was no longer relevant in your life. All of these changes culminated around 1999, when you stepped into a whole new sandbox. In fact, things were so different that many of you changed your daily wardrobe around that time as well. In what appears to be your own good fortune, just when you were on new turf and unsteady terms — ta-dah! — lucky Jupiter entered your sign in July 1999, where it stayed (with the exception of a few months) until July 2000. What a welcome bonus! (Whew.)

Jupiter gave you a lovely lift while you were adjusting to a whole new scene! Shortly afterwards, a boost to your salary sweetened the pot even more. (If friendship is the bread of life, money is the honey!)

2001 – 2005

Although your earnings were getting stronger at this time, because you were in a totally new sandbox, you began to question some basic values. Essentially, you wanted to know what really matters. It's your nature to take a long-range view of things. You intend to have well-planned endings in your life. You like to buy quality items that last for a long time. What you don't want is to be looking in the mirror when you're eighty-five years old, thinking, "I blew it!" No waaaay.

This is why at this stage in your life you were thinking of different kinds of employment, different jobs, different ways of making a living, and how you could create your home. But beneath all this you were struggling to establish a value system that would serve you well in the future.

By 2002, you were busy! Short trips, errands, conversations with everyone, plus increased reading, writing, and studying kept you running around with an outboard motor on your ass. By 2003–4, you had a chance to improve your home. This was also a wonderful opportunity to buy real estate if you were lucky enough to do so. This was an excellent time to make major purchases for your home and for family members.

Many of you must have explored this because there was a three-year window in 2003–6 when residential changes, job changes, or major changes to your daily living situation likely occurred. People moved in; people moved out. A revolving door!

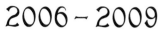

2006 ~ 2009

Despite the changes that took place in residential moves in the past few years, during this particular window of time you were determined to establish a solid home base for yourself. This meant some of you moved yet again! Those of you who had moved previously and liked where you were did not move again, but instead did major renovations to fix up where you lived. That's because the entire thrust of your values at this stage in your life was to create an anchor at home you could trust. Once you had that, then you could sally forth and conquer the world! But not without a home. Not Taurus.

By 2008, wonderful travel opportunities presented themselves, in addition to opportunities related to higher education, publishing, the media, and anything to do with medicine and the law. It was in these areas where you could really shine!

But not until 2009 did your reputation do you proud! This year, and even into 2010, provided you with chances to change how other people saw you. You improved your image in the world. Some of you even changed your appearance rather drastically with weight loss, a new wardrobe, or a totally different hairstyle, or perhaps it was what you were driving or where you lived. Something since 2008 had made people sit up and notice you in a more positive way.

Since you had this going for you, your best opportunity was to grab the baton and run! Meanwhile, this continued to be a time when increased responsibilities with children were serious. You had a lot of loose ends to work out in this area.

2010 – 2012

Currently, you're wondering what you really want to be when you grow up, regardless of how old you are. Whether you are younger or going through a mid-life crisis or retired, essentially you are trying on different career coats to see how they fit or to see how you feel inside them.[13] You want to know what it is that you should do for the rest of your life.

This is a popular time for you. Others are unusually supportive. It's a good time to enter into partnerships. In fact, all kinds of group activities will benefit you, even taking a class. Studies have shown that joining a group just once a month can affect your happiness quotient as much as doubling your income! Hard to believe, especially for Taurus, but it's true; it's because we are such social, gregarious creatures.

By 2011–12, you will swing into some kind of activity that makes you work hard. Suddenly, you're busting your buns! This period of hard work will continue for several years, but at the end of it you will get results and recognition for your efforts. In the meantime, keep singing "The Song of the Volga Boatmen": "Yo! Heave ho! . . . Now we pull hard . . . Once more, lads, once again, still once more."

Sure enough, the universe starts to reward you by June 2011, when lucky moneybags Jupiter enters your sign for the first time since the year 2000. (Yay!) You can use this break. Jupiter will remain in your sign until June 2012. (Lucky me!)

During this twelve-month period, you will easily attract opportunities and important people to you. These people will extend favours or offer you chances to do things. You want to make the most of this influence because this doesn't come along that often (once every twelve years, to be precise). Jupiter is such a positive force that by the end of 2012 your poise and your confidence in yourself will have increased. No question.

---

13. The word "career" is based on the Old French "carrière," which meant "highway." Your career is your life path. (You might or might not get paid for it.)

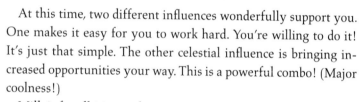

At this time, two different influences wonderfully support you. One makes it easy for you to work hard. You're willing to do it! It's just that simple. The other celestial influence is bringing increased opportunities your way. This is a powerful combo! (Major coolness!)

Milk it for all it's worth.

2013 – 2015

Most of you will encounter lovely opportunities to boost your earnings. You might increase earnings through investments or, more likely, through your own efforts, with a salary raise or through personal income if you are self-employed. This benefit will be felt primarily in 2013, but also in 2014 for some of you. Because this influence indicates heightened cash flow and a stronger focus on money, many of you will be making major purchases as well. You're not a spendthrift, but you love to buy gorgeous, quality items.

This lovely, beneficial influence will be felt in another way as well. Not only does it mean you will either earn more money or buy things you want, it also means you have the ability to actualize what you most value in life. It's like you've got the power of the Tooth Fairy! So whatever it is you value most is likely where your greatest gains will happen. This positive boost could be in a relationship, or a chance to fight for justice, or the blessing of a birth. This is also a good time to take a look at your goals, to make sure you are working toward what you want. You don't want to wake up in a few years, thinking, "What am I doing here?"

By around 2014, many of you will start to get the acknowledgement and recognition you deserve for all of the hard work you put into the past few years. This is an unusually empowering time for you! But as you step out into the world and assume more power for yourself, existing partnerships will likely be upset because you're changing the balance of power. To put it another way, you might say you are changing the way others perceive you.

Think back: since 1999, you've been reinventing yourself. You searched for and established your values, you figured out where to live, and you struggled to find a job that was meaningful. Those who were close to you watched this process. Now, at this stage in your life (starting around 2012), you are ready to step out into the world in a bigger way! But guess what? This change might be too much for those who are close to you. They don't want you to change that much. They want the old you. (Sorry, that ain't gonna

happen.) Because of this, many partnerships and close friendships will undergo serious stress at this time. Those relationships that are shaky will probably bite the dust. Those that are meant to endure will definitely have to undergo major readjustments. The reason for this is that you are changing! And that's perfectly okay.

From 2014–15 onward, you are slowly going to reach a serious career peak, one that you've been working for since 2005–6. ("Forward ho!")

Something else that is important to know: the years 2015–16 are the best time in more than a decade for real-estate improvements, real-estate speculation, and real-estate purchases. So whether you want to buy real estate for your financial advantage or to make a residential move, or buy beautiful things for your home, or fix up where you live — these are all supremely perfect things to do during this window of time. Whatever you do will tend to bring you future profit and benefit as well as pleasure. Furthermore, an ideal time like this one won't come again for another twelve years. (Make hay while the sun shines!)

2016 – 2017

This window of time is perfect for a vacation! You're ready to have fun. You love so many kinds of vacations — anything from camping to a weekend in Las Vegas — but one of your favourite holidays is a cruise, because you love good food and creature comforts. Incidentally, one of the reasons Taurus goes on vacations more than other signs is because you like to know that when you're out doing wild and crazy things in an exciting place, everything is nice and neat back home, just as you left it. You're much more inclined to push the envelope when you're away from home. You're friendly with everyone because you know they're not going to come knocking at your door tomorrow.

This is also a wonderful time for meeting a new love, enjoying saucy flirtations, and even setting up secret romantic trysts. Some of you will meet the love of your life, while others will deepen existing partnerships and relationships.

Children are also a source of joy for you. Some of you might have recently expanded your family (in the previous year), while others will likely expand their family during this time period through marriage, birth, or adoption.

This is also a very good time for financial speculation. In fact, when it comes to playing with money, at this time you can play at almost anything and win. Therefore, all forms of creativity will be rewarding, either personally or financially, or both.

The not-so-good news is that during this window of time (even though you're having fun, flirting, enjoying your kids, and relaxing on vacation), you might feel the pinch because the resources of others are either diminished or finished! ("Whaaat?") This might mean that partnerships have changed and you are no longer getting the support you used to get. (This is not surprising, considering that you are now taking your power and changing the balance in existing partnerships, so some of these partnerships are ending.) However, some of you will receive less from a partner because your partner decides to go into business, or retires, or gets laid off. Nevertheless, do not worry, because whatever diminishes

your resources now does not affect your own earnings or even your ability to invest money. You're going to come out the other side of this okay.

By 2017 and into 2018, many of you will have a great chance to improve your job. You will get a better job, or better duties at your current job, or a better working situation, or a better boss. Some of these positive changes in your employment scene might simply be due to a change in your attitude. At this stage in your life, you will definitely find your work more fulfilling and rewarding.

For those of you who are retired, this period will still represent a time when you find greater satisfaction and gratification in whatever daily tasks you do. And most certainly — and this applies to all of you — this is a wonderful window of time when your health can improve. The only downside is that you might gain weight with desserts and sweets. ("I never met a chocolate I didn't like.")

2018 – 2020

Partnerships get a lovely lift now. Some people may pop the question. Casual relationships could become committed. Even business partnerships and professional associations are blessed. This is a wonderful time to enter into a new partnership. Even dealing with the public will be positive for you. People tend to see you as upbeat, successful, and affluent. They want to be in your presence.

The good news is that by 2019 you are no longer cut off from the resources of others. (Yay!) Partners who were laid off are now employed again. Or issues are resolved so you have a better understanding of what you can expect from others. In fact, the lack of support you felt from others has swung 180 degrees — now you *are* getting support from others! Expect to receive inheritances, gifts, money back from the government, insurance payouts, or increased money or benefits through partners. You might benefit indirectly because your partner makes more money or gets a bonus.

Privately, you're feeling unusually passionate and sexy now. Naturally, you are a sensuous, earthy sign, but during this window of time your gonads are in overdrive! In fact, you're passionate about many things in life, and sex is certainly one of them. (Woody Allen says, "Having sex is like playing bridge. If you don't have a good partner, you'd better have a good hand.")

In a more serious vein (the other arm), something subtle yet important is nicely taking place. You are at a stage in your life when you're approaching the achievement of a cherished dream. It is not yet within your grasp, but you know what you want. You can see your goals. Furthermore, you get what you're doing. You know the rules of the game. There is much less uncertainty in your life.

In fact, some of you will probably explore higher-consciousness schools of thought, perhaps through groups, because you want to fully develop yourself. You have a strong sense of having achieved something, although it is not yet complete. But you know you are close!

Travel opportunities are quite wonderful in 2020. In particular, long-distance travel and longer trips are more likely. Others will explore wonderful opportunities in higher education. You sense that you've reached a pinnacle in your life, and you want to be fully prepared for whatever is at hand. If you have a career in publishing, the media, medicine, or the law, this is also a wonderful time for you to expand your learning in these areas, as well as to explore further opportunities.

You're definitely on a roll now and it feels wonderful!

2021 – 2022

Omigawd. This window of time is the career peak you've been working toward over the past fourteen years. When you look back, you see significant changes that took place around 1999. Then around 2005, you tried everything to establish a home base and make yourself feel more secure. Then around 2012, partnerships were difficult (ya think?), but that was when you truly started to take your power and really go for it. Now you're at a point in your life when you know your dreams can come true! Depending on how old you are and at what stage of your career, this is a time of graduation, marriage, or the birth of your first child (especially if having children is important to you). However, traditionally, for most this is a time of promotions, kudos, awards, approbation, and recognition in your job and your career.

Nevertheless (arms in the air with fingers in a V formation), "Let me say this about that." This time, to be more precise, is a time of *harvest*. We all know that sometimes a time of harvest is when you see which crops have failed. Bummer. If this is the case for a few of you, do not be discouraged. Don't get all hung up on the failure aspect. Consider it a lesson well learned. Your first loss is your cheapest loss. In other words, cut your losses and move on.

Even if you do experience loss in some area of your life, other areas will definitely show the fruition of seeds that were well planted. You are a sign who plans well. You have good discipline. You might think because you love your good food and good wine you're a bit debauched. But not really. You know when to party and when to work.

Do take note: several influences are at work right now. Even though this is a time of harvest, another completely different influence is bringing you good luck, beautiful opportunities, and a chance to boost your reputation in a marvellous way. This latter boon will apply to all Tauruses, even those who are disappointed with some aspect of their harvest.

Therefore, without question, for many of you, this will be the most powerful time in your life! ("Did you get the hi-float bal-

loons?") This will be a time when doors open for you, important people want you by their side, offers will be extended, and kudos, praise, and increased earnings will be yours.

The year 2021 is also a popular year for you. (This popularity boost will occur in 2022 for Tauruses who were born later in the sign.) Suddenly, everybody wants to see your face! This is the perfect time to join clubs, groups, and any kind of professional association. It's even a great time to take a class or join a gym, because it means the interaction you have with others is particularly rewarding at this time. Even partnerships will favour you.

Your interactions with others help to boost your confidence. In turn, this allows you to be more ambitious with your dreams and hopes for the future. You are starting to think big! ("I can do this.")

2023 – 2025

The time of success, popularity, and increased confidence plateaus somewhat, but it does continue. You feel more confident and, dare we say, smug? (We dare.) And just as a good thing seems to build on what went before, in May 2023, lucky moneybags Jupiter enters Taurus for the first time since 2011. Now you are really laughing all the way to the bank! Jupiter is going to stay in your sign until May 2024, bringing all kinds of increased opportunities, as well as attracting powerful people to you. On a more subtle level, it increases your confidence in yourself, which very soon shows in your increased poise.

This is also the beginning of a twelve-year cycle of growth when you are going to learn new things — mostly the kinds of things that expand your experience of the world and make you wiser. Some will also become involved with people from another country or a different culture — either professionally or through a romantic commitment.

Even the spiritual dimension of your life will expand. You will be wiser, kinder, and more big hearted to others. In part, this is because you have enjoyed recent successes, which (for most people) increases your compassion for others as well as your joie de vivre.

Life is fortunate.

Around 2024–25, your earnings will increase. It also appears you have greater cash flow in general, which means many of you are spending more money buying goodies for yourself and your loved ones. You feel richer and more affluent — and it shows!

In other ways, it seems you can manifest (almost magically) what it is you really want. Your chickens are coming home to roost! Indeed, this is a powerful time when so much in your life is coming together because you worked hard to make it happen!

Small wonder that by 2026 (taking a peek down the rabbit hole) you will enter a time when you decide to streamline, downsize, and let go of what is no longer relevant in your life. Whatever seems to be baggage and extra weight will go. This purging will

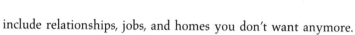

include relationships, jobs, and homes you don't want anymore. You are gearing up for a whole new beginning in 2028.

"Good night and good luck."
EDWARD R. MURROW
American Broadcast Journalist
(APRIL 25, 1908–APRIL 27, 1965)

Famous Taurus Personalities

Lionel Hampton	April 20, 1908–2002
George Takei	April 20, 1937
Ryan O'Neal	April 20, 1941
Jessica Lange	April 20, 1949
Toller Cranston	April 20, 1949
Carmen Electra	April 20, 1972
Brent Seabrook	April 20, 1985
Queen Elizabeth II	April 21, 1926
Charles Grodin	April 21, 1935
Patti LuPone	April 21, 1949
Andie MacDowell	April 21, 1958
James McAvoy	April 21, 1979
Yehudi Menuhin	April 22, 1916–1999
Aaron Spelling	April 22, 1923–2006
Glen Campbell	April 22, 1936
Jack Nicholson	April 22, 1937
William Shakespeare	April 23, 1554–1616
Joseph M. W. Turner	April 23, 1775–1851
Halston	April 23, 1932–1990
Roy Orbison	April 23, 1936–1988
Lee Majors	April 23, 1939
Tony Esposito	April 23, 1943
Michael Moore	April 23, 1954
Dev Patel	April 23, 1990
Shirley MacLaine	April 24, 1934
Sue Grafton	April 24, 1940
Barbra Streisand	April 24, 1942
Jean-Paul Gaultier	April 24, 1952
Kelly Clarkson	April 24, 1982
Edward R. Murrow	April 25, 1908–1965
Al Pacino	April 25, 1940
Hank Azaria	April 25, 1964
Renée Zellweger	April 25, 1969
Carol Burnett	April 26, 1933

Joan Chen	April 26, 1961
Jet Li	April 26, 1963
Kevin James	April 26, 1965
Stana Katic	April 26, 1978
Jack Klugman	April 27, 1922
Coretta Scott King	April 27, 1927–2006
Sheena Easton	April 27, 1959
Dinara Safina	April 27, 1986
Ann-Margret	April 28, 1941
Alice Waters	April 28, 1944
Jay Leno	April 28, 1950
Ian Rankin	April 28, 1960
Penélope Cruz	April 28, 1974
Jessica Alba	April 28, 1981
William Randolph Hearst	April 29, 1863–1951
Duke Ellington	April 29, 1899–1974
Celeste Holm	April 29, 1917
Zubin Mehta	April 29, 1936
Michelle Pfeiffer	April 29, 1958
Dale Earnhardt	April 29, 1951–2001
Jerry Seinfeld	April 29, 1954
Kate Mulgrew	April 29, 1955
Daniel Day-Lewis	April 29, 1957
Mike Babcock	April 29, 1963
Andre Agassi	April 29, 1970
Uma Thurman	April 29, 1970
Jonathan Toews	April 29, 1988
Willie Nelson	April 30, 1933
Annie Dillard	April 30, 1945
Jane Campion	April 30, 1954
Paul Gross	April 30, 1959
Kirsten Dunst	April 30, 1982
Kate Smith	May 1, 1907–1986
Glenn Ford	May 1, 1916–2006
Judy Collins	May 1, 1939
Rita Coolidge	May 1, 1945
John Woo	May 1, 1946
Tim McGraw	May 1, 1967
Benjamin Spock	May 2, 1903–1998
Engelbert Humperdinck	May 2, 1936
Donatella Versace	May 2, 1955

Dwayne "The Rock" Johnson	May 2, 1972
David Beckham	May 2, 1975
Bing Crosby	May 3, 1903–1977
Pete Seeger	May 3, 1919
Sugar Ray Robinson	May 3, 1921–1989
Frankie Valli	May 3, 1934
Doug Henning	May 3, 1947–2000
Dulé Hill	May 3, 1975
Audrey Hepburn	May 4, 1929–1993
Robin Cook	May 4, 1940
Randy Travis	May 4, 1959
Søren Kierkegaard	May 5, 1813–1855
James Beard	May 5, 1903–1985
Tammy Wynette	May 5, 1942–1998
Michael Palin	May 5, 1943
John Rhys-Davies	May 5, 1944
Sigmund Freud	May 6, 1856–1939
Rudolph Valentino	May 6, 1895–1926
Orson Welles	May 6, 1915–1985
Willie Mays	May 6, 1931
George Clooney	May 6, 1961
Martin Brodeur	May 6, 1972
Randindranath Tagore	May 7, 1861–1941
Gary Cooper	May 7, 1901–1961
Eva Perón	May 7, 1919–1952
Johnny Unitas	May 7, 1933–2002
Harry S. Truman	May 8, 1884–1972
David Attenborough	May 8, 1926
Don Rickles	May 8, 1926
Gary Snyder	May 8, 1930
Peter Benchley	May 8, 1940–2006
David Keith	May 8, 1954
Enrique Iglesias	May 8, 1975
Mike Wallace	May 9, 1918
Barbara Ann Scott	May 9, 1928
Glenda Jackson	May 9, 1936
Candice Bergen	May 9, 1946
Billy Joel	May 9, 1949
Steve Yzerman	May 9, 1965
Rosario Dawson	May 9, 1979
Fred Astaire	May 10, 1899–1987

Barbara Taylor Bradford	May 10, 1933
Gary Owens	May 10, 1936
Wayne Dyer	May 10, 1940
Gaétan Boucher	May 10, 1958
Bono	May 10, 1960
Ryan Getzlaf	May 10, 1985
Irving Berlin	May 11, 1888–1989
Martha Graham	May 11, 1894–1991
Mort Sahl	May 11, 1927
Nancy Greene	May 11, 1943
Frances Fisher	May 11, 1952
Natasha Richardson	May 11, 1963–2009
Florence Nightingale	May 12, 1820–1910
Jiddu Krishnamurti	May 12, 1895–1986
Katharine Hepburn	May 12, 1907–2003
Farley Mowat	May 12, 1921
Yogi Berra	May 12, 1925
Burt Bacharach	May 12, 1928
George Carlin	May 12, 1937–2008
Gabriel Byrne	May 12, 1950
Emily VanCamp	May 12, 1986
Joe Louis	May 13, 1914–1981
Bea Arthur	May 13, 1922–2009
Harvey Keitel	May 13, 1939
Ritchie Valens	May 13, 1941–1959
Stevie Wonder	May 13, 1950
Stephen Colbert	May 13, 1964
Bobby Darin	May 14, 1936–1973
George Lucas	May 14, 1944
David Byrne	May 14, 1952
Tom Cochrane	May 14, 1953
Tim Roth	May 14, 1961
Cate Blanchett	May 14, 1969
Sofia Coppola	May 14, 1971
Amber Tamblyn	May 14, 1983
Katherine Anne Porter	May 15, 1890–1980
James Mason	May 15, 1909–1984
Richard Avedon	May 15, 1923–2004
Madeleine Albright	May 15, 1937
Lainie Kazan	May 15, 1940
Brian Eno	May 15, 1948

Mike Oldfield	May 15, 1953
Henry Fonda	May 16, 1905–1982
Woody Herman	May 16, 1913–1987
Liberace	May 16, 1919–1987
Pierce Brosnan	May 16, 1953
Debra Winger	May 16, 1955
Janet Jackson	May 16, 1966
Corey Perry	May 16, 1985
Megan Fox	May 16, 1986
Dennis Hopper	May 17, 1936–2010
Bill Paxton	May 17, 1955
Sugar Ray Leonard	May 17, 1956
Enya	May 17, 1961
Craig Ferguson	May 17, 1962
Alan Doyle	May 17, 1969
Sasha Alexander	May 17, 1975
Tessa Virtue	May 17, 1989
Omar Khayyám	May 18, 1048–1131
Bertrand Russell	May 18, 1872–1970
Perry Como	May 18, 1912–2001
Margot Fonteyn	May 18, 1919–1991
Pope John Paul II	May 18, 1920–2005
Reggie Jackson	May 18, 1946
Rick Wakeman	May 18, 1949
Diane Duane	May 18, 1952
George Strait	May 18, 1952
Chow Yun-Fat	May 18, 1955
Tina Fey	May 18, 1970
Malcolm X	May 19, 1925–1965
Jim Lehrer	May 19, 1934
Nancy Kwan	May 19, 1939
Nora Ephron	May 19, 1941
Grace Jones	May 19, 1948
James Gosling	May 19, 1955
Kyle Eastwood	May 19, 1968
James Stewart	May 20, 1908–1997
Stan Mikita	May 20, 1940
Joe Cocker	May 20, 1944
Cher	May 20, 1946
Dave Thomas	May 20, 1949
Timothy Olyphant	May 20, 1968

GEMINI

MAY 21 – JUNE 20

GEMINI THE TWINS
(MAY 21 – JUNE 20)

"I THINK."

"Only those who attempt the absurd will achieve the impossible.
I think it's in my basement . . . let me go upstairs and check."
M. C. ESCHER
Dutch Graphic Artist
(JUNE 17, 1898–MARCH 27, 1972)

"People do not seem to realize that their opinion of the
world is also a confession of character."
RALPH WALDO EMERSON
American Philosopher, Essayist, and Poet
(MAY 25, 1803–APRIL 27, 1882)

Element: Air
Ruling Planet: Mercury
Quality: Mutable
Opposite Sign: Sagittarius
Symbol: The Twins
(Castor and Pollux, Twin Sons of Zeus and Great Warriors Who Were Devoted to One Another; Castor Was Human and Pollux Was Immortal)
Glyph: The Two Pillars, Representing Both Sides of Your Nature
Lucky Gems: Aquamarine, Agate, Beryl, and Tiger's Eye[1]
Flower: Lily of the Valley
Colour: Yellow
Parts of the Body: Fingers, Hands, Arms, Shoulders, and Lungs

You Like: Witty people, lively conversation, pens, maps, bookstores, magazines, travel, elegant sports, literary pursuits, and the outdoor life. You also love to gossip.

You Don't Like: Bores, routine, monotony, drudgery, feeling trapped, and people who tear pages out of dictionaries or phone books. (Heresy!)

Where You Shine: Charming, entertaining, adroit, informed, communicative, bright, clever, musical, adaptable, and adventurous. And you're good with your hands! (You devil.)

So Who's Perfect? Argumentative, fickle, deceitful, nosy, and inconsistent.

---

1. Different texts will name different gems for different signs. Frankly, I take all of this with a grain of salt. (Actually, I'd prefer vodka with a small bowl of Planters peanuts.)

What Is Gemini-ness?[2]

The quickest way to get a handle on your sign is to understand what your ruling planet means in astrology. The ruling planet of Gemini is Mercury, the planet named after the winged messenger to the Roman gods. The Greeks called this god Hermes. They also saw him as the patron of travellers, shepherds, and cowherds (which is handy to know if you own this kind of stock).

Both the Greeks and the Romans associated Mercury with trade and commerce. (His motto was: "I can get it for you wholesale.")

"Cogito ergo sum."[3]

In astrology, Mercury rules how you talk, think, speak, and communicate. It rules your nervous system, lungs, fingers, hands, and arms. This is why you're always talking and gesturing with your hands. (All Geminis are Italian.)

In a word (actually, in many words — after all, we are discussing Gemini), you are the supreme communicator of the zodiac. You are the wordsmith. If you cannot speak (using your lungs) you will write, use sign language, or gesture with your hands. But you will communicate!

You are the most articulate, quick-witted, clever sign of them all.

Some people have a way with words, some not have way.

However, there is another astrological reason (beyond the fact that Mercury rules all forms of communication) that you're so keen to communicate. It is because you are a Mutable Air sign. (Don't worry — this is not contagious.)

All twelve astrological signs are Mutable, Cardinal, or Fixed. The Fixed signs (Taurus, Leo, Scorpio, and Aquarius) like a predictable outcome and tend to be traditional. (They also can't have children.) The Cardinal signs (Aries, Cancer, Libra, and Capricorn) shoot from the hip and are dynamic. (They arrive with five extra pals to formal sit-down dinners.) The Mutable signs (Gemini, Virgo, Sagittarius, and Pisces) — this means you — are shape-shifters. You quickly conform to whatever is happening. If you walk into a room and everyone is laughing, you're laughing! If you walk into a room and everyone is solemn and silent, you laugh very quietly to yourself.

---

2. No one is just one sign because everyone's chart is made up of different planets. Therefore, this section captures the Gemini archetype — the qualities of "Gemini-ness." Many other signs will have Gemini characteristics as well. Therefore, the discussion of one sign is not an exact description of that person; rather it is a description of the qualities of that sign.
3. *Cogito ergo sum* is Latin for "I think, therefore I am." Not to be confused with the oft-used *Cogito ergo porc pan*, which means "I think, therefore I'll have this pork bun."

Meanwhile, back at the laboratory, all twelve signs also represent one of the elements: Air, Water, Fire, or Earth. You are an *Air* sign. All Air signs are extremely *intellectual*. (The three Air signs are Gemini, Libra, and Aquarius.)

When we cross-reference these two categories, it is immediately apparent that you are the *only* Mutable Air sign. (You knew you were special.) No other sign has this particular combination. This is why you are highly intellectual while, at the same time, able to adapt constantly to your surroundings and everything in your world. To say you can think on your feet is an understatement. Plus you have the ability to laugh at yourself, which is why you're always amused.

Just by looking at your astrological ruler Mercury, and what it represents, we see that you are a fast-talking, clever, articulate neologist[4] who is always on the go and can fit in anywhere at a moment's notice (or less).

Mercury Retrograde

We cannot discuss your ruler, Mercury, without delving into the phenomenon of Mercury retrograde.[5] Three (sometimes four) times a year for about three weeks, your ruler, Mercury, appears to be going backwards in relation to planet Earth. (Of course, it is not actually going backwards, it just appears to be doing so.)

Nevertheless, during these times, everything that Mercury rules also seems to go backward or suffer from delays. (Cars, trucks, buses, trains, bikes, mail delivery, anything to do with phones, computers, messages, clocks, appointments, maps, meetings, plus encounters with siblings, relatives, and people from your past.)

During these times we have flat tires, dead batteries, or car troubles; we miss buses and planes; we wait at the wrong Starbucks to meet someone, or we arrive late. Our phone gets cut off or goes dead just when we really need it. Ditto for our camera. Silly errors and goofy forgetfulness become maddening. We can't find things. And when we go look for them, instead we find *other* things we lost a long time ago! (Go figure.)

People from our past suddenly appear. Ex-lovers, partners, bosses, teachers, and friends. (Even in our dreams.) Sometimes it's great seeing these faces, sometimes it isn't. You're in a video store, and you suddenly see an ex-lover *avec* current *paramour* across the room. (Panic!) You are "alone" and in your grubby sweats. (Groan) You hide in the comedy section, and after staring at the same movie titles foreeeverrr, you exit quickly only to bump into the happy couple at the cash register. (Aaagghh!)

Most people dread Mercury retrograde because these are the times when you misplace things and have confused communications. (You're waiting to pick up your mother at the wrong casino, and she doesn't have a cellphone.)

Fortunately, Mercury retrograde periods are not a complete write-off. As a matter of fact, they are excellent times to finish what is already on your plate. Finish that book. Finish that thesis. Finish putting the car back together.

4. I knew you'd like this one. A neologist is someone who coins phrases or makes up words. Obviously, it was a Gemini neologist who came up with this term in the first place!
5. "Retrograde" is Latin for "What the hell is happening?"

"Wait a minute, Doc. Are you telling me you built a time machine
out of a Delorean?" — Marty McFly

MICHAEL J. FOX

Canadian Actor and Author

Film's *Back to the Future* Trilogy and TV's *Spin City*

(B. JUNE 9, 1961)

We are also more introspective during a Mercury retrograde time. It's easier to go back into the past. Therefore, these are excellent times to study history, do research, or have revealing discussions with your shrink about your first sexual experience. ("Whaaat?")

The best advice for dealing with Mercury retrograde is to try to do damage control ahead of time and stay on top of potential car repairs. Allow extra time for travel. Double-check appointments, meeting places, times, dates, and addresses. Avoid making major expenditures that are Mercury related — i.e., cars, trucks, bicycles, computers, phones, and anything related to communications.

Mercury retrograde is also a very poor time to open a business or initiate a new deal. However, it's an excellent time to close a deal that was already on the table.

I personally don't worry too much about Mercury retrogrades. When I get flat tires, misplace things, and make errors at work, I just say, "Classic Mercury retrograde." (Actually, I say a few other things, too.) However, I would not buy cars, computers, or cellphones during these times. Definitely not.

Naturally, I hide from ex-lovers in video stores as well, but not in the comedy section! There's nothing funny about this.

Four Big Clues about Gemini

To get a broader (but still very superficial) understanding of Gemini, in addition to the description of Mercury, there are four big clues to describe Gemini:

1. Need to Flex Your Intellectual Muscles
2. Curious and Curiouser
3. "I'll Take Two"
4. Need for Freedom

Need to Flex Your Intellectual Muscles

You have a finely tuned intellect. You're sharp, quick-thinking, fast-talking, and an extremely quick study. You love information, and you are happiest when you are learning something new and thought-provoking. (You particularly love having epiphanies.)

In fact, learning *invigorates* you! When you learn about something that excites you, your pulse quickens. You're rapacious about reaching out for more information. You have books and magazines everywhere — by your bed, in the living room, in the bathroom, on your dining-room table, in your kitchen, in the hallway, and on the back seat of your car. You particularly like magazines, because you can get current information in quick hits. You read more than one book at a time.

> "We are always looking for the book it is necessary to read next."
> SAUL BELLOW
> American Author and Winner of the Nobel Prize in Literature (1976)
> *The Adventures of Augie March, Herzog*, and *Ravelstein*
> (JUNE 10, 1915–APRIL 5, 2005)

When you meet others, you ask questions. You discover what they did in the past, what they're doing now, and what they plan to do. Your interest in others brings you amazing discoveries. And your interest is genuine because you like people!

You also love to meet celebrities and VIPs because you're fascinated by their achievements. What are they really like? Are they any happier with their fame and money? What provoked them to pursue this path? Was their childhood different or unique? You want to know! Plus — *quelle surprise* — rubbing elbows with the rich and famous makes for a far more entertaining story. What juicy tidbits to sprinkle in your conversations. You love it!

Your interest in others gives you chances to discover treasure troves of facts, anecdotes, tips about books to read, places to go, and people to contact. *This enriches your life!*

> "It has long been an axiom of mine that the little things
> are infinitely the most important."
> SIR ARTHUR CONAN DOYLE
> Scottish Physician and Writer; Creator of Sherlock Holmes
> (MAY 22, 1859–JULY 7, 1930)

Small wonder you are a raconteur and a storyteller! (Many of you are working to help stamp out and abolish redundancy and repetition.) You entertain everyone you meet with fascinating tales and the latest information about whatever is current. This is why others find you intriguing!

You can glance at the dust jacket of a book, and later that evening, at some sophisticated soiree, you will brilliantly regale others about the author and the role this literary genre fulfills in the changing society of today.

All Geminis are chatalogical. Yada, yada, yada.

Not only do you learn easily and quickly, you also pick up languages by osmosis! After a weekend in Paris, you return home entirely bilingual. This is because you have an ear for words. You learn languages quickly, you remember the lyrics to songs, and invariably know what group is playing, no matter how obscure. If you hear "Gabba gabba hey!" you'll casually say, "That's the Ramones doing 'Pinhead.'" (Who *knows* these things?)

But it pleases you to be able to display your intellect. Oh yes! You take pride in having a fine mind. You're not being pretentious and you're not being a show-off. You value your mind and your sharp intellect and, because of this — you like to flex your brainy muscles! You like others to know that you're smart, because you *are*.

Artists need appreciation for their creative efforts, and in the same way you want recognition for how lightning swift your mind is and how intelligent you are to see the relationships and connections you perceive, which so many miss! Unfortunately, it also means your brilliance too often goes unnoticed because others fail to appreciate your mental agility. They can't keep up!

> "Mediocrity knows nothing higher than itself,
> but talent instantly recognizes genius."
> SIR ARTHUR CONAN DOYLE
> Scottish Physician and Writer; Creator of Sherlock Holmes
> (MAY 22, 1859–JULY 7, 1930)

You vibrate with life. You're intrigued by people, information, discoveries, and above all you love music. Many of you work in publishing, communications, retail, or the music industry.

You take pleasure in displaying your knowledge, but you are happiest when you are learning. However, a very close second is when you impart to others what you have learned.

> "Knowledge is the function of being."
>
> PLATO[6]
>
> Greek Philosopher and Mathematician
>
> *The Republic*
>
> (428/427 B.C.–348/347 B.C.)

Curious and Curiouser

You are curious about absolutely everything — for five minutes.

It's important to understand how much curiosity drives you. It is one of the main factors that shapes your life. We know how knowledgeable you are. We know you pick up languages the way others pick up viruses. You can do all these things — why? Because you are *interested*!

Astrology books discuss how curious about everything in life Geminis are. It's because you are alive with curiosity! You might think this sounds obvious or axiomatic, but many people have surprisingly little curiosity about other people and other things. (It's kinda sad.) *Did you know that medium coffee has more caffeine than dark-roast coffee?*

You want to know about the people around you. You want to know what they think about things, where they came from, and what their hopes for the future are. You want to know about their associations, and who they're related to, and if they're single, married, or divorced. *Did you know that Jesse James, H. G. Wells, Edgar Allen Poe, and Jerry Lee Lewis all married their first cousins?*

You love trivia. *Julia Child was a Gemini Rising, and was six feet two. Her sister Dorothy was two inches taller!*[7]

You want to know how things work, why they are broken, and how they get repaired. You want to know what others are thinking about and what the details of their lives are. You want to know what everybody's talking about. You want to know about geography, cities, and different cultures. You want to explore other systems of thought.

---

6. He lectured, he wrote, and he never stopped talking. There is no way to prove that Plato was a Gemini, but I'm sure he was one.

7. Julia Child (August 15, 1912–August 13, 2004) was Gemini Rising, with Sun in Leo and Moon in Libra. Because Mercury is the ruler of Gemini and she was Gemini Rising, this meant Mercury was Lord of her chart; i.e., Mercury had "extra power" in her chart. And what does Mercury represent? Speech! In Julia's chart, her planet Mercury was poorly aspected. It was square Jupiter and square Saturn. This meant she had difficulty talking (Saturn) in an overly exuberant way (Jupiter), which she did! When he first met her, her husband Paul described her as "a bit hysterical" (and he didn't mean "funny").

You love biographies. You like to see how lives unfold and what shapes people's choices. You love to see the relationship between things and people. You're as interested in the lives of famous people as you are in the lives of your neighbours. It's all grist for the mill.

You stay in touch with others. You send emails, phone messages, and text messages, in addition to tweeting and blogging. You water your trapline regularly.

You have your favourite hangouts, which you visit at the same time of day. This keeps you in touch with the gang! Neighbourhood pubs and coffee houses are classic meeting places. You chat with familiar pals. You meet new faces. And if "no one" is there, you read the book you always carry, or browse through magazines, or do crossword puzzles and Sudokus. (You love playing mental games and doing puzzles.) You might snack on finger food — your favourite kind. (A nibble of this, a nibble of that.) *The chocolate chip cookie was invented in 1930 by a Gemini dietitian named Ruth Graves Wakefield (June 17, 1903–January 10, 1977).*

GADGETS

You're a gadget freak. You want something that rivets your attention, and, hey — it's useful, too! You love the brief challenge of figuring out how something works. Then you marvel that someone invented this contraption. ("A label maker!"[8]) You love to see what other minds can create. ("What will they think of next?") Your home is full of things that were interesting to buy but are getting dusty somewhere or now lie hidden at the back of a drawer.

Of course, you love old-fashioned gadgets as well as modern ones. Compasses, watches, hourglasses, astrolabes, timepieces, maps, pens of all kinds, any instrument of calibration, globes, slide rules, abacuses, and anything you would find in the study of Benjamin Franklin or on the desk of Noah Webster. Gemini goodies and treasures!

You also like games because you're a prankster at heart. You're extremely fun-loving and playful! Geminis are the Peter Pans of the zodiac. You never really grow up. You are childlike and youthful forever.

If you can't pick the brains of somebody else, and you're not into your book, magazine, or puzzle — there is always the requisite laptop or smart phone to keep you busy. Why all this fascination with stuff? Because you must be kept busy! Busy is important.

You don't do boring.

---

8. My father was a Gemini and he loved his label maker! He put those ugly labels on everything, most which didn't need to be labelled. He just loved using it. He always wrote with a fountain pen with green ink. He was also a ham radio operator. He read everything, but his great love was mathematics. "It's like candy to me." He also read the early sci-fi writers, who he said were (for the most part) mathematicians as well.

"Imperfection is beauty, madness is genius, and it's better
to be absolutely ridiculous than absolutely boring."

MARILYN MONROE

American Actress, Singer, and Model

Gentlemen Prefer Blondes, How to Marry a Millionaire, and *The Seven Year Itch*

(JUNE 1, 1926–AUGUST 5, 1962)

"I'll Take Two"

The symbol for your sign is the Twins, and, sure enough, Geminis have a strong relationship to the number two. You like to have two homes and two cars, and many of you have two jobs. When you're shopping, if you have trouble making a choice, you often take both.

Years ago, someone said to me, "Happiness is having alternatives."

I was in a bar in Port Townsend, Washington. (It was the bar that was in the movie An Officer and a Gentlemen.) *Although I am not a Gemini, I have a lot of Gemini in my chart, and the minute I heard that sentence it rang true! Whenever I'm debating with myself about something or someone else is trying to make a decision, perhaps about which item to bring along, I say, "Why not take both? Happiness is having alternatives!"*

Your Gemini penchant for two extends even further. Basically, you love to live in two worlds! You might live in the city and at the same time also have a country home or a cottage on an island. (Or you live in the country and keep a pad in the city.) You adore bouncing back and forth between two separate realties. Naturally, you will *keep your two worlds apart.* After all, if they're not kept separate, then they will get all mushy and blurry and become *one world.* Oh no!

What you want is *contrast* and *variety*. You love to be in one world where you know everyone, and you schmooze, and shop, and attend events, and perhaps work there — it's all quite wonderful. And then — ta-dah! — you need a change. So you slip into your other world, where you schmooze with others, and shop, and attend parties and events, and possibly work there — it's all quite wonderful. Ideally, neither world knows very much about the other. This is what gives you that refreshing change!

You need fresh hits of different places. When you get tired of one, you switch to the other.[9] And when that one starts to pale, you go back to the first. ("I forgot how much I love the city!" or "God, this peace is perfection!")

> "You have to see a building to comprehend it.
> Photographs cannot convey the experience, nor film."
> ARTHUR ERICKSON
> Canadian Architect and Urban Planner
> (JUNE 14, 1924–MAY 20, 2009)

Need for Freedom

You are a freedom-loving person. You're not the rolling stone that Sagittarius is. And you're not the rebellious iconoclast that Aquarius is. You simply need to be free to do your own thing!

And what is your thing? You like to meet new people, discover new events, travel to new places, and, above all, be free to learn, so you are constantly stimulated. You particularly like to observe other cultures.

> "I had all the usual ambition growing up.
> I wanted to be a writer, a musician, a hockey player.
> I wanted to do something that wasn't nine to five."
> MICHAEL J. FOX
> Canadian Television and Film Actor and Author
> Film's *Back to the Future* Trilogy and TV's *Spin City*
> (B. JUNE 9, 1961)

This is why you travel. Although some Geminis roam the globe, most prefer frequent shorter trips. What you seek is variety and stimulation! Plus, you have to stay in touch with your cohorts.

Essentially, you prefer to be footloose and fiancé-free. Security is not a big issue for you, although, admittedly, money is your ticket to travel, learn, and be free to do what you want.

---

9. I was told that the wonderful international architect Arthur Erickson (June 14, 1924–May 20, 2009) never liked to stay in one city for more than ten days.

But there are two exceptions. Gemini is sandwiched in between Taurus and Cancer, as any quick glance at a horoscope column will reveal. Meanwhile, astrology calls Mercury and Venus the "personal" planets because they are so close to the Sun. Therefore, whatever sign the Sun is in, there's a good chance that Mercury and Venus are also in the same sign. But if Mercury and Venus are not in the same sign as the Sun, they won't be too far away. They will likely be in one of the two signs on either side. So one Gemini person might have the Sun in Gemini as well as Mercury and Venus in Gemini. This person will be the Peter Pan Gemini. ("I'll never grow up!")

However, another Gemini person might have Mercury or Venus or both in Taurus. This Gemini, unlike many other Geminis, wants to own land, preferably acreage. Or instead, a Gemini might have Mercury and Venus in Cancer. If this is the case, then this particular Gemini will strongly value home, family, cooking, and gardening. So many kinds of Geminis!

The reason I started off with the term "Gemini-ness" was to discuss the Gemini archetype, as opposed to the Gemini individual. Nobody is strictly Gemini because *nobody is just one sign.*

The archetype of Gemini is to remain free and unfettered so that one has a future full of possibilities and choices. To most Geminis, security means being trapped. ("I had to gnaw off my left elbow to break free!") This is also why so many of you choose to be self-employed. You want to call your own shots. You want the freedom to be spontaneous, because you know you are very likely to change your mind.

If others accuse you of changing your mind, you react with amazement. The truth is you take pride in your ability to be mentally flexible. You are not being wishy-washy or inconstant. *Au contraire!* Your adaptable nature shows you are alive and growing, and constantly responding to the changing world around you! Besides, isn't life sweetened by risk?

"The thing about acting is you don't want to let on how enjoyable it is or everybody would want to become an actress. But it really is. It's a pleasure to go and exchange your identity."
GENA ROWLANDS
American Film, Stage, and Television Actress
Gloria and *A Woman Under the Influence*
(B. JUNE 19, 1930)

Gemini in Love

"I am good, but not an angel. I do sin, but I am not the devil.
I am just a small girl in a big world trying to find someone to love."
MARILYN MONROE
American Actress, Singer, and Model
Gentlemen Prefer Blondes, How to Marry a Millionaire, and *The Seven Year Itch*
(JUNE 1, 1926–AUGUST 5, 1962)

Did you know your ruler, Mercury, was also known as the god of sex? (Would I kid you?) You are, after all, the sign of Marilyn Monroe, Angelina Jolie, John Wayne, Gena Rowlands, Isabella Rossellini, Errol Flynn, Johnny Depp, Joan Collins, Isadora Duncan, Rupert Everett, Tony Curtis, and Josephine Baker, all of whom have swooning fans.

You love an adoring peanut gallery. It's so nice to know that others are eager to hear from you and they want to know what you're doing. Furthermore, they want to invite you to lunches, parties, and interesting events.

However, when it comes to one-on-one relationships, what you really seek is a meeting of the minds. You have a fine mind, and you want to find an equally fine mind to play with! You parry and thrust with words. You want someone who can appreciate your clever repartee! You want an intellect equal to yours with which to exchange clever ideas! This is why romantic seduction for you is all about conversations, letters, notes, and poems. You keep in touch almost hourly with text messages, voicemail, and phone calls, as well as handwritten notes hidden in suitcases, briefcases, lunch kits, and under pillows, and written in lipstick on the bathroom mirror.

You give your loved one the books you love, as well the books you think they will enjoy. You slowly become linked to your lover intellectually so that you each have no one but the other almost constantly on your minds.

And let us not forget cards! Cards tucked under windshield wipers, cards taped to bicycles and motorcycles, cards delivered in the mail or by hand, or left to be discovered in a favourite magazine.

But if you do not feel an immediate simpatico in your exchange of ideas and values — *phffft!* — it's nothing more than a one-night stand. Or two. (You do like doing things in pairs.)

Sexually, all the Air signs are a bit kinky. This doesn't mean you don't take a plain vanilla approach to sex — because you might. But it is a fact that Geminis are playful, curious, and experimental in bed, especially if they read about it somewhere, like in the Kama Sutra. (I have the Coles Notes version.)

One area where you reign supreme is *la bouche*. Geminis are the best kissers in the world! (All that lip activity without calorie content.) Hardly surprising, considering you can talk your way into and out of anything so smoooooothly!

However, it is in the realm of sexual attraction, love, and romance that we encounter your greatest contradiction. To begin with, we all know how much you love variety. ('Tis the spice of life!) So when it comes to romance, you are thrilled to have more than one adoring lover. (This is where your pack mentality comes into play.) You like to think that even though you are ensconced and totally involved with one person, there are others out there pining for you, throwing love letters over the fence or slipping them under your door. This is why you're in no hurry to cut off all ties, even when you encounter your true love. You like to have a few possibilities dangling around to boost your morale and hedge your bets. ("It's nice to know somebody out there loves me.")

Another reason you hesitate to raise the drawbridge is you're so busy! After all, it's easy for you to juggle people. (Why not?) You like to have two dates on one night. I know two different Gemini people (there's that number again), one male, one female, who actually slipped out of bed while their partner was sleeping, jumped into their car, and drove off to a rendezvous with another person, only to return before sun-up and slip back between the sheets, cuddling up to partner number one, who was none the wiser. I suspect this is a common Gemini scenario, and that many of you are nodding and grinning lasciviously. (You devil.)

Another reason you can be sly and devious with lovers is you're a big fibber. (Oh, admit it.) Even if you're not stretching the truth to save your own skin, you always embellish your stories! (You think it's a shame to ruin a good story with the facts.) Needless to say, you can talk fast if you have to save your tush!

So this is one side of Gemini. It's your fickle twin.

> "A wise girl kisses but doesn't love, listens but doesn't believe,
> and leaves before she is left."
> MARILYN MONROE
> American Actress, Singer, and Model
> *Gentlemen Prefer Blondes, How to Marry a Millionaire,* and *The Seven Year Itch*
> (JUNE 1, 1926–AUGUST 5, 1962)

But there is also a completely different side to Gemini (read on, Macduff), and it is based on the fact that your symbol is the Twins. Something deep inside of you resonates with this symbolism. In fact, it is why you like to have two of everything! (Including lovers.)

But if we explore the concept of the Twins more deeply, we discover that, right from the womb, you have been seeking your other half. You are seeking that which will complete you. Initially, as a young child, your family fulfilled this role. Your family became your "other half." This is why even if your family was horribly abusive to you, you will remain loyal to this bunch of jerks![10]

As you grow older, your need to complete yourself eventually becomes your deep search for your soulmate. Many signs seek their soulmate, but none so fervently and passionately as Gemini. And just as you demonstrated extreme loyalty to your family (whether they deserved it or not), you will likewise demonstrate total and complete loyalty to your soulmate. You demand only one thing in return — that you are the number one person in the life of your partner. No one comes before you.

So you embody this strange contradiction. I think of it as the fickle twin and the faithful twin. It's true that you can be fickle. A variety of partners titillates you and puffs up your sense of self-worth. It's thrilling to be wanted by many. You enjoy the excitement of keeping others at bay, waiting for a word from you, wanting to see you, hoping for a note, a call, a mere acknowledgement of their devotion to you. (You love it.)

Yet you are also the person who so very keenly and deeply wants to find your true love — your soulmate. And when you do, you are utterly loyal to this person because this person is not just an "other" — this person is the other half who completes you in this lifetime.

---

10. This scenario is not uncommon for abused Geminis.

The Gemini Boss

"As long as you're going to be thinking anyway, think big."
DONALD TRUMP
American Businessman, Socialite, Author,
and Television Personality on *The Apprentice*
(B. JUNE 14, 1946)

Your Gemini boss is overbooked, and probably absent a lot of the time going to meetings, doing research, touching base with others, and learning whatever is possible about the competition. If important people call, this boss wants to know! If something important happens, interrupt this boss. They can handle interruptions. They multitask!

The Gemini boss will scan email, talk on the phone, and sign documents, all the while listening to a conversation going on outside the office door. These talkers will know when they hear the boss sing out, "I highly doubt they'll be serving beer at this time of day."

The Gemini boss knows everything that's going on. (Well, sort of.) Because Geminis crave variety, stimulation, and a busy schedule, they do miss some things — but not much.

The Gemini boss wants to know office gossip, office romances, and anything that might affect turnover. However, make your reports and conversations brief, because this is a busy person! (Not only is this boss busy, this boss gets bored easily.) The right type of administrative assistant will always run interference for their Gemini boss by shutting the door to bores! (Are you kidding?)

Geminis are casual about money, so if your Gemini boss is taking you out for lunch, make sure cash or credit cards are available. If not, you might have to pick up the tab.

The Gemini boss works very well with a partner. This boss needs the stimulation of conversation and the exchange of ideas. Think-tank meetings and brainstorming sessions are the ticket.

Expect this boss to change their mind at a moment's notice. (It's a Gemini prerogative.) They like to be greeted in the morning; they like to know when you leave at the end of the day.

You can make their day by bringing them a pertinent magazine article they might have missed, which, admittedly, is unlikely.

The Gemini Employee

"A little alarm now and then keeps life from stagnation."
FRANCIS CRICK
British Biologist, Physicist, and Neuroscientist
One of the Discoverers of the Structure of the DNA Molecule
(JUNE 8, 1916–JULY 28, 2004)

Mercury, the ruler of Gemini, is related to the Latin word *merx* (merchant, commerce), which means you will often find Gemini employees in the retail trade. In addition to retail establishments and restaurants, there are four areas that strongly beckon to Geminis: (1) driving taxis, buses, and trucks for a living; (2) working for newspapers, magazines, and publishing houses (*quelle surprise*); (3) teaching; and (4) working in the travel industry.

Just like the Gemini boss, the Gemini employee hates to be bored! So the marvellous thing about your Gemini employee is that they are excellent at multitasking. Furthermore, they're happy to be busy. They will not be flabbergasted if you throw lots of different kinds of jobs their way. Don't be fooled by the youthful appearance of many Gemini employees, who could be approaching retirement. (Geminis never really grow up.)

Your Gemini employee is great at writing reports, closing sales, talking to others, attending meetings, getting the scoop on insider information, networking, and doing research. However, don't put this person in a room all by themselves. Big mistake. Geminis need others to talk to! In fact, Geminis work best in pairs. (Yes, this sounds silly, but it's true.)

This is an amazingly versatile employee. However, if you exile them to routine or boring work, they will make a lot of mistakes and then quit.

Geminis like surprise gifts of pens, personalized paper, and curious things from other countries, like pagan fertility gods.

The Gemini Parent

"If I had influence with the good fairy who is supposed to preside over the christening of all children, I should ask that her gift to each child in the world be a sense of wonder so indestructible that it would last throughout life."

RACHEL CARSON

American Marine Biologist, Nature Writer, and Environmentalist

The Silent Spring

(MAY 27, 1907–APRIL 14, 1964)

The Gemini parent can be an absolutely marvellous, wonderful parent, primarily because a part of the Gemini parent is still a child.[11] Not only is the Gemini parent playful, witty, and humorous, their curiosity can match that of a child. Together, the Gemini parent and child will eagerly explore the universe, whether it's looking into the heavens through a telescope, poring over a book from the library, or holding a fascinating conversation at the dinner table.

The Gemini parent is always holding forth, teaching, illuminating, and, at times, teasing. This is an understatement. My Gemini father turned everything into a teaching session, but it was fun, invigorating, and stimulating.

The Gemini parent will certainly encourage reading, and will also provide pencils, pens, compasses, rulers, crayons, paints, watches, clocks, flashlights, hammers, nails, scissors, and any other kind of support material for children to write, create, build, or record their ideas. The appreciation and enjoyment of music is another area the Gemini parent will encourage.

However, the main thing the Gemini parent can offer is the role model of being curious about everything in life, of being eager to learn more of whatever is out there, and the notion that if you don't know something, all you have to do is ask.

A Gemini parent is like having a home teacher as well as a loving mom or dad.

"Kids are at my level. I like goofing around with them."

JOHN GOODMAN

American Film, Television, and Stage Actor

Film's *The Big Lebowski* and TV's *Roseanne*

(B. JUNE 20, 1952)

---

11. My Gemini father was a wonderful man. Long after my brother and sister and I had left home, very young neighbourhood children were still knocking on our front door to ask if he would come out to play.

The Gemini Child

"Once there was a little bunny who wanted to run away.
So he said to his mother, 'I am running away.'
'If you run away,' said his mother, 'I will run after you.
For you are my little bunny.'" — Excerpt from *The Runaway Bunny*
MARGARET WISE BROWN
American Children's Author
(MAY 23, 1910–NOVEMBER 13, 1952)

Most Gemini children walk early, talk early, and get into everything! These are bright little kids! Do not think they are just being mischievous (although they can be); Gemini children are curious about everything. They're hungry and eager to learn anything new — *anything*.

This is a child who needs a lot of stimulation, but not the passive stimulation of television. (Television just gives you the illusion you have a life.) This child needs to engage very personally with the world with outings to parks, having their own library card, taking music lessons, and above all by being read aloud to. Gemini children love the printed word and they love to read. But, even more than that, they treasure having someone they love read to them.

Be patient with their questions. This is the kind of child who wants to know why the sky is blue. They're not stalling or trying to annoy you. The Gemini child is unbelievably curious and, at the same time, extremely playful!

Talk to this child like an adult. You might be surprised at how adult your answers can be and still make sense to this fresh young mind. If possible, introduce this child to other languages. Geminis learn new languages extremely quickly!

This is a social child who needs the company and stimulation of others. If this child wants to hang out with the adults, don't discourage them by suggesting they run along and play outside. Geminis go wherever they find life is most interesting!

"It is a great thing to start life with a small number of really
good books which are your very own."
SIR ARTHUR CONAN DOYLE
Scottish Physician and Writer; Creator of Sherlock Holmes
(MAY 22, 1859–JULY 7, 1930)

How to Be a Happier Gemini

You are a lover of life. You're captivated by everything in the world around you, and you want to *do* everything! It's as if you are skipping from rock to rock across water, or from mountaintop to mountaintop across a continent, eagerly reaching out for whatever you can grasp next.

This is an exciting, admirable way to live. What promotes this driving force can be attributed to the symbol of your sign, the Twins. You are always looking for your other half — something to complete you. Without that "something," you feel incomplete. This means you are constantly energized by a restless, driving force. In fact, you use this energy to explore as much of life as you can.

However, this driving force often yields hollow victories. Whatever you reach out for and whatever you successfully grasp is just some "thing." It does not fulfill your need for completion. You don't feel satisfied.

> "The delusion of entertainment is devoid of meaning.
> It may amuse us for a bit, but after the initial hit we are
> left with the dark feeling of desolation."
> ARTHUR ERICKSON
> Canadian Architect and Urban Planner
> (JUNE 14, 1924–MAY 20, 2009)

Essentially, what is at play is this: because you are unconsciously seeking your twin, something that will "complete" you, you are constantly chasing after something to make you feel fulfilled. You believe that if you could marry that person, or write that book, or have that job, or build that house, or drive that car, or win that prize, or get that promotion, or grasp whatever wonderful thing out there it is that you want — *then you would be happy.*

This is the great fallacy of Gemini, the Twins.

Basically, you are a victim of the "grass is greener" syndrome. It colours everything you do in your life. Imagine that you are going to shop for a new winter coat. You enter a store and, in two minutes flat, you find the perfect coat! Are you going to buy it, content that your shopping trip took only ten minutes? Oh no. You will ask the sales clerk to hold it. "I'm sure I'm going to buy this coat, but could you please hold it for me for two hours?" Then you will run around and check out other stores to make sure you don't find a coat you like better. Of course, there's a remote chance you will find a coat that is better, but probably not, so you return to the first store and buy the first coat you saw.

This scenario plays out in many other aspects of your life, especially your love life. You tend to hug your loved one, all the while looking over their shoulder, in case someone "better" comes along.

This reluctance to commit might be misconstrued as your need for freedom. But really, it's a kind of paralysis. You're afraid to commit to something right now in case you regret it later, because something better might come along. (You often want to know what other people are going to order at a restaurant, in case when the food arrives their order looks better than your choice.)

Therefore, this "grass is greener" fixation is always driving you, creating a constant sense of dissatisfaction and mistrust with what you currently have or what is currently available to you.

Now here is the sobering truth: *you are absolutely right*. If you commit to this particular person, a year from now, someone better might come along! If you do spend all of your money on this house, or car, or coat, you might eventually see a better house, or car, or coat. You were right! (Whaaat?)

The truth is, *there is no end to better*. There will always be younger, richer, taller, bigger, more beautiful, more delicious, more famous . . . The list is endless. There is no end to better.

So what can you do? You are, after all, in the real world. This is not just a dress rehearsal. You will have to accept the fact that this is how reality works. Every human being on the face of this planet makes committed decisions, despite the fact that "something better" might come along. This ability to commit is called *contentment*.

Negativity is wanting things to be different from the way they are. Or, to put it another way, if you are content with the way things are, then there is no negativity.

Consider these two realities: First, because there is no end to better, you have to get off the merry-go-round of waiting for something better, because this never ends. If you do want to buy something, or have a partner in your life, or whatever — you have to make a commitment. You have to live your life! Just accept this. We all live with this reality. The second thing to be aware of is, whether you appreciate what you have or focus on what you don't have makes all the difference in the world to being happy or unhappy. Quite literally, happiness is wanting what you have, just as unhappiness is wanting what you don't have.

The encouraging aspect of all this is that you can actually play with both of these approaches because they both exist in your mind. This is why someone with surprisingly little in life can be content and happy, and someone with great riches and fame can be miserable.

So it's up to you. Once you accept that there is no end to "better," and that you have to get out of this vicious, never-ending headspace, this is a huge leap ahead! It allows you to realize you have to make decisions in the *now*. All of us are subject to this diabolical "no end to better." It's a harsh truth, just like aging is a harsh truth. Acceptance is the quickest way for peace of mind when you're dealing with something that is unavoidable.

Likewise, a mental state that is constantly discontented will make you miserable! Look around you — appreciate who you are and what you have. I pray daily for this quality — that I and others can appreciate who we are and what we have. (And, if I don't have time, I have Dial-a-Prayer on speed dial.)

> "If the stars should appear but one night every thousand years, how man would marvel and stare."
> RALPH WALDO EMERSON
> American Philosopher, Essayist, and Poet
> (MAY 25, 1803–APRIL 27, 1882)

Years ago, a wonderful teacher named Dhyani Ywahoo[12] spoke at the Orpheum Theatre in Vancouver. I could not go, but I met someone who did attend the talk and asked her, "Hey, in twenty-five words or less, what did she say?"

My friend replied, "She said the most important meditation we could do daily was appreciation."

> *Do not like; do not dislike.*
> *All will then be clear.*
> *Make a hair's breadth difference,*
> *And heaven and earth are set apart.*
> EASTERN PROVERB

---

12. Venerable Dhyani Ywahoo is a spiritual leader, peacemaker, and author of *Voices of Our Ancestors*. She is Chief of the Ani Yun Wiwa (Cherokee) and founder of Sunray, an international NGO dedicated to planetary peace.

GEMINI
YOUR 40-YEAR HOROSCOPE
1985 – 2025

Why Go into the Past?

I want you to have faith in your predictions. The only way you can believe what I say is to test it for yourself. This is why I start with brief highlights from the past twenty-five years. If anything in these past twenty-five years resonates with you, then what I say about your future will have the same validity. It is all one long timeline — your life.

The past predictions generally apply once you have left home or are "running your life" and making your own decisions. Prior to that, the major events in your life were dictated to you by other people, likely your parents.

1985 – 1989

Many of you will remember that since the early 1980s, partnerships were a roller-coaster ride. (How could you forget?) Breakups and shaky relationships were definitely the tone of the 1980s. (Yikes!)

A major reason for this was that in February 1981, explosive Uranus moved directly opposite your sign where it stayed until December 1988. It was inevitable that this would inspire you to break away from anything that restricted you or prevented you from feeling free. Conflict with others was dramatic! (And you've got entertaining stories to prove it.)

Relationships with enemies and legal entanglements were unexpected, maybe even shocking. This was the decade that taught you that a lie is the only substitute for the truth. But surely, you learned something? "Yes, I did. Marriage is not a word — it's a sentence."

One nice touch was that travel and anything to do with college or university gave you a lovely bonus in the mid 1980s. (Something exciting was happening!) In fact, this was also a very good time to explore opportunities in publishing, the media, medicine, and the law (which many of you did since you were busting your buns then).

By the late 1980s, even though support from partners and other sources dried up — from July 1988 to the summer of 1989 — lucky Jupiter was in your sign making you strong and unusually hopeful about your future. Ah yes, as Jean Kerr wryly observed, "Hope is the feeling you have that the feeling you have isn't permanent."

1990 – 1993

And your feelings of hope were justified because 1990 brought good news! Many of you earned more money. Something made you feel richer. Ironically, you might have spent money to increase your assets; and perhaps *this* made you feel richer, even though you had to foot the bill. ("Yeah, I'm rich but I'm broke.")

Actually, it was good you felt richer this year, because the support from others (especially from partners) might have dwindled or disappeared. (Groan.) This meant it was now up to you. You were being tested to show you could stand on your own four feet.

By 1992, it became easier to believe in yourself ("I believe in me. I saw me in the bathroom mirror this morning."), and your positive vibes attracted others to you so that you enjoyed increased popularity and exciting new contacts. (You love your peanut gallery.)

By 1993, you were finally out from behind the eight ball with respect to suffering from a lack of support from partners and other sources. Now you could breathe a sigh of relief! In fact, you started to prepare for something because you could sense you were going places! Some of you went back to school. Others travelled to learn more about the world.

At home, warm, fuzzy feelings began to surround your family and domestic life. 1993–94 was also an excellent time to buy real estate, or expand where you lived, or buy beautiful things for your home. In fact, this sense of abundance and increase might have actually brought new members to your family through birth, or marriage, or adoption. (Hmmm. Was somebody born then? Did somebody move in with you or your family then?)

1994 – 1996

By 1994–95, you had a sense of having arrived! Certainly, something you had been working on for a long time (since 1986, or perhaps even 1977) came to fruition. Some of you graduated; others got a special job or a wonderful promotion. Yet again, some married, especially if marriage was something you had wanted.

This was a time of harvest; you were reaping whatever seeds you sowed in the past. Quite literally, in the Biblical sense, where you planted well, you got rewards. And where you planted poorly, you saw, "This ain't working!" If this was the case, it was a smartening-up time. Now you know. Move on!

1994 was also a year when love and romance could blossom! Vacations were fun. You enjoyed social events, sports, and playful times with children. Life was thrilling! Your phone was ringing! This was also a good time for the arts and creative activities. Speaking of creative activities — this was also a time for babies! (Children or grandchildren.)

By 1995, you had a chance to improve your job. You got a better job, or better duties, or found a better working situation, or got a more attractive workspace, or your evil boss disappeared like the Wicked Witch of the West. ("I'm melting! Melting!"[13])

At this time, around 1995–96, lucky Jupiter was directly opposite your sign, which meant you were on top of your game. You were able to promote your good name among your peers and create a positive reputation for yourself. It was also a wonderful growth-oriented time.

By 1996, partnerships flourished. (This doesn't mean you never squabbled with partners or loved ones, because no partnership is ever perfect. However, you definitely appreciated your partnerships, and realized how valuable and enriching they were to you.)

Later this year (and perhaps into 1997), you benefitted from the wealth and resources of others. Inheritances, gifts, favours,

---

13. Margaret Hamilton (December 9, 1902–May 16, 1985) played the green-skinned Wicked Witch of the West in *The Wizard of Oz*. She was a Sagittarius, which is 180 degrees opposite Gemini; however, she had Pluto in Gemini, which is more of a generational distinction. She also had a remarkable nose!!

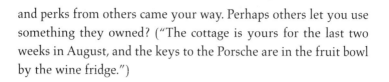

and perks from others came your way. Perhaps others let you use something they owned? ("The cottage is yours for the last two weeks in August, and the keys to the Porsche are in the fruit bowl by the wine fridge.")

1997 – 1998

For lucky Geminis, sex was hot, heavy, and abundant! (Hey, it's the most fun you can have with your eyes closed.) Certainly, your sex drive was revved at this time. But your challenge (out of bed) was to find that happy balance between respecting your own needs and boundaries and yet at the same time respecting the needs and demands of others. There's a fine line between helping others and co-operating with people versus selling out!

Travel opportunities began to look promising. Many of you had a chance to see new places and discover new cities and countries. Others travelled for business, or to learn something new. This was a great year to take advantage of educational opportunities. Perhaps you went back to school, took courses, or got further training.

Interaction with people from other cultures and different countries might have been meaningful. And sexy! (Fun way to learn a new language.)

By 1998, moneybags Jupiter was travelling across the top of your chart, bringing all kinds of opportunities to you, in addition to introducing you to powerful, important people who could make a positive difference in your life. This was a strong time for you.

1999 – 2000

A popular time! This continued to be a good time for a promotion at work or increased public recognition. Your success might have triggered an important transfer or residential move for you.

Soon, you became more involved with groups by joining classes, clubs, and organizations. You made new friends. This was definitely a good time to talk to others about your cherished dreams for the future, because their feedback was helpful to you.

By 2000, you had entered a two- to three-year window when you started to dismantle much of what you had created since around 1987–88. It was time to move on. (Perhaps this was your choice, perhaps it wasn't.) Either way, you were going through cupboards, closets, garages, and lockers to get rid of what you no longer needed or wanted. ("I'm certainly keeping my baseball cards and my wok.")

2001 – 2003

Ah ha! The time of the good, the bad, and the ugly. Perhaps there was no "ugly," but very often when we have to let go of things it's painful. We're creatures of habit. We like to keep that which is familiar. ("I was very fond of that fifty-dollar bill. It had sentimental value for me.")

This continued to be a time of letting go and saying goodbye. Even if you didn't want to, it happened. When you saw certain people or did familiar things, the old thrill was just not there. It's as if the same activities that you had always done for years no longer gave you the same results. (Whaaat?)

Actually, the time between 1996 and 2009 was particularly fractious for partnerships. Relationships were getting blown out of the water. (However, once you passed this window of time, this painful influence would never again occur in your lifetime.[14] Whew!)

That was the bad part.

The good part was that from July 2000 to July 2001, lucky moneybags Jupiter was mostly in your sign.[15] (Yay team!) You needed that boost of luck! Sure enough, by late 2001, your poise and self-confidence had increased, along with your appreciation of who you were and what you could do. ("The name is Bond, James Bond, and I like my women stirred, not shaken." Bond's creator, Ian Fleming, was a fellow Gemini.)

Fortunately, your earning power became stronger around 2002–3. You got a better job, or earned more money, or figured out how to make a little extra on the side. Some made major expenditures in this year. No matter how you cut it, your wealth increased. Ka-ching!

This was the time when your world dramatically changed. Suddenly, you were in a whole new sandbox: a new city, a new

---

14. This is not to say that all Geminis will never split up in the future. But it is safe to say that this unusual and very tough influence on partnerships is gone for good. The lesson you were meant to learn is this: you have to stop blaming others for whatever happens to you — good or bad. You have to acknowledge that, quite likely, you are triggering all kinds of things with unconscious cues and expectations. ("Me?" Yes, you.)
15. The last time that Jupiter was in Gemini was in 1989–90.

country, a new job, a new relationship — *something*. In fact, for many, the change was so dramatic that your daily uniform changed! ("Do you think this room makes my ass look fat?")

2004 – 2005

Ironically, the financial boost that you got last year sort of evaporated! Now you were struggling to make a buck. (Another day, another dollar.) However, you had entered a three-year window where you had to seriously determine some important values — *what really matters in life.* (You certainly don't want to have regrets when you are ninety and can barely reach for the remote.)

The good news is that everything to do with your home, family, and your domestic scene started to look better. Either you had better digs or your family relationships were more upbeat, more positive, more joyful.

This was also a good time for real-estate deals. If you bought property for yourself, it would later prove to be profitable. This also applied to speculative property. (*Has that pup tent served you well?*)

Ooh la la! Romance was promising at this time! Some of you met the love of your life! Romance, love affairs, and thrilling flirtations made your heart go ka-thunk, ka-thunk! (Forget pitter-patter!)

This was also a great time for vacations and wonderful getaways. Anything to do with sports was cool. (Who doesn't love a hockey game with a hot dog and a beer?)

New children might have entered your world through birth, adoption, or relationships. And while all these warm, fuzzy things were going on, the arts were similarly blessed! ("I know it's toxic, but I still prefer cadmium red.")

Your theme was grabbing all the pleasure you could hold! (Mom always liked you best.)

2006 ~ 2007

At this stage, some of you were in the throes of changing jobs and residences. (For others, this happened later.) This was a two- to three-year window when your life was very much up in the air! Your friends kept your address in pencil.

Basically, you were coming down the home stretch of a journey you began around 2001. This journey was a transformation from who you were around 2000 to who you would be by 2008.

In the early stages of this journey (around the beginning of the millennium), you were scrambling to create a new identity in terms of your image, your wardrobe, and the look you wanted to present to the world. ("I'm giving up Spandex.")

Then you wrestled with what kind of job you should get or how you should earn your money or, for that matter, how much money *do* you need anyhow? After all, what really matters in life? (It's difficult to have both time and money. Not many people can kick back, relax, *and* be rich!)

However, now you were experiencing different surroundings through changing jobs or changing residences and a constantly changing daily milieu. ("If it's Tuesday, this must be the bathroom.")

All these changes were intended to put the finishing touches on the new you: how you think, how you speak, and how you see your daily world. Fortunately, romance was still strong and life was full of fun-loving play, hot sex, and vacations. It was good to be alive!

Oh oh! By 2007, you were singing "Get a haircut and get a real job" (we love you, George) as you searched for the right job, or the right place to live, or both. But life was still so unsettling! Fortunately, you love the stimulation that change brings to your life.

What was fortunate now was the fact that your employment scene was looking up! (Just when you needed it.) This *was* a good year to get a better job, a better boss, or a better something! And (there's more?) your health was improving as well. Perhaps all that hustling pumped your muscles and amped your enthusiasm for life?

2008 ~ 2010

By 2008, you began to feel a celestial benefit though partnerships, both professional and intimate. (The sexy ones were more fun, but more maddening!) Close friendships also sprang up. (All so cozy.) Naturally, this made you feel good, because the twin in you is always seeking its other half. ("Romulus!" "Remus!" "Ann!" "Abigail!" "Ashley!" "Mary-Kate!" "Flossie!" "Freddie!")

It also felt like the tooth fairy had arrived. Gifts, goodies, and the financial and/or tangible support of others were a blessing! Inheritances, money back from the government, insurance payouts, or just living off the fat of somebody else's land benefitted you. Of course, whatever came your way was the result of the seeds that you planted in the past. In other words, you deserved this! (Awriiiight!)

Those born later in Gemini were perhaps still searching for a place to live or a different job. Change was still in the air! However, early Geminis had already identified a place they wanted to call home. If so, they were fixing up their digs in a major way, or doing renovations, or fixing the roof or the basement — something substantial.

Marvellous travel opportunities also existed this year, as well as opportunities to go back to school or get further training in some way. This was a great year to sign up for a course or perhaps meet a foreign lover and learn a new language. Who said learning wasn't fun? (The only phrase I know in Spanish is *"Me gusta mucho tu esplendito cuerpo!"* Very handy to know if you're lost and need directions. Everyone was so kind and helpful!)

By 2010, you were laughing. This was one of the best years in a decade for you to capitalize on career opportunities and promote your good name. Some of you got a promotion or some kind of public recognition. You certainly got increased respect from your peers.

While all this was happening, you began to feel more confident about yourself. The gods were smiling on you! (Oh my goodness! There's Smarticus! And Acidophilus! And Testicles!)

2011 – 2013

Your confidence in yourself is stronger now, in part because you feel increasingly stable in your home environment. (Finally, you have a warm feeling in your tummy.) This is so important! If things are willy-nilly at home, how can you sally forth to conquer the world? Despite the fact that you appear to others to be a butterfly going from flower to flower, the truth is you need stability in your home environment. You need something to hang on to that you can trust. You always have and you always will.

Not only do you feel increasingly satisfied with where you live, your relations with family members are much better now than they were several years ago. Thank gawd!

Naturally, nothing is perfect, because nothing is ever perfect. Get real.

This is a popular time for you! Suddenly, everyone wants to see your face! People think you're "pretty and witty and wiiiiiise," and for some reason (but why would anyone doubt this?) you have cachet.

Now is the time to join clubs, groups, and organizations. Enjoy attending classes. Any kind of group dynamic will bless you. In turn, you'll feel confident and successful dealing with groups, whether they're as casual as a meeting or as formal as Parliament. Others sense that you're willing to be part of the team and that you want their success to be your success.

Some will meet people from different backgrounds and other cultures. Travel is also likely at this time.

At home, you're involved in home repairs and shoring up the solidity of your home base. And you feel good about this.

Soon, you'll experience something that triggers an increased interest or exploration in your inner world. You might start asking questions about spirituality or your belief system.

Some kind of external experience will cause you to mature and respond to others with compassion and skillful means instead of the knee-jerk reaction that you might have displayed in the past. That's why you find it increasingly easier to take the high road. You'll put

the interests and needs of others before your own. This isn't being sacrificial. It's actually being wise. By putting the interests of others before your own, you benefit enormously. You grow in ways that are the most meaningful. By 2013, you'll be a far more "quality" person — a finer individual — someone others value knowing.

(None of my Gemini friends paid me to say this.)

In June 2012, lucky Jupiter enters your sign, where it stays for the entire year! (Until June 2013.) This is fabulous news. (The last time Jupiter was in your sign was from July 2000 until July 2001.)

Jupiter takes twelve years to go through all the signs, which means that every twelve years you have a winning ticket! When Jupiter is in your sign, it enormously boosts your confidence. Jupiter also has a social component, and, because of this, you are more inclined to draw people and auspicious circumstances to you.

Jupiter is also associated with higher learning and wisdom. That is why this is the beginning of a major cycle of growth for you. Once again you are exploring a new cycle of discovering deeper aspects of yourself, along with what you're truly capable of. Jupiter is a blessing! It offers you divine protection. It blesses all your relationships with others. What's not to like?

In your family and private life, some might take on a parental responsibility with someone. You'll play the role of teacher or caretaker.

But, more importantly, this stage in your life marks the end of a time of preparation that began approximately around 2001. If you look back, you'll see you have reinvented yourself! What you're involved with now, and the person you appear to be to others, and the choices you make, are all very different from who you were in the year 2000.

This is the end of a time of relative obscurity where you strived to figure out who you were, and what you wanted, and where you would live. This is a turning point! From here on, you will work steadily toward achieving your goals. Because now you're more confident about who you are, and what you value, and where you live. Such freedom!

That's why this time in your life is a beginning! *Bon voyage!*

2014 ~ 2015

You're starting to get serious about work now. (It's a popular method of earning money.) At this time, most of you will be earning more. This could mean you might get a better job, or you earn more money at your current job, or you start to make money on the side. In fact, it would appear that your assets increase, which means you will be buying things that you like.

In addition, this year or next year, you are slipping into serious work mode. Suddenly, you're a slave driver — driving yourself. In part, this is because you feel you're being tested. Nevertheless, you will achieve a lot.

From 2011 to 2019, at different times (according to the actual day of your birth), you'll experience several years of stimulating change. Various opportunities will suddenly arise that give you greater independence, greater freedom, and greater control of your life.

You will also have a chance to advance yourself in whatever work you're doing. This favourable influence might only happen a couple of times in your life.

By 2015, even though you're working hard, you're happy! You feel more optimistic about your life than you have in ages. Relations with siblings and relatives are positive. Plus many of you will meet a new friend who is a real character. Fun new contacts will definitely add a little zing to your life!

2016 – 2018

At this point in your life, good things are starting to happen. Many of you will feel a major breakthrough in your life. This will occur within a two-year window, depending on your birthday. (It might even happen in 2015 for some.)

Think back to around 2000–1. You had just come out of a stretch where you had given up people, places, and possessions. This happened either by choice or by necessity. Immediately following that, you entered a whole new world — very gingerly, and perhaps with great hesitation and fear. (Maybe not.)

Whether you knew it or not, at that point you were setting off on a journey of reinventing yourself, your surroundings, your values, and even where you lived and worked. By around 2007, to a large degree, you had a sense of who you were. You certainly knew who you weren't. ("I know I'm not Johnny Depp, even though he's a Gemini.")

This particular stage in your life is something different, however. Ever since the turn of the millennium, you have been in a relatively obscure and less powerful position with respect to your chart. Now you are going to leap out like a jack-in-the-box! ("Honey, I'm home!")

The past fifteen years were a time to redefine and establish yourself and finally prove what you could do. All of this was a kind of preparation in order to set the stage for the next fifteen years, which are more of a focus on your external world. Now you're going to go for the gold!

The year 2016 is an excellent time for real-estate deals. In fact, 2015–17 is a wonderful window of time for relations with family as well as your own relationship to where you live. Buy goodies for your home! Do whatever you can to enjoy where you live. Entertain at home. This is a happy, heartwarming time for you.

Many of you will explore love affairs, romance, and fun social schmoozing. The arts will flourish. Theatre, movies, literature, music, and any other kind of creative expression will appeal. You

can do well in sports. In fact, sports and playful times with children will be rewarding.

There's one tiny caveat. (Funny how there's always a fly in the ointment.) As you start to take your power by stepping out into the world in a bigger and bolder way, this could upset your ongoing partnerships. Partnerships that are in trouble will definitely dissolve at this time. Fear not. Partnerships that are good will endure, but they will have to undergo readjustments. ("There's a small charge for alterations.")

Many of you will look back at this time of your life as a benchmark.

2019 ~ 2020

Both last year and this year, you have a wonderful opportunity to improve your job. You need to get a better job, or better duties, or a better work scene — something! Perhaps it's your attitude that changes? It's one of your luckiest times in more than a decade with respect to your health and your employment. Some will also get lots of enjoyment from small pets. (We're not talking silver-fish here.)

However, difficulty in partnerships might still be a major issue in your life. In fact, some of you could be letting go of old partner-ships and pursuing new ones.

By 2020, you seem to be getting a lot of enjoyment from part-nerships, and yet, at the same time, you're dealing with disap-pointments and disputes about shared property or something to do with your partner's earnings. It's a mixed bag!

An ongoing theme for this decade has to do with a major trans-formation in your life. It could involve embracing another belief system or encountering a teacher you greatly respect. You're seeking big answers to big questions. It's also a time when you have to come to terms with the values of others, even if they don't agree with your own values. ("Does this mean I have to wake up and smell the coffee? I hate smelling the coffee!")

2021 – 2022

You're approaching a very successful time in your life now. In terms of the so-called big time, you're not quite there — yet. Nevertheless, life is awfully good in 2021–22, because lucky Jupiter is travelling across the top of your chart, attracting opportunities to you. Not only that, Jupiter is the planet of wisdom and wealth, so it projects these same qualities on you (in the eyes of others). This means people notice you more than usual, and they see you as being affluent, successful, wise, and really getting your act together. (Cool.)

This is a once-in-twelve-years deal, so do make the most of it. Milk it for all it's worth. The end result should be that your public persona, your reputation (especially among your peers), and even your relationship with bosses, parents, teachers, and VIPs improve hugely. People are impressed with you. (As my dear friend JuJu once said, "The interesting thing about happiness is that it is so observable.")

Soon your popularity rating will increase. Who's surprised? Success always attracts attention, doesn't it? And whether it's "nothing succeeds like success" or "nothing succeeds like the appearance of success," either way your mailbox is full!

Nevertheless, that time of harvest, that career peak that you've been working toward, has still not yet arrived.

2023 – 2025

It's curious that the end of your predictions (in this book) happens to be one of the most powerful, fortunate times in your life! It looks like it was planned that way, but, of course, it wasn't. This is just how your Gemini life is unfolding.

The year 2023 is extremely powerful and rewarding for two reasons. The most obvious reason is that this is finally your time of harvest! For the next five years or so, you are on a roll! For some, especially younger people, you might be graduating, or getting married, or having a child, or buying your first home, or landing a really good job. Whatever occurs makes you feel proud of your achievements.

For other Geminis, this is that so-called career peak you've been working toward all your life. (Well, at least the last thirty years.) It's when your cherished dreams come true. Kudos, promotions, and personal success in whatever areas matter most to you now begin to come your way, and will continue to do so for the next several years. (Yay!)

However, be prepared. A time of harvest is also when you see which crops have failed. Wherever you planted poorly in the past will be very evident now. Nevertheless, for most people, this is your time of success, a time when whatever you wanted now comes true. (The last time a similar cycle happened for you was 1994–97. However, that cycle would not be entirely the same because many other planets were in different places at that time.)

Your spiritual world is enriched in 2023. Perhaps your successes make you realize the value of appreciation — of appreciating who you are and what you have. By 2024, you're laughing, because lucky Jupiter is in your sign for the first time since 2012–13. Jupiter coincides with your sign once every twelve years, generally for about a year, and it's always a happy event. No question.

Jupiter will attract good things to you: good fortune, good luck, good people, good circumstances, and good opportunities to improve your life in practically any way you want. It also signals

that this is the beginning of a new twelve-year learning and growth process, one that will enrich you and teach you greater wisdom. In fact, when Jupiter is in your sign, the only downside is that you might gain weight, because Jupiter attracts so many goodies to you! ("I never met a piece of chocolate I didn't like.")

By 2025, your money scene improves. (Yay!) This is because moneybags Jupiter now begins to attract increased earnings to you, or a better job, or a way to earn money on the side, or a raise, or money-making ideas. This is also a time when you will feel richer and more affluent because you are spending money as well. Perhaps you're buying furniture, cars, clothing — whatever — but your assets are increasing. (Money is so handy when you want to buy things, isn't it?)

You are really enjoying the fruits of your labour now, even though you're busy with lots of responsibilities. After all, he who would eat the kernel must crack the shell.

"The laughs mean more to me than the adoration. If two girls walk up to me and one says, 'You're cute,' I'll say, 'Thank you.' But I appreciate it much more when the other one says, 'You make me laugh so much.'"

MICHAEL J. FOX
Canadian Television and Film Actor and Author
Film's *Back to the Future* Trilogy and TV's *Spin City*
(B. JUNE 9, 1961)

Famous Gemini Personalities

Henri Rousseau	May 21, 1844–1910
Fats Waller	May 21, 1904–1943
Harold Robbins	May 21, 1916–1997
Raymond Burr	May 21, 1917–1993
Judge Reinhold	May 21, 1957
Fairuza Balk	May 21, 1974
Mary Cassatt	May 22, 1844–1926
Sir Arthur Conan Doyle	May 22, 1859–1930
Sir Laurence Olivier	May 22, 1907–1989
Harvey Milk	May 22, 1930–1978
Paul Winfield	May 22, 1941–2004
Naomi Campbell	May 22, 1970
Shane Koyczan	May 22, 1976
Scatman Crothers	May 23, 1910–1986
Artie Shaw	May 23, 1910–2004
Rosemary Clooney	May 23, 1928–2002
Joan Collins	May 23, 1933
Marvin Hagler	May 23, 1954
Drew Carey	May 23, 1958
"Ricardinho" Pozzi Rodrigues	May 23, 1976
Queen Victoria	May 24, 1819–1901
Bob Dylan	May 24, 1941
Patti Labelle	May 24, 1944
Roseanne Cash	May 24, 1955
Kristin Scott Thomas	May 24, 1960
Ralph Waldo Emerson	May 25, 1803–1882
Beverly Sills	May 25, 1929–2007
W. P. Kinsella	May 25, 1935
Ian McKellen	May 25, 1939
Mike Myers	May 25, 1963
Stacy London	May 25, 1969
John Wayne	May 26, 1907–1979
Peggy Lee	May 26, 1920–2002
James Arness	May 26, 1923

Miles Davis	May 26, 1926–1991
Stevie Nicks	May 26, 1948
Pam Grier	May 26, 1949
Lenny Kravitz	May 26, 1964
Helena Bonham Carter	May 26, 1966
Isadora Duncan	May 27, 1878–1927
Dashiell Hammett	May 27, 1894–1961
Vincent Price	May 27, 1911–1993
Christopher Lee	May 27, 1922
Henry Kissinger	May 27, 1923
Louis Gossett, Jr.	May 27, 1936
Bruce Cockburn	May 27, 1945
Joseph Fiennes	May 27, 1970
Jamie Oliver	May 27, 1975
Ian Fleming	May 28, 1908–1964
Johnny Wayne	May 28, 1918–1990
Rudy Giuliani	May 28, 1944
Gladys Knight	May 28, 1944
John Fogerty	May 28, 1945
Lynn Johnston	May 28, 1947
Kylie Minogue	May 28, 1968
Bob Hope	May 29, 1903–2003
John F. Kennedy	May 29, 1917–1963
Annette Bening	May 29, 1958
Rupert Everett	May 29, 1959
Melanie Brown	May 29, 1975
Benny Goodman	May 30, 1909–1986
Keir Dullea	May 30, 1936
Michael J. Pollard	May 30, 1939
Meredith MacRae	May 30, 1944–2000
Colm Meaney	May 30, 1953
Wynonna Judd	May 30, 1964
Walt Whitman	May 31, 1819–1892
Rainier III, Prince of Monaco	May 31, 1923–2005
Clint Eastwood	May 31, 1930
Joe Namath	May 31, 1943
Gregory Harrison	May 31, 1950
Sienna Guillory	May 31, 1975
Colin Farrell	May 31, 1976
Brigham Young	June 1, 1801–1877
Andy Griffith	June 1, 1926

Marilyn Monroe	June 1, 1926–1962
Charles Wilson	June 1, 1933–2010
Morgan Freeman	June 1, 1937
Paul Coffey	June 1, 1961
Heidi Klum	June 1, 1973
Alanis Morissette	June 1, 1974
Johnny Weissmuller	June 2, 1904–1984
June Callwood	June 2, 1924–2007
Carol Shields	June 2, 1935–2003
Sally Kellerman	June 2, 1937
Jerry Mathers	June 2, 1948
Dana Carvey	June 2, 1955
Josephine Baker	June 3, 1906–1975
Colleen Dewhurst	June 3, 1924–1991
Tony Curtis	June 3, 1925–2010
Allen Ginsberg	June 3, 1926–1997
Marion Zimmer Bradley	June 3, 1930–1999
Larry McMurtry	June 3, 1936
Curtis Mayfield	June 3, 1942–1999
Anderson Cooper	June 3, 1967
Rosalind Russell	June 4, 1907–1976
Dennis Weaver	June 4, 1924–2006
Geoffrey Palmer	June 4, 1927
Cecilia Bartoli	June 4, 1966
Noah Wyle	June 4, 1971
Angelina Jolie	June 4, 1975
Evan Lysacek	June 4, 1985
Pancho Villa	June 5, 1878–1923
John Maynard Keynes	June 5, 1883–1946
Richard Scarry	June 5, 1919–1994
Bill Moyers	June 5, 1934
Ken Follett	June 5, 1949
Suze Orman	June 5, 1951
Mark Wahlberg	June 5, 1971
V. C. Andrews	June 6, 1923–1986
Robert Englund	June 6, 1949
Holly Near	June 6, 1949
Sandra Bernhard	June 6, 1955
Cam Neely	June 6, 1965
Paul Giamatti	June 6, 1967
Paul Gauguin	June 7, 1848–1903

Jessica Tandy	June 7, 1909–1994
Gwendolyn Brooks	June 7, 1917–2000
Dean Martin	June 7, 1917–1995
James Ivory	June 7, 1928
Tom Jones	June 7, 1940
Liam Neeson	June 7, 1952
Prince	June 7, 1958
Frank Lloyd Wright	June 8, 1867–1959
Jerry Stiller	June 8, 1927
Joan Rivers	June 8, 1933
Scott Adams	June 8, 1957
Keenen Ivory Wayans	June 8, 1958
Julianna Margulies	June 8, 1966
Cole Porter	June 9, 1891–1964
Les Paul	June 9, 1915–2009
Michael J. Fox	June 9, 1961
Johnny Depp	June 9, 1963
Natalie Portman	June 9, 1981
Saul Bellow	June 10, 1915–2005
Philip, Duke of Edinburgh	June 10, 1921
Judy Garland	June 10, 1922–1969
Maurice Sendak	June 10, 1928
Brent Sutter	June 10, 1962
Jeanne Tripplehorn	June 10, 1963
Jacques-Yves Cousteau	June 11, 1910–1997
Gene Wilder	June 11, 1933
Jackie Stewart	June 11, 1939
Hugh Laurie	June 11, 1959
Sandra Schmirler	June 11, 1963–2000
Shia LaBeouf	June 11, 1986
Anne Frank	June 12, 1929–1945
Jim Nabors	June 12, 1930
Chick Corea	June 12, 1941
Timothy Busfield	June 12, 1957
Adriana Lima	June 12, 1981
William Butler Yeats	June 13, 1865–1937
Dorothy L. Sayers	June 13, 1893–1957
Malcolm McDowell	June 13, 1943
Richard Thomas	June 13, 1951
Tim Allen	June 13, 1953
Ally Sheedy	June 13, 1962

David Gray	June 13, 1968
Natalie MacMaster	June 13, 1972
Harriet Beecher Stowe	June 14, 1811–1896
Che Guevara	June 14, 1928–1967
Donald Trump	June 14, 1946
Boy George	June 14, 1961
Steffi Graf	June 14, 1969
Waylon Jennings	June 15, 1937–2002
Jim Belushi	June 15, 1954
Helen Hunt	June 15, 1963
Courtney Cox	June 15, 1964
Bif Naked	June 15, 1971
Neil Patrick Harris	June 15, 1973
Geronimo	June 16, 1829–1909
Stan Laurel	June 16, 1890–1965
Joyce Carol Oates	June 16, 1938
Roberto Durán	June 16, 1951
Brad Gushue	June 16, 1980
Igor Stravinsky	June 17, 1882–1971
M. C. Escher	June 17, 1898–1972
Vern Harper	June 17, 1936
Barry Manilow	June 17, 1943
Greg Kinnear	June 17, 1963
Venus Williams	June 17, 1980
Red Adair	June 18, 1915–2004
Roger Ebert	June 18, 1942
Paul McCartney	June 18, 1942
Isabella Rossellini	June 18, 1952
Kurt Browning	June 18, 1966
Guy Lombardo	June 19, 1902–1977
Lou Gehrig	June 19, 1903–1941
Gena Rowlands	June 19, 1930
Salman Rushdie	June 19, 1947
Kathleen Turner	June 19, 1954
Paula Abdul	June 19, 1962
Lillian Hellman	June 20, 1905–1984
Errol Flynn	June 20, 1909–1959
Martin Landau	June 20, 1931
Anne Murray	June 20, 1945
Lionel Richie	June 20, 1949
Nicole Kidman	June 20, 1967

CANCER

JUNE 21 – JULY 22

CANCER the CRAB
(JUNE 21 – JULY 22)

"I FEEL."

"I live to laugh and I laugh to live."
MILTON BERLE
American Comedian and Actor
(JULY 12, 1908–MARCH 27, 2002)

"The basic fact is that all sentient beings, particularly human beings, want happiness and do not want pain and suffering."
THE DALAI LAMA
Tibetan Buddhist Leader
(B. JULY 6, 1935)

Element: Water
Ruling Planet: The Moon
Quality: Cardinal
Opposite Sign: Capricorn
Symbol: The Crab
Glyphs: The Breasts of the Mother or the Claws of the Crab
Lucky Gems: Moonstone and Pearl[1]
Flowers: Jasmine and Honeysuckle
Colours: White and Silver
Parts of the Body: Stomach and Breasts

You Like: Sailing, boats, bargains, collecting, the arts, the past, mysticism, books, and home. Many of you also like to cook and garden — or at least steal flowers from other people's gardens. ("It was on the sidewalk!")

You Don't Like: Wasted food, rude behaviour, ridicule, being forced to try something new, and sourpusses.

Where You Shine: Caring, compassionate, responsive, sympathetic, tenacious, inspired, nurturing, humorous, and charismatic.

So Who's Perfect? Defensive, insecure, contrary, temperamental, moody, untruthful, caught in denial, and prejudiced.

---

1. Different astrology texts list different gems and flowers for different signs. These cannot be trusted.

What Is Cancer-ness?[2]

There's no question the easiest way to understand your sign is to know what your ruling planet means in astrology. Once you have a handle on your ruling planet, you will see the *archetype* of your sign. And once you grasp this, you can figure things out for yourself and make observations about others. "Hmmm, I think that person is a Cancer." Or "Hmmm, so that's why I do this," or "Hmmm, so that's why I hate this!" Or "Hmmm, I think it's time for a little nosh."

The Moon is the ruler of Cancer. (Of course, the Moon is not a planet, but for the sake of ease, astrologers refer to the Sun and Moon as planets. Forgive us our transgressions.)

In my Preface, I mention I do not believe the planets actually physically affect us. But the Moon, ah ha! The Moon is something else because it's sooooo close. Hey — we have actually gone to the Moon!

The reason the Moon affects us is because it has a gravitational pull on bodies of water (hence, the tides), and we are about 90 percent water (including beer). This effect is why emergency wards in hospitals and police records show heightened activity during the Full Moon.

So let's take a look at that old devil Moon.

To begin with, the Moon has extremes in temperature. The side facing the Sun is about 280 degrees Fahrenheit, whereas the side of the Moon facing away from the Sun is minus 280 degrees Fahrenheit. (Yikes.) So the temperature of the Moon is highly changeable. Does this sound like anyone you know?

Cancer is the most moody sign in the zodiac. It doesn't mean there's anything wrong with you. It doesn't mean you're always in a bad mood. It doesn't mean you're unstable. It simply means you swing through a wider range of moods more quickly than others. You can be happy, worried, despondent, then relieved, all before lunch. You're a *feeler*.

Did you know some people actually plan their wardrobe a week in advance? ("I'll wear the suede on Monday, and the brown combo on Tuesday, and my leather on Wednesday, and that blue suit on Thursday, and my jeans on casual Friday. I love how it removes the decision making every morning!")

You could *never* do this! You have no idea how you are going to *feel* on Wednesday. You might feel powerful Manhattan (black turtleneck, black leather jacket, and

---

2. No one is just one sign. This is impossible. Therefore, this is a discussion about the Cancer archetype — the qualities of "Cancer-ness." Many other signs will have Cancer qualities as well. Therefore, the discussion of one sign is not an exact description of that person, but rather, it is a description of the qualities of that sign.

black pants) or you might feel vulnerable and nervous (blue sweater, blue jeans, and a baby blue blanket). Not until you gaze into your jammed closet do you have any idea what you're going to wear. Even then you might try something and change it twice because it doesn't "feel" right.

In astrology, every planet (including the Moon) represents certain aspects of ourselves. Astrology assigns rulership to everything in the world. For example, Mercury rules how we think, talk, and communicate. Mercury also rules cars, trucks, and ground transportation. Every person has Mercury in their chart somewhere in one of the twelve signs.

The same goes for the Moon. Every person has the Moon somewhere in their chart. And for every person the Moon symbolizes the same thing, regardless of whether they're an Aries, a Leo, a Scorpio, or a Cancer. The Moon represents their *feelings*.

This bears repeating: the Moon is all about your *feelings*. The Moon in anyone's chart not only represents their feelings and their emotional response to life but also their earliest, most primal feelings about their mother (or primary caregiver) and their family.[3]

John Bradshaw[4] would call the Moon your "inner child." Why? Because how you responded to others when you were young became your emotional footprint in life. It conditioned your responses for years to come.

So even though everyone has the Moon somewhere in their chart, only the sign of Cancer is *ruled by the Moon*.

Now you can see why you react to your environment in such a sensitive manner and why your feelings get hurt so easily. Of course, it's not cool to show this at times, so you suffer in silence. Generally, you leave an uncomfortable situation. You withdraw. If you are upset at any event, you leave quietly, with no fuss or fanfare, and you might cry all the way home.

You never have to say to a Cancer, "You need to get in touch with your feelings." You're *always* in touch with your feelings!

Furthermore, the sign of Cancer rules the stomach. (It also rules the breasts.) So the first place Cancer people often feel tension is their stomach. They lose their appetite or feel out of sorts when they're flooded with emotions.

The funny thing is you don't *look* this way. You've got your act together! You learned by the time you were three years old to suck it up. But, internally, you will always be *super-sensitive*.

There is an upside. Because you're so sensitive, especially to the dynamics of family and the dynamics of relationships, you have the best sense of humour in the world! Humour grows out of pain, and you know how to see the funny side of life. Some

---

3. I recall doing a phone reading for someone in New York. The aspects to her Moon were harsh and I said so. She quickly replied, "I was raised by wolves."
4. John Bradshaw is an author, educator, counsellor, and motivational speaker. He is the author of six books. According to an entry in Wikipedia (gotta love Wikipedia), in 1999, Bradshaw was nominated by a group of his peers as "One of the 100 Most Influential Writers on Emotional Health in the 20th Century."

signs do mimicry. Some signs act comically. But you grasp the essence of what is funny in life. In fact, I think many great comedians who have different Sun Signs are probably Cancer Rising or have Moon in Cancer.

Consider the following Cancers who made a living being funny:

Mel Brooks	June 28, 1926
Gilda Radner	June 28, 1946–May 20, 1989
Dan Aykroyd	July 1, 1952
Rube Goldberg	July 4, 1883–December 7, 1970
Neil Simon	July 4, 1927
Merv Griffin	July 6, 1925–August 12, 2007
Marty Feldman	July 8, 1934–December 2, 1982
Steve Lawrence	July 8, 1935
Tom Hanks	July 9, 1956
Fred Gwynne	July 10, 1926–July 2, 1993
Milton Berle	July 12, 1908–March 27, 2002
Bill Cosby	July 12, 1937
Cheech Marin	July 13, 1946
Will Ferrell	July 16, 1967
Phyllis Diller	July 17, 1917
Red Skelton	July 18, 1913–September 17, 1997
Don Knotts	July 21, 1924–February 24, 2006
Robin Williams	July 21, 1951
Jon Lovitz	July 21, 1957
Dan Rowan	July 22, 1922–September 22, 1987

(Incidentally, Phyllis Diller has Sun in Cancer and Moon in Cancer.)

"Tragedy is when I cut my finger. Comedy is when you
fall into an open sewer and die."
MEL BROOKS
American Director, Screenwriter, Actor, and Producer
Blazing Saddles, *The Producers*, and *Young Frankenstein*
(B. JUNE 28, 1926)

"If you're going to tell people the truth, be funny or they'll kill you."
BILLY WILDER
Austrian-Born Artist, Filmmaker, Director, and Producer
Some Like It Hot, *The Apartment*, and *Sabrina*
(JUNE 22, 1906–MARCH 27, 2002)

You are also a born storyteller, in part because you have a fabulous memory. I recall a talk I gave in Vancouver where people had their charts in front of them. I said,
"Mercury in Cancer is the strongest placement for memory. Would anyone here
who has Mercury in Cancer please raise your hand?" About a dozen people raised
their hands. I nodded at a white-haired man with a full white beard and said, "Can
you please tell us your earliest memory?" He paused, looked around the room, and
said, "Childbirth." (Whaaat?) I'm proud I can remember the names of some classmates from Grade 2! But childbirth? Was he kidding? No, the Cancer memory is
truly amazing.

So you're sensitive and you have a fabulous sense of humour and a great memory. You also have a touchy stomach and you worry. (Oy vey.)

However, you are the most warm, friendly sign! Cancers have perfected the art
of casual chit-chat, the proverbial over-the-fence gossip. You talk to strangers about
the weather, sports, whatever. You schmooze to perfection!

Three Big Clues about Cancer

To get a deeper understanding of your sign, let's add three symbols to the Moon, because it's easy to remember these.

1. The Big Tit (Your Deep Nurturing Quality)
2. The Barnacle (Your Tenacity)
3. The Crab (Your Ability to Circumvent and Manoeuvre)

The Big Tit

> "There can be no keener revelation of a society's soul
> than the way in which it treats its children."
>
> NELSON MANDELA
> President of South Africa (1994–1999)
> Winner of the Nobel Peace Prize in 1993 after Having Been Imprisoned
> for Twenty-Seven Years
> (B. JULY 18, 1918)

Please take no offence. Male or female, any Cancer is the "big tit" because you are — hands down — the *nurturer* of the zodiac. You take care of babies, children, friends, relatives, family members, and plants, as well as a soup on the stove that isn't quite zesty and delicious. You also take care of office feuds, dead appliances, stalled cars, zombie gardens, corporate woes, and broken hearts.

Once you understand your nurturing quality, you'll get a better appreciation of who you are. Cancer rules the breasts, which is where we get our *first meal in life*. Our next meal comes from the kitchen. Ergo, Cancer rules the *kitchen*. By extrapolation, the kitchen is situated in a house. Sure enough, Cancer rules the *home*. And this home is sitting on a patch of terra firma, and Cancer rules the *land*! (This is why Cancer rules *real estate*.) But this piece of land is part of a larger *community*, which in turn might be part of a city and finally a *country*. Cancer rules all those levels of homes as well.

To put it another way, if you're going to go home tonight, that's where you live. If you're going to go home for Thanksgiving, that's probably your family home, where you grew up or where your parents live. If you've been living abroad for awhile and you say, "I'm going home next month," that's probably your country of origin. All of these homes are under the domain of Cancer.

"Give me your tired, your poor,
Your huddled masses yearning to breathe free."
(Verse Inscribed on the Statue of Liberty)
EMMA LAZARUS
American Poet, Born in New York
(JULY 22, 1849–NOVEMBER 19, 1887)

Meanwhile, back in the kitchen, you are going to feed everyone, but where is the food? Ah ha! Cancer can garden. So part of this nurturing quality of Cancer is the ability to cook and garden, although many of you don't. But you *could*.

But what if the stove breaks down? Or the plow is broken? You can fix it because you will feed your family! Cancer is the most mechanical sign in the zodiac.[5]

So you can cook and garden, and you're also mechanical. That covers it all. The Cancer host will *cook* you a fabulous meal from the *food they grew* in their garden, and serve it to you on the *table they built*. This is no mean feat. Who could top this?

You regard eating as an art. You're interested in food, how it's prepared, how it's spiced, how much it costs, and where it comes from.

"I really believe food has to look good by itself. If you buy good,
fresh green beans, you don't have to line them up in a row or anything like
that. Just put them out on a nice-looking plate."
WOLFGANG PUCK
Austrian-Born Celebrity Chef, Author, and Restaurateur
(B. JULY 8, 1949)

Your need to nurture takes you into nursing and other professions where you help to care for people or help them heal in some way. You can nurse anything and anyone back to health.

"Caring is the essence of nursing."
DR. JEAN WATSON
Developed the Theory of Human Transpersonal Caring
(B. 1940)

Nevertheless, you value family first. Your success in life is primarily due to your desire to nurture and take care of your family. (Can we go back to your place and have dessert?)

Your knee-jerk reaction is to be solicitous and concerned about others. You urge someone to take an umbrella, or, if it's chilly outside, you say, "Is that all you're

---

5. Whenever I had a female client with Jupiter in Cancer, I would say, "You're so mechanical, if something is wrong with your car, you will *actually look* under the hood." Invariably, their reply would be, "Oh, I don't really work on my car. Maybe just minor things like changing the oil." Changing the oil? If something is wrong with my car, I just want a cellphone.

wearing?" You offer blankets, sweaters, and gloves and send people home with left-overs, pies, and sandwiches for the road.

All this is dismissed as nothing. (*Phffft!*) No effort at all. It's the same way when you cook. When people ask you how you make something so delicious, you say, "It's easy. I used whatever was in the fridge. I added spinach and cheese to this."

You cannot fathom that my fridge has nothing but tonic water, mustard, ketchup, and peanut butter. (The peanut butter is there because thank gawd I went shopping!)

The Barnacle

Why the Barnacle? Not because you like water, which you do. In fact, you love to live near the water, or sail on it, or work on it, or hang out near docks and marinas. You even like long baths! But no, the reason you are the Barnacle is because you *can't let go* of anything! You hold on for dear life.

For starters, you can't throw anything away. You save your leftovers.[6]

You save glass jars, rubber bands, string, screws, those white plastic buckets that no-name ice cream comes in, large coffee tins, old lamps, any piece of fabric, clothes that don't fit (but hey, the buttons are great), wool, *National Geographic*s, birthday cards, photographs, negatives, report cards, yearbooks, receipts, letters, keys, old cutlery, pots and pans (even after you get new ones), kettles, dishes — and I haven't even started on the collectibles. Oh, you *love* collectibles! Why? Because you cannot let go of the past.

You're sentimental. You have old corsages, racetrack tickets, theatre programs, and love letters in boxes, trunks, and drawers. Stuff from the twenties, thirties, for-ties, and fifties (not to mention that antique clock from the eighteenth century — what a score!). Your cupboards and closets and basements and garages are *full*!

And guess what else you do to hold on to the past? You take a picture! Almost all Cancers own at least two cameras in their lifetime (and probably more).

> "The departure of our boys to foreign parts with the
> ever-present possibility that they might never return, taught the real
> value of photography to every father and mother."
> LOUIS FABIAN BACHRACH
> American Photographer
> (Bachrach comes from a family of photographers. His father photographed
> President Abraham Lincoln; his son photographed Senator John F. Kennedy.)
> (JULY 16, 1881–JULY 24, 1963)

6. This reminds me of the guy who said, "When I was growing up all we had was leftovers. We never had the original meal."

Since you nurture, feed, and house everyone, your penchant for holding on to stuff makes good sense. After all, you are the nester of the zodiac. You not only hold on to everything that comes your way — "just in case" or because "I might need this someday" — you hold on because you are frugal.

You hold on to your money.[7] You save for a rainy day. Not only do you save, you buy life insurance, you shop for bargains, and you rarely pay retail. You know all the best thrift shops, second-hand stores, and consignment outlets. And you *invented the garage sale.*

"That man is rich whose pleasures are the cheapest."
HENRY DAVID THOREAU
Author, Poet, and Naturalist
Walden
(JULY 12, 1817–MAY 6, 1862)

I never go to garage sales. They depress me. Plus I feel intrusive, like I'm poking around in the bowels of somebody else's life. I also hate asking how much something costs. I will never bargain or dicker. The whole uncertain money thing is too nerve-wracking. (That's because I am Libra Rising.) Then, you might ask, why am I at a garage sale? I'm there because I'm driving somewhere with my Cancer friend Crazy Bob, and he insists on stopping. It's so humiliating. If he sees an item for twelve dollars (perhaps a George Foreman grill), he will hold it up and yell out across the yard, "I'll give ya fifty cents!"

Your Barnacle quality makes you the most tenacious sign in the zodiac. Cancers never quit. Once you set your mind on something, you persevere to the nth degree. In fact, your dogged perseverance earns you the reputation of being a dark horse. Initially, you display little flash and dazzle. You are easily overlooked. But, as the years go by, the proof is in the pudding. A large number of Cancers are on the boards of large corporations, and they are there because of their staying power. Your long-term success might also be due to that wonderful sense of humour of yours.

After all, he who laughs lasts ...

The Crab

Cancer the Crab. This is a very apt symbol for you, because you hide behind a shell to protect yourself from life's vicissitudes, boring guests, and bad art. Your deep nurturing instincts help you protect yourself. (Think of the instructions an airline attendant gives to passengers. Parents are instructed to put the oxygen mask on themselves first, before they put the masks on their children, because if the parent passes out, no one gets a mask!) You know that if you don't take care of yourself, you will be of little use to anyone else.

---

7. If you save a little money each day, at the end of a year you'll be surprised at how little you have.

Your desire to nest and create a wonderful home for yourself and your family is tied up with being a crab. You are most relaxed (and creative) in familiar surroundings, especially your home. You are safe in your shell. Under stress, you hide!

Furthermore, like the crab, you approach something sideways; you rarely confront a situation head-on. You are far too diplomatic (and kinda sneaky) for that. You won't risk rejection or being rebuffed. If you want to go to a movie with someone, you won't just say, "Hey, do you want to go to a movie?" Instead, you'll casually ask, "Are you busy tonight?" You rarely ask for anything directly.[8] Like the crab, you approach situations from an oblique angle.

Also like the crab, you are drawn to water. Many of you choose professions related to marinas, lakes, rivers, and the ocean. You would love to have your own boat, no matter what size. It soothes you to be in or around water.

> "It isn't that life ashore is distasteful to me. But life at sea is better."
> SIR FRANCIS DRAKE
> Second-in-Command of the English Naval Fleet against the Spanish Armada
> (1540–JANUARY 27, 1596)

This water element also represents the unconscious, which is very much tied up with your sign. You are governed far more by your unconscious feelings than you might ever guess. So much of you is "hidden" behind your crab shell. This is why sometimes you cannot act. You freeze in a situation because you're waiting for your intellect to catch up to your feelings.

When you meet someone new, you will talk about anything under the sun because you're really trying to get a "feel" for that person. You know you can trust your gut. (Ah, that Cancer stomach.)

> "And now here is my secret, a very simple secret; it is only with the heart that one can see rightly, what is essential is invisible to the eye."
> ANTOINE DE SAINT-EXUPÉRY
> French Writer and Aviator
> *The Little Prince*
> (JUNE 29, 1900–JULY 31, 1944)

Now I'm going to contradict myself because, of course, we all have our contradictions. While it's true you approach life gently, sensitively, and in a rather indirect way, nevertheless you are a Cardinal sign.[9] This is the part of you of that is full of derring-do!

---

8. However, if you are Scorpio Rising or Leo Rising, this is another matter. ("Ten-shun!")
9. All signs are Cardinal, Fixed, or Mutable. Cardinal signs are active doers. They take action! They initiate. (Aries, Cancer, Libra, and Capricorn are Cardinal signs.) Fixed signs are stable, traditional, and bossy. A Fixed sign makes an entrance! (Taurus, Leo, Scorpio, and Aquarius are Fixed signs.) Mutable signs are shape-shifters and communicators. They slide in and out of situations with ease. They adapt. (Gemini, Virgo, Sagittarius, and Pisces are Mutable signs.)

"Greetings, and death to our enemies."
DAN AYKROYD
Canadian Comedian, Actor, Screenwriter, and Musician
The Blues Brothers and *Ghostbusters*
(B. JULY 1, 1952)

It's ironic, because even though you have your own protective shell, you're unusually bold about reaching into the lives of others. You don't hesitate to initiate something or get the ball rolling in a way that amazes people. You're ambitious. You want success! Because success means money, and money means safety, protection, and security, especially for your home and family.

I am going to reveal my own bias here (and despite their objections to the contrary, every astrologer has some biases). If I had to tackle an important project, I would want a lot of Cancer people on my team. You have common sense and you're down-to-earth. These are necessary qualities in the real world. Your fabulous sense of humour guarantees a fun and lighthearted approach to everything. (It's important to see the funny side of life.) But, most of all, your ability to see how something should be done, and to tackle it with intelligence, and then finish the job because you have unparalleled perseverance and follow-through — these qualities are invaluable. You're extremely supportive. Anyone would consider themselves lucky to have you on their side!

(Crazy Bob paid me to say this.)

Cancer in Love

"A woman needs to be a cook in the kitchen and a whore in the bedroom."
JERRY HALL
American Model, Actress, and Former Long-Term Partner of
Rolling Stones Front Man Mick Jagger
(B. JULY 2, 1956)

You're a romantic, and you're extremely sentimental. You hold on to keepsakes and mementos of every special moment you've shared with a lover. (Even a previous lover.)

Fortunately for your love life, you are one of the most likeable signs in the zodiac. You're easy to talk to, and, since you're so sensitive, you're likewise very considerate about the feelings of others.

When in love, you display all your warm Cancer qualities. You nurture your lovers. You cook for them, run them a bath, and fix things for them. You help them in any way. You are sweet, supportive, tender, and caring.[10] Of course, your Barnacle side really holds on to someone! You can be possessive, even clingy at times.

"People who care about each other enjoy doing things for one another. They don't consider it servitude."
ANN LANDERS (PEN NAME OF ESTHER "EPPIE" LEDERER)
American Advice Columnist, 1955–2002
(JULY 4, 1918–JUNE 22, 2002)

Most astrology books claim Cancers are loyal. And you are — to a point. But I know many of you stray from the nest! You don't go out looking to score. That's not your style. Remember the Crab? It's not your nature to be so direct. You wait for the other person to make the first move. And when they do, even if you are in a relationship, you find it hard to rebuff someone if you're fond of them. You hate to hurt their feelings. It's almost as if you hate to "let them go" even if you're not in a relationship yet. You are governed by your feelings, remember? Not your intellect. You might be having something on the side yet still be hugely possessive of your partner. (What's good for the goose is good for the goose.)

---

10. You can tell when two Cancers are hugging each other because they are both patting and rubbing each other's backs at the same time. Cancers are the best huggers.

"At every party there are two kinds of people: those who want to go home and those who don't. The trouble is, they are usually married to each other."
ANN LANDERS (PEN NAME OF ESTHER "EPPIE" LEDERER)
American Advice Columnist, 1955–2002
(JULY 4, 1918–JUNE 22, 2002)

The Cancer infidelity is not a flash-in-the-pan one-night stand. It's another on-going relationship. After all, you like to play house. It is not uncommon that a Cancer infidelity is where one partner discovers their Cancer mate has been seeing someone else for twelve years! Sometimes all three parties are aware of each other. ("Now we need a fourth for bridge.")

When it comes to expressing your earthy passions, you are not what you appear. You look so respectable! God, motherhood, and the flag. Pearls thrown in for a classic touch. We can take you home to dinner. But in the bedroom — you are insatiable.

Nevertheless, your personal approach to love is surprisingly laissez-faire. Oh yes, you want love. You need love. You seek love. But you can be rather casual, no? You might keep several lovers on the string and not see a big problem with this, not really. I mean, everybody's happy, right? You're more than wonderful to them — no question. You're hardly a monster; you *care* about these people!

You're a practical romantic. You never let your loved one down. You're extremely loyal to your loved one — even if this loyalty is not in the society's accepted terms of fidelity. Of course, it's a different matter if the reverse is happening. (Of course!)

Now we come to a classic Cancer phenomenon. You are infamous for staying in the wrong relationship too long. (I heard that gasp.) One obvious reason is you cannot let go. It's not in your Barnacle nature.

But there's another reason you stay in these relationships too long. You're so sympathetic and caring, you "understand" when someone is being a jerk. You "know" why they acted that way. If they drink too much, or are rude, you rationalize, "Hey, they lost their job, they're licking their wounds, they don't really mean it." Your empathy for someone lets you forgive bad behaviour.

It's important to realize if you're in a relationship that is holding you back, this relationship is holding the other person back *as well.* Give yourself permission to leave. *Now!*

Cancers are heady, emotional lovers. You're affectionate, cuddly, and totally focused on pleasing your partner. You know how to make someone feel adored and special. And, yes — you do play with food. Think whipped cream, honey, and Scotch.[11]

But you hover! You like to know where your other half is at all times. (You want a warm feeling in your tummy about the relationship.) No matter how gorgeous you are, you can be surprisingly insecure. If your partner has a cellphone, they're on an electronic leash.

---

11. I've heard interesting stories about how exciting cold Coca-Cola can be. Apparently, "You can't beat the feeling."

However, the right partner won't mind, because you're a catch. Who else can create such an inviting, warm home environment? Who else can wonderfully feed someone, pet them, and make them laugh? Who else will be there with practical and loving support when the chips are down?

You are all anyone needs in life.

"All married couples should learn the art of battle as they should learn the art of making love. Good battle is objective and honest — never vicious or cruel. Good battle is healthy and constructive, and brings to a marriage the principles of equal partnership."

ANN LANDERS (PEN NAME OF ESTHER "EPPIE" LEDERER)
American Advice Columnist, 1955–2002
(JULY 4, 1918–JUNE 22, 2002)

The Cancer Boss

"Ridiculous yachts and private planes and big limousines
won't make people enjoy life more, and it sends out terrible messages to
the people who work for them."

SIR RICHARD BRANSON
British Industrialist and Chairman of Virgin Group
(B. JULY 18, 1950)

Although you're not driven to be the boss in the same way Aries or Leo or Scorpio might be, the truth is you would rather be the boss than the employee. You have savvy, experience, common sense, and skillful means when dealing with others. Therefore, you should be the boss!

I have said a lot about how sensitive you are, and every word of it is true. Nevertheless, you are ambitious. Oh yes! And you're tenacious. You're totally ready to go after what you want. Think of Julius Caesar, John D. Rockefeller, Nelson Mandela, Sir Edmund Hillary, Tom Cruise, Sylvester Stallone, Harrison Ford, Gerald Ford, John Glenn, Babe Zaharias, and Helen Keller. These people are not wusses!

But you're inclined to be a cheapskate. Admit it. You push your workers to be cost-conscious and you're tight on budget allocation, generally by setting a good example yourself. Of course, your superiors are impressed with your tight-fisted management style.

You reward loyalty, and you don't like turnover. Obviously, you hate firing people unless you have to. You also hate when employees quit or leave you. You don't like to let go!

The Cancer Employee

"The thing with high-tech is that you always end up using scissors."
DAVID HOCKNEY
British Painter, Draftsman, Set Designer, and Photographer
(B. JULY 9, 1937)

You are an excellent employee because you have enormous stick-to-it-iveness! You are reliable, conscientious, and hard working, and you are excellent on follow-through. You don't get lippy with your boss, even if you don't agree with them, and you're surprisingly co-operative. Because you stay in the same job for a long time, you acquire years of experience and invariably become a valuable asset to any team or organization.

"The pen is mightier than the sword, and considerably easier to write with."
MARTY FELDMAN
British Writer, Comedian, and Actor
(JULY 8, 1934–DECEMBER 2, 1982)

You're naturally resourceful and mechanical. Not only do you know how to fix things, you are also one of the first to see the most practical way of doing something. ("Wouldn't it be easier to blow the balloons up *in* the gymnasium rather than transport them there?")

You're also cost-conscious. You hate to waste materials and money. If you have to stick to a budget or buy material for your job, you're thrifty and economical. (Bosses like this.) Plus you have a genuine concern for the environment.

"Caring about the environment has always been a big part of my life.
When you grow up in a really beautiful place and you hear that it is
jeopardized, you want to do something."
K. T. TUNSTALL
Singer, Songwriter, and Guitarist
(B. JUNE 23, 1975)

Your easygoing chit-chat style guarantees harmony and co-operation among co-workers. You're a great hire!

The Cancer Parent

"Every single decision I make about what material I do,
what I'm putting out in the world, is because of my children."
MERYL STREEP
American Actress Who Has Received the Most Nominations for Film and Stage
Kramer vs. Kramer, Sophie's Choice, The Bridges of Madison County,
and *The Devil Wears Prada*
(B. JUNE 22, 1949)

Few signs come so naturally prepared for the role of parent. To nurture others is one of strongest, most wonderful qualities you have. You were born for the job. You love to cuddle, caress, and care for someone who needs you. You take to the role of parenting like a duck to water, because now there is an even greater and more noble reason to constantly feather your nest — your children need you!

This is why the Cancer parent makes sacrifices for his or her child. You will go without good clothing, good shoes, or fine furniture so your children can get a good education, or go to summer camp, or have the tools or musical instruments they need.

You never hesitate to make the sacrifice, in part because you always take the long-range view of things. You are in this for the long haul, remember? You care strongly about making it work today, and tomorrow, and tomorrow, and tomorrow. Your children will sense this and feel secure in the home you create. No question.

Naturally, you create a homey environment and provide delicious and nutritious meals for your child. You take parenting seriously, but also very much in stride. This role comes naturally because you are happy to cook or garden (you generally hate housework), and this creates stability at home.

There's no question the kitchen is the heart of the home. Therefore, any home will be vital, bustling, and alive with energy if the kitchen is bountiful. And Cancers know how to do this!

"It's the sense of what family is at the dinner table. It was the joy of knowing Mother was in the kitchen making our favourite dish. I wish more people would do this and recall the joy of life."
PAUL PRUDHOMME
American Celebrity Chef; Famous for His Cajun Cuisine
(B. JULY 13, 1940)

However, the Cancer parent can be smothering. (Yes, you.) But beware! When you smother your children — and, of course, you do this out of love — you might inadvertently send a message to your kids that they're inadequate to take up the task of living. Even if you encourage them with words, they will sense your concern and suspect it is justified. Of course, in time they will grow to understand that this is just you being you. But what if this realization doesn't occur until they're forty?

As your children get older, it's often difficult for you to let them go. You see their growing independence as a loss for you. It's painful when they leave home. But this is just something that goes with the territory. Hopefully, little grandchildren will soon follow!

Parenting ain't for sissies.

The Cancer Child

"Any kid will run any errand for you if you ask at bedtime."
RED SKELTON
American Comedian, Radio Personality, and Television Actor
(JULY 18, 1913–SEPTEMBER 17, 1997)

The Cancer child needs a lot of hugging. I cannot emphasize this enough. This is a very sensitive child who wants to feel protected — indeed, *needs* to be protected emotionally and psychologically until he or she can build their own little crab shell. They need physical contact and a sense of belonging. They want very much to feel safe at home.

As part of their attempt to create what is familiar and "homey" in their environment, they will become attached to certain things. (Remember, this young person will grow into an adult who can't let go. We're talking Baby Barnacle.) Therefore, do not force this child to give up a bottle, or a soother, or their baby blue blanket, or their teddy bear, or anything else they've grown attached to and that gives them comfort. I guarantee they will be horrified if as young teenagers, you throw out their ratty jean jacket, smelly sneakers, or favourite piece of clothing. These children become very attached to certain things. These things have *meaning* for them. (I know more than one grown Cancer male who still has his childhood teddy bear high up on a shelf in his den.)

As adults, these children feel sentimental about many of their childhood treasures; therefore, you must respect this need by saving these mementos. (Yeah, tough if you're a Virgo or Scorpio parent.)

Do try to laugh and appreciate their lame jokes as they fumble their way toward cultivating humour when they are four and five years old. They are testing their ability to be funny. They know this skill exists, and they know they have it, but they're not sure how it works. Later, they will entertain you royally at dinnertime! Cancers are marvellous dinner companions.

Do not force your Cancer children to eat anything they don't want to eat. They have a strong relationship with food, and many of them will grow up to be great chefs. Stay clear of this delicate realm of fascination, and let them enter it with genuine interest and joy. I know a Cancer woman who was forced to eat her porridge as a child. As she grew up, she was a dutiful daughter to her parents. (Unusually so.) Nevertheless, at her father's funeral, she knelt down and quietly slipped some oatmeal into his coffin. She had never forgotten.

By all means, let them help you cook. Let them help you garden. Give them mechanical toys, little tea sets, and cooking sets, plus dolls and stuffed animals to nurture. But do not be critical of them. This is a very sensitive child whose feelings are hurt very easily.

"How old would you be if you didn't know how old you were?"
LEROY "SATCHEL" PAIGE
American Baseball Player
The Oldest Rookie (at Age Forty-Two) to Play Major League Baseball
(JULY 7, 1906–JUNE 8, 1982)

How to Be a Happier Cancer

> "I feel that it is healthier to look out at the world through a window than through a mirror. Otherwise, all you see is yourself and whatever is behind you."
>
> **BILL WITHERS**
> American Singer-Songwriter
> "Just the Two of Us" and "Ain't No Sunshine"
> (B. JULY 4, 1938)

Few would guess how keenly (and privately) you react to the hurts you experience. You are pained by subtle words and slights others slough off. People accuse you of taking small things too seriously. But it's just who you are. You will always react with great sensitivity to what others say or do. As I see it, your tender Cancer nature can suffer too easily in two ways:

1. Your sensitivity to minor slights
2. Your inability to let go of painful situations

Dealing with Minor Slights

Here is something most people don't know. The twelve signs of the zodiac are really on six planes or planks. Each plank has a sign on either end.

Aries...................Libra
Taurus ....Scorpio
Gemini............Sagittarius
Cancer ....Capricorn
Leo ....Aquarius
Virgo ....Pisces

You are a Cancer and your opposite sign is Capricorn. But, really, you have a lot in common with Capricorn (love of family, for example) because you are actually *two ends of the same plank. Capisce?*

You both are expressions of the same energy. Now, here is an astrological truth: in order to gain greater skilful means for living our lives, we should all strive to be more like our opposite sign. This is how we grow beyond our own boundaries and limitations. This means it is wise for you to observe the Capricorn approach to life, just as it is wise for the Capricorn to observe your approach to life.

The Capricorn approach to life is "no pain, no gain." Even a glance at the Capricorn section (or just the quotes) will give you a quick picture of very different style of living and set of values. The opening quote to the Capricorn section by J. R. R. Tolkien is a real cutie:

> *March on. Do not tarry. To go forward is to move toward perfection.*
> *March on, and fear not the thorns or the sharp stones on life's path.*

Whaaaat? Capricorns are stoic! Their "suck it up, Princess" attitude might sound cold and unfeeling to you, but, hey, it's just the other extreme of where you are coming from. Somewhere in the middle — between both of you — is the ideal.

Your extra-sensitive reactions, especially to minor slights, only make you miserable. Of course, the only person it hurts is *you*. Your choice of response is actually adding to your suffering. And you *do have a choice*.

In fact, have you noticed that your response is related to how much else is going on in your life? If you're very busy with major events, you more easily ignore an insensitive comment. You don't have time to give it much thought. But if you do have the time — oh, how you brood!

I agree, it's not easy to simply tell yourself the insensitivity of others is no reason to suffer. But it's a beginning. You might even go one step further and realize these people are actually sadly ignorant. (They're boors.)

Therefore, for the sake of your own happiness — and, by extension, your own productivity and effectiveness in the world — try not to take minor things so seriously. It's a matter of perspective.

Your reaction to pain will also depend on how involved you are in a world beyond your own world. When you think about the problems of loved ones or those who are suffering in your city or in another country, then by comparison your problems will shrink. Your awareness of the suffering of others will diminish your own troubles. Anyone who has visited Darfur or Chad or Haiti immediately realizes how good they have it back home.

Pain is relative. Once your mind embraces the greater suffering of others, it will diminish your own problems. This awareness does not come overnight. It is cultivated. Exposure to and a greater awareness of the suffering of others always puts things in perspective.

Dealing with Painful Situations

Suffering is a natural part of life. Nobody escapes suffering. You can't assume being rich or famous makes you happy. If this were true, then rich and famous people would be happy. But many rich and famous people commit suicide or lead miserable lives. Nobody gets through life without suffering.

Remember your Barnacle quality? You hold on! You tenaciously hold on to pain. You replay events over and over in your mind, refusing to let go. You're hurt, and you're not going to pretend the pain isn't major, because it *is*. If someone has injured or betrayed you, you're not letting them off the hook that easily!

You have the illusion that, by suffering, you're not letting the other person off the hook? (Whooaa!) The truth is the other person might be oblivious to what they did to you or they have long forgotten. They might even be dead. Why are you holding on?

When you hold on to your pain, it's like holding on to a hot pot. You don't want to let go of the pot, and yet, as you keep holding on to it, your hands are burning. Too often, you would rather "nurse" this grudge or painful memory than let it go. To just let it go seems to diminish the gravity of the event.

I have heard Cancer clients speak with bitterness about a partner. They would agonize and sometimes weep. And, many times, they were discussing events that happened *years* before.

> "Most people are prisoners, thinking only about the future
> or living in the past. They are not in the present, and the present is
> where everything begins."
> CARLOS SANTANA
> Mexican-American Rock Guitarist of the Band Santana
> (B. JULY 20, 1947)

You have power over your own state of happiness. To let go of suffering has nothing to do with dismissing what someone else did or even what you did. It has nothing to do with the past. It has everything to do with the present and certainly the future.

How many years do you have left to live — maybe eighty? Probably less. None of us knows how long we will live or when we will die. Why be miserable? No matter how tough your situation is, you might as well be as happy as you can be.

The purpose of life is to be happy.

Fortunately, everything is impermanent — even suffering. Nothing stays the same. It's important to remember that your suffering *will diminish*, if for no other reason than the sheer passage of time. But you can hasten this by actively choosing to let go.

The end of all rising is falling.
The end of all saving is spending.
The end of all living is dying.
The end of all meeting is parting.
EASTERN PROVERB

Consider a profound observation from the opposite end of your plank — Capricorn Dr. Kary Mullis: "There is a place in your brain, I think, reserved for 'melancholy of relationships past.' It grows and prospers as life progresses, forcing you finally, against your better judgment, to listen to country music."

CANCER
YOUR 40-YEAR HOROSCOPE
1985 – 2025

Why Go into the Past?

I want you to believe and have faith in your predictions so you can derive benefit from them in guiding your future. The only way you can believe what I say is to test it for yourself. This is why I start with brief highlights from the past twenty-five years. If anything in these past twenty-five years resonates with you, then what I say about your future will have the same validity. It is all one long timeline — your life.

The past predictions generally apply once you have left home or are "running your life" and making your own decisions. Prior to that, the major events in your life were dictated to you by other people, likely your parents.

1985 – 1990

This was a time when many of you were questioning what you wanted to do with your life. Some of you had increased responsibilities with children. (Inheritances and help from others were a good thing.) In 1986, travel and higher education were favoured. Ditto for publishing and the media. By now, you had sunk your teeth into something and were working hard. The fruits of your labour began to pay off in 1987, as influential people plus your own accomplishments beautifully boosted your reputation. Now you started to get the recognition you deserved!

Increased popularity around 1988, along with involvement with clubs, groups, and professional associations, kept you busy. This was a time when you met new people. Perhaps this put a strain on partnerships and close friendships that began and blossomed by 1989. This might have been difficult. No question. Some relationships bit the dust, but in August 1989, lucky Jupiter returned to your sign for the first time since the late seventies. Glory hallelujah! This boosted your confidence and made you feel lucky and blessed. It was a great help at this time when partnerships were so challenging. (Challenging partnerships are such a bummer.)

1991 – 1996

It's a good thing you had a chance to boost your earnings, because difficulties with partnerships made you let go of some things, including the practical support you previously enjoyed.

By 1992–93, your belief in yourself was stronger. You saw there was a future! And 1993 was also a wonderful time when you had a chance to improve your home and your family scene, and possibly buy real estate. Whatever happened, your family and personal life were enriched.

Fortunately, by 1994, the prior loss you had suffered seemed to fade, and was now less important. You were on your own two feet. In fact, things were looking so good, you could plan a vacation! Certainly 1994–95 was a wonderful time for higher education, publishing, the media, and travel for pleasure. This was also a great time to fall in love. New romance was exciting! You also had opportunities to express your creative talents. Life was good.

By 1995, opportunities to improve your job were at hand. You either got a better job, or made the job you already had work for you. Small wonder that, by 1996, things began to turn in your favour. This was the year when relationships and partnerships were blessed. Some of you made a permanent commitment at this time.

This was also a time of harvest, when your reputation started to blossom in a positive way. Finally, you felt a sense of victory after slogging it out since 1983. Whew!

1997 – 2000

Things continued to go along very well for you. You saw what was working and what was not. Wills, inheritances, insurance payouts, money back from the government, and direct assistance from others really helped you. You received the benefit of the support of others. Hey — they *believed* in you!

Basically, 1998 was a fabulous time. Travel for pleasure plus opportunities in higher education, medicine, the law, publishing, and the media were juicy. You got accolades and applause for your achievements. That is when you felt proud of what you could do, and others were equally aware of your success.

Naturally, this was followed by an increase in popularity. (Nothing succeeds like success. And success often leads to excess!) "Jump in! The water's fine!"

By the turn of the millennium, one of your challenges was learning how to keep everyone happy, plus continue to deal with groups and yet, at the same time, save a little time and energy for yourself! After all, you count, too! It was difficult juggling your own success as well as your popularity with others. (It's tempting to sell out.)

2001 – 2005

For whatever reason (according to the details of your personal life), at this stage in your life, you knew you had to start to downsize and let go of things. This was not easy for you! For many Cancers, external events grabbed you by the throat, forcing you to give up possessions, homes, jobs, and even relationships. (Yikes!) You did not do this willingly, unless you have Scorpio in your chart.

Fortunately, in the summer of 2001, moneybags Jupiter entered your sign, where it stayed for the next twelve months. This helped you because it made you happier and more optimistic. Nevertheless, letting go of things is never easy for you. Especially relationships. It's also very difficult for you to let go of homes and the plans you had. All those hopes and expectations.

By 2003, many of you improved your earnings, or you felt wealthier because of increased assets. Perhaps you bought yourself some toys? You might have introduced changes at home that made you feel richer. Whatever happened, by 2005, you *did* feel richer at home. This was a wonderful window of time for you to invest in real estate.

All aspects of your family life took a positive turn by around 2005. There was more joy in your home, more joy in family relationships, and perhaps joy at the expansion of family through birth, adoption, or marriage. This was an enriching time for you, despite what you had to give up!

2006 – 2010

If you look back at 2005–6, you see a significant change taking place in your life. Following a time of loss, and giving things up, and saying goodbye, you began to swing your life into a new direction where you started to reinvent yourself. By 2006, vacation plans and travel for pleasure looked sweet! This was also a great time for love affairs, romance, sports, playful times with children, and a chance to explore opportunities in the arts and show business.

After this lovely little reward, no wonder you were ready to get down to work and improve your job scene. All this became possible in 2007. At this time, you got a better job, or improved your job, or your evil boss was transferred to Buzzard Roost, Mississippi.

However, by 2008–9, big changes were in the wind. Residential moves and job changes suddenly appeared — without expectation, might I add — and this created changes on your home front. Fortunately, while you were undergoing this kind of upheaval, partnerships and close friendships were suddenly enormously supportive. (Well, that's a relief!)

It's times like this that make you realize what goes around comes around. You are an unusually caring, supportive, loyal friend to others (including partners). Now when you were frazzled and needing the support of others, it was *there*! You earned these brownie points from the universe.

The aftershock of residential and job changes continued all the way through 2009–10, yet you continued to benefit from others. But by 2010, travel for pleasure, plus an opportunity to promote yourself in publishing, the media, medicine, or the law, looked sweet.

Some of you began to work for or with foreign countries or to make new friends with people from very different backgrounds (romantic or otherwise).

Many of you now turned your efforts to major renovation projects. Next on the agenda was to establish a firm base for yourself in your world. ("I want a nice waterfront nest, with four bathrooms with heated floors, with a great barbecue, and a big deck with steps down to my own private dock.")

2011 – 2014

Ever since 2003, you have been reinventing yourself. Initially, you fiddled around with your image, experimenting with different hairstyles, clothes, and anything that projected a different look. This new look might have been unconscious, or it might have been contrived or planned for, or it might have related to job or residential changes.

Now, you're in the final throes of reinventing the new you! As such, you're putting the final touches on this so-called product. Whatever takes place now is meant to hone and refine how you talk, think, communicate, and listen to others. In order to do this, life will throw you into a different daily milieu. This might happen because of job changes, residential moves, or both. Without question, you're still in a state of flux.

Fortunately, lucky moneybags Jupiter is sailing across the top of your chart in 2011, bringing you all kinds of opportunities to explore, as well as benefit from events and contacts with others (especially important people). This beautifully boosts your reputation in a positive way! Something this favourable hasn't happened since the year 2000.

By 2012, you'll become even more serious about putting down roots somewhere. You're a nester, and for the first time since the early eighties, you're determined to create a home for yourself that you can rely on. Something to give you a cozy feeling in your tummy. (Domestic security is vital to you.)

This is why many of you will renovate where you live or fix things up in a major way (e.g., by repairing the roof or the basement). Major changes to your family relationships might also take place.

Meanwhile, your popularity is increasing, which means entertaining at home is a given. Everybody wants to see your face! Many of you will join clubs, groups, classes, and different associations at this time as well. (Something has to account for your increased schmoozing with everyone.)

As you settle in and start to feel comfortable with where you're living, many of you will get in touch with a deeper aspect of yourself. You will plumb your feelings about life and your values. You might meet a powerful teacher, or play this role for others. The years 2013–14 are a particularly spiritual time for you.

Bravo! In the summer of 2013, lucky moneybags Jupiter is back in your sign! This is marvellous news. "I love me!" (The last time this happened was 2001–2.) Jupiter is the largest planet. For example, you can fit all the other planets in the solar system into Jupiter. Jupiter represents magnification, increase, wealth, growth, and wisdom. It also represents luck and good fortune! Naturally, everybody wants Jupiter to be in their sign!

During this time, your self-confidence and poise will increase. You'll develop a greater faith in yourself and your ability to do things. This is because others will treat you with greater respect. Since they see you in such a positive light, they will expect *more* from you as well. They think you can *deliver*! This is a tremendously positive influence for you, and it attracts wonderful opportunities to you as well. Say yes to what comes your way. You will be able to fulfill the expectation of others. In fact, you will shine!

2015 ~ 2017

Now your focus begins to turn seriously to work and earning money. For starters, 2015–16 is a time when you can boost your earnings. Yay! Some of you will get a better job. Others will just get more money staying where you are. Some will figure out ways to earn more on the side. Whatever the case, your earnings and assets are bound to increase. Naturally, your sense of wealth and richness could be due to serious purchases you make yourself (even though you pay for it). Nevertheless, you feel pretty swell driving a fancy car or enjoying your beautiful home full of fresh, elegant touches.

Ironically, while all this is going on, you might still feel uneasy about what it is you really want to be when you grow up. At this time, increased responsibilities with children are likely. This could be due to family expansion or kids moving back home.

Not until 2017 do you start to see a viable plan for yourself. Once you focus on this, you will start to work hard. We're talking busting your buns! You're also unusually enthusiastic now.

You're busy with short trips, schmoozing, wheeling and dealing, buying and selling, and talking to everyone. Some of you will also be reading, writing, and studying more than usual. There might be an increased emphasis on teaching, acting, training, or even driving.

You're no longer worried about your home scene. Things are settled there. Now you're trying to prove to others what you can do.

2018 – 2020

Since the fall of 2017, and for most of this year, your real-estate opportunities are fabulous! This is a great time to buy a home. It's also a great time to buy property for speculation. Similarly, it's an excellent time to augment or improve your home. Whatever you do to your home will add to its value, and your future profit if you ever sell it.

Because everything is going swimmingly in your domestic scene, naturally, relationships with family members are better than ever. (Even your brother-in-law — and that's saying something.) Family reunions, family gatherings, and just everyday family situations are rewarding and joyful. And yes — you're still busting your buns. It was ever thus.

Enter stage left: A vacation. A fun getaway! White sands, turquoise waters, yummy drinks with little pink parasols. ("Walk this way.")

Sometime during 2018–19, you will take a well-deserved vacation! Factoid. This is also a marvellous time for love affairs, romance, parties, and all kinds of fun stuff. In fact, this is an extremely beneficial time for the hospitality industry, the arts, show business, and the entertainment world. It's your turn to live it up! By all means, do so — you worked for this — and you deserve it.

After you return refreshed, romantically sated (ooh la la), and happier with life, who is surprised that you'll conclude that all your hard work is starting to pay off!

Later in 2019, you will get a better job, or better duties, or a better boss, or better working conditions — the operative word is *better*. We like better. Best is even nicer, but we never refuse better!

Along with your job scene improving, your health scene will improve as well. This is not surprising, considering how one's health and job are so often linked, especially if you're a high-wire aerialist.[12]

Enjoy your good fortune!

---

12. Which brings to mind: if at first you don't succeed — skydiving is not for you.

By 2020, small wonder your partnerships and close friendships are shaping up beautifully. Something will happen to confirm to you that you're in the right partnership. You feel all comfy-like. You also feel greater respect for partners and close friends.

Others will enter into close partnerships, marriage, or even professional partnerships at this time, with someone older, more established, richer, or more sophisticated in the ways of the world.

This is all good stuff. But, hey — you earned it. You reinvented yourself. You got your home scene settled. You busted your buns. Then you took a vacation and enjoyed playful times with children, while some of you met the love of your life. Life has been good!

This is why you are about to make your debut. Ta-dah! (Drum roll here.)

2021 – 2022

For the past fifteen years, you were sort of *under* the table, trying to prove to everyone who you were and what you could do. Now you're jumping on *top* of the table! You're willing to be much more high-viz. It's as if you're announcing to the world, "Hey! Deal me in! I'm a player!" You are becoming more *empowered*!

Quite likely, your recent experience of working hard brought you rewards so that you feel more confident and you believe in yourself. Promotions and positive feedback from others are forthcoming now.

Be careful, because this is a very significant turning point in your life. As you move forward to accept increased successes, you'll quite likely have to let go of things that aren't working.

This is a hugely challenging time for existing partnerships. Partners feel threatened because of how you are gaining power, and liking it! Perhaps they want you to be the old you? But you're not going to do this. Oh no! You're out of the box, and you intend to stay here. This means partnerships that have outlived their usefulness will probably end in 2020–21, or roughly at this time. Partnerships that are meant to endure will undergo major re-adjustments.

This is why many of you will notice that by 2022, financial, practical, emotional, and psychological resources from others are either diminished or removed. Naturally, this throws you back on your own resources. But you have never been *stronger*! For starters, in 2021, gifts, goodies, and favours from others, including inheritances, will benefit you. For some, this will be a settlement in your favour from a separation.

By 2022, travel opportunities and chances to improve something in publishing, the media, medicine, and the law abound. Many of you will go back to school, or travel, or both, because this is definitely a time of broadening your horizons.

2023 – 2025

The year 2023 is a mixed bag, but a very interesting mixed bag! For starters, lucky moneybags Jupiter is crossing the top of your chart for the first time since 2011–12. Yay! Nothing wrong with this! *C'est bon!* Whenever Jupiter moves across the top of your chart, it totally boosts your profession, your career, your social status, and definitely your reputation. ("I'm so great.") Kiss, kiss, hug, hug.

This is the typical time when people get promotions, or public recognition for their achievements, or the increased esteem of their colleagues. I mean, it's really nice. Ya know? We all love positive strokes.

Many will get more travel opportunities connected with their work, or they might find themselves dealing with foreign countries and foreign people more than usual. Others will switch to a new field that is Jupiter related — i.e., higher education, medicine, healing, the law, or world travel.

So there's that.

Now for the mixed part. (Who ate all the cashews?) This is where you're hurting. Actually, in the past few years, partnerships have been in the toilet. So many of you are now fighting over shared possessions, and who owns what, and who owes whom. *C'est la vie.*

The resources of others — government support, support from partners, money back from certain situations, insurance deals, red-tape stuff — do not look good. (Don't you hate this part?)

Finally, in 2024–25, there's a light at the end of the tunnel, and it's not a train, thank gawd! The squeeze play you felt from others now fades from being important. The next few years are definitely a time of preparation. You're getting ready for your aria. (Your diva moment will arrive in 2027.)

So play this hand as best you can. Do whatever you can to prepare for this wonderful moment (2027) that is just a few years away. Get further training or education, and learn whatever you can through travel. The year 2024 is a wonderful time for meeting

groups and joining clubs, associations, and professional organizations. It's schmooze city!

What is important is that all this schmoozing has a subtle influence on you. You feel loved. You feel important. You feel that what you do is significant. And because of this, you start to modify your goals so they are more properly magnificent. Oh yes!

You are two years away from a pinnacle of achievement.

"The most technologically efficient machine
that man has ever invented is the book."
NORTHROP FRYE
Canadian Literary Critic and Theorist
(JULY 14, 1912–JANUARY 23, 1991)

Famous Cancer Personalities

Jean-Paul Sartre	June 21, 1905–1980
Jane Russell	June 21, 1921
Maureen Stapleton	June 21, 1925–2006
Mariette Hartley	June 21, 1940
Benazir Bhutto	June 21, 1953–2007
Erica Durance	June 21, 1978
Prince William of Wales	June 21, 1982
Billy Wilder	June 22, 1906–2002
Bill Blass	June 22, 1922–2002
Kris Kristofferson	June 22, 1936
Meryl Streep	June 22, 1949
Cyndi Lauper	June 22, 1953
Dan Brown	June 22, 1964
Edward, Duke of Windsor	June 23, 1894–1972
Alfred Kinsey	June 23, 1894–1956
June Carter Cash	June 23, 1929–2003
Vint Cerf	June 23, 1943
Frances McDormand	June 23, 1957
Fred Ewanuick	June 23, 1971
Zinedine Zidane	June 23, 1972
Jack Dempsey	June 24, 1895–1983
Jeff Beck	June 24, 1944
Mick Fleetwood	June 24, 1947
Mercedes Lackey	June 24, 1950
Sherry Stringfield	June 24, 1967
Lionel Messi	June 24, 1987
George Orwell	June 25, 1903–1950
Celia Franca	June 25, 1921–2007
Carly Simon	June 25, 1945
Roméo Dallaire	June 25, 1946
Anthony Bourdain	June 25, 1956
Ricky Gervais	June 25, 1961
George Michael	June 25, 1963
Pearl S. Buck	June 26, 1892–1973

Babe Didrikson Zaharias	June 26, 1911–1956
Chris Isaak	June 26, 1956
Chris O'Donnell	June 26, 1970
Gretchen Wilson	June 26, 1973
Derek Jeter	June 26, 1974
Ogyen Trinley Dorje	June 26, 1985
Helen Keller	June 27, 1880–1968
Bob Keeshan	June 27, 1927–2004
Charles Bronfman	June 27, 1931
Vera Wang	June 27, 1949
Isabelle Adjani	June 27, 1955
Margo Timmins	June 27, 1961
Tobey Maguire	June 27, 1975
King Henry VIII	June 28, 1491–1547
Mel Brooks	June 28, 1926
Gilda Radner	June 28, 1946–1989
Kathy Bates	June 28, 1948
John Cusack	June 28, 1966
Mary Stuart Masterson	June 28, 1966
Antoine de Saint-Exupéry	June 29, 1900–1944
Nelson Eddy	June 29, 1901–1967
Slim Pickens	June 29, 1919–1983
Gary Busey	June 29, 1944
Maria Conchita Alonso	June 29, 1957
Matthew Good	June 29, 1971
Lena Horne	June 30, 1917
Vincent D'Onofrio	June 30, 1959
Mike Tyson	June 30, 1966
Michael Phelps	June 30, 1985
Allegra Versace	June 30, 1986
Leslie Caron	July 1, 1931
Geneviève Bujold	July 1, 1942
Deborah Harry	July 1, 1945
Dan Aykroyd	July 1, 1952
Princess Diana	July 1, 1961–1997
Pamela Anderson	July 1, 1967
Liv Tyler	July 1, 1977
Hermann Hesse	July 2, 1877–1962
Wisława Szymborska	July 2, 1923
Medgar Evers	July 2, 1925–1963
Ron Silver	July 2, 1946–2009

Jerry Hall	July 2, 1956
Evelyn Lau	July 2, 1971
Johnny Weir	July 2, 1984
George M. Cohan	July 3, 1878–1942
Franz Kafka	July 3, 1883–1924
Rohinton Mistry	July 3, 1952
Laura Branigan	July 3, 1957–2004
Tom Cruise	July 3, 1962
Thomas Gibson	July 3, 1962
Patrick Wilson	July 3, 1973
Steven Foster	July 4, 1826–1864
Meyer Lansky	July 4, 1902–1983
Ann Landers	July 4, 1918–2002
Neil Simon	July 4, 1927
George Steinbrenner	July 4, 1930
Bill Withers	July 4, 1938
Richard Garriott	July 4, 1961
P. T. Barnum	July 5, 1810–1891
Jean Cocteau	July 5, 1889–1963
Katherine Helmond	July 5, 1928
Robbie Robertson	July 5, 1943
Huey Lewis	July 5, 1950
Edie Falco	July 5, 1963
Kathryn Erbe	July 5, 1966
Frida Kahlo	July 6, 1907–1954
Bill Haley	July 6, 1925–1981
The 14th Dalai Lama	July 6, 1935
Sylvester Stallone	July 6, 1946
Geoffrey Rush	July 6, 1951
Hilary Mantel	July 6, 1952
Marc Chagall	July 7, 1887–1985
Simone Beck	July 7, 1904–1991
Robert A. Heinlein	July 7, 1907–1988
Pierre Cardin	July 7, 1922
Ringo Starr	July 7, 1940
Kirsten Vangsness	July 7, 1972
Michelle Kwan	July 7, 1980
Elisabeth Kübler-Ross	July 8, 1926–2004
Jeffrey Tambor	July 8, 1944
Wolfgang Puck	July 8, 1949
Anjelica Huston	July 8, 1951

Kevin Bacon	July 8, 1958
Toby Keith	July 8, 1961
Beck Hansen	July 8, 1970
Barbara Cartland	July 9, 1901–2000
Mervyn Peake	July 9, 1911–1968
Mercedes Sosa	July 9, 1935–2009
Dean Koontz	July 9, 1945
Jimmy Smits	July 9, 1955
Tom Hanks	July 9, 1956
Nikola Tesla	July 10, 1856–1943
Marcel Proust	July 10, 1871–1922
John Wyndham	July 10, 1903–1969
Alice Munro	July 10, 1931
Arthur Ashe	July 10, 1946–1993
Arlo Guthrie	July 10, 1947
Adrian Grenier	July 10, 1976
Jessica Simpson	July 10, 1980
E. B. White	July 11, 1899–1985
Yul Brynner	July 11, 1920–1985
Giorgio Armani	July 11, 1934
Liona Boyd	July 11, 1949
Leon Spinks	July 11, 1953
Sela Ward	July 11, 1956
Henry David Thoreau	July 12, 1817–1862
Pablo Neruda	July 12, 1904–1973
Milton Berle	July 12, 1908–2002
Andrew Wyeth	July 12, 1917–2009
Pierre Berton	July 12, 1920–2004
Gordon Pinsent	July 12, 1930
Bill Cosby	July 12, 1937
Julius Caesar	July 13, 100 B.C.– 44 B.C.
Wole Soyinka	July 13, 1934
Paul Prudhomme	July 13, 1940
Patrick Stewart	July 13, 1940
Harrison Ford	July 13, 1942
Cheech Marin	July 13, 1946
Cameron Crowe	July 13, 1957
Robert Gant	July 13, 1968
Gustav Klimt	July 14, 1862–1918
Northrop Frye	July 14, 1912–1991
Woodie Guthrie	July 14, 1912–1967

Ingmar Bergman	July 14, 1918–2007
Pema Chödrön	July 14, 1936
Princess Victoria of Sweden	July 14, 1977
Iris Murdoch	July 15, 1919–1999
Linda Ronstadt	July 15, 1946
Arianna Huffington	July 15, 1950
Jesse Ventura	July 15, 1951
Terry O'Quinn	July 15, 1952
Forest Whitaker	July 15, 1961
Roald Amundsen	July 16, 1872–1928
Barbara Stanwyck	July 16, 1907–1990
Ginger Rogers	July 16, 1911–1995
Will Ferrell	July 16, 1967
Duncan Keith	July 16, 1983
Erle Stanley Gardner	July 17, 1889–1970
James Cagney	July 17, 1899–1986
Art Linkletter	July 17, 1912–2010
Donald Sutherland	July 17, 1935
Camilla, Duchess of Cornwall	July 17, 1947
Ryan Miller	July 17, 1980
William Makepeace Thackeray	July 18, 1811–1863
Hume Cronyn	July 18, 1911–2003
Nelson Mandela	July 18, 1918
John Glenn	July 18, 1921
Margaret Laurence	July 18, 1926–1987
Richard Branson	July 18, 1950
Kristen Bell	July 18, 1980
Edgar Degas	July 19, 1834–1917
Brian May	July 19, 1947
Atom Egoyan	July 19, 1960
Jared Padalecki	July 19, 1982
Edmund Hillary	July 20, 1919–2008
Diana Rigg	July 20, 1938
Carlos Santana	July 20, 1947
Josh Holloway	July 20, 1969
Sandra Oh	July 20, 1971
Ernest Hemingway	July 21, 1899–1961
Marshall McLuhan	July 21, 1911–1980
Robin Williams	July 21, 1951
Sarah Waters	July 21, 1966
Josh Hartnett	July 21, 1978

LEO

JULY 23 – AUGUST 22

LEO THE LION
(JULY 23 – AUGUST 22)

"I WILL."

"Experience is not what happens to you; it's what you do
with what happens to you."
ALDOUS HUXLEY
British Writer
Brave New World
(JULY 26, 1894–NOVEMBER 22, 1963)

"Houston, Tranquility Base here. The Eagle has landed."
NEIL ARMSTRONG
Aviator and Astronaut
First Person to Step on the Moon
(B. AUGUST 5, 1930)

Element: Fire
Ruling Planet: The Sun
Quality: Fixed
Opposite Sign: Aquarius
Symbol: The Lion
Glyphs: The Swirl of the Lion's Mane or Tail or the Energy Rays of the Sun
Lucky Gems: Ruby, Peridot, Topaz, and Onyx[1]
Flowers: Marigold and Sunflower
Colour: Orange
Parts of the Body: Heart and Spine

You Like: Movies, compliments, the theatre, sports, teaching, offering help, entertaining, being pampered, games, attention, splendid surroundings. You often wear animal prints, large chunky jewellery, and comb your hair back from your forehead (no part). You expect to be treated with respect.

You Don't Like: Cheapskates, petty-mindedness, dishonest behaviour, giving up, and being nagged, mocked, or ignored.

Where You Shine: Generous, principled, honourable, warm-hearted, forthright, energetic, positive, brave, witty, and intelligent. You always pick up the tab.

So Who's Perfect? Arrogant, proud, extravagant, ostentatious, egocentric, patronizing, opinionated, didactic, and uncompromising.

---

1. Different texts will name different gems for different signs. (Is nothing sacred in this world anymore?)

What Is Leo-ness?[2]

To truly understand a sign, look to the planet that rules that sign, because this planet will give you a wealth of clues! The ruling planet of Leo is the Sun. When you understand what the Sun represents in astrology, you'll get a quick feel for the archetype of Leo.

First, an important distinction: Everyone's "sign" is actually their Sun Sign. If you're a Gemini, it means you have your Sun in Gemini. If you're a Taurus, it means you have your Sun in Taurus. If you're a Leo, it means you have your Sun in Leo. (And each sign has their Moon in a sign, and their Mercury in a sign, and their Venus in a sign, and so on. That is how astrology works.) So when you say your "sign," you're actually saying the sign where your Sun is. *Capisce?*

Therefore, everybody has a Sun Sign, *but only the sign of Leo is ruled by the Sun.* Big difference!

Ah yes, the glorious Sun! (No wonder you're hot stuff!) For starters, the Sun *shines* on everyone and everything. It catches us in its brilliant light. This means Leo people are inexplicably in the limelight, whether they seek this out or not.

In her book Bittersweet, *Susan Strasberg describes walking along the streets of Manhattan with Marilyn Monroe (who was Leo Rising). Suddenly Marilyn turned to her and said, "Do you want me to do her?" Marilyn shook her head and adjusted her shoulders while she continued walking. Suddenly people were screaming, "There's Marilyn Monroe!" and clamouring for her autograph.*

---

2. No one is just one sign. This is impossible. Everyone's chart is made up of different planets. Therefore, this is a discussion about the Leo archetype — the qualities of "Leo-ness." Many other signs will have Leo qualities as well. Therefore, the discussion of one sign is not an exact description of that person; rather, it is a description of the qualities of that sign.

Leos can control their high-viz *Star Quality*. You can slink into a restaurant unnoticed, or make an entrance that causes everyone to rubberneck your arrival.

However, the maddening thing is this star quality also means Leos are extremely self-conscious, often painfully so. They believe others are watching them. Naturally, because Leos feel they're in the spotlight, they're aware of how they enter a room, a restaurant, a bar, or a classroom, or even how they enter the kitchen in the early morning if others are present. They think others are noticing them, even if this is not the case! (Kinda pathetic in a way.)

So what does it mean if you think everyone is noticing you? You *care* about your appearance! You're *aware* of your wardrobe. If you wear clothes that are drab or dumpy, you feel depressed. If you're self-conscious about being overweight, you will lack energy to the point where you'll be less effective in your job and in your relationships with others. ("I hate myself!") Leos who have gained weight will cancel social engagements because they can't stand how they look. They don't want to go out and be judged. After all, Leo is the sign of royalty! And the sooner everyone recognizes this, the easier everyone's life is going to be. ("Has the carriage arrived?")

"There are people who have money and people who are rich."
GABRIELLE "COCO" CHANEL
Pioneering French Fashion Designer and Founder of the House of Chanel
(AUGUST 19, 1883–JANUARY 10, 1971)

You like to dress well and have a snappy wardrobe. You never have enough clothes. (Have you noticed whenever you get something new, you switch to wearing that item? It makes you wonder what you wore before you bought it!) You like shopping, because spending money on what you want is your opportunity to exercise your freedom. Furthermore, because you think you are being noticed all the time, not only do you want to dress well, you choose to dress in a way that is special. Leos like large, one-of-a-kind pieces of jewellery. They dress in animal skins, capes, and velvet, and add other dramatic touches to their wardrobes.

"I am a deeply superficial person."
ANDY WARHOL
Painter, Printmaker, Filmmaker, and Public Social Figure
(AUGUST 6, 1928–FEBRUARY 22, 1987)

I can spot a Leo by the metallic handbag, or the animal-print scarf or sweater, or the hair pushed carelessly back off the forehead. Their style of dress is sporty and casual. (The sign of Leo rules sports, theme parks, golf courses, and vacations, as well as show business and the entertainment world.) A Leo never does up the top button on a shirt. Too straight, too conservative, too confining! Nevertheless, because Leo is royalty, they can be lavish in their dress at times. (Think Coco Chanel, Yves Saint Laurent, and Jennifer Lopez.)

Leos *love to make an entrance*! They will spend money on their appearance, and especially on their hair — their lion's mane. They love signature sunglasses (like famous Leo Jacqueline Kennedy) and large handbags. We're talking serious diva mode here, but tasteful.

Shy Leos suffer painfully because of this quality of feeling in the limelight. But they, too, need to be noticed, even if they can't stand it. *(Quel tough!)* They have Walter Mitty daydreams of heroic achievements — their moment in the Sun! However, when cornered, shy Leos avoid being caught by refusing all invitations. They cannot take the pressure they feel when they're out in the company of others. Nevertheless, secretly, every Leo wants to be a star!

Once again, think of the Sun "shining" on this person. This is why many Leos choose occupations where they are the centre of attention. They go into acting, teaching, training, or doing something where they stand up in front of other people to perform, show, guide, entertain, illustrate — whatever. Never lose sight of the idea that Leos have their ruler, the Sun, shining down on them in full dazzle!

However, there's another quality of the Sun. The Sun *radiates* enormous energy in an *outward* direction. This is why Leo people easily radiate enthusiasm, encouragement, and warmth to others. *They are like the Sun.* This is obvious when you see their success in teaching, entertaining, or reaching out to others. They want to inspire! They almost feel it's their duty to do so.

"If there's a silence in a room, I'll try to fill it as soon as humanly possible."
MATTHEW PERRY
American-Canadian Television and Film Actor
TV's *Friends*
(B. AUGUST 19, 1969)

My Leo Aunt Betty[3] was the first person I ever heard say this. She said if there was a lull in the conversation, she felt she had to jump in to fill it. (I was a kid at the time and did not know about Leo.)

We all know that the Sun is the giver of all life. Without the Sun, there is no plant or animal life. This sustaining, thriving approach to life is what Leos are all about. Leos are huge givers! They give their time, their energy, their money, their possessions, and their knowledge to the world.

---

3. My Aunt Betty was married to my Aries Uncle Jack. They had fire and pizzazz! I loved to visit them when I was a child.

Three Leo Qualities

If we look more deeply at your ruling planet, the Sun, you will easily see three broad qualities of Leo:

1. Creativity
2. Warmth, Radiance, and Generosity
3. Leadership and Need for Recognition

Creativity

Naturally, each sign is creative. But with Leo, creativity is a driving purpose in life. A *raison d'être*. Leos not only want to create, they *need* to create — be it an event, a situation, a person, a play, a movie, a party, or an experience.[4] In astrology, everything in life comes under the domain of one sign or another. (Astrology classifies the entire world this way — by the rulership of a planet or sign.) When we see what Leo rules in the world, it is quickly evident how creative Leo people are!

> "Pick up a camera. Shoot something. No matter how small,
> no matter how cheesy, no matter whether your friends and your sister star
> in it. Put your name on it as director. Now you're a director.
> Everything after, you're just negotiating your budget and your fee."
> JAMES CAMERON
> Canadian Filmmaker, Director, Producer, Screenwriter, Editor, and Inventor
> *Titanic* and *Avatar*
> (B. AUGUST 16, 1954)

SO WHAT DOES LEO RULE?

Leo rules all the arts. It rules the theatre, show business, and the entertainment world. Furthermore, it rules professional sports. Any time you are being entertained by any event, or any person, or any thing — you are having a Leo experience. If you pay money to go anywhere or be entertained, you are having a Leo moment. You are

---

4. In the movie *Wag the Dog*, Dustin Hoffman (who is a Leo) plays the role of Stanley Motss, a successful Hollywood producer. Hoffman's character was based on Robert Evans, who has been called the Godfather of Hollywood. Evans has his Moon in Leo and, although his time of birth is unknown, I would not be surprised if he is Leo Rising. (Nor would any of his seven wives.) Hoffman emulated Evans's work habits, mannerisms, quirks, clothing style, hairstyle, and look, right down to his signature large, square-framed eyeglasses. Apparently the real Evans is said to have declared, "I'm magnificent in this film!"

in the Leo world of parties, social events, movie theatres, playhouses, theme parks, stadiums, arenas, and golf courses.

Leo also rules the hospitality industry. It doesn't rule food per se. Rather, it rules the idea of giving a person the experience of going out to eat or going away to stay somewhere. Therefore, it rules restaurants,[5] hotels, and resorts. Anything from the MGM Grand Hotel in Las Vegas to a small B&B in rural Manitoba is Leo. Anything from Disney World to a little pitch-and-putt in Parksville, British Columbia, is Leo. Leo is constantly trying to create a situation to dazzle and entertain others. This is because Leo wants to create! Leo constantly gives birth to ideas, which, in turn, become events to entertain and delight others.

This is also why every work of art falls under the domain of Leo creativity. But, hey, when it comes to creativity, what is the ultimate work of creativity in the world? A human being! "It walks! It talks!" Therefore, Leo rules children. Anyone who works with children or teaches children has a Leo profession. Just as anyone who acts, directs, works in the movies, or works in the theatre (whether you're an usher or a star) is doing a Leo job.

When you see how all of these creative things in the world are under the domain of Leo, naturally it follows that Leos are creative people! (Ya think?)

"In order to be irreplaceable one must always be different."
GABRIELLE "COCO" CHANEL
Pioneering French Fashion Designer and Founder of the House of Chanel
(AUGUST 19, 1883–JANUARY 10, 1971)

No matter what they do for a living, Leos do things with style, drama, and theatricality. To be sure, many Leos work in so-called "Leo fields," i.e., the entertainment world, or the hospitality industry, or teaching, or the arts, or sports. But, obviously, there are Leo cab drivers, Leo plumbers, Leo scientists, and Leo chefs. What distinguishes them from anybody else doing that same job is they do it with flair, creativity and enthusiasm. They'll put a razzle-dazzle spin on it!

Warmth, Radiance, and Generosity

Leo people have a natural warmth and radiance. Just as the Sun gives warmth, so do they. This is why Leos are one of the most generous signs. In fact, they radiate enthusiasm to the point of being bossy! ("Are we all having fun?")

Leos are big-hearted and they have memorable smiles! In fact, their smiles are dazzling! (Think of Sandra Bullock, Ben Affleck, Halle Berry, Jennifer Lopez, Martin Sheen, Maureen O'Hara, Barack Obama, and Loni Anderson.)

You love to entertain and to be entertained. (Everyone wants to sit at your table.)

---

5. The Moon rules restaurants as well. The Moon rules the food aspect of eating. Leo rules the aspect of going out to a restaurant to see others and to be seen. This is why Leo- and Cancer-types make going to restaurants a hobby.

You will go over the top to offer a memorable experience to anyone, and, because you're so generous, you spend waaay too much money doing this. Leos think nothing of borrowing money or going into debt to show others a good time. Leos are quick to pick up the tab. You'll order expensive wine and great food for others even if you can't afford it. And you will especially do this if you know you're treating people who would normally not have this luxury. Please note: this is not about impressing others, although it might look like that. (This is where the generous Leo nature is often misunderstood.) You *genuinely want others to enjoy pleasure and have a good time*! Leos will go into debt to make sure everyone is happy! (Curious, but true.) They believe it is their purpose in life to encourage others.

One of the reasons Leos have such a generous impulse is actually based on the Leo need to "create a production," because every Leo is constantly creating a memorable moment for somebody else. (Think of every Leo as having a Cecil B. DeMille impulse.) It is their essence to constantly give birth to a new moment.

But this has its downside. Since Leos are scripting a moment (whether it's a dinner party, an Oscar party, or a birthday party), they expect their participants to play their respective roles. (Oh yes!) If it is a sit-down dinner for eight, the Leo host will be horrified (but never show it) when a Cancer guest shows up with three extra pals in tow. Naturally, this ruins the seating arrangement the Leo host has so carefully planned. Leos appear spontaneous, but *they really aren't*. They are creative, fun-loving, and theatrical, but surprisingly timid. They like a menu, a program, an idea of what is unfolding. The only surprise they really like is the one they plan for others.

Leo's impulse to create vibrant moments in life naturally means they give ideas, information, money, experiences, food, and gifts to others, as well as lend their clothes, cars, and homes to others.

The minute several Leos are on the scene, this totally boosts the energy and enthusiasm that is present in any room. If several Leos are in an audience, they will enthusiastically applaud the performer, because they're sympathetic with the performer's attempt to entertain. *They can relate!* ("I'm on fire! What an audience! There's Sean Penn, Madonna, Arnie, Kevin Spacey, Dustin Hoffman, Mick Jagger, and Denis Leary loving my jokes! *I'm magic!*")

Guess whose bathroom mirror is covered in kisses?

"I don't want to live. I want to love first and live incidentally."
ZELDA FITZGERALD
American Novelist, Icon of the 1920s "Flapper" Era, Literary and Social Celebrity,
and Wife of Author F. Scott Fitzgerald
(JULY 24, 1900–MARCH 10, 1948)

Likewise, Leos are big tippers, especially if the service is great. They applaud the efforts of anyone who goes out of their way to create a wonderful experience for people, because that's what Leos believe life is all about.

This warmth and radiance is sustaining. Leos are very loyal. They are not fair-weather friends. It's their nature to encourage others. Not only are Leos fabulous actors, they're great teachers. They enjoy holding forth because they love an audience, and they love to *share* their knowledge.

Always remember the ruling planet to grasp the essence of a sign. Since the Sun is the ruler of Leo, you can think of a Leo person as someone who is beaming energy out into the world, hoping to make little seeds sprout. These seeds can be people, or ideas, or just moments in time. Leo wants to make things grow! They bring balloons to parties, knowing how to help set the stage for everyone else to have fun.

However, here is where Leos kid themselves. They imagine themselves to be shrewd judges of character. Ha! In fact, Leos are gullible and naive. They are a trusting sign, because they themselves are trustworthy and loyal. They can be conned by anyone who is lavish with their praise. At times, they think they are being sly and devious, but they're an open book! (You are so busted!)

> "We're overpaying him, but he's worth it."
> SAMUEL GOLDWYN
> American Film Producer
> (AUGUST 17, 1879–JANUARY 31, 1974)

Leadership and Need for Recognition

Leo is actually the most balanced and complete of all the signs. (Yeah, yeah, all the other signs can eat their hearts out.) I repeat, *you are the most balanced sign in the zodiac*. One of the reasons for this is that you express the energy of the Sun without a filter. (Every other sign has their Sun being expressed though a Capricorn filter, or a Virgo filter, or a Gemini filter. *Capisce?*)

Consider the Sun. In addition to giving energy to grow and create things, and to radiate warmth — the Sun also *illuminates*. And get this. The illumination of the Sun shines on the rich and the poor alike, without distinction. The Sun gives vitality, warmth, and light without discrimination.

In the same way (even though Leo is "royal"), you happily befriend people of every class and walk of life. Sure, it is true you are easily star-struck. ("I just saw Bruce Willis!") Nevertheless, you think nothing of having close friends from a wide variety of backgrounds. Leos are not snobs; they just look that way! You might be arrogant, vain, and regal, but you are not a snob. Leos love all classes of people.

Since Leo is ruled by the Sun, naturally, Leos love *to be seen*. This makes sense when you realize that Leo rules the entertainment world and the hospitality industry. A big reason people go out to have fun is they *want to see* other people, and they *want to be seen*. It's reciprocal social juice!

"Drama is life with the dull bits cut out."
ALFRED HITCHCOCK
British Filmmaker, Producer, and Director
Rebecca, *Rear Window*, and *Psycho*
(AUGUST 13, 1899–APRIL 29, 1980)

Therefore, this Leo need to be recognized often dictates their choice of profession. Ideally, they need to be recognized on a *daily* basis. That's why they love praise! (You can never compliment a Leo too much. Even if you shower them with false flattery and they know it, they're still pleased that you cared enough to make the effort.) Leos want to be recognized for what they do, and they certainly want to be recognized for their excellence. They take pride in their ability to entertain you and their skill in pleasing you, and, above all, they want to be recognized for their generosity.

This need for recognition is not shallow. What is the point of writing something if it is never read? What is the point of making a movie if nobody sees it? What is the point of acting if there's no audience? The whole idea of Leo creativity and Leo warmth and radiance is that it reaches out to touch others and involves a *reciprocal* element. Something has to bounce back. The light must be reflected. Something has to give some affirmation and acknowledgement, or else, "What's it all about, Alfie?"

There's another reason for the Leo need for recognition. Leo is the sign of royalty. This is why all Leos have a kind of nobility. Shy Leos (and even brash Leos) display a certain dignity that is natural to them. And because Leo is the sign of nobility, Leos easily take the helm! Leos are natural managers and executives. They are quick to see the big picture because they understand the theatre of the moment. Leos immediately see why a restaurant, or a play, or an event either works or doesn't work. They know what the public wants.

You see how easy it is when you start to grasp the planet that rules the sign? Then you can expand further and come up with different examples of how that planet works and why you are a certain way.

"Elementary, my dear Watson."[6]

---

6. This phrase in fact never appeared in the novels of Arthur Conan Doyle. It first showed up in the Sherlock Holmes movies. A phrase that Doyle *did* write was, "It was very superficial, my dear Watson, I assure you." Doyle, who was a Gemini, had Saturn in Leo.

Leo in Love

"The secret of a happy marriage is finding the right person. You know they're right if you love to be with them all of the time."

JULIA CHILD[7]

American Chef, Author, and TV Personality

Introduced French Cuisine to America Through Her Cookbooks

(AUGUST 15, 1912–AUGUST 13, 2004)

Leo is *the* sign of romance. What else would you expect from the sign that rules the arts, the theatre, literature, music, movies, and anything dramatic and over the top? If romance doesn't fall into this category, what does?

Leos take their love affairs verrrrry seriously! They become totally consumed with romantic ardour. In fact, Leos are in love with being in love! I remember a client, who was Leo Rising, who told me that she and her psychiatrist were in love with each other. I wasn't surprised to hear she was in love with her shrink, but I was surprised that it was reciprocated. I said, "You mean, he has actually *told* you he loves you?"

She laughed confidently and said he always said he was *not* in love with her, but she *knew* this was just his way of denying what he truly felt. The more she explained it to me, the more clearly I could see that her shrink had done *everything* he could to convince her he was not in love with her, but she refused to believe it! That was my first inkling, which was later confirmed many times, that Leo Rising people always think people are in love with them.

"I like restraint, if it doesn't go too far."

MAE WEST

American Actress, Playwright, Screenwriter, and Sex Symbol

(AUGUST 17, 1893–NOVEMBER 22, 1980)

The Leo lover wants to be adored. Correction: the Leo lover *needs* to be adored. Daily. Not only with words, but also with actions. You must express your adoration to the Leo lover with gifts of flowers, wine (preferably champagne, because then it's an *occasion*!), tickets to the theatre, treats to movies, and little (and big!) gifts to show how much you care.

---

7. I recommend a wonderful book about Julia Child — *Appetite for Life* by Noël Riley Fitch (New York: Anchor Books, 1997). Julia is a hero of mine, and I've read four biographies about her, including her autobiography. However, I thought *Appetite for Life* was absolutely inspirational!

I recall another Leo client who supported her boyfriend. She picked up the tab for everything. However, whenever she returned home, she was greeted with lit candles (even outside), music, drinks, and canapés to welcome her. To be welcomed *in such a romantic way* every time she came home was the *special* attention she needed to satisfy her Leo desire to be adored and appreciated. Of course, he did all the cooking. (He had her number.)

Nevertheless, beware! Leos hate cheapskates. That's because they are so generous. They love to give gifts. They love to buy you what you want. They love to treat you to movies, dinners, and the theatre. If they interpret your frugality as being "cheap," they are *so* not impressed.

Leos are hot lovers! They like sex. (Some astrology texts say Leos are the sexiest sign.) They're not particularly kinky, but they like to have fun. Female Leos will splurge on lingerie. All Leos will spend lots of money on fabulous sheets, bedding, and duvets because they understand the theatre of sex. They know how to create a romantic setting.

I have a dear Leo friend who went to Los Angeles after her divorce and spent about three thousand dollars on lingerie. Her optimism paid off! In no time, she was in an affair with a guy who took her on a mad, passionate weekend to Whistler. (They never left their room.) The first night, she made a wonderful entrance with a knockout peignoir ensemble from her goodie bag, and they had a wild time in bed. Then she showered and reappeared in another outfit. More passion! And then later, another outfit! More passion! And later, another outfit! During one day and two nights, she made six entrances in six different delectable costumes. (The guy was kinda stunned and amazed, but, hey, was he complaining?) Ha! Classic Leo.

"Too much of a good thing can be wonderful!"
MAE WEST
American Actress, Playwright, Screenwriter, and Sex Symbol
(AUGUST 17, 1893–NOVEMBER 22, 1980)

Leos are impulsive and dramatic. I recall a story about a Leo woman who was splitting up with her lover. It was their last date and somehow they ended up with another couple at a club. She didn't want to dance with the man she was leaving, so she got up on the dance floor and danced alone. Soon, a stranger joined her, and together they created magic on the dance floor.

When she returned to the table, she decided she had to give her phone number to this stranger, so she went to the washroom, intending to drop a piece of paper with her number on it at his table on her way back to her group. While she was in the washroom writing her number down, the door burst open, and in rushed the dancer! Immediately they were in each other's arms. While they were still embracing, the door to the women's washroom burst open again, and behold! It was the guy from the other couple at her table! He recovered quickly and said, "I have to have your number!" Caught unawares (and Leo is a surprisingly naive sign), she gave it to him!

As an interesting footnote, in a strange coincidence, they both called her about eight weeks later, on the same night, at the same time. And once again the dancer was first, and once again the second guy actually asked the operator to interrupt the long phone call. Yet again, he barged in! This kind of drama is what Leo is all about. The love lives of Leos are the stuff of movies.

You can keep your Leo lover happy with praise; thoughtful, romantic gestures; and an attitude of constant adoration. If you don't think you can keep this up — move on. However, you may never again find yourself in such a romantic movie. Think twice before heading for the Exit.

The Leo Boss

"I don't want any yes-men around me.
I want everyone to tell me the truth — even if it costs him his job."
SAMUEL GOLDWYN
American Film Producer
(AUGUST 17, 1879–JANUARY 31, 1974)

Being the boss comes naturally to Leo, because, after all, who is the King of the Jungle? It's Leo the Lion!

There are three reasons Leos make great bosses:

- They are quick to see the whole picture — the bottom line
- They can inspire others with their charismatic leadership
- They instinctively know how to bring out the best in people

For starters, Leo is faster than any other sign to immediately see the big picture. They quickly see what is needed and they just as quickly see what is wrong. This means they know instantly what needs to be done![8] Fortunately, every Leo has great organization skills.

"I am sometimes a fox and sometimes a lion. The whole secret of government lies in knowing when to be the one or the other."
NAPOLEON BONAPARTE
Emperor of France May 18, 1804–April 11, 1814
and March 20, 1815–June 22, 1815
(AUGUST 15, 1769–MAY 5, 1821)

Good management is getting things done through other people, and Leos know how to do this! Leos are great at inspiring others. In fact, their talent for doing this is almost magical.

The reason Leo assumes this role so naturally is because Leo is the sign of royalty. This means every Leo has a sense of noblesse oblige. Leo expects to be respected, and in turn, every Leo has a kind of dignity that commands respect.

---

8. I speak to you personally from the heart. Isn't it frustrating when you are in a situation that suddenly changes, and you know immediately what is the first and most critical thing that needs to be done — and others cannot comprehend it? Utterly maddening!

Leo is a charismatic leader. Barack Obama; Bill Clinton; Henry Hoover; Simón Bolívar; Benito Mussolini; Arnold Schwarzenegger; Queen Elizabeth, the Queen Mother; Cecil B. DeMille; Napoleon Bonaparte; Henry Ford; Casey Stengel; Stanley Baldwin; Fidel Castro; Marshall Field; and T. E. Lawrence (Lawrence of Arabia) — all Leos.

Furthermore, Leos are excellent at spotting the skills and aptitudes of the people around them. They see the creative potential in others. The Leo manager knows to send the soldier to war and the accountant to the bank, whereas less effective managers send the soldier to the bank and the accountant to war.

Leos know how to bring out the best in those around them. Leo directors, teachers, and managers can get results from people that others cannot. (Can you hear the Leo actor gushing to the Leo director: "The reason I was the best Hamlet the stage has ever seen is because you are God!")

Employees like to work for Leo bosses. Since Leos like praise, they know how to give praise. They know the value of positive encouragement. Furthermore, Leos are generous. They're not cheapskate bosses. They believe in paying well, and they believe in bonuses. Leos are great managers and executives who show their appreciation for those who work for them.

Another reason it's easy to work for a Leo boss is because Leo works hard! Quite literally, Leos are capable of working themselves to death (scary but true). They have a finger in everything. No detail is too insignificant. Once they're excited about the product, or the event, or the result, they give it *their all* because — hey, it has their name stamped on it!

Take note: the Leo boss will feel betrayed by criticism.

The Leo Employee

There's an upside and a downside to the Leo employee. The upside is that Leos are loyal and they quickly see the big picture, so they know what needs to be done. Furthermore, Leos are not lazy! Don't get me wrong; Leo the Lion is a big fat cat who knows how to relax and pamper itself. But, when there's work to be done, Leos are extremely productive. In fact (remember how giving Leo is), Leos can actually work themselves to death. (I do not say this casually.)

"You can scream at me, call me for a shoot at midnight, keep me waiting for hours — as long as what ends up on the screen is perfect."
ARNOLD SCHWARZENEGGER
Austrian-Born Bodybuilder, Actor, Businessman, and Politician
(B. JULY 30, 1947)

Leo employees are full of bright ideas and enthusiasm. The downside is that if they aren't recognized or appreciated, they quickly get discouraged. Leos will give you everything, but they have to be *appreciated*! If you don't praise them or acknowledge their efforts, they'll quit. Or if they're a prisoner of golden handcuffs, they'll be very tough to manage.

Another downside is that, because Leos are natural managers, they chafe under poor management. They hate working for people who don't know what needs to be done or how to get things done. This frustrates the hell out of them! After all, Leos are excellent managers as well as organizers!

In the 1960s, Douglas McGregor of the MIT Sloane School of Management developed a system that describes two very different attitudes toward workforce motivation. It involves what he classified as Theory X and Theory Y.

Theory X assumes people are inherently lazy. Give them an inch and they will take a mile. When the cat's away the mice will play. This kind of manager tends to micromanage and supervise their employees.

By contrast, Theory Y assumes people are actually hard working if they're motivated. (Look how hard people work at playing tennis or mountain climbing.) Theory Y assumes if you give people enough room for self-direction, they will perform better.

Leos definitely function better under a Theory Y management style. That's because, at heart, every Leo *is* a manager. Therefore, Leo needs the opportunity to manage their own job and receive acknowledgement and praise for doing it well.

(Money is nice, too, because Leos burn through their cash entertaining others and giving gifts to everyone.)

"An idealist is a person who helps other people to be prosperous."
HENRY FORD
American Founder of the Ford Motor Company
Father of the Modern Assembly Line
(JULY 30, 1863–APRIL 7, 1947)

The Leo Parent

"Since I had the baby I can't tolerate anything violent or sad."
LISA KUDROW
American Television and Film Actress
TV's *Friends*
(B. JULY 30, 1963)

Leo parents are great parents. In part, this is because Leo rules the sign of children, which means Leos like kids! Let me clarify this: Leos don't necessarily like to babysit other people's kids, although they're extremely sympathetic to children in general. They are appalled at cruelty or indifference to children, and, when it comes to their own children, they're extremely indulgent.

However, do take note: *never criticize their children*! Even if a Leo parent speaks critically of their own children, they will take huge offence if anyone else does so. (Think of the proud Leo lion.)

Leos want their children to be well-rounded, especially in the arts. Leos will pay for piano lessons, guitar lessons, acting lessons, drum lessons, and dance lessons, as well as take their children to plays, parades, movies, the theatre, and theme parks. Leos want their kids to have fun! But, more than that, they want their kids to understand the creative process of the entertainment world in general. They want them to know that the creative process is, in fact, a big aspect of *life*. Shakespeare was right:

All the world's a stage,
And all the men and women merely players;
They have their exits and their entrances,
And one man in his time plays many parts,
His acts being seven stages . . .
AS YOU LIKE IT

As a Leo, you also want your children to feel a Walt Disney moment if possible. You're a romantic! I knew a single (and broke) Leo mother who received money from her in-laws one Christmas to buy clothing for her kids. Instead, she took them to a boutique toy store and said, "You can have anything you want in the whole store!" (She told them to pick one thing.) She explained, "I wanted my kids to have the thrill of walking into a toy store and picking out anything they wanted." A typical Leo move: extravagant, impractical, and totally theatrical — something that was almost make-believe.

You might not be the most practical parent, but you're a strong contender for being the most fun!

"Health food may be good for the conscience,
but Oreos taste a hell of a lot better."
ROBERT REDFORD
American Actor, Director, Producer, Environmentalist, Philanthropist,
and Founder of the Sundance Film Festival
Butch Cassidy and the Sundance Kid, *All the President's Men*, and *The Candidate*
(B. AUGUST 18, 1936)

The Leo Child

"A grown-up is a child with layers on."
WOODY HARRELSON
American Television and Film Actor
(B. JULY 23, 1961)

The Leo child is an easy child to raise. They exhibit warmth and radiance at an early age, and their winning style makes others like them. Even when very young, they embody elements of dignity and nobility that their Leo royalty bestows on them. They're less inclined than other children to have temper tantrums or meltdowns. It's beneath them.

Furthermore, their naturally generous nature makes them want to co-operate with family and parents. In fact, as soon as the Leo child can earn money, they will come home with gifts for their parents and siblings. This is how strong the Leo generosity is. *It's a way of being.*

However, it's important to know that the Leo child needs constant praise! This is a creative child who can do so much more if there is encouragement. In addition, the Leo child benefits from dancing lessons, piano lessons, guitar lessons, and good sports equipment, because, after all, Leo rules the arts and sports.

Goethe's advice applies to all children, but most especially to Leo children: "Correction does much, but encouragement does more."

Harsh criticism will dash the confidence of the noble little Leo. Be very careful here.

Leo children will be happier if their home supports their need to entertain. I recall a Leo client who fondly remembered that once a week she could invite friends over for Sunday dinner. This was an important memory. She had big birthday parties and teenage dances where, once again, her mother provided food and drink. (Aren't moms great?)

Never forget that your Leo child is at heart a performer, even if they are shy. Every encouragement to explore this desire is a positive thing! It will boost the young Leo's confidence and help the child to discover how Leos come alive once they have an adoring audience.

"I have a simple life. I mean, you just give me a drum roll,
they announce my name, and I come out and sing."
TONY BENNETT
American Singer
(B. AUGUST 3, 1926)

Never forget that the Leo child, who will grow up to be a Leo host, needs lots of opportunities to practice entertaining others when they're young!

How to Be a Happier Leo

Leo is associated with royalty and nobility. Leo is also a natural leader or executive. Because of this Leo almost expects preferred treatment. (And generally gets it!) It doesn't take much to connect the dots to see that pride and arrogance can be Leo's downfall. ("I am King! All bow down before me!")

Pride is a tricky thing. There's good pride and there's bad pride. Good pride might be described as divine pride. This is because, in order to achieve anything, we need confidence and pride in our abilities. We have to believe in ourselves, especially if we have to encounter a particularly challenging job. If you think you have excellent abilities and you don't, then that is arrogance. If you think you have excellent abilities and you do, then that is confidence. This is an important distinction.

Of course, there's what we call plain old pride, the Biblical version, but it doesn't sound as bad as hatred, greed, or malice, does it?

> "When did I realize I was God? Well, I was praying
> and I suddenly realized I was talking to myself."
> PETER O'TOOLE
> Irish Stage and Screen Actor
> *Lawrence of Arabia*
> (B. AUGUST 2, 1932)

However, there is definitely a downside to pride! I think there are four major drawbacks.

The first thing pride does is it separates one from others. If you feel superior to those around you, then it follows that you think they're inferior to you. Naturally, others will sense your feeling of superiority. ("I wonder what the little people are doing tonight?") You create distance between yourself and others instead of closeness. This kind of pride is not ideal.

A second disadvantage of having a prideful attitude is that it's difficult to learn anything. If you think you know it all, you're hardly receptive to new ways of looking at things or being open to new information. ("Been there. Done that. Got the T-shirt.")

We all know the story about the Harvard professor who travelled to Japan to meet a Zen roshi. The professor was ushered into a simple, clean-swept room where the roshi sat. The professor sat down and immediately started talking. He enthusiastically expounded upon his theories, and what he thought Zen was all about.

Meanwhile, the roshi, still silent, picked up a metal teapot and started to pour tea into the professor's cup. He kept pouring and pouring while the professor kept talking and talking. Soon the cup overflowed and the tea was spilling onto the table. The professor looked down and cried, "Stop! Can't you see it's full? You can't get any more in!" The roshi set the teapot down and said nothing. That was the end of the interview. One hopes the professor got the message! His mind was so full, there was no room for anything new to enter. Pride can do this.

A third disadvantage is that, when you're full of pride, you look *pathetic*! Does a Leo ever want to look pathetic? No! You want to took talented, capable, generous, caring, aware, intelligent, and, above all, modest in an unassuming but ever-so-appealing way.

The fourth disadvantage is subtle but real. When your mind is clouded with pride, you really miss out on a lot. Your nose is in the air. You refuse invitations. You remain aloof. Being above the riffraff means you lose out on many rich, fabulous experiences!

Clearly, this pride thing is a bummer. Each time it arises it leaves a negative footprint on your mind or your life. So, what can you do about it?

First, you can do a reality check. Are you really that special? Is every other Leo you know really that special? Could you be looking in the mirror of the evil witch? ("Mirror, mirror, on the wall, who is the fairest of them all?") *Get real*! Even the Leo emperor Napoleon Bonaparte said, "A throne is only a bench covered with velvet."

Second, simple intelligence (and you are smart) tells you we are all more alike than we are not. We all want happiness. Nobody wants to suffer. What makes us happy might differ according to culture and background, but big deal. We are all basically cut from the same cloth. (Yeah, yeah, you're raw silk.) Embrace your humanity; you are part of the human race.

Gratitude is the most important daily meditation you can do. Be grateful for who you are. You are special — *but so is everyone!*

> "After the game, the king and the pawn go into the same box."
> **ITALIAN PROVERB**

You know in your big, warm heart that this is true. Acknowledge everyone's unique place in the world and move on. It's not that you have to be humble. You just have to be *real*.

> "O Great Spirit, whose voice I hear in the winds,
> I come to you as one of your many children.
> I need your strength and your wisdom.
> Make me strong, not to be superior to my brother,
> but to be able to fight my greatest enemy: Myself."
> **CHIEF DAN GEORGE**
> Chief of the Tsleil-Waututh Nation, Actor, and Author
> (JULY 24, 1899–SEPTEMBER 23, 1981)

LEO
YOUR 40-YEAR HOROSCOPE
1985 – 2025

Why Go into the Past?

I want you to have faith in your predictions. The only way you can believe what I say is to test it for yourself. This is why I start with brief highlights from the past twenty-five years. If anything in these past twenty-five years resonates with you, then what I say about your future will have the same validity. It is all one long timeline — your life.

The past predictions generally apply once you have left home or are "running your life" and making your own decisions. Prior to that, the major events in your life were dictated by other people, likely your parents.

1985 – 1987

This was a good year for partnerships. However, the difficulties and increased responsibilities with children might have been onerous for some Leo parents. Nevertheless, exciting travel opportunities, plus anything to do with publishing, the media, medicine, the law, and higher education, were blessed.

By 1987, you entered a very strong time. Certain major events boosted your confidence. Parents, teachers, bosses, and VIPs renewed their respect for you. It was easy to look like a winner! Basically, life was pretty good.

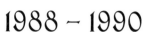

1988 – 1990

At around this time, you began to bust your buns to prove your worth. At times, what you were doing seemed overwhelming. You doubted if you could pull it off. But you did, in part because your popularity was very strong then. Others were prepared to help you. In addition, lots of opportunities came your way through powerful people. Bosses, parents, teachers, and VIPs were ready to assist you.

Because of your own hard work, and also because of some recent good fortune (or, at least, good wishes from others for your benefit), many of you explored your spirituality more deeply at this time. I'm not saying you necessarily found God, but you probably discovered His neighbourhood.

1991 – 1993

This was a very good time for you in many respects. Whatever happened (especially in 1991) enormously increased your self-confidence and your poise. In your personal life, many opportunities and people were attracted to you. You were the lucky star!

However, life always has cycles within cycles. While all these good things were going on, partnerships and close friendships were in the toilet. This was the classic time for an important relationship to go belly up. If a partnership did not end at this time, then it certainly had to undergo major readjustments to endure.

Nevertheless, this was a pivotal time in your life. It represented the culmination of something. For about fourteen years, you had been busy figuring out who you were, what your values were, where you wanted to live, and what you could do. Now your sights swung to the heavens. You started to give serious thought to your career and your reputation in the world.

1994 – 1996

Your private life became increasingly richer at this time, as the fates began to bless your home, family, and domestic situation. In fact, your family life was happier! Many of you literally expanded your family through birth, adoption, or marriage, or perhaps some other reason. Your private life had much joy at this time, even though, ironically, the financial and practical support from other sources was drying up! (Whaaat?)

(When it comes to support being withdrawn, I always think of something I read years ago about a young boy at college who sent a telegram to his father. "No mon. No fun. Your son." The father replied, "Too bad. I'm sad. Your dad.")

This was also a great time for vacations and romance, even though the support from others was diminished. Soon your job improved as well. (Thank gawd!)

1997 – 1998

Your job scene continued to improve even more. And, along with your job, your health also improved at this time. You felt increasingly encouraged about your ability to get ahead in the world. Some of you took courses or got further training to make the most of a situation that was soon to blossom in your favour.

Partnerships and close friendships were also improving at this time. In fact, entering any kind of professional or intimate partnership was rewarding. Finally, the resources of others started to help you. The tide had turned! (Once again — thank gawd!)

1999 – 2000

This was an extremely powerful time in your life. It was a time of culmination, when you could see clearly what was working and what was not. Many of you received a promotion, a better job, accolades, or some kind of applause and recognition for your efforts.

Success in travel, publishing, and higher education, as well as medicine and the law, also boosted your happiness with increased opportunities. You were really hitting your stride!

By 2000 and into 2001, your confidence increased (for various personal reasons) and you were looking hot! Others thought so, too. You were on top of your game and, for some, this manifested in wonderful moments of romance and vacations in the sense of having arrived. ("I'm somebody!")

This was a good time for partnerships, both intimate and professional. (Yum, yum. Ain't love grand?)

2001 – 2003

Your popularity was really increasing now. You were pushing further outward and meeting new people, possibly through groups, clubs, and organizations. You made new contacts, acquaintances, and friends.

In addition, your goals became quite ambitious! You were not afraid to tackle major projects. You believed you were capable of doing something bigger than you had ever dreamed possible. You were The Little Engine That Could. ("I think I can. I think I can.")

Your ability to work with others both socially and professionally became so demanding that one of your challenges was how to maintain your own privacy, integrity, and independence, and yet at the same time work successfully with others. A slippery slope.

This was also a time when you increased your capacity to learn more. You encountered people who taught you things. In turn, you might also have been the teacher to those around you. (A role you often play.)

By 2003 you were laughing! By then, it was apparent to you just how much you could accomplish. ("I'm too sexy for my shoes!")

2004 – 2005

During the past several years, you had been so successful in your many achievements, you began to experience what the I Ching[9] wisely points out — when you reach the mountaintop and you want to keep going, the only place to go is down. Hence, you entered a window of time (perhaps two to three years) when you began to dismantle much of what you had created since around 1989–90. It was time to let go of people, places, relationships, and possessions. You started going through everything you owned to get rid of what was no longer relevant. Some of you moved residences, some changed jobs, some changed partners, and some changed countries!

But this was not really a time of loss. It was more a time of major reorganization in your life. In fact, many of you earned more money at this time. Ka-ching!

---

9. The I Ching is also known as *The Book of Changes*; it is an ancient Chinese text commonly used for divination in the West.

2006 – 2007

Your world took a serious turn at about this time. Different things occurred that, in fact, made you feel older. You might have felt creaky in your joints or concerned with wrinkles in the bathroom mirror (actually, get real — they were on your face!).

You had a sense of beginning something that was very major, and this was true! You were starting a new thirty-year cycle around 2006. This was a cycle that would lead you on a journey of completely reinventing yourself.

Fortunately, along with the serious aspects that were occurring, your home life improved beautifully! At this time, you felt richer and more fortunate with your family situation. You liked where you were living. Perhaps you moved to something bigger, or you expanded your home, because you certainly felt richer! This was a marvellous time for real estate, whether for your own personal use or for speculation.

Family was a source of increased joy. You bought balloons and threw parties.

2008 – 2010

The bleak news around this time was that many Leos started to lose money. For some reason, your earnings either disappeared or were diminished. You had to work harder for the same money or less. (Whaaat?)

Therefore, it was no surprise many of you started to explore new sources of income. Of course, some readjusted an extravagant lifestyle. The fact is, although you are considered to be an extravagant sign (and, let's face it, you are), you know how to live very well on less. You have panache! By the same token, if you're suddenly determined to achieve something, you can save money. Oh yes! The secret is that you have to be super-motivated.

So, at this stage in your life, you were giving a lot of thought to money, which is why my forecasts for your sign at this time were encouraging you to get out of debt. When you're out of debt, it's easier to be broke.

On the bright side, relationships were very enriching! Personal partnerships were a source of joy. Yeah, yeah, there's always friction and disappointment, but, in the main, friendships and partnerships were supportive.

Finally, by 2010, a break in the clouds appeared, and you were once again very much on top of your game. Career opportunities and numerous chances to promote your reputation and your good name were suddenly at hand. You were loved and adored once again!

Thank gawd.

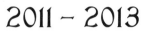

2011 – 2013

You are now entering a time of considerable flux and change in your life. You will recall that, around 2003–5, you had to give up a lot. You got rid of a lot of stuff — possessions, places, and even friendships. ("Bye! Write if you get work!")

Then, around 2005–6, you entered an entirely new phase of your life. It was the beginning of a major thirty-year cycle. Mainly, the beginning of this phase was all about inventing the new you. This will be readily apparent by 2013–14, when you will be able to look back at 2003 and confirm for yourself how dramatically your life has changed. ("Gads! I can't believe it!")

Now, *at this time*, you are still in this process of redefining yourself. The final details of this process primarily involve the finishing touches, which are honing and refining your mental process, your style of communicating with others, how you talk and think, and even how you listen. In order to achieve this refining process, life is going to force you to change your daily milieu in some way. That is to say, the bathroom you see every day will be different, or the car you drive every day, or the people you talk to every day, or the workplace you go to every day. Something in your daily environment is going to change.

By logical extension, a residential move or a job change (or both) is likely to take place in order to make this happen. *Capisce?* Some of you will give up things to go into something new. Others will simply add new acquaintances, new places, and new activities to what they already have. But things will change!

And here is the part where Leo luck shines once again. Could it be the Sun is always on your side? (You'll be humming "On the Sunny Side of the Street" or "You Are the Sunshine of My Life.") Corny, but maybe not. How else to explain that just as you are going through this time of change (which might be taxing), and change is always work, lucky Jupiter is at the very top of your chart, bringing wonderful opportunities to promote yourself in the world! You aced this one again! In other words, just when you need to make changes, opportunity is knocking at your door. How

auspicious can this be? (You're covered in horseshoes.)

Furthermore, this good fortune leads to increased popularity for your sign, especially in 2012–13. New faces, new organizations, and new interests will appear in your life. People from other backgrounds and different cultures will enter your world. Some of these could blossom into romantic involvements. Other contacts will be the result of travel and interacting with people whom you would not normally meet. These contacts will trigger something or encourage you to broaden and expand your goals for the future. You'll expect more for yourself because you will genuinely see and believe it is within the realm of possibility. "I can do this!"

Small wonder that, as these experiences evolve, your capacity to learn more about yourself, as well as learn more about dealing with others and dealing with the world around you, will increase. You will become wiser, more experienced, and — dare we say — more humble. (I think the humble part comes with the wisdom.)

Impressive stuff!

2014 ~ 2015

All these exciting changes will have ramifications in various areas of your life. Not only that, but they will also force you to reassess one of the most basic aspects of your life, namely, where are you going to live? During this particular window of time, you will be determined to establish a home you feel very happy about. After all, you are royalty and your home is your castle.

You want to feel good about where you live. You want to feel secure. And you want all of this to apply to your family and loved ones as well. That's why some of you will move yet again during this time frame, while those of you who are happy where you are will do major repairs to where you live. These repairs will be things like fixing the roof, or fixing the basement, or a major renovation. You will do whatever is possible to secure your home base.

In the same way, as you are undergoing changes in your physical home structure, major changes in your family structure might also take place. The dynamics might change through birth, death, divorce, or meeting new people. To give you an idea, the last time you addressed this sort of thing was around 1983–86. Older Leos might think back to what they did then to secure their home anchor and also how their family dynamic might have changed then.

Once again, lucky Leo gets horseshoes! By 2015, moneybags Jupiter is back in your sign for the first time since 2003. So, no matter what happens, you're laughing! Ultimately, whatever you experience will increase your confidence, your self-assurance, and your poise. You will feel that, despite the challenges you go through at home and within your family structure, you are blessed! The world has your back.

This is also a time when your health is good, partly because you feel so optimistic. You're actually beginning a twelve-year cycle of growth. Many of you will travel more than usual. Others will take up a new study. Whatever happens, you will get the feeling your freedom is increasing. Yay!

At this time, you feel closer to being the person you really are. Success is not so scary.

2016 – 2017

How sweet it is! You're back in the money again. You might not fly to L.A. to spend three thousand dollars on lingerie, but you could. For the first time in more than a decade, your earnings are growing! And for those who do not notice an increase in earnings, it's because instead you will choose to change jobs. Of course, some lucky Leos will do both. They will change jobs and get more money. Sweet!

Meanwhile, back in the crib, children will become an increased responsibility. This means some of you will become parents and others will become grandparents. It also means some of you will realize you should never lend your car to anyone to whom you have given birth. Or you're horrified to discover your teenager is attending Stiletto High.

Privately, despite your recent successes (or perhaps because of them), and despite your recently boosted income, deep down you are secretly wondering what you really want to do with your life. Perhaps you have the feeling that you've been there, done that. Or you might be just starting out, and, after a great beginning, realize this isn't quite what you wanted. You want something different.

Romance, of course, swoons dizzily on, as it always does in the life of Leo. Some of you will have love affairs with someone older or someone of a different age. Whichever way it works, it will be a learning experience.

And, on the work scene, you'll work hard for anything you achieve right now. But not as hard as you are about to!

Fear not; by 2017, a celestial shift wonderfully boosts your sense of optimism, as well as your confidence about what you are capable of doing. Many of you will receive increased training, or go back to school, or be very involved in post-secondary education. Others will be successful writing, editing, teaching, acting, or even driving for a living.

The year 2017 is also a great year to relate to siblings and relatives. In fact, siblings might give you money and gifts! (My favourite colour is the hundred-dollar bill. Admittedly, the fifties are kinda cute, too.)

2018 ~ 2020

Ah ha! This is a marvellous time for real-estate deals. Now is the time to buy, or sell and buy, or do anything to improve your home situation. You can't go wrong. Some of you will buy wonderful goodies for your home so you feel richer about where you live. Others will do something to feel like they're living in a bigger place, and some of you will literally move into a bigger home or have more land.

Just as your physical living structure seems to be bigger, nicer, richer, and more enjoyable, your experience of family will similarly improve. Family members will be a source of joy. Furthermore, family members will be generous to each other. You might travel with your family at this time. Another logical extension of this "expansive family feeling" is your family might really expand! This is the logical time for the birth of new family members or the increase of family through marriage or adoption.

While all of this is taking place in your private life, you're working hard at your job or at any important task. In fact, during 2018–20, you're putting out a lot of effort. You might work so hard you'll feel overwhelmed. Don't worry. Just as you survived the hard work of the late 1980s, you will survive this stint as well.

Around 2019–20, expect to take a wonderful vacation. Yay! You'll have no trouble justifying this to yourself, because you'll know you deserve it! (Work is the curse of the drinking class.)

This is also a fabulous time for romance and love affairs. Although much of your social toing and froing will be lighthearted and casual, some of you will meet the love of your life. (Be still, my beating heart.)

In typical Leo fashion, when you're on a roll, you do it all! By 2020, you'll have wonderful opportunities to improve your job, or get a better job, or improve your job surroundings ("I've got a corner window!"). Or you might simply change your attitude to your job. Whatever happens, the result is you feel greater rewards and joy from your work. And by work, I mean whatever it is you

do every day. You might not get paid for it. It could be employment or it could be your daily personal work.

Nevertheless, you are still busting your buns! You're working hard because you sense big rewards are almost within your grasp.

2021 – 2022

All that hard work is starting to pay off now. Since 2005, you have been focused on your private life and your inner world. You have gone through many changes, giving up things and then moving in a new direction, which included job changes and residential moves. Around 2014–16, you solidified your home base. Since then, you have worked hard to prove you could do something. But all of these activities were primarily about personal and internal challenges, or challenges to do with your home life and your private world.

At this point, it's almost as if you now leap onto the stage of life, declaring, "I've arrived! Fresh horses and whisky for my men!" That's because the next fifteen years will focus much more on your external world, your reputation, your career, and your ability to make a name for yourself.

The major reason you can finally cross over from a primarily interior world (the past fifteen years) into an emphasis on an external world (the next fifteen years) is that you're more confident! (You're eating razor blades for breakfast.) And while this new enthusiasm and confidence feels right, it might be a bit much for partnerships. (Oh yeah. You have *changed*.)

The result will be that partnerships and close friendships will be challenged. Those that have outlived their usefulness, or are no longer relevant in your life, will fall by the wayside and be history. ("Slip out the back, Jack.") This is not to say all serious relationships will end now. *Au contraire!* Lasting relationships will simply undergo readjustments so they can endure.

What really sweetens the pot now is you can benefit from the wealth of others. Many of you will receive inheritances, money back from the government, gifts, goodies, the use of other people's possessions, scholarships, or bursaries, or you might benefit indirectly because of bonuses and increased wealth of partners and family members. "Oh, how the money rolls in."

Around 2022, travel plans look promising and delightful. Some of you will go to school or get further training, because anything to do with higher education is beautifully blessed. Others will meet people from different countries and become romantically or professionally involved. Through your travels or your interactions with people from different cultures, something will cause you to transform your world view. You'll drop prejudices and faulty ideas because you learn new information!

This is also an excellent time for publishing and anyone who works in the media, medicine, or the law. Since 2019–20, early Leos have been giving serious thought to self-employment and striking out on their own. As this decade progresses, many more Leos will explore the independence of self-employment or perhaps consulting. This is because, for the first time in your life, unpredictable Uranus is at the top of your chart. I repeat, this has never happened before in your life (at least your adult life) because Uranus takes eighty-four years to complete its cycle.

Invariably, Uranus introduces radical change to your professional world. It also dramatically changes your identity, or your reputation, or your social status. You might regard authority figures as repressive. (Ya think?) Many of you will rebel and quit your day job!

Fortunately, this same influence can bring sudden opportunities to work in different fields, especially those related to aviation, computer technology, radio, and non-profit organizations.

Uranus wants change — change for the better. But, often, people will continue in an unhappy situation rather than risk the insecurity of breaking free. The danger of losing is too scary. It's important to have the courage to take a leap at this time, because if you don't go gracefully, Uranus will force you to make the change! (Gulp.)

2023 – 2025

Once again, your lucky stars are at play. (Frankly, until I did this long timeline for the sign of Leo, I was not aware of how much good fortune you would have whenever you encounter adversity. It's as if the universe took something away with the right hand but, at the same time, offered you something with the left. Curious, but wonderful.)

At this point, you will start to experience diminishing support — practical, emotional, and psychological — from other sources. Perhaps partnerships no longer give you the practical support you used to enjoy. Scholarships and bursaries might dry up. This will be a hard time to get a loan, for example. It's as if the resources of others are not available to you in the same way they were before. Naturally, this throws you back on your own resources, which can be a strengthening and maturing process (but who really wants to be that strong or mature?).

Nevertheless, once again the cavalry arrives! While you undergo a lessening of support from others (including partners), lucky moneybags Jupiter returns to sail across the top of your chart, just as it did in 2011, 2000, and 1988. Rescue is at hand!

When Jupiter is at the top of your chart — and this lasts for about eighteen months — you will naturally try very hard to move ahead in the world. Your ambition is aroused in a positive way. You're enthusiastic about what is possible. In turn, you have even more enthusiasm because whatever you hoped could be possible is a reality! Important people and opportunities now present themselves to you.

Expect a promotion at work; or public recognition for your efforts; or, possibly, fame, and certainly adulation or approbation. This journey of Jupiter invariably makes you feel at home with what you're doing, and unusually confident in your own skin. You believe in yourself, and you feel good about how life is unfolding.

This is a wonderful boost to counteract external resources that are drying up (which has nothing to do with your own earnings, but rather the support of others). It also brings opportunities to

shift to a field related to Jupiter, like travel, healing, or working in medicine, the law, publishing, or higher education.

You also have the confidence to explore self-employment, if this is your choice. Another offshoot is that Leos will enjoy increased popularity with others in 2024–25. Friends will benefit you. Groups, clubs, and organizations will be a source of joy, enthusiasm, and much activity. Contact with others will expand your goals and strengthen your resolve to reach for what you want.

This is a powerful influence and it has a tricky way of working. If what you do improves the lives of others as well as your own life, the results will be greater and more long-lasting. However, if what you do improves only your own life, the results will be lesser and more short-lived. In other words, what you put out will come back to you magnified.

What goes around, comes around.

"These are the voyages of the Starship *Enterprise*. Its five-year mission . . . to boldly go where no man has gone before."
GENE RODDENBERRY
Screenwriter, Producer, and Creator of *Star Trek*
(AUGUST 19, 1921–OCTOBER 24, 1991)

Famous Leo Personalities

Raymond Chandler	July 23, 1888–1959
Don Drysdale	July 23, 1936–1993
Woody Harrelson	July 23, 1961
Philip Seymour Hoffman	July 23, 1967
Charisma Carpenter	July 23, 1970
Marlon Wayans	July 23, 1972
Michelle Williams	July 23, 1980
Daniel Radcliffe	July 23, 1989
Amelia Earhart	July 24, 1897–1938
Chief Dan George	July 24, 1899–1981
Zelda Fitzgerald	July 24, 1900–1948
Ruth Buzzi	July 24, 1936
Lynda Carter	July 24, 1951
Jennifer Lopez	July 24, 1969
Anna Paquin	July 24, 1982
Patrice Bergeron	July 24, 1985
Maxfield Parrish	July 25, 1870–1966
Estelle Getty	July 25, 1923–2008
Walter Payton	July 25, 1954–1999
Matt LeBlanc	July 25, 1967
Javier Vázquez	July 25, 1976
Gracie Allen	July 26, 1885–1964
Aldous Huxley	July 26, 1894–1963
Stanley Kubrick	July 26, 1928–1999
Jason Robards, Jr.	July 26, 1922–2000
George Bernard Shaw	July 26, 1856–1950
Vivian Vance	July 26, 1909–1979
Carl Jung	July 26, 1875
Blake Edwards	July 26, 1922
Mick Jagger	July 26, 1945
Helen Mirren	July 26, 1945
Dorothy Hamill	July 26, 1956
Kevin Spacey	July 26, 1959
Sandra Bullock	July 26, 1964

Kate Beckinsale	July 26, 1973
Norman Lear	July 27, 1922
Jerry Van Dyke	July 27, 1931
Bobbie Gentry	July 27, 1944
Peggy Fleming	July 27, 1948
Alex Rodriguez	July 27, 1975
Jonathan Rhys-Meyers	July 27, 1977
Jacqueline Kennedy Onassis	July 28, 1929–1994
Beatrix Potter	July 28, 1866–1943
Rudy Vallee	July 28, 1901–1986
Sally Struthers	July 28, 1948
Clara Bow	July 29, 1905–1965
Dag Hammarskjöld	July 29, 1905–1961
Peter Jennings	July 29, 1938–2005
Bill Forsyth	July 29, 1946
Geddy Lee	July 29, 1953
Martina McBride	July 29, 1966
Emily Brontë	July 30, 1818–1848
Henry Ford	July 30, 1863–1947
Henry Moore	July 30, 1898–1986
Casey Stengel	July 30, 1890–1975
Peter Bogdanovich	July 30, 1939
Paul Anka	July 30, 1941
Arnold Schwarzenegger	July 30, 1947
Jean Reno	July 30, 1948
Delta Burke	July 30, 1956
Kate Bush	July 30, 1958
Laurence Fishburne	July 30, 1961
Lisa Kudrow	July 30, 1963
Vivica A. Fox	July 30, 1964
Simon Baker	July 30, 1969
Tom Green	July 30, 1971
Hilary Swank	July 30, 1974
Geraldine Chaplin	July 31, 1944
Michael Biehn	July 31, 1956
Wesley Snipes	July 31, 1962
J. K. Rowling	July 31, 1965
Dean Cain	July 31, 1966
Dom DeLuise	August 1, 1933–2009
Jerry Garcia	August 1, 1942–1995
Yves Saint Laurent	August 1, 1936–2008

Sam Mendes	August 1, 1965
James Baldwin	August 2, 1924–1987
Myrna Loy	August 2, 1905–1993
Carroll O'Connor	August 2, 1924–2001
Peter O'Toole	August 2, 1932
Isabel Allende	August 2, 1942
Sam Worthington	August 2, 1976
Edward Furlong	August 2, 1977
Rupert Brooke	August 3, 1887–1915
Anne Klein	August 3, 1923–1974
Leon Uris	August 3, 1924–2003
P. D. James	August 3, 1920
Tony Bennett	August 3, 1926
Martin Sheen	August 3, 1940
Martha Stewart	August 3, 1941
John Landis	August 3, 1950
Brent Butt	August 3, 1966
Evangeline Lilly	August 3, 1979
Louis Armstrong	August 4, 1901–1971
Raoul Wallenberg	August 4, 1912–1947
Maurice "Rocket" Richard	August 4, 1921–2000
Billy Bob Thornton	August 4, 1955
Barack Obama	August 4, 1961
John Huston	August 5, 1906–1987
Neil Armstrong	August 5, 1930
Loni Anderson	August 5, 1946
Maureen McCormick	August 5, 1956
Patrick Ewing	August 5, 1962
Adam Yauch	August 5, 1964
Lucille Ball	August 6, 1911–1989
Robert Mitchum	August 6, 1917–1997
Andy Warhol	August 6, 1928–1987
Michelle Yeoh	August 6, 1962
M. Night Shyamalan	August 6, 1970
Geri Halliwell	August 6, 1972
Garrison Keillor	August 7, 1942
David Duchovny	August 7, 1960
Charlize Theron	August 7, 1975
Sidney Crosby	August 7, 1987
Emiliano Zapata	August 8, 1879–1919
Dino De Laurentiis	August 8, 1919

Esther Williams	August 8, 1921
Dustin Hoffman	August 8, 1937
Connie Stevens	August 8, 1938
Keith Carradine	August 8, 1943
Sam Elliott	August 9, 1944
Melanie Griffith	August 9, 1957
Whitney Houston	August 9, 1963
Gillian Anderson	August 9, 1968
Eric Bana	August 9, 1968
Juanes	August 9, 1972
Kevin McKidd	August 9, 1973
Rosanna Arquette	August 10, 1959
Antonio Banderas	August 10, 1960
Alex Haley	August 11, 1921–1992
Ian McDiarmid	August 11, 1944
Marilyn vos Savant	August 11, 1946
Steve Wozniak	August 11, 1950
Hulk Hogan	August 11, 1953
Cecil B. DeMille	August 12, 1881–1959
William Goldman	August 12, 1931
George Hamilton	August 12, 1939
Pete Sampras	August 12, 1971
Casey Affleck	August 12, 1975
Hayley Wickenheiser	August 12, 1978
Cindy Klassen	August 12, 1979
Alfred Hitchcock	August 13, 1899–1980
George Shearing	August 13, 1919
Fidel Castro	August 13, 1926
Tal Bachman	August 13, 1968
Steve Martin	August 14, 1945
Danielle Steel	August 14, 1947
Gary Larson	August 14, 1950
Earvin "Magic" Johnson	August 14, 1959
Halle Berry	August 14, 1966
Napoleon Bonaparte	August 15, 1769–1821
Edna Ferber	August 15, 1885–1968
Julia Child	August 15, 1912–2004
Mike Connors	August 15, 1925
Melinda Gates	August 15, 1964
Debra Messing	August 15, 1968
Ben Affleck	August 15, 1972

Natasha Henstridge	August 15, 1974
Quinton Aaron	August 15, 1984
Robert Culp	August 16, 1930–2010
Eydie Gormé	August 16, 1932
Lesley Ann Warren	August 16, 1946
Kathie Lee Gifford	August 16, 1953
James Cameron	August 16, 1954
Angela Bassett	August 16, 1958
Madonna	August 16, 1958
Timothy Hutton	August 16, 1960
Steve Carell	August 16, 1962
George Stroumboulopoulos	August 16, 1972
Samuel Goldwyn	August 17, 1879–1974
Mae West	August 17, 1893–1980
Robert De Niro	August 17, 1943
Sean Penn	August 17, 1960
Rosalynn Carter	August 18, 1927
Robert Redford	August 18, 1936
Patrick Swayze	August 18, 1952–2009
Denis Leary	August 18, 1957
Madeleine Stowe	August 18, 1958
Edward Norton	August 18, 1969
Christian Slater	August 18, 1969
Coco Chanel	August 19, 1883–1971
Ogden Nash	August 19, 1902–1971
Gene Roddenberry	August 19, 1921–1991
Willie Shoemaker	August 19, 1931–2003
Jill St. John	August 19, 1940
Bill Clinton	August 19, 1946
Robert Plant	August 19, 1948
Peter Gallagher	August 19, 1955
Adam Arkin	August 19, 1956
Kyra Sedgwick	August 19, 1965
Matthew Perry	August 19, 1969
Jacqueline Susann	August 20, 1918–1974
Isaac Hayes	August 20, 1942–2008
Connie Chung	August 20, 1946
Al Roker	August 20, 1954
Amy Adams	August 20, 1974
Kim Cattrall	August 21, 1956
Alicia Witt	August 21, 1975

Hayden Panettiere	August 21, 1989
Dorothy Parker	August 22, 1893–1967
Ray Bradbury	August 22, 1920
Honor Blackman	August 22, 1925
Valerie Harper	August 22, 1940
Adewale Akinnuoye-Agbaje	August 22, 1967
Giada De Laurentiis	August 22, 1970

VIRGO

AUGUST 23 – SEPTEMBER 22

VIRGO THE VIRGIN
(AUGUST 23 – SEPTEMBER 22)

"I ANALYZE."

"'Come to the edge,' he said.
They said, 'We are afraid.'
'Come to the edge,' he said.
They came.
He pushed them — and they flew."
GUILLAUME APOLLINAIRE
French Poet and Playwright
(AUGUST 26, 1880–NOVEMBER 9, 1918)

"Why is it that when we talk to God we're said to be praying,
but when God talks to us we're schizophrenic?"
LILY TOMLIN
Actress, Comedian, Writer, and Producer
(B. SEPTEMBER 1, 1939)

Element: Earth
Ruling Planet: Mercury
Quality: Mutable
Opposite Sign: Pisces
Symbol: The Virgin
Glyph: An "M" with a Closed Loop, Representing the Reproductive Organs
Lucky Gems: Sapphire, Agate, and Peridot[1]
Flowers: Azalea and Lavender
Colours: Navy and Neutrals
Parts of the Body: The Nervous System and the Intestines

You Like: Pets, plants, books, cleanliness, soaps, cookery, being busy, helping others, picnics, creating order, vitamins, and self-help books. You're sexy and hot in the sack.

You Don't Like: Inefficiency, waste, crude behaviour, criticism, needing help, being dependent, and laziness.

Where You Shine: Altruistic, sincere, analytical, helpful, dependable, discerning, humorous, and clever. And you know so much about so much!

So Who's Perfect? Fault-finding, prudish, critical, fussy, hypochondriacal, doubting, skeptical, cynical, and jaded.

---

1. Different texts will name different gems for different signs. Ditto for flowers. Beware!

What Is Virgo-ness?²

Wonderful smarty-pants Virgo! You are one of the brainiacs of the zodiac. You are so smart, the main function of your body is just to carry your head around.

However, if you want to get a broader grasp of what your sign is all about, look to your ruling planet for all the clues. Your ruling planet is Mercury. In astrology, Mercury rules both Gemini and Virgo. However, these two signs are considerably different. How could this be? How could they have the same ruler?

The god Mercury was greatly revered by ancient societies. The Greeks called him Hermes, and the Romans called him Mercury (based on the Latin *merx* — to merchandise). Not only was Mercury considered to be the messenger of the gods,³ but he was also closely linked to commercial success. Both Hermes and Mercury were clever tricksters!

However, the Mercury that rules Virgo is likely more in tune with the Egyptian god Thoth. The Egyptians claimed that Thoth (or his girlfriend) invented writing. Thoth was the primary god worshiped by the Egyptian scribes. No surprise, therefore, that so many great writers are Virgos: Leo Tolstoy, H. G. Wells, D. H. Lawrence, Johann Wolfgang von Goethe, A. S. Byatt, and Stephen King, to name a few.

Mercury rules the intellect. It rules the mind and the nervous system, and it also rules ideas, words, thoughts, conversations, study, reading, writing, printing, books, maps, and newspapers. It rules the quality of taking something from point A to point B, which obviously includes ideas and words, whether spoken aloud or in writing. Mercury also rules taking objects from point A to point B. Hence, Mercury rules the delivery of anything — parcels and packages — and, therefore, it rules postal systems and courier services. Goods and services also go from point A to point B; thus Mercury rules retail, wholesale, service industries, and all forms of trade and commerce.

It follows that all forms of ground transportation fall under the domain of Mercury as well: cars, trucks, trains, buses, cabs, bicycles, motorcycles, scooters, and pogo sticks. Mercury is all about ideas, words, things, and people *on the go*!

Mercury is about "busyness" as well as "business."

---

2. No one is just one sign because everyone's chart is made up of different planets. Therefore, this section captures the Virgo archetype — the qualities of "Virgo-ness." Many other signs will have Virgo characteristics as well. Therefore, the discussion of one sign is not an exact description of that person; rather, it is a description of the qualities of that sign.

3. When NASA launched their missile to Mercury on August 3, 2004, they named it Messenger. (Those guys are clued in!)

"I used to be the fastest telegram messenger boy in all Fresno. My nickname was 'Speed.' Finally, I said, 'Take back your nickname. This pace is killing me.' Anyway, I still write fast — it's my impatient Armenian nature. I'm keen to find out how my plots end, and if I write faster I'll find out sooner."

WILLIAM SAROYAN

Armenian-American Author and Dramatist

(AUGUST 31, 1908–MAY 18, 1981)

Details! Details! Details!

Since you are ruled by busy, information-based Mercury, you rely completely on your intellect to control your world. To begin with, you *notice* everything! You're a detail person. Nothing escapes your attention. If a complete stranger walks by wearing different-coloured socks, you notice. Not only do you notice everything, you also absorb all kinds of details, and you *remember* them forever!

You've got this huge filing cabinet in some deep recess of your brain. You know more trivia than all the other signs combined.

Your sponge-like ability to take in all this information is curious, because you don't even really try. You have a natural penchant for analyzing everything around you — who is there, what they're wearing, what they plan to do, where they're going, and what they said. You're like this big, ongoing recorder constantly taking in data.

"I am a camera with its shutter open, quite passive, recording, not thinking."

CHRISTOPHER ISHERWOOD

British-American Novelist

A Single Man

(AUGUST 26, 1904–JANUARY 4, 1986)

Fortunately, all this information comes in very handy, because you are one of the most self-sufficient, independent signs. Think of the lengths that Greta Garbo (September 18, 1905–April 15, 1990) went to to control her privacy — "I vant to be alone."[4]

You're not pushy and you appear modest, but you do control your world by your uncanny ability to notice things. When you meet someone, you subtly control the conversation with your questions and observations. You can chat with a casual stranger for twenty minutes and, afterwards, you will know *everything* about this person, but they will know *nothing* about you. This is not about power. It's about survival. You keep others at bay with questions, observations, and appropriate comments. This ability *protects* you. You buffer yourself. You maintain your comfort level with the world by using your brain and your incredible *powers of observation and analysis*.

---

4. Apparently, she in fact never said that. She later explained, "I only said, 'I want to be left alone.'"

"As soon as you trust yourself, you will know how to live."
JOHANN WOLFGANG VON GOETHE
German Writer, Playwright, Poet, and Philosopher
Faust
(AUGUST 28, 1749–MARCH 22, 1832)

Because your mind is so intelligent, so flexible, and so analytical, your speech is equally clever. Virgos are the best mimics in the zodiac! You can use your vocal skills to entertain others for hours! Think of these Virgos with their clever verbal antics: Peter Sellers, Donald O'Connor, Adam Sandler, Bill Murray, Jane Curtin, Bob Newhart, Anne Bancroft, Peter Falk, and Paul Reubens. Who wouldn't want to sit down to dinner and listen to these wonderful wits?

"When I was younger and did a stand-up gig, it would take me two weeks to recover. Sometimes I'd get so panicked that I would stutter."
ADAM SANDLER
American Actor, Comedian, Singer, Musician, Screenwriter, and Film Producer
(B. SEPTEMBER 9, 1966)

Mercury is the smallest planet, and it moves very quickly. It orbits the Sun in only eighty-eight days. This is why you have such a fast, quick-thinking mind. Think of the speed of Mercury! Its tiny size is symbolic of the fact that nothing is too inconspicuous or innocuous for you to notice. I think Virgos are like Sherlock Holmes; however, Holmes's creator, Arthur Conan Doyle, was a Gemini. (Nevertheless, there's that Mercury again! And who knows? Doyle might have been Virgo Rising.)

Four Big Clues about Virgo

There is so much to say about your extremely intelligent sign. However, to better understand Virgo, I've reduced your fabulous qualities to four broad categories:

1. Drive for Perfection
2. Discriminating Intelligence
3. Desire to Serve and Be Useful
4. Health and Hygiene Awareness

Drive for Perfection

No sign more than yours is constantly striving to be perfect! Because you're an Earth sign, the perfection you strive for is tangible and real.

> "We're going to try and recruit the very best people we can and produce the best papers we can, and publish them to the highest standards we can."
>
> **CONRAD BLACK**
> Canadian-British Newspaper Publisher, Author, Historian, and Columnist
> (B. AUGUST 25, 1944)

To begin with, you obviously want to have a perfectly organized environment. You want everything in its place or filed away. You want useful items and tools ready to hand. You want your books categorized and your CDs alphabetized. You'd like to think you're making your life, and the lives of those around you, easier by creating order out of chaos.

> "It seems to me that the problem with diaries, and the reason that most of them are so boring, is that every day we vacillate between examining our hangnails and speculating on cosmic order."
>
> **ANN BEATTIE**
> American Short Story Writer and Novelist
> (B. SEPTEMBER 8, 1947)

We all want to feel good about ourselves, and each sign chooses a different avenue or approach to life to get this feeling of self-respect and inner pride. Your ability to create order so that your world functions better gives you a sense of purpose and also a sense of achievement.

"There is nothing you can't do, if you set your mind to it.
Anything is possible."

RICK HANSEN

Canadian Paralympian and Activist

Best Known for His "Man in Motion" World Tour

(B. AUGUST 26, 1957)

Candy Spelling (b. September 20, 1945), wife to the late TV producer Aaron Spelling and mother of Tori Spelling, has one room in her house devoted entirely to wrapping gifts. (Hey, she has a BIG house.) A rich array of gift wrap hangs on the wall, and every detail she needs to do a superb job of wrapping her gifts is there waiting for her. A Virgo dream!

One Virgo who has made money telling others how to live more efficiently is Shirley Conran (b. September 21, 1932), author of the bestselling Superwoman. *The following excerpt is taken from Becky Pugh's interview of Shirley Conran in the* Telegraph.

"'I'm not at all worried by clutter,' [Conran] assured me, 'as long as it is in the place where clutter goes.' She wasn't joking. In her tiny dressing room, serried ranks of colourful clothes and shoes stand to attention. Her jewellery and accessories live in two skinny-drawered filing cabinets, in which her earrings are individually sorted in plastic ice-cube trays. A cupboard in the master bedroom houses neat piles of wrapping paper, ribbon, bags, boxes, and gifts she picks up throughout the year. My eyes were on stalks."

This is not to say that all Virgos are fabulously organized and that nothing is ever out of place. Each sign has its flipside. Virgos can be slobs, but these guys are the exception. (Or they're depressed Virgos.)

If you are reading this, the odds are you are a Virgo or you are Virgo Rising. But there are people of any sign who might have their Saturn in Virgo.

What does this mean? We each have *all the planets* in our astrological charts. Therefore, we each have Saturn in one of the signs somewhere in our chart, and Saturn shows where we are *challenged* — it's where we have a lot to learn. This is where we do *not* have our act together. In other words: Saturn-in-Virgo people desperately want to be like people with Sun in Virgo! They, too, want to memorize sundry pieces of information, and learn everything, and figure out how to stash all the details of their life so that they can be effortlessly retrieved in the future at a moment's notice. Magic!

But they can't.

Instead, Saturn-in-Virgo people have huge piles of papers, magazines, clippings, and books *everywhere*. Their desk at the office is a veritable *mound* of paper. It's impossible for them to find anything. And where do you think their passport is at home? They have *no idea*! (Just a vague hope.)

I have a dear friend who has Saturn in Virgo. One September she said to me, "Well, I've *finally* found my garden hose. What a pain!" I asked, "What do you mean?" She said, "At the beginning of the summer, I bought a new garden hose, and then, all summer, I couldn't *find* it. I looked *everywhere*!" I said to her, "Was it out in that shed?" (She has one of those little metal sheds jammed full of stuff.) "No." She took a deep breath. "And you won't believe it when I tell you where it was." She lowered her voice conspiratorially. "It was on my kitchen table."

I rest my handbag.

That is a story of Virgo gone wrong. Too much clutter! Your drive for perfection and your motivation to create a more organized environment where you work and where you live make you the envy of others. When people visit you, they reap the rewards of your smooth-running environment.

This quest for perfection colours everything you do. It's your basic drive in life. You look anywhere and you think, "What's wrong with this picture?" In other words, "How can I make it better? How can I make it perfect?" This is why the greatest critics in the world are Virgos. You are the best literary critics, art critics, movie critics, architectural critics — you name it. You're intelligent. You're analytical. You notice everything. And you know how to make appropriate assumptions from this information. (And, while you're doing so, you're picking lint off the jacket of the person standing next to you.)

Virgos are fabulous editors, proofreaders, inspectors, quality control experts, testers, researchers and professionals who analyze anything in their field.

Ironically, your drive for perfection has a lovely tangent to it — it makes you humble. Who better than you knows how impossible perfection is? Very, very few Virgos are arrogant. You have a gentle, modest quality that appeals to others. You are not given to braggadocio or booming displays of confidence. Like fellow Virgos Peter Falk and Bob Newhart, you display your skill with an offhand shrug that implies you don't take yourself too seriously.

> "Colin is the sort of name you give your goldfish for a joke."
> COLIN FIRTH
> British Film, Television, and Stage Actor
> *Pride and Prejudice*, *Bridget Jones's Diary*, and *A Single Man*
> (B. SEPTEMBER 10, 1960)

(Ah, gorgeous Colin. Don't you know how many adoring fans would love to have you as their pet?)

Unfortunately, your drive for perfection makes you a constant worrier! Every morning, before your feet even hit the floor, you're determined to make your world right. "Today is the day!"

In your morning shower, you go over your litany of everything you intend to give up because it's harmful, and everything you hope to do because it would be helpful. Those who live with you cringe, because they can't even finish their morning coffee without hearing about your list of how to fix something, improve something, and make sure no one has cavities and all the kids get A's.

This is why you *love* lists. Lists give you a sense of power! They give you the illusion that you're gaining control of your world. Actually, you use your lists. In fact, very often Virgos go through old papers and come across a list they made years ago. Invariably, they're pleasantly surprised to see how much of that list they have accomplished.

This is why you create routines and have habits you value. Once you discover a new method, if you think it makes your life easier, you immediately adopt it. And you're right! This is wise.

I know one Virgo who has a rule that whenever she loses something, no matter what she is doing, she stops everything and starts looking for the lost item. She could be on the way to an important meeting and discover she is missing one leather glove. That's it. She will immediately search the car, ignoring the protests of fellow travellers who say, "Find it later!" *This is her rule.* She says you have to look for something the minute you realize it is missing because that's when the trail is hottest.

Virgos love their routines.

221

Discriminating Intelligence

Naturally, every sign is intelligent. A person's intelligence is linked to their Mercury and depends upon the placement of Mercury in their chart. Nevertheless, tons of Virgos are unusually intelligent.

"There is only one time that is important — NOW! It is the most important time because it is the only time that we have any power."

LEO TOLSTOY
Russian Novelist, Essayist, Dramatist, and Educational Reformer
War and Peace and *Anna Karenina*
(SEPTEMBER 9, 1828–NOVEMBER 20, 1910)

To put a finer point on it (you love the finer points), Virgo intelligence has a discriminating quality. You know how to *assess* information. You appreciate the details of description, composition, lighting, situation, locale, and relationship, and you weigh their values. You know how to discriminate this from that. You discern subtle nuances and minute distinctions.

Again, this very clear intelligence, combined with your drive for perfection, makes you a fabulous critic! When it comes to your ability to criticize, you can be extremely objective, detached, and, therefore, rather *scathing*. It would be wise to remember that people who abhor honest criticism are family, friends, acquaintances, and strangers. *Capisce?*

However, your discriminating intelligence becomes the yardstick by which you make all your decisions. Now I realize this doesn't sound like a bad thing, but what of the decisions that require spontaneity, passion, creativity and — sometimes — sheer recklessness?

This is why many Virgos are loath to leave a steady, secure job, even if they're offered a once-in-a-lifetime opportunity to do something grand! "But what if . . .?" It has to make *sense* to you. You don't like risk. This is why your clear intellect will always dominate your decision-making process.

"It takes twenty years to build a reputation and five minutes to ruin it."

WARREN BUFFETT
American Industrialist and Philanthropist,
and One of the World's Most Successful Investors
(B. AUGUST 30, 1930)

Desire to Serve and Be Useful

Many of you know Virgo is the sign of service. You find delight in being able to serve someone in precisely the ways they prefer. It might be as minor as giving them a cup of tea with just the right amount of milk in it (milk for tea, cream for coffee), and with just the right amount of marmalade on their toast. You will also feel satisfaction from your desire to serve your community, your city, or your country.

"The vocation of every man and woman is to serve other people."
LEO TOLSTOY
Russian Novelist, Essayist, Dramatist, and Educational Reformer
War and Peace and *Anna Karenina*
(SEPTEMBER 9, 1828–NOVEMBER 20, 1910)

We all do things to garner self-respect. Some want victory, some want wealth, some want fame, some want prestige, and so on. Naturally, most of us, to varying degrees, want all of these things. So when I discuss the archetype of a sign, I am discussing what that particular archetype *values most*, and the archetype of Virgo, the driving force behind Virgo, is *achieving personal satisfaction from being intelligently useful.*

To you, actions speak louder than words.

"It's a joy to labour for those you love."[5]
PROVERB

You give good hotel. This is for many reasons. For starters, it's an obvious demonstration of how intelligent and observant you are. How else could you know how to please someone if you haven't observed, and made an effort to remember, what they need or want? The other person is flattered that you are aware of their preferences, their size, their favourite soap, wine, food, colour, whatever. Fabulous service is no mean feat!

However, there is more involved: you like to feel *needed*. You like to be useful to others. When you are *fulfilling* a needed function, you have a warm feeling in your tummy. Just the fact you can beautifully do something that needs to be done (and probably do it better than anyone else) gives you great self-satisfaction.

---

5. I saw this phrase painted on a beautiful plate in Spirit Lake, Iowa, at the summer cottage of my husband's family.

I often travel with a Virgo friend. When we arrive at a hotel, she pulls out bags of herbal tea, exotic little coffees, and packages of nuts, in addition to which she gives me high-end little bottles of shampoo, lotions, and whatnot that are superior to whatever the hotel offers. It's her way of wanting to bring an added special touch to our trip.

And, when things go wrong, Virgos know how to survive! They have a snow shovel in their trunk along with jumper cables and tire chains, plus their flashlights work! (And they have backup batteries.) Of course, they also have all the right tools for the job.

I recall showing a Virgo friend a book with a spine that had come loose. It was a beautiful book about Tibet and I wanted to keep it. He said, "That's no problem." He opened a cupboard door. On the shelf were four or five little cosmetic train cases from the 1950s — those lunchbox-style cases that zip, with little handles on top. "I pick these up at garage sales for fifty cents," he said. Then he reached for one of the train cases, saying, "This one has all my glues related to paper products."

Meanwhile, I'm thinking, Whaaat? I have to scramble to find glue, let alone a train case devoted exclusively to glues related solely to paper products! That's Virgo.

"A useless life is an early death."
JOHANN WOLFGANG VON GOETHE
German Writer, Playwright, Poet, and Philosopher
Faust
(AUGUST 28, 1749–MARCH 22, 1832)

Health and Hygiene Awareness

"Never eat more than you can lift."
MISS PIGGY
Character from TV's *The Muppet Show*

Every sign rules one part of the body. For example, Aries rules the head, Taurus rules the throat, Gemini rules the lungs and hands, and so on. The sign of Virgo rules the nervous system and the intestines. This is why you are unusually aware of diet and hygiene.

Virgos wash their hands a lot. It's not a silly compulsion. You are well versed in bacteriology and the transmission of disease through germs. You know one of the simplest things you can do to stay healthy is to wash your hands throughout the day.

(Okay, I confess I know a Virgo who not only washes his hands a lot but also uses a paper towel to grab the doorknob on the men's washroom as he leaves. This guy's not taking any chances!)

Virgos are always experimenting with their diets. You'll explore being a vegetarian, or try a macrobiotic diet, or eat for your blood type, or try anything else that's trendy or intelligent. The whole process of digestion is very high on the Virgo awareness level.

"I'm on a new tranquilizer diet — I haven't lost a pound, but I don't care."
UNKNOWN

Virgos who suffer from stress or who worry too much (their numbers are legion) can suffer from irritable bowel syndrome. You're very tuned in to your whole digestive process. As a result, you take vitamins, drink cod liver oil, and eat kelp. You make smoothies out of powdered protein and acerola-cherry concentrate (naturally buffered). I always say if I wanted to throw a stick and hit the most Virgos, I would throw it at any health food store. Virgos own the store, they work in the store, and they're certainly customers of the store.

"I can spend hours in a grocery store. I get so excited when I see food,
I go crazy. I spend hours arranging my baskets so that everything fits in
and nothing gets squashed. I'm really anal about it, actually."
CAMERON DIAZ
American Actress
The Mask, *There's Something about Mary*, and *Charlie's Angels*
(B. AUGUST 30, 1972)

Virgos spend money on health products and other goodies that live in the medicine cabinet. You don't necessarily eat them or use the stuff. It's sort of like making a list. You feel good about being on top of the latest thing that is going to be beneficial, and so you immediately buy it. Sometimes you actually *try* it. Very often, however, these containers are never even opened. (But you *have* them!)

Virgo is the sign most associated with "wellness." You believe that an ounce of prevention is worth a pound of cure. Never scoff at this Virgo fascination for health products. Virgos look young! They take care of themselves!

This is not to say you never indulge in junk food or wine and cheese. But, when you do, you *know* it. You don't kid yourself. I know a Virgo who always has a cigarette with her protein smoothie. Her response? "We all have our contradictions."

If you read my description of Rising Signs in Chapter 2, you now know that your Rising Sign governs your appearance. Needless to say, Virgo Rising is one of the *youngest-looking* Rising Signs of all! Raquel Welch is Virgo Rising. Lucille Ball was Virgo Rising. This youthful appearance in later years is mainly because Virgos are not excessive. You endorse moderation. You're aware of what you eat. You practise good hygiene. Basically, you guys take care of yourselves! This is why Virgos look wonderfully young in their sixties, seventies, eighties, and nineties.

Hey, that discriminating intelligence pays off!

Virgo in Love

"A kiss is a lovely trick designed by nature to stop speech
when words become superfluous."
INGRID BERGMAN
Swedish-Born Actress
(Three Academy Awards, Two Emmy Awards, and One Tony Award for Best Actress)
Casablanca
(AUGUST 29, 1915–AUGUST 29, 1982)

Let us lay this "Virgo the Virgin" bit to rest right now. *Phffft!* You are an Earth Sign, and all Earth signs are sensuous, horny, highly tactile, and full of ardour! The image of Virgo the Virgin actually refers to your ability to be self-sustaining and independent, which includes emotional independence.

"Do not give in too much to feelings.
An overly sensitive heart is an unhappy possession on this shaky earth."
JOHANN WOLFGANG VON GOETHE
German Writer, Playwright, Poet, and Philosopher
Faust
(AUGUST 28, 1749–MARCH 22, 1832)

Naturally, you want to be cuddled in somebody else's arms just as much as anyone else. No question. However, remember that discriminating intellect of yours? Essentially, you make your decisions with your mind, not your heart. This means you do not *trust* being carried away by your emotions. It's kinda scary. After all, who's going to be in charge? And who knows where this might lead? One moment, you're in bed with someone and the next moment, you're close-dancing!

"There comes a moment in the day when you have written your
pages in the morning, attended to your correspondence in the afternoon,
and have nothing further to do. Then comes that hour when you are bored;
that's the time for sex."

H. G. WELLS[6]

British Author, Pacifist, and Science Fiction Writer
The Time Machine and *The War of the Worlds*
(SEPTEMBER 21, 1866–AUGUST 13, 1946)

One of the major things to deal with in your romantic relationships is your desire for perfection. Down deep, you're looking for someone who is perfect. ("Duh!") Ironically, because of your critical powers of observation, even if you *found* someone who was almost perfect, you would keep looking for what's wrong.

On your first date with someone, you're already wondering if they are the person with whom you want to share weekend custody of your unborn kids.

This Virgo quality is like the story of John, who wants to borrow his neighbour's lawn mower. As he slowly walks down his driveway and across the street toward his neighbour's house, he imagines a future scenario. What if he's late in returning the lawn mower? What if the neighbour gets lippy? And what about the time the neighbour kept John's snow shovel for months? As this conversation continues back and forth in John's head, John gets more and more steamed up about what could go wrong. He rings the doorbell. The neighbour opens the door. John looks at him and says, "Oh, hell! Keep your damned mower!"

Virgos are a little bit like this when they first encounter a possible sexual partner. Before the date is even over, they're running future scenarios in their mind about everything that could go wrong. In addition, they keep looking at this person with a critical eye. The result is that Virgos often shy away from relationships. To you, relationships are frequently *more trouble than they're worth.*

But there is also something else at play. You have a fantastic critical ability, which you can use to your advantage in your job — but it backfires in romance. Oh yeah!

When you're anxious for somebody else's approval, you turn your critical eye inward on yourself. Invariably, you come up wanting. You're unworthy. You're not beautiful enough, handsome enough, rich enough, tall enough, skinny enough, or whatever. You can't take the pressure! Even if you can fake it for the first few dates, eventually you will be *found out*! You'll be exposed, warts and all. Agghh.

As a result, you do a complete 180. Instead of looking for that perfect partner, you subconsciously decide that someone else — someone very far from perfection — would be the right person for you. Less pressure. (Whew!) This is why you often

6. H. G. Wells, although married, had a number of affairs with illustrious women, two of whom were also Virgos: American birth control activist Margaret Sanger (September 14, 1879–September 6, 1966) and Australian novelist Elizabeth von Arnim (August 31, 1866–February 9, 1941).

date people who are "beneath" you. It's for two reasons. The first reason is you feel less threatened. How can *they* criticize *you*? Like, hello?

The second reason is your desire to improve things. It's classic Virgo style to make a silk purse out of a sow's ear. I remember a Virgo girlfriend saying, "Give me a manager, and in three years I'll give you a vice-president."

Sometimes Virgos will sustain a long relationship that is completely without commitment. (Probably, the other person is waiting and hoping.) Virgo is ostensibly playing the field even though they're not seeing anyone else. They just want to coast, because they want the sex. Because Virgos do like sex!

In fact, your modest, mild-mannered, gosh-golly-gee Virgo is often into bondage. (Blindfolds are fun.) In an effort to try to explore this, I asked a Virgo friend of mine if he had ever tried bondage. "Oh yeah," he said nonchalantly. "My girlfriend used to tie me to a rocking chair. She used duct tape on my ankles and my wrists." Wide-eyed, I nodded politely. He added, "It was fun."

> "I wouldn't call him a slave. I don't whip him when he does something wrong. Just when he does something good."
>
> **SHANNON ELIZABETH**
> American Actress and Celebrity Poker Player
> *American Pie*
> (B. SEPTEMBER 7, 1973)

You often choose to live alone because it seems to be easier. There are fewer complications, and you can keep to your routine. Nobody else messing up the bathroom, or bringing gear in and leaving stuff everywhere. (Never forget how much comfort Virgos get from having a sense of order.)

Now hear this! If someone really wants to make a *big* impression on you, all they have to do is *do* things for you! They must perform a needed service!

(Tip to woo a Virgo: If something needs to be done, *do* it. Fix what needs to be repaired. Because now you're talking Virgo language to the Virgo. *Capisce?*)

Here is a classic pipe dream for the Virgo female: Mary lives in an old house, and in the basement her clothes dryer is no longer working. Too broke to buy a new one, she is reduced to drying her clothes on a wooden clothes horse and on a clothesline strung across the basement. She hates doing this. Enter her new beau, Mr. Soon-to-Be-Perfect.

One day, Mary returns home and notices a large cardboard box in the backyard. She goes down to the basement, and lo and behold! Someone has bought her a new dryer! Not only that, they got rid of the old one! And now for the pièce de résistance: they built a little shelf above the dryer for soap and bleach. On top of the dryer is a note: "Hope you don't mind. I left the cardboard box in the backyard because I thought Jimmy would have fun playing in it."

Major score! Mary is putty in his hands from that moment on. Anyone who goes to those lengths to notice what she needs, and then do all this just for her — just to help her and make her life easier — is Mr. Perfect!

I myself have Venus in Virgo (although I am not a Virgo). It means I have a bias for Virgo people and Virgo activities (I buy lots of vitamins), and when it comes to romance I am very Virgo-ish! I recall someone saying to me, "Wow, if I had known that painting your kitchen cupboards was foreplay, I would have done it long ago!"

To show affection, Virgo will wait on you, and serve you tea, coffee, drinks, and healthy food. Virgo will do your laundry, or fix your car, or help you move. After a while, you'll realize how tough life would be without this devoted Virgo in the picture!

Hey, is a bit of duct tape and a rocking chair that big a deal?

The Virgo Boss

"Whenever you're sitting across from some important person,
always picture him sitting there in a suit of long red underwear.
That's the way I always operated in business."
JOSEPH P. KENNEDY
American Businessman, Political Figure, and U.S. Ambassador to Great Britain
(SEPTEMBER 6, 1888–NOVEMBER 18, 1969)

A stupid boss is a terrible thing. I think there should be a law against it. Fortunately, you're intelligent. This quality alone goes a long way to making you very effective in directing the energy of others.

I think the single biggest thing that makes you an excellent boss is that you're not afraid to get your hands dirty. (Kinda funny, considering how often you wash them.) Virgo is not above any kind of work. You will do whatever it takes to get the job done. People who work for you know this, and they will respect you for this. They figure if you're going to do it, they can do it, too.

You're fair-minded. You're also a good communicator. You're extremely practical, and you know the shortest distance between two points.

You know what your Achilles heel is before I even say it. You can be too critical! You expect too much of others. It's important to remind yourself that the people who work for you put their pants on one leg at a time, just like you. *We are all frail mortals.*

Furthermore, keep in mind that not everyone is as concerned about little details as you. Others don't even *see* them! And before you get judgemental about what they fail to see, remind yourself of what you might fail to *feel*, or experience, because you're made from a different cloth than them. Think of it this way: Maybe you are rice. But the people who work for you are potatoes, or bread. Naturally, a potato is not going to be so aware of a grain of rice. It's not in their nature, even if, to you, it is very obvious. You have to cut others some slack!

You can do this because, basically, you're personable and easy to get along with. Since you are sensitive, you are likewise sensitive to the feelings of others.

One of your big strengths is that you don't have a big ego. You don't have to strut around the place like a prison guard with mirrored aviators. (I actually had a part-time job working for someone like that when I was in university, and he *had* been a prison guard.)

But your lack of ego can be a bit problematic in your role as a manager. You're not into grabbing personal power. You work for the satisfaction of the job itself, not for the glorification of your ego. In fact, you are sometimes reluctant to take a promotion that gives you a broader range of power over more people.

However, your willingness to pitch in and demonstrate that you will do any job plus the fact that you are a compassionate person combine to make you an effective manager. People are *lucky* to work for a Virgo because you yourself have such a great work ethic.

The Virgo Employee

"Coffee, tea, or milk?"

A Virgo employee is a dream come true. There are so many reasons for this. To begin with, you're reasonable, you're intelligent, you notice things, you're awake, you're aware of what's going on around you, and, hey, avoiding the stupidity factor is a big plus for any employer!

Because Virgo is the sign of service, you genuinely enjoy doing a good job, and doing it right, and giving someone what they're looking for. Your employer *loves* you! (Unless they know you're doing priceless imitations of them behind their back.)

Virgos have the inspiring quality of being willing to do yucky jobs. I knew a seventeen-year-old Virgo who worked as a busboy at the Sheraton Landmark in Vancouver when it had a revolving restaurant on the forty-second floor. (The employees used to throw rolls of toilet paper off the top floor to make flying streamers.) It was his first job. One night, one of the customers, an old man who had difficulty walking, asked this boy to help him to the washroom. Just as the old man reached the washroom door, he soiled himself. This Virgo lad, in his white shirt and black tie, calmly helped the old man clean himself up. Not a pleasant job. He then helped the man down the elevator and out of the restaurant to the sidewalk, where he hailed a cab for him. He told me that just as the man was about to enter the cab, the cab driver protested, once he got a whiff of the situation. Nevertheless, the boy firmly put the man in the cab, and told the driver to take him home.

I admired that kid. Many would not have gone out of their way to help someone in such a messy situation. Ya think?

Virgos will work long hours. But one of your specialties is anticipating what others need. You are punctual. You are reliable. And you're an efficient worker! Because it's in your nature to enjoy being useful, as well as to delight in offering good service, it's obvious you are a stellar employee.

And let us not forget that some of the greatest researchers are Virgo. Plus you are wonderful working with handicapped people or doing physiotherapy. You like to help. You like to be needed.

If human resources departments ever clued in to what a great hire you are, they would do everything they could to recruit Virgos.

The Virgo Parent

"Of course if you like your kids, if you love them from the
moment they begin, you yourself begin all over again, in them, with them,
and so there is something more to the world again."
WILLIAM SAROYAN
Armenian-American Author and Dramatist
(AUGUST 31, 1908–MAY 18, 1981)

The wonderful thing about the Virgo parent is that they give their children
a sense of security about the world, because the Virgo parent will provide a regular routine. Children need this. Children like boundaries and steady rhythms. The
Virgo parent is punctual and serves meals at a regular time, and likewise, establishes
a regular bedtime. Children flourish with this kind of order in their environment. It
makes them feel safer. They understand what to expect.

The Virgo parent is also aware of hygiene and health issues. Very few Virgo parents
will indulge a child's yearning for junk food. The children of Virgo parents have
protein smoothies and fresh fruit for breakfast. They might be on a vegetarian diet.

I recall cooking breakfast for a sweet little four-year-old of a Virgo parent who
was visiting my house.

He chowed down eagerly on his plate of food, then suddenly looked up. "Wow!
This is good! What do you call this?"

"Bacon," I said.

Naturally, the Virgo parent has to be careful about *being critical*. Of course, you do
not see it as criticism. You think it is constructive advice. Constant, ongoing, helpful
advice. (Ha!) But all this advice has the implication that the child is inadequate. Why
would you want to send this message to your child?

The Virgo parent has to learn to curb their tongue. Your kids aren't going to be
perfect, because nobody's perfect, including you. Lighten up!

Virgo parents are sometimes not physically demonstrative with their affection,
even though they love their children with all their heart. Naturally, your children
will know you love them because of all the things you do for them. But they still
need hugs and gestures of affection. Everyone does. Even the family dog.

Remind yourself that most of the criticism you constantly offer doesn't make a
difference. It really *doesn't*. It sounds like nagging. (And there are none so deaf as
those who are wearing headphones.)

Your great strength as a parent is being a wonderful role model. Your children are not going to do what you tell them; they are going to do what you do.

"Love begins by taking care of the closest ones — the ones at home."

MOTHER TERESA

Albanian-Born Catholic Nun, Humanitarian, Founder of the Missionaries of Charity, and Winner of the Nobel Peace Prize (1979)

(AUGUST 26, 1910–SEPTEMBER 5, 1997)

The Virgo Child

"You only have to do a very few things right in
your life so long as you don't do too many things wrong."
WARREN BUFFETT
American Industrialist and Philanthropist,
and One of the World's Most Successful Investors
(B. AUGUST 30, 1930)

Many Virgos are little hams when they're young. Their amazing ability for mimicry is with them right from the beginning! They need a supportive environment to experiment and tap into their talent. Yes, they need encouragement to perform, but they also need a safe place to make mistakes.

You have to be extremely careful about criticizing a Virgo child. Believe it or not, this little person is already self-critical! Imagine a little kid who's already trying to be *perfect*. Naturally, by virtue of being a child, failing at everything you try for the first time is par for the course, whether it's walking, talking, trying a new sport, or playing an instrument. Can you see how tough it is to be a Virgo kid?

The Virgo child is so quick to put themselves down. They get discouraged so easily! In fact, as incredible as this sounds, little Virgo children are worriers! They worry about school. They worry about their teachers. They worry about bullies in the neighbourhood. Essentially, the Virgo child is gentle and does not throw their weight around. They're happy to just fit in.

But, most of all, Virgo children *want to feel useful.* They want to feel they're doing a good job helping you. Look for ways in which they can take on a task and do it well. This will build their confidence, and it will also give them a sense of reward and self-satisfaction. They feel so proud of themselves when they can successfully help you and be useful at home.

Ideally, the Virgo child does not need to hear heavy-duty news about the plight of the world. If, as a parent, you are concerned about society, do not burden your Virgo offspring with your anxieties. Remember, they are little worriers. They take things very seriously.

Above all, the Virgo child needs an excellent education. This is a kid with a bright, discriminating mind! They learn very quickly. And, because of this, school can be a positive experience. However, if teachers are critical or the child's contemporaries are overbearing, they will withdraw and lose their footing in the bigger scheme of things. Very often, Virgos demonstrate an interest in mathematics and science. Try to give them the books, tools, and support to further explore these areas. Virgos are bright kids!

The Virgo child loves a regular routine. She likes everything to be in its place. Try to establish a sense of order with everything they use: where their toothbrush is, where their pyjamas are, where the food is that they get for themselves. They feel secure when everything is familiar and stays the same. They like routine.

This gentle child can often appear to be surprisingly self-sufficient, even aloof. Nevertheless, your Virgo child needs just as much hugging and cuddling as any other child. Therefore, be demonstrative. Offer lots of hugs and affection.

Please take note: Virgo children are often fussy eaters. So what? Don't make a big deal about this. They don't have to try everything. They might go for several years and never eat eggs, or broccoli, or their bread crusts. Don't get your belly in a rash over any of this, because their *digestive system is sensitive*. Remember: Virgo rules the intestines.

Meals should not be times of criticism or discussions about family problems or what's going wrong at school, and certainly not times when the Virgo child is forced to eat food they don't want to eat! (I think forcing kids to eat food is a power issue; it's about who is in control. I say, let it go.) Make mealtimes happy times. (Even if it's in front of the TV.)

The joke is, when they grow up, they're going to know far more about food and nutrition than you ever did! They're very cautious about the whole area of eating. Just relax.

"Definitely, it's a fear of failure that drives me."
JERRY BRUCKHEIMER
American Film and Television Producer
Armageddon, Pirates of the Caribbean, and TV's *CSI* series
(B. SEPTEMBER 21, 1945)

How to Be a Happier Virgo

"A lifetime of training for just ten seconds."
JESSE OWENS
American Track and Field Athlete Who Won Four Gold Medals at the 1939 Olympics
(SEPTEMBER 12, 1913–MARCH 31, 1980)

Your Virgo drive for perfection has a boomerang quality of making you aware of your *imperfections*. If I could advise the world on how to talk to Virgos, I would say, "Never criticize them! They are already doing a great job of that by themselves."

You know you find it easy to critically appraise others and so, naturally, when you look in the mirror, you don't notice your gorgeous eyes, or your fit physique, or your great complexion. You see a zit, or love handles, or wrinkles, or bags under your eyes. Or you hate your hair, or your nose, or your waistline. Bummer!

On top of this, you're a worrier. You are constantly trying to improve your surroundings and meet the demands of others — and all the while you have to keep all these balls in the air! Oy vey! You think about all this at night in bed, and you think about it first thing in the morning. It's very hard for you to just kick back and let it be.

In a nutshell, you're dealing with a challenge to your feelings of self-worth. In fact, you are so full of self-doubt, especially when you're younger, that you constantly footnote whatever you say. Instead of just stating your opinion, you'll say "studies indicate," or you'll quote a book or another source. It's as if your own opinion doesn't carry enough weight, so you have to back it up with something in print. You have to get an expert on board. (Does this ring a bell, Pavlov?)

So, what can you do to reverse this impulse to be self-critical? It's a costly habit, because it counters your ability to appreciate who you are and to value your precious life. And you are precious; every person is.

Love involves your capacity to care for or have feelings for others. This kind of thing doesn't materialize out of thin air. It's actually an *energy*. And this energy-comes from *within* you. It all begins in you.

Now here's the sweet part (and I think a lot of people don't know this). To develop this energy — call it love, call it compassion (it has many names) — is a *learned* process. That's right. You can learn how to do it. And, wow, if there ever was a quick learner, it's you!

There are actual exercises you can do to develop this energy in your heart. (I say "heart" because it sounds better than "your left armpit.")

One renowned spiritual teacher suggested the following method. (It takes about thirty seconds. And you only have to do it once a day. Hey, thirty seconds — love? Pretty efficient use of your time!)

Here is the method:

Sit somewhere quietly, preferably alone (although I have done this in a crowd).

Then, visualize yourself on your right, sitting there. There you are. (I always imagine myself in whatever I am wearing at the moment.) There you are, and you want to be happy. You certainly don't want to be unhappy. And you have every right to be happy!

Now, on your left, visualize a huge group of people. These people are in great suffering. They might be war victims, or earthquake victims, or burn victims. They might be starving children. Their number is huge. If you personally know someone who is suffering, put them in this group.

Now, *you* are in the centre. You are like an all-powerful judge, with godlike powers. You know that the person sitting to your right (which is you) wants to be happy, and doesn't want to suffer. But you know that the huge group on your left also wants to be happy and they want to be free from their terrible pain and suffering.

You in the centre have the power to *choose*. Which side is it going to be?

Fortunately, Virgos are intelligent. Furthermore, you appreciate the value of being able to do something for others. Therefore, you will choose the group on the left. *You will choose them over yourself.* And. when you make this choice, for a tiny nanosecond the energy within your heart will get a boost. I guarantee this.[7]

If you take thirty seconds and do this exercise every day, even though you already *know* what your choice is going to be, you will get that tiny boost of energy in your heart. And, slowly, this energy will build. And love will build in your heart — love for yourself and, eventually, for others.

You have to actually *do* the visualization and go through the exercise. It's not just an *idea*. It's not just a mental process. It's something you're actually *doing*. That's because we are verbs not nouns.

Every time you elect to *make that choice,* to choose the group that is suffering over your own individual self, you will develop the energy within you that creates love.

What have you got to lose by trying?

---

7. In 1981, I heard the Dalai Lama explain this exercise in a talk he gave at the Hyatt Regency in Vancouver. Shortly after, he was also going to speak at Christ Church Cathedral in an interdenominational service. I arrived at the church early and waited in a pew. There was a beautiful bouquet of flowers on a table at the front of the church, about forty feet from me. Since I was just sitting there waiting, I decided to try the exercise I had just heard about in the previous talk. I visualized myself to my right, and a large group of burn victims to my left, and I also placed my brother, who was dying, in that group. While I did the exercise, I was staring at the bouquet of flowers. The exact instant that I chose the group — for a *nanosecond* the flowers sort of ballooned and became more vivid in colour. No question. Super fast, super subtle, but I *saw* it. I believe that when I tapped into this higher energy — the cultivation of love — my senses expanded their capacity to perceive the world.

"I would rather have a competent extremist
than an incompetent moderate."

LEON JAWORSKI

Special Prosecutor During the Watergate Scandal (Appointed November 1, 1973)

(SEPTEMBER 19, 1905–DECEMBER 9, 1982)

VIRGO
YOUR 40-YEAR HOROSCOPE
1985 – 2025

Why Go into the Past?

I want you to have faith in your predictions. The only way you can believe what I say is to test it for yourself. This is why I start with brief highlights from the past twenty-five years. If anything in these past twenty-five years resonates with you, then what I say about your future will have the same validity. To me, it is all one long timeline — your life.

The past predictions generally apply once you have left home or are "running your life" and making your own decisions. Prior to that, the major events in your life were dictated to you by other people, likely your parents.

1985 ~ 1987

This was definitely a time of flux, when job changes and residential moves were at hand. The good news was that many of you improved both your health and your job at this time. Partnerships and relationships also improved.

In fact, many of you benefitted from the wealth and resources of others through inheritances, gifts, direct assistance, or indirect benefits from partners who got bonuses or a better deal. Sweet!

1988 – 1990

Job changes and residential moves continued to keep you on guard. It was hard to count on anything. Eventually, your total focus was simply to establish a firm anchor for yourself in the world. You needed a home you could rely on. Inevitably, this involved repairs, moves, buying and selling, and doing whatever you could to feel secure. You were sanding floors, painting walls, and making your digs tickety-boo. (One of your favourite words.)

Travel was wonderfully rewarding then. Ditto for higher education and publishing. You were able to learn and do things that were truly meaningful. Some of you might have taken the trip of a lifetime!

Soon your job, career, and reputation started to take off. People were impressed! Nevertheless, increased responsibilities with children were sobering, but something you didn't hesitate to shoulder. And, hey, your popularity soon began to soar!

1991 – 1993

This is when you really started to bust your buns to show others what you could do. And you did. In fact, 1992 was a particularly successful year for you! Accolades, praise, achievements, and good times landed in your lap. Hey, you worked hard for it — you deserved it.

Opportunities to earn money also started to increase. Yay! However, partnerships were becoming increasingly challenging. Oy vey. These partnerships were personal, professional, or even with your job.

What the large print giveth, the small print taketh away.

1994 – 1996

It's a good thing you were relatively optimistic at this time, because it was difficult getting along with others, mainly significant others, in your life. Close friendships and partnerships suffered. In part, this was because you started to *take your power*. When this happens, it upsets the existing balance in any relationship.

Ever since the early eighties, in a way, you had been building up to this moment. And now it was time to fly! For the previous fourteen years, you had been working on who you were, your values, where you lived, and what you would do. You were getting training and proving yourself. Now you were stepping out into the world for real. "And now, for our next contestant . . ."

Even though partnerships and friendships were ending or undergoing big readjustments, family life was enriching. Some of you moved to bigger digs. Others expanded family through birth, marriage, adoption, or people arriving on your doorstep for various reasons. Some of you were able to get away on a wonderful vacation.

This was also a time when romance, love affairs, and serious flirtations started. (Zis was zee time for loff!)

1997 – 1998

As your confidence grew, you *liked* yourself more. You felt better about being who you were. You felt stronger at work, stronger in your job, and stronger with the potential opportunities that were available to you. Speaking of feeling stronger — even your health improved!

The downside was that support from others — financial, practical, psychological, or emotional — diminished. This threw you back on your own resources. Fortunately, you handled it.

However, another curious influence began at this time. Uranus, the planet of earthquakes, volcanoes, dynamite, and unpredictable events, started a slow journey through the part of your chart that relates to health and employment. (And also small pets.) From this point until 2004–5, you encountered sudden changes with your job, with your health, and, likewise, with small pets in your care.

1999 ~ 2000

At this time, benefits from others came your way to help you explore opportunities in higher education, medicine, the law, publishing, and the media, as well as enjoy the thrill of travel! Yay!

Stimulating, exciting things were swirling around you! Some of you fell in love, or had an affair with someone from a different background. ("She ate the whole crab! Shell and all!") Essentially, this was a time when you expanded your experience of the world through teachers, travel, or exciting events. Some of you explored new religions or philosophies and human-potential movements.

Your excitement at this time was your sense of anticipation. You sensed you were going to attain something that was important. Almost there!

2001 – 2003

Finally! Now you started to hit your stride. You were proud of your achievements. Graduation, a promotion, or a chance to start your own business was thrilling. Others were getting married, buying their first house, or making whatever special dream they hoped to achieve a reality. ("Yay me!")

This was a lovely time of harvest. You felt proud of your achievements, but, like any harvest, you also saw what was not working. Hopefully, you just moved on. This was not the time to dwell on failures. (But who doesn't brood over failures?) Ah yes, the vultures circle, and as that Chinese proverb goes, "Everyone pushes a falling fence."

2004 – 2005

The year 2004 was a lovely turning point. Your confidence certainly was boosted then! You started to feel better about yourself. People noticed you; it was easy to attract important people to you, and there were also more opportunities available.

By 2005, many of you had gotten a better job or discovered ways to boost your income. (For some, this financial advantage occurred in 2006.)

At this time, a celestial influence began that would last until around 2011. This stirred up things with partnerships and close friendships. Some of you who were celibate or single suddenly met someone who turned you on! Perhaps there was an age difference (especially younger). Something was different and unusual, because, for you, it was a *stretch* to relate to them. As a result, you felt life was more exciting. You felt younger, wilder, and more alive!

Soon, opportunities to boost your earnings also grew. (Money is so handy if you want to buy something, and it certainly upgrades despair.)

2006 – 2007

A curious shift started to occur around this time as you began to downsize and streamline your possessions. You went through cupboards, drawers, garages, attics, storage places, and lockers, deciding what to keep and what to turf. When Virgo is on a roll, Virgo is extremely thorough. You probably went through your entire home getting rid of stuff and reorganizing everything. Sheesh!

Some went so far as to give up friends, jobs, and relationships. (This was when you were doing a serious overhaul.)

2008 – 2010

Now you entered a pivotal time in your life, one of those bench-mark periods. Your life was changing, and, as you gave up things in one area, you gained things in other areas. For example, where you lived improved. Family life improved. Many of you moved to bigger or nicer digs. On the heels of this came fun and excitement! Romance, love affairs, vacations, travel for pleasure, sports, the arts, and fun activities with children were a source of enjoyment. For many of you, this was *party time*!

And these good times were soon followed by a chance to won-derfully improve both your health and your job scene. In fact, practically every aspect of your life started to improve, which was ironic because it followed so much loss. Go figure.

2011 ~ 2013

Two interesting influences are taking place at this time, and they will help each other in a mutually beneficial way. To begin with, you are entering a two- to three-year span of time when, essentially, you will be questioning your values. It's a time in your life when you're wondering what it's all about. What really matters? Where do I place my bets? You don't want to make a big, bad decision you'll later regret.

Generally, when a person is going through redefining their values and reprioritizing things, they often focus on the external expression of this — making money. Therefore, in the next few years, you will definitely be thinking about how you should earn a living, how you can make more money, and if *how* you are making money is a *worthy* effort. If you're retired and beyond the "day job/slave wage" lifestyle, you'll still be wondering about how to best use your resources and the things you own.

But the bottom line is still, *what really matters?*

Fortunately, as mentioned above, the second influence that is present now is an opportunity to travel, to go back to school, to explore other cultures, to learn more about different religions, and to tap into different belief systems. It's very fortunate that, at the very time when you're wondering about your basic values, you will have many opportunities to explore different ways of living, either through travel or study. Bonus!

Others will use this beneficial influence to make headway in publishing, the media, medicine, or the law.

Some of you will also fall in love with someone from another culture or another country. (Now there's a fun way to learn a new language.)

Sometimes we prepare for success, and sometimes success catches us off guard and drags us along for the ride. That's probably what's going to be happening in 2012. This is a year full of wonderful opportunities. It's as if you're suddenly lucky! You attract opportunities as well as important people to you. You might even win things rather easily. It's as if a fairy godmother

were perched on your shoulder. Therefore, at this time, when you are questioning your values, your successes might crystallize your decisions.

Increased popularity in 2013 will be fun. Now is the time to get out and schmooze. Join clubs, groups, and organizations. This is not a year to go it alone. Form working units, because partnerships of any kind, intimate and professional, will totally benefit you.

It's important to stay light on your feet now. That's because you're entering a time of uncertainty from 2014 to 2016.

2014 ~ 2015

This is definitely a time of flux and change, with residential moves and job changes. No question. Things are uncertain, but do take note. Many times when I tell people they will have a job change or a residential move, they are positive that they won't. In my experience, it generally happens at least 90 percent of the time. (Actually, the ones who deny it so vehemently are the most shocked when it happens.)

This is your *window of change*. Not only that, some of you might move more than once. Sort of a hippity-hop situation. This is because you will not seriously settle down until 2016–17. In this particular time frame, you are sort of "trying on" new situations. The same pattern can apply to jobs. You get one, you take one, you start one, then you leave.

What beautifully offsets this hectic instability is an increased popularity with others. But wait: not only do others want to share your company, they're willing to *help* you! Yes, they will help you pack and move. (Not move the bodies, only the furniture.) Therefore, join forces with others. Become part of groups, clubs, and organizations. All kinds of partnerships or working units will benefit you.

In addition, this is a time when you feel greater optimism about what is possible for you in the future. Suddenly, you're confidently entertaining big goals! Big dreams!

Perhaps this is why you enter a brief time (about a year) of exploring spiritual and mystical ideas and schools of thought. One might say that you are searching.

"I'm not that tough; I'm not that smart. I need life telling me who I am, showing me my mind constantly. I wouldn't see it in a cave."

RICHARD GERE
American Actor and Producer
American Gigolo, An Officer and a Gentleman, and *Pretty Woman*
(B. AUGUST 31, 1949)

2016 – 2017

As if to confirm that moments of searching can lead to something meaningful, 2016 is a bonus year for you! Influential people, opportunities, plus lots of fun and pleasure suddenly start to come your way. Thank gawd! About time! The primary reason things are going so well for you this year is that lucky moneybags Jupiter is in Virgo for the first time since 2003. Ta-dah! Needless to say (but I will), by the end of 2016, your confidence will have increased, along with your self-assurance and poise. A series of small successes can do wonders for the ego!

Meanwhile, back at the ranch, you are now very serious about establishing a solid anchor for yourself in terms of where you live. ("I must! I must!") You might move again. You might sell and buy. You might buy for the first time. If you stay where you are, or even if you move again, you will likely be fixing up your home in a major way, perhaps fixing the roof or the basement or doing major renovations.

Travel opportunities are likely now. You're actually entering a new twelve-year cycle of growth. Speaking of which, since this is a time when you attract good fortune and opportunities to you, you might put on weight. You are quite literally "attracting" flesh to the bone. (Go easy on seconds of dessert.)

Note: dire warnings about calories never apply to dark chocolate.

This is also a significant time for family relationships, especially with parents. (By the way, my parents turned out Okay. How about yours?)

Finally, all this good stuff leads to what is really practical — yes, the green stuff. Moolah. Scratch. Coin. Loot. Dough. Cabbage. Lettuce. Bread. Bacon. Clams. It's almost enough to make you break out singing, "Food, glorious food! Hot sausage and mustard!" Depending on if you're an early Virgo or a later Virgo, your earnings will be boosted in 2017 or 2018.

Delicious!

2018 – 2020

In the next few years, increased responsibilities with children are likely. Some of you will pursue lessons or learn a technique related to acting, the performance arts, or music. Basically, this is a time when discipline and training can help you express your creativity. (Start practising those arpeggios.) You won't need much encouragement to do this, because you're unusually optimistic now. Your future seems promising! You *believe* in yourself.

In truth, although you have this optimism about your future, you're also secretly wondering what you really want to be when you grow up. You're mentally trying on different careers, and imagining yourself successful in different ways.

Some lovely news is that 2019 ushers in a time that is excellent for real-estate deals. Hopefully, you saved the scratch from the past two years, or got a better-paying job to justify a good mortgage, because this is the time to buy land. ("Buy land" was always Mark Twain's advice. "They aren't making it anymore.")

You might want to buy your own home, or land, or property for speculation. Whatever you enter into or initiate during this time (in terms of real estate) will almost surely bring you a profit in the future.

By the same token (love that token!), everything to do with your family will give you increased joy and perhaps even wealth. You'll enjoy entertaining family where you live. Your family relationships will be happier. And, in fact, your family might expand through marriage, birth, adoption, or people who visit and just never leave. (That's a tough one.) It's your fault for giving such good hotel!

This is the classic time for making major purchases or changes to your home to make you feel richer, more affluent, and more comfortable with your living space. ("Fit for a king!") Your home and family will be a greater source of joy.

Have you noticed that when things are happy at home, many other things seem to be possible? Perhaps that is why 2020 is a wonderful year for a vacation. It's also a great time to explore the

arts. (Perfect — you've been practising!) It's also a wonderful time for sports, the entertainment world, show business, and anything to do with the hospitality industry.

In addition, 2020 is a great year for romance. Ta-dah! Something fun and playful can begin. (Could it be your 20/20 vision?) Whether or not this romance turns serious is entirely up to you.

2021 – 2022

A curious thing is taking place right now: both Jupiter, the planet that represents wealth, good fortune, abundance, and increase, and Saturn, the planet that represents obstacles, limitations, restrictions, and serious learning, are in the same sign. When we look at this double whammy for your sign, we see that, in one way, you'll be working harder than ever before. In fact, this hard work will continue for the next two to three years. You'll put out so much effort that at times you'll feel overwhelmed. Nevertheless, you *will* do it.

But, at the same time, at least for the first eighteen months, lucky Jupiter is going to bring you enormous good fortune in anything that relates to your job. In other words, you might get a better job or, if you don't get a better job, you will get better duties, or a happier situation, or a better workplace. At the very least, your evil boss will be transferred to the Orkneys. However, another tangent of this influence might simply be that your attitude to your work changes. Whatever the cause, the bottom line is you will find that your work is more rewarding and more satisfying than ever before. Hopefully, it will pay better, too!

While all these good things are happening to your employment scene, your health will also improve. (With a few exceptions.) On the whole, you will feel more optimistic and buoyant, physically speaking. However, your bone structure could suffer from stiff joints. You might also need dental work during this time. (Hey, if you're going to really take a bite out of life, be prepared.)

By 2022–23, partnerships are a bonus. Existing partnerships will definitely improve in a reassuring way. Intimate partnerships will be more cozy. Professional partnerships will feel solid and reassuring. In fact, even your dealings with the general public will be more positive and more successful.

This is also a time in your life when you will feel things are coming to a head. Something reaches a culmination of sorts. You know that further hard work will make your successes more public and more easily recognized.

How sweet it is!

2023 – 2025

Now you enter a time of good fortune. In part, this is due to your hard work. But it's also due to the increased recognition and knowledge that you received last year and this year as well.

Perhaps this is why gifts, goodies, inheritances, money, favours, and benefits from others will come to you around 2023. However this happens, you will benefit from the resources and wealth of others. You can count on this! Some of you will benefit indirectly through bonuses or improved situations for your partner. Either way, you're laughing all the way to the bank.

And yes, you're still working hard. However, by 2024, things start to change. For starters, partnerships and close friendships will be challenged as never before. Those that have outlived their usefulness will probably end. Those that are meant to endure — and they will — will have to undergo major readjustments.

The year 2024 marks a *huge* change for you. That's because for the previous fourteen years, you were busy creating your inner world: your identity, your values, your home, and, finally, your work. But this year marks a time when you step out into the world in a more public way. Despite challenges with partnerships, you're moving forward! You might get recognition for something or increased acknowledgement in some way.

This is the beginning of a span of fourteen years when you will create and develop your *external* world as opposed to your *internal* world. Now your focus will be on career, public reputation, and the role you play in your community, in your city, and perhaps even in your country.

Your increased ambition and willingness to take your own power is one of the reasons existing partnerships are challenged. It's true that, at the end of the game, the pawn and the king go back in the same box, but relationships are different. You have no intention of *going back*. From 2024 onward, you're *going forward*!

This is also a great year for travel or higher education. Grab every opportunity to return to school, take courses, or learn anything that

broadens your horizons. Publishing, the media, medicine, and the law are also areas that promise positive growth and opportunities. This is an exciting time! (The last time anything similar occurred was around 1994.)

By 2025, you are riding high! Important people notice you. Opportunities from many areas are presented to you. This is your best chance in more than a decade to boost your reputation and make a name for yourself. Most of you will do this. However, some will elect to use this powerful time to change careers. If so, you may go into something related to travel, dealing with foreign countries, or a healing profession. Legal opportunities will also present themselves. If you change professions, you might not reach the level of success that this year promises; instead, you will simply have the opportunity to switch to what you really want to do.

But it's all good!

"I like living. I have sometimes been wildly, despairingly, acutely miserable, racked with sorrow, but through it all, I still know quite certainly that just to be alive is a grand thing."

AGATHA CHRISTIE
British Crime Writer
Created Hercule Poirot and Miss Jane Marple, and
Also Wrote Short Stories and Plays
The Mousetrap
(SEPTEMBER 15, 1890–JANUARY 12, 1976)

Famous Virgo Personalities

Gene Kelly	August 23, 1912–1996
Vera Miles	August 23, 1929
Barbara Eden	August 23, 1934
Keith Moon	August 23, 1946–1978
Rick Springfield	August 23, 1949
Queen Noor of Jordan	August 23, 1951
River Phoenix	August 23, 1970–1993
Jay Mohr	August 23, 1970
Eliza Carthy	August 23, 1975
Kobe Bryant	August 23, 1978
Jorge Luis Borges	August 24, 1899–1986
Arthur "Big Boy" Crudup	August 24, 1905–1974
Alex Colville	August 24, 1920
René Lévesque	August 24, 1922–1987
Yasser Arafat	August 24, 1929–2004
Kenny Baker	August 24, 1934
Stephen Fry	August 24, 1957
Steve Guttenberg	August 24, 1958
Cal Ripken, Jr.	August 24, 1960
Marlee Matlin	August 24, 1965
Chad Michael Murray	August 24, 1981
Leonard Bernstein	August 25, 1918–1990
George Wallace	August 25, 1918–1998
Monty Hall	August 25, 1921
Sean Connery	August 25, 1930
Regis Philbin	August 25, 1933
Tom Skerritt	August 25, 1933
Anne Archer	August 25, 1947
Martin Amis	August 25, 1949
Gene Simmons	August 25, 1949
Elvis Costello	August 25, 1954
Tim Burton	August 25, 1958
Billy Ray Cyrus	August 25, 1961
Blair Underwood	August 25, 1964

Rachael Ray	August 25, 1968
Claudia Schiffer	August 25, 1970
Rachel Bilson	August 25, 1981
Christopher Isherwood	August 26, 1904–1986
Mother Teresa	August 26, 1910–1997
Zipporah Dobyns	August 26, 1921–2003
Geraldine Ferraro	August 26, 1935
Rick Hansen	August 26, 1957
Branford Marsalis	August 26, 1960
Macaulay Culkin	August 26, 1980
Friedrich Hegel	August 27, 1770–1831
Alice Coltrane	August 27, 1937–2007
Tuesday Weld	August 27, 1943
Cesar Millan	August 27, 1969
Johann Wolfgang von Goethe	August 28, 1749–1832
Leo Tolstoy	August 28, 1828–1910
Robertson Davies	August 28, 1913–1995
Jack Vance	August 28, 1916
Scott Hamilton	August 28, 1958
Shania Twain	August 28, 1965
Jack Black	August 28, 1969
Jason Priestley	August 28, 1969
Ingrid Bergman	August 29, 1915–1982
Richard Attenborough	August 29, 1923
Elliot Gould	August 29, 1938
Michael Jackson	August 29, 1958–2009
Rebecca De Mornay	August 29, 1959
Todd English	August 29, 1960
Mary Shelley	August 30, 1797–1851
Raymond Massey	August 30, 1896–1983
Warren Buffett	August 30, 1930
Jean-Claude Killy	August 30, 1943
Cameron Diaz	August 30, 1972
Lisa Ling	August 30, 1973
William Saroyan	August 31, 1908–1981
Daniel Schorr	August 31, 1916
Alan Jay Lerner	August 31, 1918–1986
Van Morrison	August 31, 1945
Richard Gere	August 31, 1949
Scott Niedermayer	August 31, 1973
Sara Ramírez	August 31, 1975

Edgar Rice Burroughs	September 1, 1875–1950
Yvonne De Carlo	September 1, 1922–2007
Rocky Marciano	September 1, 1923–1969
Lily Tomlin	September 1, 1939
Gloria Estefan	September 1, 1957
Marge Champion	September 2, 1919
Terry Bradshaw	September 2, 1948
Mark Harmon	September 2, 1951
Guy Laliberté	September 2, 1959
Keanu Reeves	September 2, 1964
Salma Hayek	September 2, 1966
Sami Salo	September 2, 1974
Ferdinand Porsche	September 3, 1875–1951
Eileen Brennan	September 3, 1932
Valerie Perrine	September 3, 1943
Charlie Sheen	September 3, 1965
Shaun White	September 3, 1986
Craig Claiborne	September 4, 1920–2000
Mitzi Gaynor	September 4, 1931
Damon Wayans	September 4, 1960
Beyoncé Knowles	September 4, 1981
Darryl F. Zanuck	September 5, 1902–1979
Bob Newhart	September 5, 1929
Raquel Welch	September 5, 1940
Werner Herzog	September 5, 1942
Freddie Mercury	September 5, 1946–1991
Loudon Wainwright III	September 5, 1946
Vincent Lam	September 5, 1974
Swoosie Kurtz	September 6, 1944
Jane Curtin	September 6, 1947
Michaëlle Jean	September 6, 1957
Jeff Foxworthy	September 6, 1958
Elizabeth Vargas	September 6, 1962
Anika Noni Rose	September 6, 1972
Queen Elizabeth I of England	September 7, 1524–1603
Grandma Moses	September 7, 1860–1961
Taylor Caldwell	September 7, 1900–1985
Buddy Holly	September 7, 1936–1959
Beverley McLachlin	September 7, 1943
Evan Rachel Wood	September 7, 1987
Antonín Dvořák	September 8, 1841–1904

Grace Metalious	September 8, 1924–1964
Peter Sellers	September 8, 1925–1980
Patsy Cline	September 8, 1932–1963
David Arquette	September 8, 1971
Pink	September 8, 1979
Alexandre Bilodeau	September 8, 1987
Cliff Robertson	September 9, 1925
Otis Redding	September 9, 1941–1967
Hugh Grant	September 9, 1960
Adam Sandler	September 9, 1966
Henry Thomas	September 9, 1971
Michael Bublé	September 9, 1975
Arnold Palmer	September 10, 1929
Karl Lagerfeld	September 10, 1938
José Feliciano	September 10, 1945
Margaret Trudeau	September 10, 1948
Amy Irving	September 10, 1953
Colin Firth	September 10, 1960
D. H. Lawrence	September 11, 1885–1930
Brian De Palma	September 11, 1940
Lola Falana	September 11, 1942
Harry Connick, Jr.	September 11, 1967
Taraji P. Henson	September 11, 1970
Maurice Chevalier	September 12, 1888–1972
Jesse Owens	September 12, 1913–1980
Michael Ondaatje	September 12, 1943
Barry White	September 12, 1944–2003
Jennifer Hudson	September 12, 1981
Laura Secord	September 13, 1775–1868
Claudette Colbert	September 13, 1903–1996
Roald Dahl	September 13, 1916–1990
Jacqueline Bisset	September 13, 1944
Stella McCartney	September 13, 1971
Ivan Pavlov	September 14, 1849–1936
Margaret Sanger	September 14, 1879–1966
Walter Koenig	September 14, 1936
Sam Neill	September 14, 1957
Amy Winehouse	September 14, 1983
Agatha Christie	September 15, 1890–1976
Fay Wray	September 15, 1907–2004
Jackie Cooper	September 15, 1922

Tommy Lee Jones	September 15, 1946
Oliver Stone	September 15, 1946
Prince Harry of Wales	September 15, 1984
Alfred Noyes	September 16, 1880–1958
Lauren Bacall	September 16, 1924
Charlie Byrd	September 16, 1925–1999
B. B. King	September 16, 1925
Peter Falk	September 16, 1927
Ed Begley, Jr.	September 16, 1949
Mickey Rourke	September 16, 1952
Amy Poehler	September 16, 1971
Alexis Bledel	September 16, 1981
Mary Stewart	September 17, 1916
Hank Williams, Sr.	September 17, 1923–1953
Roddy McDowall	September 17, 1928–1998
Stirling Moss	September 17, 1929
Anne Bancroft	September 17, 1931–2005
Ken Kesey	September 17, 1935–2001
John Ritter	September 17, 1948–2003
Alexander Ovechkin	September 17, 1985
Greta Garbo	September 18, 1905–1990
Rossano Brazzi	September 18, 1916–1994
Frankie Avalon	September 18, 1939
James Gandolfini	September 18, 1961
Lance Armstrong	September 18, 1971
Jada Pinkett Smith	September 18, 1971
William Golding	September 19, 1911–1993
Cass Elliot	September 19, 1941–1974
Jeremy Irons	September 19, 1948
Twiggy	September 19, 1949
Joan Lunden	September 19, 1950
Daniel Lanois	September 19, 1951
Trisha Yearwood	September 19, 1964
Jimmy Fallon	September 19, 1974
Upton Sinclair	September 20, 1878–1968
Jelly Roll Morton	September 20, 1885–1941
Sophia Loren	September 20, 1934
Guy Lafleur	September 20, 1951
Kristen Johnston	September 20, 1967
H. G. Wells	September 21, 1866–1946
Leonard Cohen	September 21, 1934

Jerry Bruckheimer	September 21, 1945
Stephen King	September 21, 1947
Bill Murray	September 21, 1950
Faith Hill	September 21, 1967
Jim Byrnes	September 22, 1948
Andrea Bocelli	September 22, 1958
Joan Jett	September 22, 1960
Bonnie Hunt	September 22, 1961
Elizabeth Bear	September 22, 1971
Ronaldo	September 22, 1976
Tom Felton	September 22, 1987

LIBRA

SEPTEMBER 23 – OCTOBER 22

LIBRA THE SCALES
(SEPTEMBER 23 – OCTOBER 22)

"I BALANCE."

"The cup of tea on arrival at a country house is a thing which, as a rule,
I particularly enjoy. I like the crackling logs, the shaded lights, the scent of
buttered toast, the general atmosphere of leisured coziness."
P. G. WODEHOUSE
British Writer of Novels, Short Stories, and Musicals
(OCTOBER 15, 1881–FEBRUARY 14, 1975)

"Time flies like an arrow.
Fruit flies like a banana."
GROUCHO MARX
American Comedian and Film Actor
(OCTOBER 2, 1890–AUGUST 19, 1977)

Element: Air
Ruling Planet: Venus
Quality: Cardinal
Opposite Sign: Aries
Symbol: The Scales
Glyph: Scales or the Setting Sun at the Fall Equinox,
when Day and Night Are in Balance
Lucky Gems: Sapphire, Diamond, and Jade[1]
Flowers: Orchid, Foxglove, and Columbine
Colours: Blues, Pastels, and Dusty Rose
Part of the Body: The Kidneys

You Like: Refined beauty, attractive rooms, gourmet restaurants, books, music, leisure and luxury, good conversation, decorating, buying linens and beautiful clothes. You schmooze with the best of them. Not only do you like to please others, you really know how to please in bed!

You Don't Like: Ugly places, bad smells, loud noises, arguments, bigotry, unfairness, shouting, violence, and squalor. And you really don't like a bad table at a restaurant.

Where You Shine: Diplomatic, charming, conciliatory, balanced, logical, informed, graceful, fair-minded, judicious, and wise. You can make any room look better: you have a fantastic eye. (And a cute butt.)

So Who's Perfect? Lazy, dissatisfied, narcissistic, procrastinating, dependent, vacillating, inconstant, and fence-sitting. It takes too long to pick out bathroom tile. ("Just make a choice! It's not like it's written in stone — er, actually, it is.")

---

1. These are not written in stone. Astrology texts disagree about which flowers and gems are in each sign. (What can we trust in this world?)

What Is Libra-ness?[2]

To quickly grasp the essential qualities of your sign, you need to understand what your ruling planet means in astrology. Your ruling planet is Venus, the planet associated with beauty! Many people think Venus is about love and romance. While this isn't necessarily wrong, it's woefully incomplete.

Technically, Venus rules relationship (singular) — the relationship of light to dark, the relationship of colour to colour, the relationship of line to line, the relationship of texture to texture, the relationship of composition, and the relationship of word to word.

It is said that a beautiful face is a face that is symmetrical. If you cover half a face in a photo, you'll be surprised at how different the two halves look (especially if you have a Polaroid of Quasimodo). So a beautiful face has a specific "relationship" within itself. *Capisce?*

Venus is not about emotions and feelings. If you want to talk about feelings, think Jackie Gleason: "To the Moon, Alice!" The Moon is the planet[3] that rules all our emotions. Admittedly, Venus is associated with our biases. (Well, who isn't drawn to beauty?)

More than any other sign, you are hugely affected by the appearances of everything around you! The view from your window matters. You feel different if your everyday view is a yard full of parked buses or a green lawn sloping down to a lake. What you perceive through your eyes affects your vitality, your health, and your happiness.

It *matters* what you see! What colours are your walls? Is there art on the walls? How is your room furnished? Is it appealing or drab? Is your car pleasant or a rusty clunker? When you look in the mirror, do you like your appearance? What does your kitchen look like? Do you want to prepare food on those countertops? Do you like your bathroom towels? Do you look forward to getting into your bed at night?

These are not frivolous questions for Libra.

---

2. No one is just one sign because everyone's chart is made up of different planets. Therefore, this section captures the Libran archetype — the qualities of "Libra-ness." Many other signs will have Libran characteristics as well. Therefore, the discussion of one sign is not an exact description of that person; rather, it is a description of the qualities of that sign.
3. Astrologers refer to the Moon and the Sun as planets. This is another reason people make jokes and point at us.

"It is a delicious moment, certainly, that of being well nestled in bed,
and feeling that you shall drop gently to sleep . . .
the limbs have just been tired enough to render the remaining in
one posture delightful; the labour of the day is gone."

LEIGH HUNT
British Critic, Essayist, Poet, and Writer
Best Known for the Poem "Abou Ben Adhem"
(OCTOBER 19, 1784–AUGUST 28, 1859)

You are totally involved with the *facade* of your world. In fact, if you had to live in squalor, you would become physically sick. This is why you want nice linens, lovely bedding, beautiful cushions on comfortable sofas, good art on the wall, and hardcover books on shelves sitting on oriental carpets.

"Go, and never darken my towels again!"
GROUCHO MARX
American Comedian and Film Actor
(OCTOBER 2, 1890–AUGUST 19, 1977)

All Librans are interior designers. You effortlessly create beautiful spaces, because you need to be in them!

Only a Libra knows there are at least eleven shades of navy blue. Your ability to discern colours and see visual distinctions is remarkable![4]

"My clothes are predominately black and my home is predominantly white."
FRAN DRESCHER
American Television and Film Actress
Beautician and the Beast and TV's *The Nanny*
(B. SEPTEMBER 30, 1957)

If you have pots of money, you'll do something stellar with where you live. If you're broke, you will still make a room wonderfully inviting with plants, posters, and baskets. You scrimp on everyday items so you can blow a wad on a painting or one stunning piece of furniture. In fact, it's hard for you to spend money on essentials like scissors, hammers, or rakes, yet you easily buy stemware and fresh flowers. (Every Libran knows if you put out fresh flowers, you don't have to dust.)

---

4. The Coen brothers created the movie *The Big Lebowski*. One of its memorable lines is "That rug really tied the room together." Ethan Coen (b. September 21, 1957) was born on the cusp of Libra and has Jupiter in Libra. He is making fun of Libran sensibilities! But the actor who played Jeffrey Lebowski, Jeff Bridges, has no Libra in his chart (except for Neptune, which applies to almost everyone born in the 1940s.) This is why we don't believe him when he says that line.

Your beautiful ambience obviously includes sound, which is why you love music! It soothes and transports you, and you use it to create the mood you want.

Consider these famous Librans:

John Coltrane	September 23, 1926–1967	John Lennon	October 9, 1940–1980
Ray Charles	September 23, 1930–2004	Sharon Osbourne	October 9, 1952
Julio Iglesias	September 23, 1943	Sean Lennon	October 9, 1975
Bruce Springsteen	September 23, 1949	Giuseppe Verdi	October 10, 1813–1901
Glenn Gould	September 25, 1932–1982	Thelonious Monk	October 10, 1917–1982
George Gershwin	September 26, 1898–1937	James "Midge" Ure	October 10, 1953
Marty Robbins	September 26, 1925–1982	Tanya Tucker	October 10, 1958
Olivia Newton-John	September 26, 1948	Luciano Pavarotti	October 12, 1935–2007
Randy Bachman	September 27, 1943	Hugh Jackman	October 12, 1965
Shaun Cassidy	September 27, 1958	Yves Montand	October 13, 1921–1991
Jerry Lee Lewis	September 29, 1935	Nana Mouskouri	October 13, 1934
Madeline Kahn	September 29, 1942–1999	Paul Simon	October 13, 1941
Johnny Mathis	September 30, 1935	Natalie Maines	October 14, 1974
Julie Andrews	October 1, 1935	Usher Raymond	October 14, 1978
Sting	October 2, 1951	Chuck Berry	October 18, 1926
Chubby Checker	October 3, 1941	Tom Petty	October 20, 1950
Stevie Ray Vaughan	October 3, 1954–1990	Dizzy Gillespie	October 21, 1917–1993
Tommy Lee	October 3, 1962	Franz Liszt	October 22, 1811–1886
Steve Miller	October 5, 1943	Annette Funicello	October 22, 1942
Bob Geldof	October 5, 1951		

Libra is also the sign that rules haute couture and fashion. You know what colour is in season, but you aren't trendy. Yet you always look pulled together and colour-co-ordinated. If you ran out of a burning building in the middle of the night, grabbing clothes on the way, you'd be the only one on the street who looked "dressed."

"It's very important to have the right clothing to exercise in. If you throw on an old T-shirt or sweats, it's not inspiring for your workout."

CHERYL TIEGS

American Model and Actress

(B. SEPTEMBER 25, 1947)

When two Librans dine out, they often agree to wait for a better table. You truly appreciate good conversation in beautiful surroundings — the rich life of epicurean leisure!

The Libran Scales

The symbol for Libra is the scales, which indicates there's a constant balancing act going on inside you. You might think the scales mean you're the most balanced people. Sorry to disappoint. It means you're constantly *striving* for balance and harmony.

These scales of justice also symbolize that Libra is the sign that rules lawyers and the legal system: the relationship of word to word, or the rights of the individual versus society, or the rights of one person versus another.

Plus Librans are given to verbosity and rhetoric. You take twenty words to say what others say in five. For example, "No" is "I hardly think so" or "I doubt that very much."

You weigh your words carefully, choosing the one with just the right nuance (which is why many of you are great writers). If Libra rules the law and rhetoric and fashion — connect the dots. A little wager?

There are two conferences going on in a large hotel. One ballroom is full of lawyers, and the other ballroom is full of engineers. In which ballroom are the main speakers likely to wear stylish suspenders? And in which ballroom are you more likely to find a pair of Christian Louboutin heels?

I rest my handbag.

Unfortunately, these Libran choices (the profession of law combined with beautiful clothes, cars, and jewellery) make you the butt of jokes like this:

> Just as a lawyer was getting into his new BMW convertible, a big semi-trailer sideswiped him. Within minutes, a cop was on the scene, where he found the lawyer bemoaning the wrecked door to his car. The cop looked at him incredulously and said, "I can't believe how materialistic you are! You're worried about losing your car door, and your arm is ripped off?" Stunned, the lawyer looked down and screamed, "My Rolex!"

Almost all great lawyers will have Libra in them — their Sun, Moon, Mercury, Venus, or Mars is in Libra, or perhaps they are Libra Rising. Pierre Trudeau (October 18, 1919–September 28, 2000) was a double Libra, which means he was a Libra with Libra Rising.[5] The media constantly remarked on the flair and flamboyance in his dress. Who can forget his buckskin jacket? And he always wore a rose in his lapel.

---

5. Check out the chart on page 5 if you know the time of day you were born to discover your Rising Sign.

Four Ways to Spot a Libra

Libra is a subtle and complex sign, but these four buzzwords will help you get a handle on this sign:

1. Teeter-Totter
2. Fence-Sitting
3. Contradictions
4. Social Conscience

Teeter-Totter

When you go to a playground, you can swing on a swing, slide down the slide, or do many things by yourself. But the minute you get on a teeter-totter, you need somebody on the other end. This is you. (Ideally, the other person is romantic and well-dressed. You like their choices in furniture and music, and they pay all the bills.)

> "The pleasure of reading is doubled when one lives
> with another who shares the same books."
> **KATHERINE MANSFIELD**
> New Zealand–Born Short Story Writer
> "The Garden Party," "The Doll's House," and "The Fly"
> (OCTOBER 14, 1888–JANUARY 9, 1923)

But everything in life is not ideal. Whether you live with someone or not, you need a running mate. You don't do solo. If you go to a movie, a restaurant, a concert, an event, or just shopping for groceries, you like someone along for company. Even if you're at home working, you find it comforting to know someone is off in another room.

Of course, many Librans do live alone. You even tell yourself how much you enjoy it. But if you could have your druthers (I never leave home without my druthers), you'd prefer to watch TV with someone, enjoy your dinner with someone, or drive somewhere with someone. It's the teeter-totter thang.

This is important to know, because your need for company shapes your behaviour. For starters, you're a pleaser. You ingratiate yourself to others. You're courteous and thoughtful. You're an excellent listener. You respect the privacy of others. You know how to entertain and make others happy, because this way you're a desirable companion! (Pretty shallow, huh?)

Librans are the most charming, articulate, witty, and delightful people to be with! *You are dessert!*

Not only do you charm but you're also attractive, handsome, and beautiful. (It's the Venus thang.) Right from the cradle, you learned how to please others with your appearance, personality, and lifestyle. Everyone wants to be in your company!

"Waaaait a minute! This makes me sound like a piece of dressed-up bait!" (You're right. My apologies, because you are so much more.)

Remember the scales? You strive to find balance. You don't want tension, conflict, and people yelling and swearing. "Who does?" you ask. Actually, many love adventure and passionate intensity. Whereas, you want a good table at a nice restaurant. You prefer stylish comfort. (To you, outdoors is where the car is.)

Therefore, you need people in your life because you like to feel *connected*. It's comforting.

Fence-Sitting

Actually, "Fence-Sitting" technically comes under the Teeter-Totter category, but, after a lot of indecision and waffling back and forth, I finally decided to give it its own section so as to explore it more fully. I hope this is the right approach. I mean, it definitely is an aspect of the Teeter-Totter section, so there's no question that, in many respects, it should remain in the Teeter-Totter category. But there is also no denying that the particular emphasis it deserves might be swallowed up by the sweeping notion of partnerships, which is so intrinsic to the Teeter-Totter part. And, hey — you're definitely not a fence-sitter when it comes to partnerships! Well, except sometimes you can be. You do want a partner in your life, we know this. Of course, we know this. The key of course is, which one? And, hey, what about when you are with someone and then later you're not so sure about them any more — aaagghh, I hate that part, don't you? But then it's such a drag to bring all this up (as if anyone wants to hear this!).

Others call this indecisiveness. I prefer "fence-sitting." "Indecisiveness" sounds almost handicapped or something. Hello? Would you apply the word "handicapped" to this group of Librans?

Lech Wałesa	September 29, 1943
Jimmy Carter	October 1, 1924
Mahatma Gandhi	October 2, 1869 – January 30, 1948
Niels Bohr	October 7, 1885 – November 18, 1962
Eleanor Roosevelt	October 11, 1884 – November 7, 1962
Margaret Thatcher	October 13, 1925
Dwight D. Eisenhower	October 14, 1890 – March 28, 1969
Friedrich Nietzsche	October 15, 1844 – August 25, 1900
John Kenneth Galbraith	October 15, 1908 – April 29, 2006

Arthur Schlesinger	October 15, 1917 – February 28, 2007
Pierre Elliot Trudeau	October 18, 1919 – September 28, 2000
Nellie McClung	October 20, 1873 – September 1, 1951
Tommy Douglas	October 20, 1904 – February 24, 1986

Confess: you do delay your decision-making process. And here are four reasons why:

1. You hate to upset others.
2. Because you're intelligent, you see more parameters to any situation. What looks simple to some looks complex to you.
3. You don't want to make a wrong decision! (Drum roll. Stage left — Enter, limping: "The Mistake.")
4. What appears as indecisiveness is really your need to talk things out. You ask everyone for advice, because when you verbalize your thoughts out loud you clarify things in your own mind.[6] You also want to sift their responses. Will you take their advice? No! You just want more input to digest.

I have a friend named Sonam who had a lovely shop in Kitsilano, the hippie neighbourhood in Vancouver. She sold books, baskets, clothing, cards, jewellery, and a fascinating array of lovely little bibelots. A Libran shop!

She had a trick to help indecisive customers.

"What I would do," she said, "is take the ring and the bracelet and put one in each hand, and put them behind my back, and say, 'Left hand or right hand?'"

The customer would choose one hand, and I would bring that hand out and open it. If they were happy — great! If they were disappointed, then I would open the other hand and say, "So this is your choice!"

6. You know how your worries are sort of like vague grumblings and rumblings in some deep recess of your brain? Sometimes when I finally voice what my concerns are, I don't even agree with me!

Not to decide is to decide.

Fence-Sitting Leads to Contradictions and Close Dancing

You have contradictions as you strive for balance. The harmony you seek ain't necessarily so! Consider these contradictions:

- Harmony versus Debate
- Perfection versus Laissez-faire
- Fence-Sitting versus Impulsiveness

HARMONY VERSUS DEBATE

You love serenity. You want to please and get along. And yet you can argue so vehemently, you leave others stunned, with their mouths gaping, gasping for breath. (Whaaat?)

Who's surprised? Libra is the sign that represents the law. The most dynamic, forceful, successful lawyers and judges have Libra in them. You can be so convincing, you're scary!

This often disturbs you because you want to keep the peace, but you can't remain silent in the face of stupidity or injustice. Afterwards you chide yourself for speaking out. But if you don't speak up, you will lose your self-respect. It's not easy being you!

PERFECTION VERSUS LAISSEZ-FAIRE

You take great pains to make where you live look attractive. Then, suddenly, you let the dishes pile up. You don't get dressed; you hang out in your robe or your pyjamas.[7] Magazines and newspapers are strewn everywhere. It all goes to hell! (You know who you are.)[8] Then one day, you leap up and beautifully pull the place together.

If you ever have the misfortune to undergo a flood or a fire, you will work tirelessly to return your home to its former glory. Likewise, when you move into a new place, you instantly create a home that functions with everything in its place.

"My gawd, the place looks great! When did you move in here?"

"This morning. But it's not finished; I had to meet some friends across town for lunch."

Another area where you're rather bizarre is money. You economize and keep track of finances. Then you're insanely casual! You go from caring a lot to caring hardly at all. It's because security is not what drives you. You want to have a beautiful life!

---

7. I recall reading an article in the *New York Times* about Anne Rice (b. October 4, 1941), who apparently writes in pink and blue flowered flannel nightgowns, of which she has dozens at the ready, still wrapped in plastic.
8. My bachelor son with Venus in Libra does this frequently. In fact, one of these strikes is going on right now as I write these words. He says he's going to need hip waders and a gas mask to enter his kitchen. If this continues, his sister and I are going to do an intervention.

Your approach to sleep is also bizarre. Most of you are night owls. Most of you sleep less than others. You party and work, and party and work, then suddenly you collapse (or faint!) and sleep for hours. You believe you have a right to your own leisure. Librans are good about coddling themselves. (Despite the disapproving gaze of Capricorns who wonder if you're going to get dressed before sunset.)

> "I love to not work. I like to travel. I work maybe half the year, no more."
> CATHERINE DENEUVE
> French Actress
> *Belle de Jour*
> (B. OCTOBER 22, 1943)

INDECISIVENESS VERSUS IMPULSIVENESS

You know you're indecisive. It's a well-known Libran trait. Nevertheless, you are a Cardinal sign (Aries, Cancer, Libra, and Capricorn are the four Cardinal signs). This means sometimes you move swiftly and make snappy decisions! (Whaaat? Yes, you!) You suddenly invite people along or initiate parties. And you think fast on your feet!

I think Libra is full of more paradoxes than any other sign.

In 1981, I travelled to Portland, Oregon, to hear a wonderful teacher speak. At the end of the talk, someone raised their hand and asked, "What do you do if you fall in love with someone and it's completely inappropriate?"

The teacher looked at him and said:

"If you act with discipline, you will have no regrets.
So if you do something and you don't regret it,
then you acted with discipline.
And if you do something (the same thing) and you regret it,
then you didn't act with discipline.
And if you don't do something and you don't regret it,
then you acted with discipline.
And if you don't do something and you regret it,
then you didn't act with discipline."

At the end of the talk, I knew the teacher would pass in front of me since I was in the front row. I wanted to prostrate to him to show my respect, but I was afraid others would roll their eyes and think, Check out the holy roller.

Then, I thought of what he had just said about acting with discipline. I asked myself, "If I get down on my knees in public, will I regret it?" I decided, yikes, I might.

Then I thought, "If I don't get down on my knees, will I regret it?" And I instantly realized I might definitely regret it! What if I never had another chance to show my gratitude and respect to this person? So I got down on my knees.

Less than a year later, that wonderful teacher was killed in a car accident.

About ten years later, on Salt Spring Island in British Columbia, I ran into the very guy who had asked the question. I went up to him and said, "I am so glad you asked that question years ago in Portland!"

He said, "What question?"

"Remember, at the end of the talk, when you asked, 'What do you do if you fall in love with somebody, and it's completely inappropriate?'"

"Oh yeah." Recognition slowly dawned in his eyes. "What did he say?"

Social Conscience

> "I am still looking for the modern equivalent of those
> Quakers who ran successful businesses, made money because they offered
> honest products, and treated their people decently . . .
> This business creed, sadly, seems long forgotten."
> ANITA RODDICK
> Founder of The Body Shop
> (OCTOBER 23, 1942–SEPTEMBER 10, 2007)

Several years ago, a Libran reader wrote to me in indignation saying, "There's more to us than good linens and great restaurants!" Of course, she was totally right.

Librans are vibrant activists, whistle-blowers, and passionate freedom fighters who work to defend and protect the civil rights of others. Because you have an innate sense of justice, and because you are an excellent debater, and because you are intelligent, and because many of you have legal training (although this is not a prerequisite) — you are incredibly effective at defending the civil liberties of humankind!

Even at the most casual level, you sign petitions, fire off emails, attend meetings and rallies, and support numerous causes to fight injustice. Because of your penchant for legal thinking, you're quick to become involved in the political process of your town, city, country, or even the world.

Consider the following Librans who worked and continue to work to make a difference for everyone:

Samuel Adams (September 16, 1722–October 2, 1803). Statesman, political philosopher, and one of the Founding Fathers of the United States.

John Marshall (September 24, 1755–July 6, 1835). Longest serving chief justice of the United States; he shaped American constitutional law and made the Supreme Court a centre of power.

Edith Abbott (September 26, 1876–July 28, 1957). American economist, social worker, educator, and author.

Brigitte Bardot (b. September 28, 1934). French animal rights activist and former actress, fashion model, and singer.

Lech Wałesa (b. September 29, 1943). Charismatic Polish politician, president of Poland (1990–1995), and trade union and human rights activist. Winner of the 1983 Nobel Peace Prize.

Jimmy Carter (b. October 1, 1924). President of the United States (1977–1981) and recipient of the 2002 Nobel Peace Prize.

Mahatma Gandhi (October 2, 1869–January 30, 1948). Spiritual and political leader of India's independence movement.

Susan Sarandon (b. October 4, 1946). American actress noted for her social and political activism.

Bob Geldof (b. October 5, 1951). Irish singer, songwriter, author, and political activist, known for his anti-poverty efforts concerning Africa.

Desmond Tutu (b. October 7, 1931). South African cleric, activist, and opponent of apartheid. Winner of the 1984 Nobel Peace Prize.

Jesse Jackson (b. October 8, 1941). American civil rights activist and Baptist minister.

Daniel Pearl (October 10, 1963–February 1, 2002). South Asia bureau chief of the *Wall Street Journal* who was kidnapped, tortured, and murdered by Al-Qaeda.

James "Midge" Ure (b. October 10, 1953). Musician and chef who co-organized Live Aid, Band Aid, and Live 8 to raise funds for famine in Africa.

Sir George Williams (October 11, 1821–1905). Founder of the YMCA.

Eleanor Roosevelt (October 11, 1884–November 7, 1962). First lady of the United States (1933–1945), author, speaker, and civil rights advocate.

Lenny Bruce (October 13, 1925–August 3, 1966). Influential and controversial American stand-up comedian, writer, social critic, and satirist.

William Penn (October 14, 1644–July 30, 1718). British-American real-estate entrepreneur (in Pennsylvania), philosopher, and early advocate of democracy and religious freedom.

Tim Robbins (b. October 16, 1958). American actor, screenwriter, director, producer, activist, and musician.

Rick Mercer (b. October 17, 1969). Canadian comedian, television personality, political satirist, and blogger.

Pierre Elliott Trudeau (October 18, 1919–September 28, 2000). Flamboyant and controversial prime minister of Canada who established the Charter of Rights and Freedoms in the Canadian constitution.

Patricia Ireland (b. October 19, 1945). U.S. administrator, feminist, and former president of the National Organization for Women (1991–2001).

Nellie McClung (October 20, 1873–September 1, 1951). Canadian feminist, politician, and social activist.

Tommy Douglas (October 20, 1904–February 24, 1986). Baptist minister who became leader of the Saskatchewan Co-operative Commonwealth Federation (CCF), leader of the New Democratic Party, and premier of Saskatchewan (1944–1961). Introduced universal public health care to Canada.

Deepak Chopra (b. October 22, 1946). American physician born in India; author and lecturer on Ayurveda, spirituality, and mind-body medicine. Former leader of the Transcendental Meditation movement.

Anita Roddick (October 23, 1942–September 10, 2007). British businesswoman, human rights activist, and environmental campaigner. Founder of The Body Shop, a cosmetics company that shaped ethical consumerism.

Librans will never let their love of beauty and the arts diminish their respect for justice and excellence. This is because Libra is essentially a social sign — a sign that loves people. Librans believe everyone should have a fair shake — and they believe this passionately.

"A man must be willing to die for justice. Death is an inescapable reality and men die daily, but good deeds live forever."
JESSE JACKSON
American Civil Rights Activist and Baptist Minister
(B. OCTOBER 8, 1941)

Libra in Love

"I once had a rose named after me and I was very flattered.
But I was not pleased to read the description in the catalogue:
no good in a bed, but fine up against a wall."

ELEANOR ROOSEVELT

First Lady of the United States of America (1933–1945)
and Prominent Author, Speaker, and Civil Rights Advocate
(OCTOBER 11, 1884–NOVEMBER 7, 1962)

All Librans are cultured. You have a refined appreciation of beauty and art. You also have a smooth gentleness. All of this comes into play when you decide to woo somebody — or be wooed. You are incredibly and tenderly romantic!

Naturally, you focus on the setting for your romantic divertissements. You will choose a wonderful restaurant, or a beautiful park, or a deluxe hotel, or you'll entertain at home with soft lighting, candles, smooth jazz, and plumped-up pillows on overstuffed furniture. Champagne and chocolate-dipped strawberries sit gleaming on a silver tray. Every detail is beautiful — the stemware, plates, napkins, flower arrangements, low lighting, and soft music. (Sigh.)

You looooove this stuff!

Nothing is too much trouble, because creating a magical reality (especially for you and your lover) is great fun! Since you're sensitive to your surroundings, you're a master at knowing how to set the right mood for a night of romantic reverie. And who more than you has a subtle appreciation of lighting, colours, textures, and fragrances?

Here is the "bare naked"[9] truth: Librans have elevated lovemaking to an art form. You are the most considerate, thoughtful, generous lover, who knows how to please your partner.

On top of this, many of you can cook! Roger Moore doing James Bond in a tuxedo epitomizes the smooth charm that Librans offer as a prelude to whatever they have planned.

Librans are knowledgeable, sophisticated, suave, charming, and wonderful conversationalists. And they're great listeners! Anyone in love with a Libra will think he or she is in heaven. You don't like coarseness, rudeness, or jarring notes. You want to enjoy relaxed leisure in comfortable surroundings.

---

9. Isn't every child redundantly bare naked? I certainly was.

Both sexes are unusually attractive. Libras have refined features and graceful movements. They're alluringly seductive. And they dress so well!

Your romantic style is a cliché copied by movies. Hollywood might be a Leo business, but its romantic lore is based on Libra know-how. Just consider a mere half-dozen Libra men and women:

Julio Iglesias	September 23, 1943
Marcello Mastroianni	September 28, 1924–December 19, 1996
Hugh Jackman	October 12, 1968
Yves Montand	October 13, 1921–November 9, 1991
Roger Moore	October 14, 1927
Ralph Lauren	October 14, 1939
Brigitte Bardot	September 28, 1934
Dita Von Teese	September 28, 1972
Angie Dickinson	September 30, 1931
Britt Ekland	October 6, 1942
Bianca Beauchamp	October 14, 1977
Catherine Deneuve	October 22, 1943

What a lineup! Dazzling, isn't it? The men are so handsome, they are almost pretty. The women are luscious in soft, appealing ways. They all have that gentle come-hither look. Wow!

And here is the amazing part: Librans are looking for partners! This seems to be too good to be true, because you are such a catch!

But life is never really that simple, is it? While it's true you're a catch (and, believe me, you are), your challenge is that you so strongly need to have someone on the other end of your teeter-totter, you compromise too much to maintain this arrangement. Librans will overlook a lot of indifference and abuse to stay in a relationship. You hate splitting up with anyone. This is because your ruler, Venus, wants to bring things together, not split them apart. Furthermore, you hate arguing and conflict. (Yeah, yeah, you can argue and debate with the best of them, but you don't like fighting.)

Therefore, you settle to keep the peace. You might have a relationship that goes on for years that is superficial but safe. It's predictable; it's polite; it's convenient. (Many movies depict a Libran love gone stale.)

The Inertia Thang

Oh yeah, the inertia thang. You find it hard to get out the door to get to work; and once you're at work, you stay late because you find it hard to get out the door to go home. You "stay" a lot. This same quality can keep you in a stagnant relationship.

This is also why Librans remain with their partners even though they're not always constant. (Oh, you try to be.) To actually split the partnership is too painful. It's like amputation.

Many of you marry more than once because you often marry young. And you remarry because you need someone on the other end of your teeter-totter.

> "I'm the only man in the world with a marriage
> license made out to whom it may concern."
> MICKEY ROONEY
> American Film Actor and Entertainer Who Has Married Eight Times
> (B. SEPTEMBER 23, 1920)

Some of you marry early and stay faithful, while others believe that chaste makes waste.

> "It is better to be unfaithful than to be faithful without wanting to be."
> BRIGITTE BARDOT
> French Actress and Activist
> (B. SEPTEMBER 28, 1934)

It's ironic that despite all the glamour that is associated with you, in the last analysis, what you want most in life is a cozy friendship with your lover. You enjoy sharing your life with someone! You want someone you can nudge in the night and someone you can have coffee with no matter how bleary-eyed you each are. You want to share your life with someone you love. In this respect, I think you are truly the most romantic of all the signs.

> "We spend so much time together, because that's how we like it.
> I never used to go on girls' nights out, even at school. And Paul has never
> liked going out for a night with the boys, either."
> LINDA McCARTNEY
> American Photographer, Musician, and Animal Rights Activist
> Married to Musician Paul McCartney, Who Is Late Virgo Rising —
> Almost Libra Rising — and Therefore Shares Birth Traits of Both Signs
> (SEPTEMBER 24, 1941–APRIL 17, 1998)

The Libra Boss

The Libra boss is tactful, diplomatic, fair-minded, and well-dressed. These are qualities that Libras value and personally exhibit. This means if you have any kind of reasonable objection to anything, you will get a sympathetic ear.

Basically, Libra is pretty easygoing in a position of authority. This is because the Libra boss wants to be liked, so they are loath to say something others don't want to hear. Nevertheless, they're not pushovers, even though they will overlook a lot. One thing they will not tolerate, however, is dissension in their group. No feuds! Libra bosses want everybody to get along. They also want their employees to be respectful of their surroundings. Librans hate slobs. (Even though they can "let things go" now and then themselves.) Wise employees of this boss will take extra care with their appearance.

If you deliver the goods, and you are polite and neat in your surroundings, and you don't cause problems, the Libra boss will give you plenty of leeway. They don't like people who rock the boat — or offend.

If you work directly for a Libra boss, of course, you might be frustrated because you can't get a fast decision. They take too long to make up their mind, or they change their mind, or they just delay, delay, delay. Librans are great procrastinators. Learn to live with it.

One curious thing: Librans don't like to discuss money. If you have to ask for a raise or complain about a budget, your Libra boss might hide behind sophisticated, diplomatic phrases that later leave you standing in the hallway wondering, "What the hell?" And you didn't get the money! If you have to make a financial plea, do it in writing. This gives your Libra boss time to think.

Librans are one of the best bosses when it comes to office parties, treats to lunch, or perks like pizza at the end of the day. That's because it's the Libran nature to entertain in style. Also, the Libra boss likes to lunch well, and always needs a luncheon companion. (Bonus!)

Furthermore, your Libran boss will create a pleasant environment that he or she likes to work in. (Unless your boss is in the penthouse and you are in the sub-basement.) Actually, the Libra boss is always aware of the ambience where their employees work.

Female Libran bosses are tougher to work for than male bosses, because the female Libran tends to be more ambitious than the male. Nevertheless, Libra is a fun-loving, contented sign, and certainly not a sign that is looking for trouble.

The Libra Employee

The Libra employee is a pleasant employee, because Librans like to get along with others. They don't want to rock the boat. They like to keep everybody happy. That's why they know how to please. Librans are marvellous in positions of service, or public relations, or event planning. And they have superb taste! Always consult them about office decor or how to decorate a space for an event.

It's important to remember this when it comes to their own working conditions. Librans cannot be productive in a drab space! They want good lighting, windows, nice furnishings, and, above all, a place that smells fresh.

Because every Libra is a Philadelphia lawyer at heart, they're not going to follow stupid orders or go along with stupid ideas. You have to do your homework and know what you're doing before you ask them to do something. Nevertheless, the Libra employee likes to please his or her boss.

When it comes to wily office politics, your Libra employee will probably be in the thick of things, because Librans like to schmooze. They talk to everyone, keeping their finger on the pulse of everything, because, basically, they are political animals!

So here is the paradox: the Libra boss hates office feuds, but Libran employees can instigate them under the guise of wanting everybody to get along. This is such a slippery slope!

It's been my observation that no matter how good you are at your job, if management doesn't like you — you'll be fired. And no matter how bad you are at your job (short of stealing), if management loves you — you'll keep your job. This is why Librans rarely get fired: Librans know how to be likable. Actually, Librans *are* likable. (What's not to like?)

The Libra Parent

The Libra parent is one of the best parents of the zodiac! To begin with, Librans are fun-loving, easygoing people. Naturally, they love to play with children and take them out to fun places, beautiful parks, and restaurants for treats, because this is what Libran parents like to do anyway. Libran parents take their kids swimming, skiing, to the movies, to the theatre, and always out to interesting places to eat.

More importantly, Librans are intelligent and fair-minded. Therefore, the Libran parent is fair in their judgements and pronouncements regarding guidance, discipline, and what is expected. Libran parents don't like fighting and misery! They will make great efforts to keep everybody happy so that there is harmony at home.

Naturally, the children of Libran parents are well-dressed and have the nicest bedrooms their parents can afford. In addition, these children will grow up in a pleasant environment surrounded by beautiful things.

Because the Libran parent is naturally artistic, they will offer all kinds of creative opportunities to their children — pottery lessons, acting classes, dance workshops, photography.

Libran parents are quite indulgent with their children. They will sacrifice to give their children beautiful things, because they believe these beautiful things empower their children.

Another big plus about Libran parents is that they are rarely coarse, or in a bad mood, or too demanding. Because Libran parents want harmony in the household, they generally exhibit qualities of reasonableness as a role model themselves.

Their love of politics encourages meetings like "family councils" or family discussions about how something should be done. Everybody gets a vote. Everybody has a voice. Fair play and honesty are big values in this household.

The Libra Child

"There is always one moment in childhood when the door
opens and lets the future in."
DEEPAK CHOPRA
Indian-American Physician, Author, and Lecturer on Spirituality
(B. OCTOBER 22, 1946)

The Libran child is a sensitive little child, and this should be respected right from the beginning. To begin with, this child needs a harmonious environment and pleasant surroundings. This does not take money. However, do let this child have input into the way their bedroom looks. (Or where their little place is.) When my daughter was three years old, I brought home a sample book of wallpaper to let her choose the paper for her bedroom. Knowing her room could end up classically "bathroom" or "kitchen" — I nevertheless persevered. To my delight (and relief) she chose a beautiful floral design that I remember to this day.[10]

Always remember your Libran child is affected by two things at home: (1) the *physical ambience*; i.e., the colours, the smells, the kind of furniture, etc., and (2) the *emotional ambience*; i.e., the levels of friction and conflict or love and laughter in the home.

Anyone who reads this will say, "Surely, this applies to every child!" And that is true. But I assure you it applies ten times more to a Libran child. Their level of vitality, development, and confidence is hugely influenced by their immediate surroundings.

Libra rules the kidneys. Therefore, it's important to encourage Libran children to drink water — lots of water.

Sleeping habits greatly vary for Librans. Your Libran child might be a night owl or need far less sleep than you think. My parents had given up on enforcing my bedtime by the time I was twelve. From then on, I was the last to go to bed. For this, I was very grateful. I am still a night owl.

Another thing parents must be aware of with Libran children is how much their wardrobe matters! Even at a young age, they know which items of clothing they prefer. They can be very proud of what they're wearing. This is not silly vanity. The whole notion of clothing and the beauty of clothes is the domain of Libra. Even if you are not "interested" in clothes — history has demonstrated there is great importance attributed to clothing and dress in different cultures and countries. Clothes matter!

---

10. As a Libra Rising, I was the Libra parent.

However, the most important thing you can do for your Libran child is minimize the amount of yelling, arguing, and conflict in the household. Of course, your Libran child needs hugging and love like every child. But you should know that the Libran child is more traumatized by listening to fighting than some other children would be.

Finally, if you can handle this — let your Libran kids have input into your living-room arrangement and how your home looks. (If they want to.) I bet they're dying to get their hands on the place! (Their first fumbling attempts won't be attractive — but, hey, you gotta start somewhere.)

How to Be a Happier Libra

"No one can make you feel inferior without your consent."
ELEANOR ROOSEVELT
First Lady of the United States of America (1933–1945)
and Prominent Author, Speaker, and Civil Rights Advocate
(OCTOBER 11, 1884–NOVEMBER 7, 1962)

Nobody is just one sign. Astrology doesn't work that way. We are actually complicated cocktails of different signs. Nevertheless, if you have your Sun in Libra or you're Libra Rising, it's important to be aware that you are not a loner. To put it simply — you need company.

If you are alone because you cannot find the love of your life or your perfect partner, please remember this is an imperfect world, full of very imperfect people, including you and me. If you can't have the surf-and-turf special, are you going to have a bowl of soup or are you going to starve?

Now your guard is up. "You're telling me to compromise. You're telling me to lower my standards!"

Actually, I'm not suggesting you lower your standards. I'm suggesting you raise them. Do not be too hasty to judge who you think should be your company. Just go out and be friendly! Talk to the people you encounter every day in a warm, friendly way, and be ready to initiate a friendship. This person doesn't have to become your lover. You don't have to end up living with them. But you might.

Librans who deny the teeter-totter principle will be unhappy. Draw others into your life! Meet them for lunch, for coffee, for dinner. Invite people home. The media have made us fearful. But, in the main, society is made up of people like you who are basically friendly. This isn't being naive — it's the truth. Go out your front door and see for yourself. Once you have a good friend, you will be much, much happier! Naturally, this person will not be perfect. Who is?

You also cannot ignore that you're hugely affected by your surroundings. Acknowledge this, accept this, and work with it. As often as you can afford to, buy yourself fresh flowers. Polish your furniture. Keep things tidy where you live and where you work. Do not — I repeat, do not — underestimate how much this will benefit you and make you happier and stronger.

Make the effort to surround yourself with beauty. This is not a lofty aim. I'm not talking *Architectural Digest*. I'm talking everyday life. The container that holds your soap in the bathroom can be pretty. Your salt and pepper shakers can be attractive. Make your furniture comfortable and pleasing to the eye with cushions, fabrics, curtains, drapes — whatever. Get area rugs, plants, wicker baskets, floor lamps, table lamps, beautiful pictures or posters — ones that make you feel good — get it all!

The dishes you use every day should be dishes you like to see. If they're dull and boring, get different ones! So often we have a jumble of mismatched cups and plates that have accrued over the years in our kitchen. I say get rid of them! Buy a matching set of something you really like. Surprisingly, everyday dishes don't cost that much. (The toughest part is getting rid of what you already have.) Ditto for your cutlery.

Maybe you're an enlightened Libran living in a beautiful environment. Great! If so, visit museums, art galleries, and beautiful buildings. Treat yourself to lunch or dinner in nice restaurants. Enjoy gardens and parks. If you can travel, take a trip. You vibrate and respond to your surroundings. If you fall into a rut, even a beautiful velvet rut, *you will get stale.* Don't do this to yourself!

Never forget the final frontier: your mind. What are you doing to stimulate your mind? You are an Air Sign, which basically means you are an intellectual. You love stimulating ideas, and most of all you love lively conversations where you can exchange these ideas! If necessary, take a class. Learn a new language, or take a flower-arranging class, or study the fine art of wine. (I am a Sudoku addict.)

In a nutshell, if you have pleasant surroundings, and someone you like for good company, and stimulating conversation with elegant meals, you're styling!

We All Have Our Contradictions

I think Libra more than any other sign has the ability to hold two opposing ideas. Think of the Libran scales of justice. How else can a great Libra lawyer fervently defend a client they know is guilty?

> "The test of a first-rate intelligence is the ability to hold two opposed ideas in the mind at the same time . . ."
> F. SCOTT FITZGERALD
> American Novelist and Short Story Writer
> *The Great Gatsby, The Beautiful and the Damned,* and *Tender Is the Night*
> (SEPTEMBER 24, 1896–DECEMBER 21, 1940)

The teeter-totter reference was a reminder that you need company in your life. But here's the catch: because of your need for others, you often give up your individuality and your power just to stay in a relationship. Might this not be too high a price?

When I was married in my twenties, I did a mind-meld with my husband. I actually stopped reading poetry and listening to music because he wasn't into it. I did what "we" did. It took me a decade to wake up and assert myself.

Libra is the classic sign for "disappearing" into a relationship, because Librans want the comfort of connectedness. Be wary! Librans are also loath to get out of a bad relationship because they hate to "do this" to the other person, and they are also afraid of being alone.

Reality check! Life is short (and fat). Time is what life is. You are born, time flies, then you die. If you are spending your time in a relationship that is not what you want, why waste your life this way? And remember that inertia is a big thing for you. You find it so it easy to just stay where you are.

Wake up and smell the coffee. Joseph Campbell, who was Libra Rising, said, "I don't believe people are looking for the meaning of life as much as they are looking for the experience of being alive." Amen.

LIBRA
YOUR 40-YEAR HOROSCOPE
1985 ~ 2025

Why Go into the Past?

I want you to believe and have faith in your predictions so you can derive benefit from them in guiding your future. The only way you can believe what I say is to test it for yourself. This is why I start with brief highlights from the past. If anything in these past twenty-five years resonates with you, then what I say about your future will have the same validity. It is all one long timeline — your life.

The past predictions generally apply once you have left home or are "running your life" and making your own decisions. Prior to that, the major events in your life were dictated by other people, likely your parents.

1985 ~ 1990

Since 1980, you'd been on a completely new journey. (Prior to that you said goodbye to a lot.) By 1985, life was looking much happier! This was a great time (give or take a year or two) for vacations, love affairs, romance — all the fun stuff. By 1986, you had an opportunity to improve your health and your job, which was good, because from 1987 to 1990, you entered a roller-coaster time of job changes, residential moves, and general instability. But, hey — you survived! (We both know that because you're reading these words.)

1991 – 1996

From 1990 to 1992, your primary focus was to find a home for yourself. After all that instability and style flexing, you needed to settle down! Fortunately, 1990 was a good time for your career and your reputation in the world. By 1991, you were proud of what you had achieved. Others might have been as well!

In 1992–93, increased responsibilities with children became more serious. Young children entered your world, or older ones moved back in! Fortunately, 1993 was a great year, because Jupiter was in your sign. You felt encouraged by life in general. It was a real lift for you. Money started to come your way by 1994 (thank goodness). From this point on, many of you felt increasing confidence in your ability to pull your act together. Nevertheless, you were definitely busting your buns in 1996!

1997 ~ 2000

The year 1997 was one of those fun years when love, romance, joy with children, vacations — all the fun stuff — were easy to attract! Some of you expanded your family through birth, adoption, or marriage. The more serious aspect of your life was that partnerships either ended or underwent a major transformation. Some close friendships also bit the dust. By 1998, wonderful work opportunities and a chance to improve your job in every way arrived. By 1999, romance, partnerships, and love once again had been resurrected in a beautiful way! (Yeehaw!)

Basically, since 1996 (which was quite challenging in many ways) you had become stronger, more focused, and more determined to go after what you wanted. Around the turn of the millennium, some kind of practical support from others was reduced or diminished, but that didn't really hold you back.

2001 - 2005

Travel opportunities were great at this time. Those of you who didn't travel went back to school or explored higher education. This was also an excellent time for publishing, the media, and anything to do with medicine or the law. By 2002, you were looking great, because lucky moneybags Jupiter was at the top of your chart! This was your chance to boost your reputation.

By 2004, you had hit the big time. At this stage in your life, you achieved something you really wanted. A job promotion, a graduation, a home, a marriage, a birth — something made you proud by 2005. Life was surprisingly sweet! Jupiter was back in your sign for the first time in twelve years, and this attracted all kinds of people, including new love, into your world.

2006 – 2010

Perhaps because of your recent success and good fortune, a lot of people and different situations were making demands on your time around now. This meant you had to learn how to juggle responding to the wants of others in order to protect your privacy and your own sense of independence and integrity. Not an easy task for eager-to-please Libra! Fun travel in 2007 was a nice boost. Ditto for time spent with siblings and relatives.

By 2008, your home life was greatly enriched. This was an excellent time for real-estate investments, or expanding your family, or spending money to enhance your home.

The year 2009 was particularly fun-loving! This was also a great time for romance, parties, movies, the theatre, sports, and having a good time. Children were a source of joy. Your chance to express yourself artistically was very strong. You were happy!

Nevertheless, this was the beginning of a two-year window when you had to start to let go of people, places, and possessions. For some of you, this meant downsizing; for others, it meant a change of residence and perhaps even country.

2011 – 2013

All of you are now totally in the throes of whatever this whole new scene is. Ironically, at the time of this writing, it is 2010, and I am getting mail from Librans asking what this big change will be. What will my new sandbox be? My best answer to them of course, is — *I don't know*!

I do know that at this time in your life, it is similar to a cycle that took place in 1980–83. Not everyone will have a residential move. Not everyone will have a job change. Some people might have a huge relationship change but remain where they are living and working. The details of what will occur are specific to the details of your own life. But I do know this is a benchmark time in your life. Oh yeah.

Last year and this year are a turning point that you will remember for years to come for some reason, although I cannot tell you what the specific reason is. When I look back to that tape loop in my own life — what happened then was that I returned to university, which in turn led to a whole series of doors opening to a completely new direction.

One very fortunate aspect about 2011 is that gifts, goodies, inheritances, money back from the government, and advantages or perks from others will come your way! Some of you will benefit indirectly through your partner, who will earn more, or get a bonus or something. It's a fortunate year for you!

In addition, this is the classic time for people to let you use something that they own — their cottage, their car, their boat, or their log splitter — depending on what you need. This is also an excellent time to get a mortgage or a loan, or to ask for any kind of assistance from others. Ka-ching!

In fact, this good fortune sails into 2012. Perhaps because the money is rolling in, you have great travel plans for 2013. You're going places! These journeys will likely not be short trips, but rather major trips that involve visiting another country or extended stays somewhere. A real change of scenery!

For those who don't travel, exploring opportunities in publishing, the media, and anything related to higher education will please you. You might go back to school or finally have success with that graduate degree. You might publish that book. It's a time when you will reach out and explore things beyond your ordinary everyday world. In doing so, you'll have an adventure and learn something new and exciting!

Not only that, but the year 2013 is also stimulating and thrilling because there's a sense of anticipation in the air. You know you're headed into something good — something you've been wanting to do or wanting to achieve. The undercurrent of this year is that feeling that you are getting dressed up for the ball! (You love this part.)

2014 – 2015

This is a stellar year for Libra! It's your turn to take a bow. Whatever you were preparing for is now yours in a beautiful way. You can expect promotions, kudos, praise, applause, and a real boost of endorsements from everyone in your circle. In fact, this is the best year in more than a decade for you to promote your reputation. Your name might be up in lights! (In fact, this could happen literally for some of you.) But all of you will feel increased respect and recognition from your peers. Needless to say, this is the perfect time to ask for a raise, or a promotion, or anything that is based upon how good you look in the eyes of others — especially authority figures.

Ironically, while all of this is going on, or because it is going on, privately you are undergoing some deep self-scrutiny about your value system. For example, if you're very successful suddenly, you might be surprised that it is not as fulfilling as you thought it would be. ("What's it all about, Alfie?")

Conversely, your increased recognition and success in the eyes of others might make you question your values in another way. You might decide you had it all wrong before, and now you are finally starting to see the light! You're undergoing a thought process that could go either way. One thing is certain: you'll be plumbing deep within yourself to determine a value system you feel you can trust.

You don't want to put your money on the wrong horse in life. You want to know what matters, then you will know where to focus. If it requires a decision on your part, no doubt you will feel some angst. You always do. (You might want to go back and read the "Fence-Sitting" part, or the page about acting with discipline to avoid future regrets.)

On a more mundane level, some of you will be changing jobs now or questioning your methods of earning money. To sum it up, on one hand you are very successful and making a splash in the eyes of others, especially parents, teachers, bosses, and VIPs. But on the other hand (you have different rings), despite this boost to your

good name, you're wondering what you should do to earn a living, and, even beyond that, what you should do in life — period!

Your increased high-viz probably creates a few waves, because 2015 is most definitely a popular year for you. Quite likely, it's one of the most popular years you've had in more than a decade. Everyone wants to see you! This is the ideal time to join clubs, organizations, classes, committees — whatever. All group activities will benefit you now. This is also why you should form working units with others. (You can't go wrong.)

Around the year 2015 is also a time to enter partnerships — both professional and intimate. Not only will you enjoy working with others and participating in group activities, you will also benefit from their expertise. Share your hopes and dreams for the future to see what others say. Get their feedback. I do not mention this casually. Their thoughts and opinions will help you! Or they may introduce you to important contacts. Sometimes we are best served by going it alone. But not this year. You need to get out in full dazzle and rally the troops!

2016 ~ 2017

Life takes an interesting turn now, because you are in a two- to three-year window when you will likely have a residential move, or a job change, or both. This is pretty major stuff! One way of testing this is to think back about thirty years (give or take a year either way). Did you move around 1986? Did you have a job change? (This is only relevant if you have already left home. In other words, you have to be making your own life decisions, and not moving or doing something as a result of your parents. Although, in many cases, I have seen it apply to a child's chart even when the parents triggered the move.)

Other things are going on now that promote a subtle (or not so subtle) new kind of awareness. Perhaps something is happening that urges you or encourages you to explore a belief system or some kind of spirituality, or even discover mysterious, esoteric, hidden knowledge. ("Hello? Hey, it's Houdini's mother asking for Harry.")

Fortunately, if you do have a job change or a residential move, the stars are smiling on you! Why? Because from September 2016 until October 2017, lucky moneybags Jupiter is in Libra! ("Yay me!")

Jupiter has not been in your sign since 2005. (Tra la, tra la, it is to laugh!) Do make the most of this! During the year that Jupiter is in your sign, all kinds of opportunities will be inexplicably drawn to you. Powerful, important people will notice you or suddenly be involved with you. Minor and major successes will occur that boost your confidence. There's no question these things will occur, because by the end of this year-long journey your self-confidence will have increased! In addition to which, your sense of poise will be noticeably stronger.

Therefore, it's a given that something positive occurs in this span of time that blesses you in a way that gives you increased inner strength. (Money is also nice, too.)

2018 ~ 2020

It's only common sense that after you receive a boost of confidence, as well as the good fortune of increased opportunities and helpful people, you can boost your earnings. That's exactly what's in the picture for you in 2018.

This year, you will not only increase your earnings, you will increase your assets in general. Many of you will make major purchases as well. Because your focus on cash flow and possessions is so strong this year, you are learning how to make the best use of what you own. Or, to put it another way, how to make what you own count! It comes down to getting the most bang for your buck. This is also a good year for investments.

Around 2019, you're prepared to do almost anything to secure a solid home base for yourself. You want a warm feeling in your tummy about where you live. Naturally, you want it to be as pleasant as possible, too. You don't need anything ostentatious. It can be small, but it must be a jewel. (One does have standards.)

This is the classic time to buy property, or land, or a condo, or a home because you want to secure your home base. Those of you who don't move this year or next year will do major renovations or major repairs to where you already live.

Just for clarity's sake — yes, I recall that many of you moved in the prior two years. (What is this? Musical chairs?) The changes that were taking place between 2015 and 2018 were actually changes that were intended to stimulate you by plunging you into a new and different milieu. That is because ever since 2010–11 you have been on a new path, and part of this new path was about completely redefining who you are in the world. As of this year, that process is pretty much finished. ("Stick a fork in me, Lord — I'm done.")

Nevertheless, in order to hone and refine your communicating style, and even how you think, you had to undergo some changes in the past few years that were primarily developmental. Some of you even moved to places where the language was different. (Like Boston.)

Your focus on your home this year, and, indeed, in the next few years, is something quite different. Now you are ready to put down roots! For those of you who like wherever you moved to during the past few years — you will stay. You will not move again. But you will fix up the place in a major way. You might also do something in the next few years to stabilize your domestic scene. Some major, basic changes might take place in your family dynamic as well.

Good news! This window of time (2020–21) is the best time you have had for real estate since 2008–9. Please make a note of this![11] Now is the time to improve where you live or invest in where you live. This is also an excellent time to speculate on real estate. It's obviously a good time to buy a new place for yourself if you can. Whatever money you put into real estate now — be it your home, speculative real estate, or new real estate for your personal use — you will appreciate a benefit and a profit in the future from this. Similarly, money invested in your domestic scene (like major purchases for your home) or family members will also please you now and in the future.

This is a wonderful time to derive joy from your family. Because everything is coming up roses, some of you will expand your family through marriage, adoption, or birth.

This is truly fortuitous, because at the very time when you should be solidifying your home base, you actually have a financial advantage to do so! How cool is that?

11. As my friend Pat says, "If you're going to fish, go where the fish are."

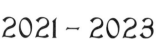

2021 ~ 2023

Once every twelve years, you might say somebody becomes the big winner of Pick the Stars, and that time has come for you! During this time in your life, you most definitely should plan for a wonderful vacation. (Whatever you can swing.) No matter how hard you're working, or what you are involved in, your main drive now is pleasure and fun! You will party, you might travel to fun places, you will enjoy playful activities with children, and you will enjoy or be more involved with sports than usual. (The beer and wine intake for many of you will be up this year!)

Needless to say, all this fun activity has to attract romance and love affairs into the lives of many of you. (Connect the dots!) This is a fabulous time to fall in love! You feel relaxed about who you are right now. No need to pretend you are anything else. This inner confidence will radiate out to others. Many of you will meet a new romantic partner. Those of you in existing relationships will rekindle your style of relating into something fun-loving, light-hearted, and more sexy. It's just like riding a bicycle, right? (But the handlebars are larger).

Businesses connected to the entertainment world, show business, and anything to do with the hospitality industry will flourish now. Also businesses or jobs connected to teaching children and anything to do with sports will get a lovely boost.

This is the classic time to introduce children into your life or to expand your family in some way. It's a time of fun, pleasure, and entertaining diversions. Some of these pleasant times most assuredly will be because of children, who are a great source of joy to you now. It's possible that many of you will feel increasing responsibilities with children, either with your own children, your grandchildren, or the children of friends. Some of you might get a job that is related to the education or care of children as well.

Take note: this might be one of the best windows for financial speculation. This might sound curious, because you're in such a party mood. However, the stars are encouraging you to "play" — and,

from the point of view of astrology, investing money is "playing" with money. Therefore, this "play" time is one of the best times for financial speculation! It's quite a different matter than earning money or inheriting money. (Astrology differentiates from these three sources of money coming into our lives.)

Wonderful opportunities to improve your job follow quickly on the heels of all this fun. Many of you will get a different job, or better duties, or a better boss, or better working conditions. If you're not working, you can look forward to better health! It's all good.

Partnerships, close friendships, and serious commitments also get a lovely boost at this time. By 2022–23, any doubts you had about a partnership are greatly dispelled. You feel more reassured about close friendships. People who are most important to you suddenly seem to be right there for you. (Yay!) That's because you're learning more about serious partnerships and what *you* really want. You're also learning more about the role you play in these partnerships. This is a time of valuable revelations and insights about how you relate to those who are closest to you.

Not only are partnerships supportive now, but gifts, goodies, inheritances, and all kinds of financial and practical benefits from the wealth of others will also start to come to you. The year 2023 is a very good year to ask for loans, mortgages, or assistance from others.

Privately, this is also a very passionate year for lovers. (Ooh la la!) It's the kind of time when you have all kinds of juicy diary fodder but no time to write. (Ain't it the truth?)

Those of you who are self-employed can more easily raise money in 2023. Similarly, those who are involved in fundraising will find it easy to tap into lucrative sources. The gravy train is coming your way!

But, privately, when you're lying in bed with the lights out, what you're really thinking about now is, "What do I really want to be when I grow up?" This question has nothing to do with your age. It's simply about where you are right now in your life.

Basically, you're trying to figure out how you can best use whatever time is left to you, which might be a little or a lot. Whatever it is, it's your lifetime! What do you most want to do with it? Partnerships and close friendships are a wonderful boon to you now. This is a good time to ask others for their support and their input.

2024 – 2025

A few of you are still on the receiving end of money, inheritances, perks, and favours from others. It's been a fortunate time for you recently in this respect. This is a good thing, because Lord knows, you are starting to work hard now. You're in a two- to three-year window of time when you are going to bust your buns! At times, you'll be working so hard, you might feel overwhelmed. Don't give in to this feeling. No matter how overwhelming your duties might seem, you will come out smelling like a rose! Make sure you get your rest. Remember how your sleep pattern gets random when you start working hard. (So what?)

Increased travel is likely for many of you right now, because a lot of travel opportunities are coming your way. Some of these are work-related; others are, hopefully, for pleasure. The good news is that many opportunities to expand your world and broaden your horizons are available to you now. For some, this means going back to school. For others, it could mean living in a foreign country or in another culture. You might learn a new language!

Publishing, the media, medicine, and the law are also areas that hold wonderful opportunities for you at this time. Writers can definitely make the most of this chance to get something published. If you work in higher education, you could get a better job, or a promotion, or a better working situation. (The opportunities in higher education apply to both students and professors and instructors.)

At this time, you feel a sense of excitement about what is to come. By 2025, lucky moneybags Jupiter starts to sail across the top of your chart, attracting even more opportunities to you. (Marvellous!) Now you will boost your reputation and your good name in the eyes of others. That's because the benevolent influence of Jupiter is so highly visible. People notice you! In particular, the people who notice you are teachers, bosses, VIPs, parents, and anyone in a position of authority. What they notice is positive! That's why this is the classic time for a promotion, praise, a raise, or something else that enhances your public reputation.

Others will benefit from this journey of Jupiter in a different way. This could be their chance to change to a Jupiter-related field like something in publishing, the travel industry, higher education — universities and colleges — or even medicine or the law. For those who have a chance to switch careers into one of these new areas, a promotion is less likely. You are using your "luck" in a different way.

This is a very positive time in your life, despite the fact that you're working so hard. One of the reasons you feel good is because you are in touch with your capabilities! In other words, you know what you can do and you're not afraid to show the world that you can do it!

"We may be surprised at the people we find in heaven.
God has a soft spot for sinners. His standards are quite low."
DESMOND TUTU
South African Cleric, Activist,
and Winner of the Nobel Peace Prize (1984)
(B. OCTOBER 7, 1931)

Famous Libra Personalities

Mickey Rooney	September 23, 1920
John Coltrane	September 23, 1926–1967
Ray Charles	September 23, 1930–2004
Julio Iglesias	September 23, 1943
Bruce Springsteen	September 23, 1949
Willie McCool	September 23, 1961–2003
F. Scott Fitzgerald	September 24, 1896–1940
Anthony Newley	September 24, 1931–1999
Jim Henson	September 24, 1936–1990
Linda McCartney	September 24, 1941–1998
Lou Dobbs	September 24, 1945
Phil Hartman	September 24, 1948–1998
Nia Vardalos	September 24, 1962
Rebecca Johnston	September 24, 1989
William Faulkner	September 25, 1897–1962
Barbara Walters	September 25, 1929
Glenn Gould	September 25, 1932–1982
Ian Tyson	September 25, 1933
Michael Douglas	September 25, 1944
Mark Hamill	September 25, 1951
Christopher Reeve	September 25, 1952–2004
Heather Locklear	September 25, 1961
Will Smith	September 25, 1968
Catherine Zeta-Jones	September 25, 1969
T. S. Eliot	September 26, 1888–1965
Marty Robbins	September 26, 1925–1982
Olivia Newton-John	September 26, 1948
Linda Hamilton	September 26, 1956
James Caviezel	September 26, 1968
Daniel Sedin	September 26, 1980
Henrik Sedin	September 26, 1980
Serena Williams	September 26, 1981
Randy Bachman	September 27, 1943
Shaun Cassidy	September 27, 1958

Gwyneth Paltrow	September 27, 1972
Avril Lavigne	September 27, 1984
Ed Sullivan	September 28, 1901–1974
Peter Finch	September 28, 1916–1977
Marcello Mastroianni	September 28, 1924–1996
Brigitte Bardot	September 28, 1934
Janeane Garofalo	September 28, 1964
Mira Sorvino	September 28, 1967
Naomi Watts	September 28, 1968
Dita Von Teese	September 28, 1972
Hilary Duff	September 28, 1987
Enrico Fermi	September 29, 1901–1954
Jerry Lee Lewis	September 29, 1935
Madeline Kahn	September 29, 1942–1999
Lech Wałesa	September 29, 1943
Bryant Gumbel	September 29, 1948
Zachary Levi	September 29, 1980
Truman Capote	September 30, 1924–1984
Angie Dickinson	September 30, 1931
Johnny Mathis	September 30, 1935
Fran Drescher	September 30, 1957
Eric Stoltz	September 30, 1961
Jenna Elfman	September 30, 1971
Walter Matthau	October 1, 1920–2000
James Whitmore	October 1, 1921–2009
Jimmy Carter	October 1, 1924
Tom Bosley	October 1, 1927
Richard Harris	October 1, 1930–2002
Julie Andrews	October 1, 1935
Randy Quaid	October 1, 1950
Mahatma Gandhi	October 2, 1869–1948
Groucho Marx	October 2, 1890–1977
Graham Greene	October 2, 1904–1991
Donna Karan	October 2, 1948
Annie Leibovitz	October 2, 1949
Sting	October 2, 1951
Lorraine Bracco	October 2, 1955
Kelly Ripa	October 2, 1970
James Herriot	October 3, 1916–1995
Gore Vidal	October 3, 1925
Chubby Checker	October 3, 1941

Stevie Ray Vaughan	October 3, 1954–1990
Tommy Lee	October 3, 1962
Clive Owen	October 3, 1964
Gwen Stefani	October 3, 1969
Neve Campbell	October 3, 1973
Damon Runyon	October 4, 1880–1946
Buster Keaton	October 4, 1895–1966
Charlton Heston	October 4, 1923–2008
Alvin Toffler	October 4, 1928
Jackie Collins	October 4, 1937
Anne Rice	October 4, 1941
Susan Sarandon	October 4, 1946
Alicia Silverstone	October 4, 1976
Steve Miller	October 5, 1943
Bob Geldof	October 5, 1951
Mario Lemieux	October 5, 1965
Kate Winslet	October 5, 1975
Thor Heyerdahl	October 6, 1914–2002
Britt Ekland	October 6, 1942
Joseph Finder	October 6, 1958
Elisabeth Shue	October 6, 1963
Amy Jo Johnson	October 6, 1970
R. D. Laing	October 7, 1927–1989
Desmond Tutu	October 7, 1931
John Mellencamp	October 7, 1951
Yo-Yo Ma	October 7, 1955
Simon Cowell	October 7, 1959
Aaron Ashmore	October 7, 1979
Shawn Ashmore	October 7, 1979
Eddie Rickenbacker	October 8, 1890–1973
Juan Perón	October 8, 1895–1974
Frank Herbert	October 8, 1920–1986
Jesse Jackson	October 8, 1941
Chevy Chase	October 8, 1943
Sigourney Weaver	October 8, 1968
John Lennon	October 9, 1940–1980
Sharon Osbourne	October 9, 1952
Scott Bakula	October 9, 1954
Sean Lennon	October 9, 1975
Thelonious Monk	October 10, 1917–1982
James Clavell	October 10, 1924–1994

Harold Pinter	October 10, 1930–2008
Nora Roberts	October 10, 1950
Tanya Tucker	October 10, 1958
Daniel Pearl	October 10, 1963–2002
Chris Pronger	October 10, 1974
Eleanor Roosevelt	October 11, 1884–1962
Elmore Leonard	October 11, 1925
Luke Perry	October 11, 1966
Jane Krakowski	October 11, 1968
Aleister Crowley	October 12, 1875–1947
Dick Gregory	October 12, 1932
Luciano Pavarotti	October 12, 1935–2007
Jane Siberry	October 12, 1955
Hugh Jackman	October 12, 1965
Yves Montand	October 13, 1921–1991
Lenny Bruce	October 13, 1925–1966
Margaret Thatcher	October 13, 1925
Nana Mouskouri	October 13, 1934
Paul Simon	October 13, 1941
Kelly Preston	October 13, 1962
Paul Potts	October 13, 1970
Billy Bush	October 13, 1971
Sacha Baron Cohen	October 13, 1971
Katherine Mansfield	October 14, 1888–1923
e. e. cummings	October 14, 1894–1962
Roger Moore	October 14, 1928
Ralph Lauren	October 14, 1939
Justin Hayward	October 14, 1946
Natalie Maines	October 14, 1974
Bianca Beauchamp	October 14, 1977
Usher Raymond	October 14, 1978
John Kenneth Galbraith	October 15, 1908–2006
Arthur Schlesinger	October 15, 1917–2007
Mario Puzo	October 15, 1920–1999
Penny Marshall	October 15, 1942
Sarah Ferguson	October 15, 1959
Emeril Lagasse	October 15, 1959
Didier Deschamps	October 15, 1968
Oscar Wilde	October 16, 1854–1900
Eugene O'Neill	October 16, 1888–1953
Angela Lansbury	October 16, 1925

Suzanne Somers	October 16, 1946
Tim Robbins	October 16, 1958
John Mayer	October 16, 1977
Rita Hayworth	October 17, 1918–1987
Evel Knievel	October 17, 1938–2007
Robert Jordan	October 17, 1948–2007
Margot Kidder	October 17, 1948
Rick Mercer	October 17, 1969
Erin Karpluk	October 17, 1978
Pierre Elliott Trudeau	October 18, 1919–2000
Chuck Berry	October 18, 1926
George C. Scott	October 18, 1927–1999
Jean-Claude Van Damme	October 18, 1960
Freida Pinto	October 18, 1984
Zac Efron	October 18, 1987
John le Carré	October 19, 1931
Marilyn Bell	October 19, 1937
Peter Max	October 19, 1937
John Lithgow	October 19, 1945
Evander Holyfield	October 19, 1962
Ty Pennington	October 19, 1965
Trey Parker	October 19, 1969
Nellie McClung	October 20, 1873–1951
Béla Lugosi	October 20, 1882–1956
Tommy Douglas	October 20, 1904–1986
Art Buchwald	October 20, 1925–2007
Mickey Mantle	October 20, 1931–1995
Tom Petty	October 20, 1950
John Krasinski	October 20, 1979
Alfred Nobel	October 21, 1833–1896
Dizzy Gillespie	October 21, 1917–1993
Whitey Ford	October 21, 1928
Ursula K. Le Guin	October 21, 1929
Carl Brewer	October 21, 1938–2001
Carrie Fisher	October 21, 1956
Doris Lessing	October 22, 1919
Timothy Leary	October 22, 1922–1996
Ann Rule	October 22, 1935
Annette Funicello	October 22, 1942
Catherine Deneuve	October 22, 1943
Deepak Chopra	October 22, 1946

SCORPIO

OCTOBER 23 – NOVEMBER 21

SCORPIO THE SCORPION

(OCTOBER 23 – NOVEMBER 21)

"I DESIRE."

"If you want to be successful, it's just this simple. Know what you are doing. Love what you are doing. And believe in what you are doing."

WILL ROGERS

American Cowboy, Comedian, Vaudeville Performer, and Actor

Young As You Feel and *Life Begins at 40*

(NOVEMBER 4, 1879–AUGUST 15, 1935)

"Happiness has a bad rap. People say it shouldn't be your goal in life. Oh, yes it should."

RICHARD DREYFUSS

American Film Actor

Close Encounters of the Third Kind and *Mr. Holland's Opus*

(B. OCTOBER 29, 1947)

Element: Water
Ruling Planet: Pluto
Quality: Fixed
Opposite Sign: Taurus
Symbols: The Scorpion, The Eagle, and The Snake
Lucky Gems: Opal, Blood-Red Carnelian, and Garnet[1]
Flowers: Geranium and Rhododendron
Colours: Red and Black
Parts of the Body: Reproductive Organs

You Like: Halloween, art, poetry, home, company, the good life, sleuthing out mysteries, boxing, finding solutions, respect, power, winning, surmounting challenges. You are the sexiest, most passionate sign in the zodiac. In fact, do you think of anything other than sex?

You Don't Like: Personal questions, betrayal, mediocrity, half-measures, lack of control, spineless indecision, restrictions, and confines. And pettiness is so, so — petty!

Where You Shine: Resourceful, accomplished, invigorating, heroic, instinctual, resilient, trustworthy, undaunted, and wholehearted. You can do anything! You have amazing determination. (Scary, actually.)

So Who's Perfect? Suspicious, jealous, vindictive, fanatical, unreasonable, and vituperative. You would make an excellent criminal.

---

1. Different texts will name different gems for different signs. (Fortunately, you have a healthy skepticism.)

What is Scorpio-ness?[2]

If there ever was a sign that wants to truly get to the bottom of something — it's you! Therefore, take note that the best way to understand the archetype of Scorpio is to study your ruling planet, Pluto.[3] When you understand Pluto's role in astrology, you will "grok" Scorpio.

In ancient times, Pluto was god of the underworld and everything that is hidden. The Greeks called this god Hades,[4] but the Romans called him Pluto. In astrology, Pluto rules all the secrets there are in life.

All of life's secrets.

When we apply this notion of "secret" to our everyday world, perhaps the first secret that springs to mind is anything that is criminal. Sure enough, Pluto rules the Mafia, the Cosa Nostra, the underworld, organized crime, criminal gangs from every nation, kidnapping, and violence.

But ah ha! In this sandbox of secrets, we also have the police — CSIS, the RCMP, the FBI, the CIA, the GRU, the KGB, Stasi, Mossad, etc. In other words, all police departments, detectives, police officers, troopers, sheriffs, constables, gendarmes, and military police are under the domain of Pluto. It's a cops and robbers thang. (Are you starting to suspect this is not the land of the *Ladies' Home Journal?*)

Pluto is all about secrets, subterfuge, crime, spying, the gathering of intelligence, and criminal detection. This is why a Scorpio can be a great criminal or a great cop. Natch! To evade the police, you have to think like the police. To catch a criminal, you have to think like a criminal.

Classic Scorpio haunts are places like tattoo parlours, strip joints, leather bars, goth night clubs, and vampire-esque hangouts, plus unsavoury places where who knows what is going down.

---

2. No one is just one sign. That is impossible. Therefore, this is a discussion about the Scorpio archetype — the qualities of "Scorpio-ness." Many other signs will have Scorpio qualities as well. Therefore, the discussion of one sign is not an exact description of that person, but rather it is a description of the qualities of that sign.
3. On August 24, 2006, members of the International Astronomical Union (IAU) voted that Pluto was no longer a planet, but rather a "dwarf planet." (It is my understanding that the majority of them were not even present at this vote, which took place on the last day of a ten-day conference in Prague. I think it was slipped in after many attendees had left.) According to BBC News Dr. Alan Stern (who leads the U.S. space agency's New Horizons mission to Pluto, and did not vote in Prague) told reporters that like-minded astronomers had begun a petition to get Pluto reinstated as a planet. Bumper stickers encouraging motorists to "Honk If Pluto Is Still a Planet" have gone on sale over the Internet, and emails circulating about the decision have been describing the IAU as the "Irrelevant Astronomical Union." From my point of view, Pluto is still a planet.
4. Christian theology later referred to Hades as the abode of the dead.

"A man is not what he says he is; a man is what he hides."
ALBERT CAMUS
French-Algerian Existential Author, Philosopher,
and Winner of the Nobel Prize in Literature (1957)
The Stranger
(NOVEMBER 7, 1913–JANUARY 4, 1960)

But crime and the police are not the only hidden things in society. Everything to do with plumbing, septic systems, and waste disposal is under the realm of Pluto, because this stuff is hidden as well! Sewers run deep beneath the streets. We don't see them or even think about them, and we certainly don't want to see or smell them! In buildings, plumbing is hidden behind the walls. In fact, plumbing is so secretive, we actually avoid the word *toilet*. Instead, we use euphemisms like "the john," "the head," "powder my nose," "spend a penny," "gotta see a man about a dog."

Garbage is another thing that is hidden. We hide the garbage under the sink, or in cans with lids. As soon as it's full, we whisk it out to bigger cans or Dumpsters. It is so offensive, it must be dispatched immediately!

Not only is garbage under the domain of Pluto, but so is "old" garbage. Therefore, Scorpio rules archaeology and anthropology. (Make no bones about it.[5])

Naturally, anything to do with locks, keys, security systems, alarm systems, safes, and hidden areas is also Scorpio.

Jewels, diamonds, and gems that are hidden deep in the bowels of the earth also come under the domain of Pluto. Therefore, anything to do with jewellery — making jewellery, selling jewellery, buying or selling gems, appraising jewellery — all of these are Scorpio.

Thus, the classic Scorpio scenario occurs when thieves (Scorpio) break the locks of doors (Scorpio) and combinations of safes (Scorpio) to steal (Scorpio) diamonds and jewels (Scorpio), and then the police (Scorpio) try to solve the crime (Scorpio).

This is fun, isn't it? Already you have a huge hit of your sign, just by knowing more about what your ruling planet Pluto is all about in astrology.

Years ago, I had an office in a heritage building called the Vancouver Block on Granville Street in Vancouver. The elevator was right outside my office. The only other businesses on my floor were several jewellers and a diamond merchant. (Since astrology is the mysterious study of "hidden knowledge," I called it the Scorpio floor.) One day, I opened the door and saw a uniformed policeman standing in the hall waiting for the elevator. On a whim, I suddenly spoke to him and said, "Hi. I'm an astrologer. Perchance, if you were just visiting a jeweller right now, I thought you might be interested to know that, in astrology, the same quality that rules jewellery also rules the police — and that quality is Scorpio." He looked at me and

---

5. I inherited my bad-puns gene from my father.

said nothing. The elevator doors opened. He stepped into the elevator, then turned to face me. As the doors closed between us, he said quietly, "I'm a Scorpio."

Ta-dah! Now we come to one of the biggest secrets of all. And yet it is hidden in plain view. It's us! All living things! We look deceptively simple because we're covered in skin, fur, feathers, or scales. But if you rip off the outer covering — aagggh! — there's all that blood, guts, flesh, bones, and organs. Poo poo caca.

Therefore, Scorpio rules everything to do with that which is *carnal* — flesh and blood.[6] This is why a classic Scorpio job is to be a butcher, a taxidermist, a mortician, or a brain surgeon. But basically, these are all the same job — you pick up a knife and slice open flesh. The butcher is looking for a pork chop; the brain surgeon is looking for a tumour.

This means the entire world of medicine is under the domain of Scorpio.

Similarly, the subtle body — the unconscious, the subconscious — is also ruled by Pluto, which means Pluto rules psychology, psychotherapy, and psychiatry. Sigmund Freud (who was a Taurus) was Scorpio Rising, and he also had his Jupiter in Scorpio. ("Hmmm, have you told Anna about your first sexual experience?")

However, the biggest secret is, of course, death. And, yes, Pluto rules death. If you sell life insurance, or work in a morgue, or drive a hearse, or sell burial plots — you're doing a Scorpio job.

I always say if you want to throw a stick and hit the most Scorpios in any city — toss it at a police station or a hospital. It's impossible to work in medicine, or in criminal detection, if you don't have Scorpio somewhere in your chart. At the very least, you have to have a strong Pluto.

Many Scorpio people look intense, but not all. Henry Winkler doesn't, and neither did John Candy or Walter Cronkite. These guys are avuncular. However, Scorpio people often have a prominent brow (like Martin Scorsese) or luscious, full lips (like Julia Roberts.) They certainly have an intense gaze. Clint Eastwood is a playful Gemini, but his Scorpio Ascendant makes him tough. Notice that all his power is in his eyes?

Now you understand why you have a special interest in medicine; or in death, jewellery, mysteries, tattoos, body piercing, and TV shows about forensics and blood spatter patterns; or in archaeology, anthropology, or plumbing. Or you know why you're an engineer in the sanitation department in Moose Jaw.[7]

Hey — Pluto rules many other things as well. It rules lasers, magnets, and atomic fission. Many physicists and research scientists are loaded with Scorpio. (Think of Madame Curie.) Their penetrating minds always burrow deep, seeking the truth. They want solutions and answers!

---

6. Scorpio people prefer art that is about people or animals. Flesh and blood. They tend to dismiss paintings of sunsets and pastoral scenes. There has to be something carnal in it — the head of a horse or a human hand.

7. This reminds me of the story of two elderly women from Kansas who were taking a bus trip across Canada. At one stop, they got off and asked someone, "Where are we?" "Saskatoon, Saskatchewan" was the reply. One woman turned to the other in amazement, and said, "Oh no! They don't speak English!"

"The power of cellular division and nuclear fission, the patterns of finger prints . . . [S]imple thoughts and observations of the nature around us take us beyond the unknown. The clues to the great mystery are all around us and deep within us."

BRYANT H. MCGILL

American Editor and Author

McGill English Dictionary of Rhyme

(B. NOVEMBER 7, 1969)

Three Big Clues about Scorpio

To get a deeper (you do deep) understanding of who you are, you might consider Scorpio in these three ways. (You already know all about the secrets.)

1. Drive for Power
2. Extremes
3. Drive for Transformation

Drive for Power

Your ruler, Pluto, was not discovered until 1930. This means that, for thousands of years, the planet Mars ruled both Aries and Scorpio. This is why Aries and Scorpio are surprisingly similar signs, although a lot of people don't know this, especially the gullible Leos.[8]

Both signs are bold and daring. Both signs never back down from a fight.[9] Both signs are alert and ready to defend or attack, because both signs are warriors! However, Aries is about *winning*. Aries loves the sweet taste of victory! Whereas, for Scorpio, it's something different. The British commander who defeated Napoleon said, "Next to a lost battle, nothing is so sad as a battle that has been won." Now that's complex. And no sign is more complex than you. Your victory is more because defeat is not an option.

Aries is the feisty scrapper with clenched fists who throws out the challenge, "Oh yeah? Wanna make something of it? Huh, tough guy?"

Oy vey. This is beneath you! Scorpio just stands there quietly and breathes — like Darth Vader. No words are necessary.

You might say the difference between Aries and Scorpio is that Aries will take a knife and stab you, and then say "I win!" Scorpio will take a knife and stab you, and then sew you up again, saying "Now you're better!"

If you really insult an Aries, their knee-jerk reaction will be to slap you in the face. If you really insult a Scorpio, they will do nothing. They will just stare at you, then ten years later, one day when you least expect it, they'll appear before you with an Uzi and obliterate you. Scorpio never forgets.

When you consider all the powerful things that Pluto rules — crime, death, violence, surgery, sex, and atomic fission — it goes without saying that the energy

---

8. I can make Leo jokes because I'm a Leo. We'll do anything for attention. (It's pathetic.)
9. I was surprised to learn how many female Scorpio Rising clients had taken up boxing to relax. They loved to hit that bag!

of Pluto is intense! "Build that bridge!" "Move that mountain!" Scorpio Rising people are so powerful they blow others away. They are often too powerful to work with others on a one-to-one basis. They work best with groups. They can pick up a megaphone and get a whole arena to do the hokey-pokey!

Scorpio has a relentless, ruthless, drive for power. The following people had such strong Scorpio energy that others followed them for good or bad. Napoleon was Scorpio Rising. General Patton was a Scorpio. General Eisenhower had Moon in Scorpio. The Desert Fox, Field Marshal Erwin Rommel, was a Scorpio. Hermann Göring had Moon in Scorpio. Joseph Goebbels was a Scorpio, as were Chiang Kai-shek, Sun Yat-sen, Leon Trotsky, Martin Luther, and Indira Gandhi. The great pacifist who gained independence for India, Mahatma Gandhi, was Scorpio Rising.

Scorpio is do or die. No ifs, ands, or buts. You mean business! You are like a tightly coiled spring, which means you hold yourself back. There is an element of disciplined restraint with Scorpio, and this controlled energy is what others sense in you. It's both sexy and scary.

> "We know what happens to people who stay in the middle of the road.
> They get run over."
>
> ANEURIN BEVAN
> British Politician
> Led Establishment of the National Health Service in Britain
> (NOVEMBER 15, 1897–JULY 6, 1960)

The irony is you're very often unaware of the strength you project. Almost every time I tried to tell a Scorpio Rising client how powerful they were, and that they could blow others away — invariably, they would look at me and say, "Who, me?" Twice I actually said, "Yes, you are powerful! One day people will call you Dragon Lady." And in both cases, the surprised women said to me, "They already do!"

Scorpios are daily heroes. You're known for your bravery and your courage. You do the jobs others can't face — like fighting fires, dealing with highway accidents, intervening in hostage situations, arresting criminals, investigating terrorism, dealing with the dead, even dealing with our garbage. Scorpios just do it. It doesn't mean you like it. It means you're a realist. You know somebody has to do it. And so you do it.

I bow before you.

Phffft! You don't care. Scorpio doesn't need fanfare. You want the power and latitude to be able to get your job done. You don't want your hands tied, unless it's kinky fun. ("I hope this time you remembered the keys to the handcuffs!")

Your intense power, drive, courage, and stamina make you the heroes of the zodiac. You're the guys who are going to save the world — if you don't destroy it first.

"All the mistakes I ever made were when I wanted to say 'No' and said 'Yes.'"

MOSS HART

American Playwright and Theatre Director

Once in a Lifetime and *The Man Who Came to Dinner*

(OCTOBER 24, 1904–DECEMBER 20, 1961)

Extremes

Oh boy! Saint or sinner? Scorpio is the sign of extremes. When you meet anyone, you love them or you hate them. There isn't a wishy-washy bone in your body. You have strong opinions about everything, which is why you won't take any advice from anyone. (Hello?)

This doesn't mean you aren't skeptical, because you are. You insist on arriving at your own data and conclusions, using your own investigatory powers because you don't trust others.

In one way, there's a good reason for this. You're extremely intelligent, plus you have a penetrating insight into things. (You can spot a phony a mile away.) You know when others aren't telling you the truth or if they have a hidden agenda. In fact, you know this not only through your perceptive, penetrating observations; you know these things because you have a sixth sense. It's spooky. You just *know*.

"Intuition will tell the thinking mind where to look next."

JONAS SALK

Medical Researcher

Developed the Polio Vaccine

(OCTOBER 28, 1914–JUNE 23, 1995)

This is one of the reasons you're attracted to the occult and mysterious, hidden knowledge. You went to see *The Da Vinci Code*, even if it did disappoint you. You read *Interview with the Vampire*.

Obsession and compulsion are totally connected with Scorpio.[10] You will go to any extreme when you really want something. Or, when you really don't want something, you do avoidance — big time. ("I'm the Queen of Denial!")

In fact, the Scorpio reticence is something to behold. Sometimes Scorpios won't even talk to you! They just stand there silently. Librans (who are eager to please) and friendly Cancers are frankly appalled. The Scorpio doesn't care. In fact, if others start to look nervous — they're perversely entertained.

Scorpio's ability to go all out is evident at Halloween. My Scorpio daughter had

10. Just because Scorpios are obsessive or compulsive, this should not be confused with someone who is obsessive-compulsive, which is an anxiety disorder that is something else altogether.

her windows decorated with ghouls and cobwebs, and thirteen pumpkins on her front step at least three weeks before Halloween. By the time October 31 rolled around — every pumpkin was rotten.

Scorpio rules sexuality, prostitution, and criminal activity. Ever notice how these Scorpio themes inspire Halloween costumes? Halloween is a Scorpio event! People *hide* behind masks. They're enamoured with blood, ghosts, death, bones, ghouls, and vampires, as well as spiders and insects and serpents (which are also under the domain of Pluto). My daughter always refers to her intuition as "my spidey sense."

Even your wardrobe is extreme! Your favourite colours are black and black, but sometimes you wear black. Leather and high boots are super cool. The boots can be heavy and menacing. (These are also surprisingly practical.) Or they can be patent leather over-the-knee stilettos. (Hot!)

This extreme quality about Scorpio means you can be the Marquis de Sade or Mother Teresa.[11] Your love-hate response to others, along with your impulse to do good or evil, is illustrated by the extremes of Billy Graham versus Charles Manson (both Scorpios) or Mahatma Gandhi (Scorpio rising) versus Joseph Stalin (Scorpio.) Sometimes your extreme behaviour lifts you to fame and success, and then pulls you down, like the talent and addictions of Scorpio Sir Richard Burton.

Your Scorpio extremes are contrasted in your ruthless drive for power and your teasing playfulness![12] Despite your tough exterior, you are not only playful, but softhearted as well. You'll make sacrifices for a great cause. You are enormously altruistic. You are also generous, but quietly generous. You don't make a big deal out of your acts of kindness. You don't need recognition for being decent.

And why?

Because Pluto is the sign that rules the masses. Therefore, the essence of Plutonian energy is to benefit society and to benefit others. It's what you do.

"Ahh, sooo." (Strokes chin gently.)

Drive for Transformation

Pluto is all about transformation: birth, maturation, and death, then regeneration — like the phoenix rising from the ashes. Pluto wants to tear things down and remove what is offensive, to makes things better. This is why Scorpio has the potential to save the planet!

In mundane terms, the transformative power of Scorpio takes something that already exists and makes it better. Therefore, Pluto rules *recovering* or *reupholstering* furniture, or *refinishing* floors, or *renovating* homes, or *restoring* art or damaged items, or *recycling* things, or *refurbishing* something. (Scorpios recycle with zeal!)

---

11. The Marquis de Sade was actually a Libra with Mercury and Venus in Scorpio; Mother Teresa had no Scorpio planets, but she might have been Scorpio Rising, which would not be surprising considering how much her work was involved with death.

12. Scorpio John Cleese (b. October 27, 1939) said, "If you want creative workers, give them enough time to play." He also said, "He who laughs, learns best."

Whereas Aries wants to begin with something fresh and new, Scorpio likes to take something that already exists and reshape it. Aries wants a new piece of fabric to sew. Scorpio modifies existing clothing. Aries builds new houses. Scorpio renovates old ones.

To improve things and introduce reforms is the natural impulse of Scorpio. This is why you are always trying to be a better person! You know there is more to life than just paying your rent, keeping a roof over your head, and feeding yourself and your family. You want to be a more evolved individual by the time you die — otherwise, what's it all about, Alfie?

You have the ability to take anything — an item, a person, a company, a town, a city, or the planet — and, by removing that which is offensive or negative, and by adding that which is beneficial or nourishing, you heal it. Simple.

You are that striving for perfection.

"Potential has a shelf life."
MARGARET ATWOOD
Prize-Winning Canadian Author, Poet, Critic, Essayist, and Feminist
Survival, *The Handmaid's Tale*, *The Blind Assassin*, and *Oryx and Crake*
(B. NOVEMBER 18, 1939)

Scorpio in Love

If you have read up until this point rather than just skipping to Scorpio in Love (and why would anyone do that? Especially a Scorpio? Confess! Your DNA is on this very page!) —

I digress.

If you have read anything previous to this page, you know what a passionate sign you are! However, if you just went for the jugular to read this part right away — you are soooo busted. Certainly this is proof positive of how passionate you are!

Scorpio rules the extremes in anyone — black or white, saint or sinner. It rules sex, death, and money. It rules lingerie and undies and everything hidden and everything carnal — everything related to flesh! And the part of the body that Scorpio rules is the genitals. (Correction: you weren't going for the jugular. My apologies.)

We're not talking Rice Krispies squares!

You're intense. Factoid. But do you know what really drives you? It's your expectations.

You expect so much from sex! You're not satisfied with just being with someone. (As a Libran might.) You're not satisfied with just being adored and loved. (As a Leo might.) You're not satisfied with the titillating fresh novelty of discovery. (As a Gemini might.) You're not satisfied with the sweet security that prestige, money, and power might offer. (As a Capricorn might.)

No! You want far, far more. You want to literally *merge* with your lover. You want the two of you to become one. You want romance and sex to be overwhelming, mind-boggling, and transcendent! (Segue to the *1812 Overture* here. The part where the cannons go off.) If you ever saw the excellent movie *Like Water for Chocolate*, the ending of that movie describes what you crave.

Of course, the big question is — is this possible?

In many ways, you know how to capture the attention of anyone you want. You invented the word *alluring*. (If you don't know this, you should: your ruler, Pluto, rules magnets. As corny as this might sound, you have the ability to *magnetize* people and situations to you.)

I had a Scorpio client who worked in television. She went down to Los Angeles, where she met a very successful director who made "big" commercials in the U.S. She said they looked at each other and the spark was there. She came back to Canada and set up a little shrine. (I thought this sounded a bit voodoo-ish. Maybe not to you.) Every day she wrote his name on a little piece of paper, then folded it and sealed it with wax, using a special seal. (Could I make this up?) She placed it on her shrine, which had candles, a bowl of water, and incense. And in five days — less than a week! — he phoned her on the pretext of scouting new locations for a commercial. Of course, he flew up, and they had a wild, passionate, memorable affair. But I never forgot how she calmly knew she had the ability to *summon* him. *Spoooooky.*

You have this ability as well.

> "I said to this priest: 'Am I expected to believe that if I went out and had an affair that God was really going to be upset? Okay, thou shalt not kill . . . steal . . . but thou shalt not commit adultery? If no one is any the wiser, what the hell difference does it make?' He was lovely. He told me the Commandments were laid down for a lot of guys living in the desert."
>
> DIANA DORS
> British Actress and Sex Symbol
> *Yield to the Night*
> (OCTOBER 23, 1931–MAY 4, 1984)

Not only are you sexually magnetic, you are a superb lover! Your playfulness leads to role-playing if your partner is willing. Since Scorpio rules everything that is "hidden," this includes lingerie and underwear because these clothes are hidden underneath outer garments. Guess who loves laced-up bodices, teddies, corsets, garter belts with suspenders, sexy heels, lace, and all that wonderful, vampy stuff.

In fact, thinking about this, I immediately checked the chart of lovely, sexy Dita Von Teese. Ah ha! She is not a Scorpio. (Surprise.) She is a Virgo, which does show in her sort of "pure" beauty. But then I saw it. Her Virgo Sun is lined up cheek by jowl with Pluto. Ah ha! This explains why she is so seduced by the allure of undergarments and, in turn, seduces others with that same allure. (Sigh.)

However, although you love to role-play, you don't need sexy clothes to feel turned on. You're confident about your ability to flirt, tease, and seduce in whatever clothes you are wearing. You know you've got what it takes.

I know a story about two police officers. (I knew one of the officers but not the other.) I don't know the Sun Signs of either officer, but there has to be a lot of Scorpio here, especially since one of them went on to do some serious undercover work. One night, one cop, who was on duty, encountered the other officer (a woman), who was off duty. One thing led to another, and soon they were heavily involved in the front seat of his squad car. Their passion intensified, items of clothing were discarded, and soon they hastily decided to switch to the back seat. It wasn't until they were happily sated that they realized they were trapped in the back of the squad car — because, of course, the doors automatically locked! And they couldn't reach the radio, which was in the front seat. They were so busted! There was nothing they could do but wait to be discovered. Which would be worse? To be rescued by a fellow colleague, or by a member of the public! Eventually, when the on-duty officer could not be contacted, an alert went out for him. (I do know he had his socks on.)

A word of caution. You are the most vulnerable of all the signs to great looks. If you meet a hunk or a serious babe you are putty in their hands, even if this person is a complete and total jerk. Hello? Where did your brains go? Just remember this.

Another client talked to me about her boyfriend, who was a Capricorn. (All Earth signs are passionate, and, in particular, Capricorns are highly sexed, and they love frequency.) I mentioned this to her, and she said, "Yeah. That's true. But he's not *hot*, ya know?"

A meaningful distinction. I never forgot that.

No sign is more jealous or possessive. (Oh yeah!) You can be a victim of the green-eyed monster to an *extreme* degree. Jealousy will make you sleepless, take away your appetite, and, finally, drive you to doing or saying something you will later regret. In part, this jealousy relates to power. Who's in control here? Are you being dismissed, or not taken seriously, or not respected? Like, whaaaat? Because, if so — "I'm outta here!"

But here is where Scorpio can *really* stun their partner. (All you have to do is remember that your sign rules garbage. Say no more.) Once you are through with someone — you *purge* them from your life. You slam that door shut, and it's over, baby. "Over!"

(The only thing that will make you open that door again is hot sex — if you're feeling deprived.) After all, you *like* recreational sex. And you're the first to admit it.

> "I never liked the men I loved and never loved the men I liked."
> **FANNY BRICE**
> American Model, Comedienne, Singer, and Theatre and Film Actress
> Best Known for the Radio Comedy Series *The Baby Snooks Show* and for
> Inspiring the Story *Funny Girl*
> (OCTOBER 29, 1891–MAY 29, 1951)

You are also passionately loyal and dedicated to your true love. You will walk over hot coals or crawl through ground glass for them. You're extremely generous to your lover. And playfully affectionate.

However, they had better not cheat on you. Baaaaad move. They'll be out on their ear so fast they won't even hear the door slam.

The Scorpio Boss

"Never tell people how to do things.
Tell them what to do and they will surprise you with their ingenuity."
GENERAL GEORGE PATTON, JR.
United States Army Officer and General During the Second World War
(NOVEMBER 11, 1885–DECEMBER 21, 1945)

You're a strong boss because you're steel-willed, disciplined, and tough. You will work extremely hard, in a no-nonsense way, and this, in turn, inspires loyalty from those who work for you. You're a shrewd judge of character, and you seem to know just how far you can push people. (And it's a lot farther than many others would!)

Your people are not only loyal to you, they have confidence and faith that you know how to problem-solve or come up with whatever solution is necessary. The Scorpio boss can give the impression that he or she can do the impossible and overcome any obstacle. (Small wonder Scorpio generals lead their troops to victory.)

However, Scorpio bosses do not necessarily win popularity contests. Your employees respect you, and they work hard for you, but they might not like you. Why? Because unless you choose to be smooth and tactful (and you certainly can be), you are often abrupt, tactless, and dictatorial. "Who me?" Admit it — you know this is true.

But hey — you get the job done! Every Scorpio boss gets results.

Before you even open your mouth, your mere gaze can rivet others to attention. ("Hi, Darth.") In fact, it's been said that a Scorpio doctor can stare at his or her patient and say, "Heal thyself," and it works! Such is the power of the Scorpio gaze. (Think *Dirty Harry*.)

Of course, the main secret in having an effective team working for you is — you have to like them. Remember how black and white you are about people? You either like them or you don't. Needless to say, if anyone is working for you and you don't like them — well, the clock is ticking on when they'll make their exit. (Oh yeah.)

In the last analysis, you are great in management, because the definition of managing is getting things done through other people. And you can do this.

The Scorpio Employee

"Lead me, follow me, or get out of my way."
GENERAL GEORGE PATTON, JR.
United States Army Officer and General During the Second World War
(NOVEMBER 11, 1885–DECEMBER 21, 1945)

It's curious. Even though you are strong-willed, determined, and very powerful, you're also very good at taking orders. (It's your respect for the military mentality.) You understand the system, and you understand how it has to work. In part, this is because you have never needed the flash and dazzle that some other signs need. You don't even need that pat on the back. What you do need is the freedom and latitude, and the right tools, to do the job. If you're handcuffed in any way — you'll be frustrated!

Your greatest talent is your resourcefulness. You're quick to see how to substitute one thing in place of another. Or you know how to take an item and give it a new use or application. Furthermore, if something breaks down, you're quick to see if it can be repaired or modified, rather than just getting rid of it and ordering a new one.

You have a basic understanding of mechanics, science, and logic. You see how things work. You're a marvellous problem solver, and you certainly know how to unclog a system.

You're very loyal to your company or your boss. However, you need to respect your boss. If your boss is weak or indecisive, you'll feel disdain. (You'll also feel frustration because you're not in their place!) Scorpio employees can easily be turned off. They like to think they're on the winning team, that they're not wasting time, and they're getting the job done. Like the Scorpio boss, you have a ruthless, no-nonsense approach to work. After all, if you're not accomplishing something — why the hell are you here? You could be somewhere else having fun!

You can be bought. You like money. And basically, you know that is why you're working. By the same token (pun intended), you need to be paid well. You particularly like perks such as watches, jewellery, tickets to games, and certainly a ham or turkey if it's appropriate. You like to win prizes — and you generally get them because you earn them through your hard work and resourcefulness!

"I always try to improve, to find new ways of expressing myself, to keep looking for truth and originality."

BURT LANCASTER

American Film Actor, Director, and Producer

Elmer Gantry, The Birdman of Alcatraz, and *Atlantic City*

(NOVEMBER 2, 1913–OCTOBER 20, 1994)

The Scorpio Parent

You love your children intensely and want the best for them. Nevertheless, you're in charge! Scorpio is all about control. You want not only self-control but control over your surrounding environment, as well as control over others, especially if they live with you, and most especially if you gave birth to them!

Scorpio parents like guidelines and rules. Your children have curfews, allowances, and rules about keeping their bedroom clean and what kind of food they may eat. There is very little over which you do not have domain.

The upside is that your children feel secure because they are in a well-run, well-organized environment with relatively few surprises. (Except for when you blow a gasket.) Your children will imitate your style because they don't get a lot of opportunities to exercise their own judgement and learn how to determine their own rules and boundaries.

In other words, living in the house of the Scorpio parent is a little bit like being in the military. Everything is all laid out. You know the rules and regulations. But what about when you are demobilized? Aye, there's the rub.

The Scorpio parent also has to be careful of jealousy. You will feel jealous if you think your children prefer your spouse, or their nanny, or their babysitter. (Remember that you are emotionally territorial.) Actually, you don't have to worry about this. The fact is you are so strong, and so decisive, and you command such respect — you are "everything" to your children. They cannot imagine their lives without you.

The Scorpio Child

The Scorpio child is extremely wilful. This is not a bad thing. (But it's challenging for a Scorpio parent who is equally extremely wilful!) When parenting a Scorpio child, do not think you have to break their will. That would be disastrous. It is the Scorpio will that ultimately leads the Scorpio adult to become a success. Why would you want to break this marvellous quality in childhood?

Instead, learn how to use this will. The Scorpio child is quite willing to follow orders and respect boundaries, rules, and regulations. All of this makes sense to the Scorpio child. However, the rules or regulations have to be *reasonable*. If you give this child unreasonable rules — he or she will figure out a way around your system.

The Scorpio child is surprisingly mature at an early age. It's as if they understand how the world works. As long as they think others are being fair and reasonable with them, they're co-operative. Friction will arise when the child doesn't want to stop doing something that is a lot of fun. Now you encounter the classic clash of wills. Nevertheless, firm logic will appeal to them.

Scorpio children like an organized environment. They tend to be neat. It's not a fussy approach. They simply want their world in working order.

The parents of the Scorpio child should be forewarned about the whole area of potty training and bathroom etiquette. Because Pluto, the ruler of Scorpio, rules plumbing, septic systems, etc., it also rules the waste system of the human body. Often a Scorpio toddler is reluctant to be toilet trained because they're not going to give up their power over that process. And even when they finally do co-operate, they're inordinately fascinated by everything related to the toilet. ("Where does it go?")

Needless to say, by the time Scorpio toddlers are five years old, they begin their never-ending love affair with scatological humour. This is the kid who roars with laughter at the word *bum*. They love talking naughty!

Most of them will go through a phase of dressing in black, getting tattoos and body piercings, and looking punk, or goth, and wearing skull-and-crossbones jewellery and belt buckles, as well as heavy-duty boots. Let's not forget the black leather. Scorpio children love insects, snakes, iguanas and reptiles.

Halloween is almost a religious rite. This can never be ignored. But if you let your Scorpio child go through all the expressions of leather, goth, skeletons, and punk rock — quite likely, they will come out the other end looking just fine. (Who knew?)

It just takes a little patience and a lot of love.

How to Be a Happier Scorpio

Your passionate intensity is your strength, but it is also your Achilles heel. It can cause you to be overwhelmed with emotions, especially when you are jealous. (No sign burns with jealousy more than you.) When you suffer, you suffer extremely! You scream, you throw things. You think of harming yourself or others. It's scary. (Even to you.)

One might think, therefore, that you would be best advised to follow the middle way — not one extreme or the other. Sounds sensible, doesn't it? But this is not realistic, because, hey — you are who you are, and you can't be who you aren't.

Years ago, I had the privilege of hearing a wise teacher talk about three approaches to enlightenment. He said that the first level, which was about avoiding harmful actions, was like *walking* to enlightenment. He said the second level, which was about not only avoiding harm but also doing good for others, was like *taking a train* to enlightenment. He said the third level, which (in my words) was the kitchen-sink reality of courageously working with whatever is on your plate and transforming it — was like *taking a rocket* to enlightenment.

You are that rocket.

You have unusually intense powers of concentration and focus. You have a laser-like mind. (Look at your desire to see the underpinnings of anything — the inner workings, the subtext, what really makes things tick.) This means once you decide you can do something, you can do the impossible very quickly! The bad news is if you go *off* course, you can get into enormous difficulties very quickly!

You have a gift — but a dangerous, powerful gift.

So now we know two things: You have your ability to intensely focus as a powerful tool at your disposal. And you have to be extremely careful how you use this laser-like ability.

There are many ways you can use your ability to focus intensely to benefit yourself, but I think the simplest is to *be here now.*[13] This means you have to be constantly *aware* of what you do, what you think, and what you say. Constantly.

Be the watcher. Be the watcher watching the watcher. Stay in the present moment as much as possible.

If you are enjoying a steak, don't think of your dinner companion. Don't think of how much the meal costs. Don't think of what just happened before dinner, or what will happen after dinner. *Just taste the meat.*

---

13. Richard Alpert, author of the book *Be Here Now,* has Pluto conjunct his Cancer Ascendant.

No matter what happens or what "loss" you experience in life — you always have the present moment. This moment right now. And if you deal with just this moment, you are in control of at least that! (It's important for you to be in control.)

You might be in control for only a moment, but that moment is *everything* because you can't leap into the future, right? You only *have* the present moment. What comes after this moment is not the next moment — it is *this* moment! Your life is a long series of "present moments." When it comes right down to it — all you ever have to do is take care of the present moment, and that is doable. It's sixty seconds! Of course, this is easier said than done. The fact is we are hardly ever in the moment, because we are always in the past or the future. Your pain is primarily a memory of the past or a fear of the future.

Something that will help you grasp a sense of the present moment is a little exercise. It's simple. You just count eleven breaths. To breathe in and out is one count. All you have to do is count eleven breaths. What have you got to lose? It takes about a minute. One minute. *Phffft!*

This one-minute exercise is deceptively powerful, because it separates what went before from what will come next. In other words, it helps to neutralize the emotions you're carrying with you. And, yes, it helps you to be right *here* — in the moment.

When you do it, it will help you to be calmer. When you begin to calm your agitated emotions, you have a better chance to see them for what they are. Every time you stop your world and count off eleven breaths, you get closer to accepting your current state of reality. And once your Scorpio determination makes an honest assessment of your current state — the only thing you will then resolve to do is to improve it! Why? Because *that is what you do!*

To constantly improve yourself is what drives all Scorpios. (It's a Pluto thang.) Your ruler, Pluto, always wants to reform and improve something to get a superior result. This is who you are!

Actually, you have no choice. You will always try to improve your life, because this is the essence of your being. The only thing that changes as you mature is your definition of *improve.*

Use the eleven-breath exercise as a braking mechanism. Nobody wants to see a train wreck. You are the most strong-willed sign in the zodiac. No question. Once you shift your focus off your pain, your relief will be surprisingly swift! The key to your happiness is your own enormous willpower.

> "I have had dreams and I have had nightmares,
> but I have conquered my nightmares because of my dreams."
>
> JONAS SALK
> Medical Researcher
> Developed the Polio Vaccine
> (OCTOBER 28, 1914–JUNE 23, 1995)

SCORPIO
YOUR 40~YEAR HOROSCOPE
1985 ~ 2025

Why Go into the Past?

I want you to have faith in your predictions. The only way you can believe what I say is to test these predictions for yourself. This is why I start with brief highlights from the past twenty-five years. If anything in these past twenty-five years resonates with you, then what I say about the next fifteen years will have the same validity. It is all one long timeline — your life.

The past predictions generally apply once you have left home or are "running your life" and making your own decisions. Prior to that, the major events in your life were dictated to you by other people, likely your parents.

1985 ~ 1990

Everything was pretty new for you around this time. However, real estate, family matters, and your domestic world were improving. Soon love and romance came along. In fact, the year 1986 was a great year for fun and vacations! After that, you had a chance to improve your job, then improve partnerships and relationships, and finally — money and goodies came to you through partners, inheritances, gifts, loans, insurance payouts, or money from the government. Looking sweet!

However, by 1989–90, residential moves and job changes kept you on your toes. But you didn't mind this because travel, education, publishing, the media, and even medicine and the law were all promising experiences for you. (Let us not forget how much you love to travel and learn.)

1991 – 1996

In the early 1990s, it was paramount for you to establish a home base for yourself. Fortunately, career opportunities boosted your reputation at that time. Everybody thought you looked swell, which is why your popularity was strong in 1992–93. (It's nice to be loved.)

By 1994, increased responsibilities with children made you sit up and take notice. However, this was also an extremely rewarding time for you in many ways. Moneybags Jupiter was in your sign that year, making you feel confident, reassured, and frankly fabulous. By 1995–96, increased earnings for many of you were encouraging. Soon, you were busting your buns to show others what you could do. *Chug, chug, chug.* "I think I can. I think I can."

1997 ~ 2000

Everything to do with family, real estate, and your home scene, plus your relations with family members, improved immensely around 1997. This was a great time to buy real estate, or to fix up where you were living. You felt happier at home. Family members were more generous to each other. This was timely, because you were still busting your buns!

New romance, love affairs, and fun vacations swept you off your feet in 1998–99. Life was good. Children expanded your world and were a source of joy. Many of you enjoyed parties, vacations, and fun getaways at this time. By 1999, your job scene looked waaaay better! You finally got the break you needed. However, partnerships were stressed or, by contrast, getting very serious. (They were either seriously breaking up or seriously getting together.) By 2000, you felt encouraged about commitment. Professional partnerships and intimate relationships were rewarding. People perceived you as doing just fine.

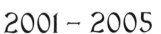

2001 – 2005

It's curious because at this stage in your life, although you did get some support from others, at the same time, some kind of practical or emotional support was also removed. Definitely a mixed bag! (You win some, you lose some.) By 2002, your world expanded to travel, higher education, or exploring opportunities in publishing, the media, medicine, or the law. Anything to do with higher education and teaching looked great (although you were still very much on your own, and relying on your own resources).

Around 2003,[14] a lot changed. Good luck started to come your way. Your reputation got a wonderful boost. And, by 2005, you started to really hit your stride. People believed you knew what you were doing. You had a sense of what you could do. You knew that success was just around the corner. On a personal level, this was a gratifying time when you also explored your inner spiritual world. You were definitely getting stronger!

---

14. All the years I state can be within a two-year window and possibly even three, depending on when you were born.

2006 – 2010

Now you entered a powerful time in your life when you could see what was working, and what was not working. In 2006, lucky Jupiter was in your sign, pumping your confidence and giving you the strength to let go of what was no longer relevant in your life. "I can do this!"

At the same time, many of you felt extremely proud of your achievements. This was a time of graduation, promotion, success, and adulation. Something confirmed to you who you really were and what you could do.

Soon, this success led to increased earnings, especially in 2007. Things were looking great! In 2008, your optimism grew and your popularity was such that your challenge was learning how to work with groups and relate to others and yet, at the same time, not lose your own personal independence and integrity. Not always easy to achieve.

Something began to enrich your home scene around 2009. This was an excellent time to buy real estate or invest in real estate. Some of you bought treats for your home so that you felt richer and more fortunate. You were also able to treat family members. This was a happy time in your personal life and your family dynamic. Some of you expanded your family at this time through marriage, birth, adoption, or the whole fam-damily moving in! Oy vey.

This could be why you took a vacation, because it was a great time to travel. It was also a good time to explore the arts, enjoy success in sports, and reap the rewards of all kinds of creative outlets, be they writing, acting, photography, working in show business, or anything to do with the hospitality industry.

This was also a fabulous time for love and romance! Many of you were really cozy with the love of your life.

2011 – 2013

At this time, a major shift begins to occur as you start to dismantle much of what you have created since 1999. In this period of time, you will be saying goodbye to partnerships and close friends. You will also be leaving behind familiar places, jobs, residences, and favourite haunts. Not all of this will happen for all of you, but some of this will happen for most of you. That's because this is a time frame when you have to let go of what is no longer relevant in your life. This includes people, places, and possessions, as well as ideas, prejudices, and ideologies.

Fortunately (except for those of you who have strong Cancer planets in your chart), letting go is surprisingly easy for you to do! In fact, letting go is something at which you excel. This doesn't mean you're not attached to people, places, and possessions. *Au contraire!* It simply means that because Pluto is your ruler, and Pluto rules surgery, garbage, and the notion of getting rid of something in order to improve things — *this* is naturally your style! You do it with relatively little anxiety. In fact, for many of you, it will be a *relief!*

In 2011–12, your job and health will improve beautifully. You will get a better job, or better working conditions, or better duties, or a better boss. Yay! Not only is this reassuring for you, but also your health can improve at this time. This is great! It puts you on solid footing, even though other areas of your life may be undergoing major changes.

It's important to know that, in the bigger picture, this is a decade when your home scene and your family life are basically confusing. You're not always sure how you want things to unfold. You're not quite sure where you want to live or what you're doing real estate–wise. Ditto for family dynamics. (For Scorpios born in October, this confusion was prominent in the late 1990s, and at the turn of the millennium. For those born between November 1 and 12, this confusion was present in 2002–6, and for later Scorpios, the domestic and family confusion or sense of uncertainty was most prominent in 2006–11.)

By 2012, relationships and partnerships are more reassuring! More yay! (When you're dealing with stuff, it's nice to know that somebody has your back.) In fact, your dealings with the general public will also be more positive. Those of you who enter committed relationships, especially in 2012, will likely do so with someone richer, older, more established, or more experienced in the ways of the world.

Take note of Zsa Zsa's advice: "Husbands are like fires. They go out if left unattaended."

By 2013, almost as if to counter what you are giving up, the universe bestows you with gifts and goodies! Inheritances, money back from the government, favours, the use of other people's property, plus the indirect benefit of increased wealth to your partner, are just some ways by which you will come out smelling like a rose.

Take note: even though this is a time when you are giving up things, this is a wonderful year to get a loan or a mortgage. Could come in handy! Never forget that you have the power to magnetize things to you — even something as tangible as money. (Actually, money isn't really that tangible, is it?)

2014 – 2015

The year 2014 will usher in a huge change in your life. Of course, the previous three years were all a preparation for this. Now you are in a completely new sandbox. In fact, the change might be so dramatic, your daily wardrobe will be different. If, prior to this year, you used to dress in tailored outfits, now you might be in sweats and gumboots. Or vice versa. ("Should I pack tropical?")

Basically, you are at the brink of a new thirty-year cycle, something similar to what happened around 1983–87. ("Omigawd! I remember that!") It's interesting to note that just when you are setting off on some kind of a new journey, where, in fact, you're going to reinvent yourself — all kinds of travel opportunities, plus chances to explore education, publishing, and the media suddenly appear for you! How cool is that? (Expect opportunities in medicine and the law as well.)

Again, Lady Luck smiles on you! Just when things are unsure in one area of your life (like being on new, uncharted turf), lucky Jupiter goes sailing across the top of your chart for the first time since 2002, bringing you opportunities to boost your good name and reputation. (We like!) Travel related to work will be likely.

In many ways, this is curious because other influences show you're beginning something new — and yet, this Jupiter influence indicates you're moving ahead and making great progress, especially with respect to your public reputation and how your accomplishments are viewed by others. (Ah, life's sweet mysteries.)

This is why 2015–16 is a great time of success and increased expansion in terms of your power and, certainly, your confidence. Something is looking extremely rosy, even though you're in an entirely new environment, or home, or job, or whatever.

One obvious explanation for this combination of newness and success occurring at the same time is that for the past three years, an urge to be self-employed has been growing within you. (And for those of you who do not suddenly spin off into self-employment, you certainly have a new attitude to your work.) It's as if you're forming a new relationship with your job. Whatever

that relationship is will free you from dull routine, and, at the same time, make you feel more autonomous and in control of your destiny. (Well, at least what you wear to work.)

2016 – 2018

This is a popular window of time! For whatever reason, many of you are joining clubs, groups, classes, or professional associations. Group situations will boost your social juices. You're definitely in the swing of things, enjoying meeting new people and enjoying being in the company of others. This interaction is a good thing.

This enthusiasm will embolden your goals, and encourage you to take on even more, or expect more for yourself. It's as if the feedback from others is all the reassuring encouragement you need to go for the brass ring.

Once again, I see this boost of confidence will enable some of you to spin off into self-employed situations. It's good to remember that your ruler, Pluto, is the planet that symbolizes all aspects of manufacturing. In other words, when you make money in a Pluto way, you make a tiny amount of profit many, many times over. (Like a small percentage of something that is sold in a high-volume way.)

Nevertheless, despite this rosy success, in this same time frame, you enter a two- to three-year window when you begin to work very hard for your earnings. (Success can be demanding!) Meanwhile, back in the dark recesses of your mind, you're starting to question what your life is all about. This is when you start asking yourself what really matters. Fame? Money? Relationships? Family? Home and real estate? Or will your final rewards be something else?

But you do know you don't want to put your money on the wrong horse. You do not intend to be looking in the mirror when you're eighty-five years old, saying, "Kid — you blew it!" This is *not* an option.

(On the other hand, according to Woody Allen, "There's nothing sexier than a lapsed Catholic.")

Once again, the fortuitous timing of lucky Jupiter comes to your rescue just as you ponder life's big questions. In October 2017, moneybags Jupiter enters Scorpio, where it stays until November 2018. How sweet it is!

"I couldn't wait for success so I went ahead without it."
JONATHAN WINTERS
American Comedian and Actor
Played the Comedic Character Maude Frickert
(B. NOVEMBER 11, 1925)

With Jupiter in your sign during 2018, lots of opportunities open up for you. (For example, the last time Jupiter was in your sign was during 2006. Think back to what happened then.) This definitely boosts your confidence!

By the end of 2018, your sense of poise and self-assurance is strengthened — no question. You will have the courage to make further changes if necessary — and, indeed, this is what will probably happen. According to Scorpio Jonathan Winters, "Nothing is impossible. Some things are just less likely than others."

2019 – 2020

Money is starting to roll in now due to increased earnings or a better job. Those of you who stepped out on your own to explore self-employment are experiencing success! *Chug, chug, chug.* "I thought I could. I thought I could."

This couldn't be more timely, because in the next two-year window, many of you will change jobs, change residences, or both. Something is going to happen that changes your daily surroundings.

Why? Because ever since 2012–13, you have been embarking on an entirely new journey. Back then, you were actually beginning to reinvent yourself. That's why you found yourself in a new sandbox. It's also why you began to question your basic values in life. Now, and in the next two years, you're ready to put the finishing touches on the new you. Your experiences will refine and hone how you talk, think, speak, and communicate. Even how you listen! In order to do this, life will plunge you into a fresh daily environment. Consider this your wake-up call.

For some, the wake-up call will be so dramatic, they'll be in an environment where the people no longer speak English! ("*¿Donde està el baño?*")

Just think of this time as a state of flux. Anything can happen. For Scorpios who are under sixty, it is almost inevitable that you will have a residential or job change. (Even if you don't think so.) For Scorpios who are older, especially people who are retired, it still might bring about a residential shift of sorts. Some people might let go of the cottage, or, alternatively, move to their winter chalet or their summer home. Something in your daily environment *will* change.

By 2020, whatever occurs pleases you very much. This is a year of increased optimism. You feel happier and more fortunate! Obviously, something in your life provokes this elevated state of contentment. Some likely causes might be that you really like where you have just moved to, or you really like your new job. After all, when you're in a state of flux vis-à-vis jobs and residences, and then suddenly you're very happy — it's a logical conclusion.

This is also an excellent time for writers, actors, teachers, and people who work in sales and marketing, as well as people who drive for a living. These particular professions are blessed around 2020.

2021 – 2023

It follows almost naturally that — after all that time of uncertainty and flux with respect to where you live and where you work — in the next few years, your major priority is to establish a firm foundation for yourself. (Ya think?) You want a home you can count on. You want security!

Therefore, if you moved in the past few years and you like where you moved, then in the next few years, you will fix up this place. We're not talking new curtains or matching towels. This is more likely a major renovation. If you bought property recently, then you will renovate, or fix the basement, or the roof, or do something substantial.

Alternatively, for those who moved recently and are not happy where you are living, the next two years will make you work fervently to move again, or find a home that fits the bill for you. Therefore, this could involve a second move. It might also involve a major real-estate transaction at this stage in your life.

Another reason some of you are moving again or renovating is because you're expanding your family through birth, marriage, adoption, children, or grandchildren. Or, maybe a brother-in-law who just won't go home — but that's rather unlikely, considering you are a firm, no-nonsense Scorpio. Scorpios are not pushovers. You're kind, generous, and certainly decent. But you're not a pushover. You don't have a gullible bone in your body.

The years 2021–22 are an excellent time for real estate. Therefore, this is a wonderful time to buy your own personal real estate, or speculate in real estate. This is also a warm, fuzzy year for family. Family relations are *definitely* happier! Family members are more generous to each other as well. It's very much a feel-good year in your home scene in general.

By around 2022, even though you might still be renovating or working to solidify your home base, you will take time off for a serious vacation. This is not just a weekend off to Vegas — this is a real, honest-to-God vacation. (You know you need one when you start to look like the photo in your passport.)

"But lo! What light through yonder window breaks?" The year 2022 is not only a wonderful year for vacations, it's a fabulous year for love, romance, parties, sports, exciting social occasions, and playful times with children. Some of you will meet the love of your life! (Be still, my beating heart.)

In part, this is because you're much more relaxed! Ever since 2013, you've been redefining who you were in the world. Now you have a sense of who you *are*; and, also, you have a strong sense of where you're living. This means you've covered the basics, and you're ready for more of life!

However, something else is at play here. About three or four years ago, wild, wacky Uranus entered the sign of Taurus, which is completely opposite your sign. Uranus will continue to oppose Scorpio until 2025. This definitely shakes things up! It could catapult some of you out of an existing partnership. ("I gotta be me!") It might also thrust some of you into an unusual relationship with someone from a very different background or a different culture. Uranus's journey through Taurus will take place over a span of about seven years. In 2018–20 it will affect Scorpios who were born in October. From 2020–22, it affects Scorpios who were born in the first ten days of November. And the later Scorpios will feel this effect most strongly in 2022–25.

One thing is certain: whatever you undergo while Uranus is opposite your sign will be a completely new experience, because the last time this occurred was in the late 1930s and early 1940s. It's a whole new ballgame!

For those of you who have been staying together for the sake of the kids, or because of some other kind of emotional dependency, or perhaps because of money — these reasons just won't cut it anymore. Suppressed tensions are surfacing! Even solid relationships, which will weather this storm, will have to make adjustments so that each partner feels less constrained and enjoys more freedom.

It's tricky. By now many of you have developed a lifestyle that you're comfortable with and you trust. You've got your little trapline, and you like it. We all get this way. That which is familiar and safe often becomes more valuable than the freedom of self-

expression. But Uranus doesn't think so! No matter how old you are, this period is going to feel like a midlife crisis. You're going to go through changes that ultimately make you feel younger, freer, and more excited about your life on a daily basis. This seven-year window is all about making a break for freedom. "To the gates!"

Perhaps that's why, by 2023, you're enjoying your job so much more. This improvement could be due to a different job, or just a different attitude to your current job, or a change in your current job. Maybe you love the money, or you love your boss, or you love your setup. Whatever it is — you're happy! (Happy is good.)

2024 – 2025

There's good news and bad news. Let's start with the bad news, because it really isn't that bad. At this stage in your life, you seem to be a bit lost about what it is you really want to do. In my columns, I refer to this as wondering what you really want to be when you grow up. It's not so much as if you're trying to get a better handle on your value system. It's not that at all. What you're seeking is a rewarding, meaningful, joyful way of expressing yourself that will hopefully bring you pots of money! (Yeah!)

You want to do your own thing — something that gives you a sense of accomplishment and at the same time feels right to be doing. Therefore, no matter how successfully you are doing whatever it is you are doing, you're starting to question it all. ("Is this what I *really* want?")

The good news is Jupiter is now entering the upper half of your chart, which means your good fortune is increasingly apparent to all! For starters, in 2024, new partnerships might form, especially with people who are richer, older, or more established than you. Certainly, existing partnerships will be more enriching and reassuring. This is a fabulous year to enter into any new partnership, be it intimate or professional.

In 2025, you continue to benefit from partnerships, but in a more tangible, financial, and advantageous way. Now your partner will earn more, which means you benefit indirectly. Or you might literally receive money, goods, favours, and the use of other things from others. The year 2025 is also an excellent time to go for a mortgage or a loan. You might receive an inheritance. In other words, you will benefit from the wealth and resources of others! Ka-ching!

What's not to like?

"All my life people have said that I wasn't going to make it."
TED TURNER
American Media Mogul and Philanthropist
(B. NOVEMBER 19, 1938)

Famous Scorpio Personalities

Pelé	October 23, 1940
Michael Crichton	October 23, 1942–2008
Ang Lee	October 23, 1954
Dwight Yoakam	October 23, 1956
Aravind Adiga	October 23, 1974
Ryan Reynolds	October 23, 1976
Moss Hart	October 24, 1904–1961
Bill Wyman	October 24, 1936
F. Murray Abraham	October 24, 1939
Kevin Kline	October 24, 1947
Amadou Bagayoko	October 24, 1954
Pablo Picasso	October 25, 1881–1973
Helen Reddy	October 25, 1941
James Carville	October 25, 1944
David Furnish	October 25, 1962
Katy Perry	October 25, 1984
Bob Hoskins	October 26, 1942
Pat Sajak	October 26, 1946
Hillary R. Clinton	October 26, 1947
Keith Urban	October 26, 1967
Theodore Roosevelt	October 27, 1858–1919
Ruby Dee	October 27, 1924
Sylvia Plath	October 27, 1932–1963
John Cleese	October 27, 1939
Fran Lebowitz	October 27, 1950
Roberto Benigni	October 27, 1952
Simon LeBon	October 27, 1958
Jonas Salk	October 28, 1914–1995
Cleo Laine	October 28, 1927
Joan Plowright	October 28, 1929
Bill Gates	October 28, 1955
Julia Roberts	October 28, 1967
Ben Harper	October 28, 1969
Brad Paisley	October 28, 1972
Joaquin Phoenix	October 28, 1974

Fanny Brice	October 29, 1891–1951
Richard Dreyfuss	October 29, 1947
Dan Castellaneta	October 29, 1957
Joely Fisher	October 29, 1967
Eric Staal	October 29, 1984
Charles Atlas	October 30, 1892–1972
Louis Malle	October 30, 1932–1995
Grace Slick	October 30, 1939
Henry Winkler	October 30, 1945
Diego Maradona	October 30, 1960
Nia Long	October 30, 1979
Sarah Carter	October 30, 1980
Chiang Kai-shek	October 31, 1887–1975
Dan Rather	October 31, 1931
Michael Landon	October 31, 1936–1991
Sally Kirkland	October 31, 1941
John Candy	October 31, 1950–1994
Jane Pauley	October 31, 1950
Peter Jackson	October 31, 1961
Dermot Mulroney	October 31, 1963
Larry Flynt	November 1, 1942
David Foster	November 1, 1949
Lyle Lovett	November 1, 1957
Fernando Valenzuela	November 1, 1960
Toni Collette	November 1, 1972
Jenny McCarthy	November 1, 1972
Aishwarya Rai	November 1, 1973
Steve Ditko	November 2, 1927
Shere Hite	November 2, 1942
Stefanie Powers	November 2, 1942
Keith Emerson	November 2, 1944
k. d. lang	November 2, 1961
David Schwimmer	November 2, 1966
Charles Bronson	November 3, 1921–2003
Martin Cruz Smith	November 3, 1942
Anna Wintour	November 3, 1949
Roseanne Barr	November 3, 1952
Kate Capshaw	November 3, 1953
Dennis Miller	November 3, 1953
Gemma Ward	November 3, 1987
Will Rogers	November 4, 1879–1935
Walter Cronkite	November 4, 1916–2009

Art Carney	November 4, 1918–2003
Robert Mapplethorpe	November 4, 1946–1989
Kathy Griffin	November 4, 1960
Jeff Probst	November 4, 1962
Matthew McConaughey	November 4, 1969
Curtis Stone	November 4, 1975
Elke Sommer	November 5, 1940
Art Garfunkel	November 5, 1941
Sam Shepard	November 5, 1943
Patricia Wells	November 5, 1946
Bryan Adams	November 5, 1959
Tilda Swinton	November 5, 1960
Tatum O'Neal	November 5, 1963
Sally Field	November 6, 1946
Glenn Frey	November 6, 1948
Ethan Hawke	November 6, 1970
Thandie Newton	November 6, 1972
Rebecca Romijn	November 6, 1972
Marie Curie	November 7, 1867–1934
Leon Trotsky	November 7, 1879–1940
Billy Graham	November 7, 1918
Al Hirt	November 7, 1922–1999
Joan Sutherland	November 7, 1926
Mary Travers	November 7, 1937–2009
Joni Mitchell	November 7, 1943
Bram Stoker	November 8, 1847–1912
Christiaan Barnard	November 8, 1922–2001
Patti Page	November 8, 1927
Alain Delon	November 8, 1935
Bonnie Raitt	November 8, 1949
Mary Hart	November 8, 1950
Alfre Woodard	November 8, 1952
Rickie Lee Jones	November 8, 1954
Gordon Ramsay	November 8, 1966
Parker Posey	November 8, 1968
Carl Sagan	November 9, 1934–1996
Tom Fogerty	November 9, 1941–1990
Susan Tedeschi	November 9, 1970
Eric Dane	November 9, 1972
Nick Lachey	November 9, 1973
Martin Luther	November 10, 1483–1546
Richard Burton	November 10, 1925–1984

Tim Rice	November 10, 1944
Ellen Pompeo	November 10, 1969
Brittany Murphy	November 10, 1977–2009
George Patton	November 11, 1885–1945
Kurt Vonnegut	November 11, 1922–2007
Jonathan Winters	November 11, 1925
Stanley Tucci	November 11, 1960
Demi Moore	November 11, 1962
Calista Flockhart	November 11, 1964
Adam Beach	November 11, 1972
Leonardo DiCaprio	November 11, 1974
Sun Yat-sen	November 12, 1866–1925
Grace Kelly	November 12, 1929–1982
Neil Young	November 12, 1945
Radha Mitchell	November 12, 1973
Ryan Gosling	November 12, 1980
Anne Hathaway	November 12, 1982
Joe Mantegna	November 13, 1947
Whoopi Goldberg	November 13, 1949
Chris Noth	November 13, 1954
Jimmy Kimmel	November 13, 1967
Steve Zahn	November 13, 1967
Gerard Butler	November 13, 1969
Frederick Banting	November 14, 1891–1941
Brian Keith	November 14, 1921–1997
Charles, Prince of Wales	November 14, 1948
D. B. Sweeney	November 14, 1961
Laura San Giacomo	November 14, 1962
Georgia O'Keeffe	November 15, 1887–1986
Ed Asner	November 15, 1929
Petula Clark	November 15, 1932
Sam Waterston	November 15, 1940
Anni-Frid Lyngstad	November 15, 1945
Beverly D'Angelo	November 15, 1951
Chad Kroeger	November 15, 1974
Marg Helgenberger	November 16, 1958
Diana Krall	November 16, 1964
Lisa Bonet	November 16, 1967
Kelly O. Benson	November 16, 1969
Martha Plimpton	November 16, 1970
Maggie Gyllenhaal	November 16, 19773
Oksana Baiul	November 16, 1977

Rock Hudson	November 17, 1925–1985
Gordon Lightfoot	November 17, 1938
Martin Scorsese	November 17, 1942
Lauren Hutton	November 17, 1943
Danny DeVito	November 17, 1944
Lorne Michaels	November 17, 1944
Tom Seaver	November 17, 1944
Mary Elizabeth Mastrantonio	November 17, 1958
Daisy Fuentes	November 17, 1966
Rachel McAdams	November 17, 1978
Christopher Paolini	November 17, 1983
Johnny Mercer	November 18, 1909–1976
Alan Shepard	November 18, 1923–1998
Margaret Atwood	November 18, 1939
Linda Evans	November 18, 1942
Alan Dean Foster	November 18, 1946
Warren Moon	November 18, 1956
Oscar Núñez	November 18, 1958
Elizabeth Perkins	November 18, 1960
Owen Wilson	November 18, 1968
Chloë Sevigny	November 18, 1974
Indira Gandhi	November 19, 1917–1984
Roy Campanella	November 19, 1921–1993
Larry King	November 19, 1933
Ted Turner	November 19, 1938
Calvin Klein	November 19, 1942
Meg Ryan	November 19, 1961
Jodie Foster	November 19, 1962
Jason Scott Lee	November 19, 1966
Jim C. Garrison	November 20, 1921–1992
Robert Kennedy	November 20, 1925–1968
Dick Smothers	November 20, 1939
Bo Derek	November 20, 1956
Josh Turner	November 20, 1977
Foster Hewitt	November 21, 1902–1985
Goldie Hawn	November 21, 1945
Nicolette Sheridan	November 21, 1963
Björk	November 21, 1965

SAGITTARIUS

NOVEMBER 22 – DECEMBER 21

SAGITTARIUS
THE CENTAUR
(NOVEMBER 22 – DECEMBER 21)

"I SEE."

"Don't worry about the world coming to an end today.
It's already tomorrow in Australia."

CHARLES M. SCHULZ

American Cartoonist

Peanuts

(NOVEMBER 26, 1922–FEBRUARY 12, 2000)

"I don't believe in astrology; I'm a Sagittarius, and we're skeptical."

ARTHUR C. CLARKE

British Science Fiction Author, Inventor, and Futurist

2001: A Space Odyssey

(DECEMBER 17, 1917–MARCH 19, 2008)

Element: Fire
Ruling Planet: Jupiter
Quality: Mutable
Opposite Sign: Gemini
Symbol: The Centaur
Glyph: The Centaur's Arrow
Lucky Gems: Turquoise, Amethyst, and Topaz[1]
Flowers: Dandelion and Eglantine
Colours: Purple and Blue
Parts of the Body: Thighs and Hips

You Like: Animals, travel, the outdoors, challenges, learning profound things, gambling, mythology, research, taking risks, keeping your options open. You also love booze, gambling, and serious partying. (I mean, you party!)

You Don't Like: Being confined, banal matters, domestic chores, possessive people, orders, apathy, injustice, and cruelty to animals. You also don't like uncomfortable formal wear and effete snobs.

Where You Shine: Broad-minded, philosophical, wise, positive thinking, joyous, mature, tolerant, gifted, and generous. You are also athletic, ecologically minded ("Save the males!"), and look great in Gore-Tex.

So Who's Perfect? Slapdash, impatient, rash, flippant, forgetful, overly optimistic, casual, and indiscreet. Guess who is a serious boozer?

---

1. Lucky gems? Flowers? Colours? These can vary according to different sources. Just so you know.

What Is Sagittarius-ness?[2]

The quickest way to understand what Sagittarius is all about is to understand what your ruling planet means in astrology. Your ruling planet is Jupiter (also called Jove). The Romans made Jupiter the patron saint of ancient Rome, and the Greeks called this god Zeus. (You're the big time, baby!)

As King of the Gods, Jupiter was depicted as a bearded older man, always naked, holding a thunderbolt because he was also King of the Sky and Thunder. His father was Saturn, and Mercury and Mars were his children, while Neptune and Pluto were his brothers. In addition to ruling the gods, Jupiter also ruled the laws in society. (He had it covered from all angles.)

Jupiter was also associated with wine festivals and he had *lots* of love affairs! ("By Jove! You don't say?")

In our solar system, Jupiter is the largest planet. It is sooooo big, you could put all the other planets inside it, and still have enough room for a sesame seed and the heart of a Hollywood producer.[3]

To get an idea of its relative size, the diameter of Jupiter is 89,000 miles, whereas the diameter of Earth is a mere 8,000 miles. This is why astrology associates Jupiter with growth, expansion, magnification, increase, and *excess*. "Excess? Does this ring a bell, Pavlov?"

Jupiter is also the ruler of luck and good fortune! It represents success, abundance, happiness, joy, and generosity. I often call it "moneybags Jupiter" because it represents wealth. Jupiter is everything everyone wants — success, luck, riches, and happiness. Yay!

No wonder your sign is breezy, upbeat, and optimistic!

> "I am an optimist. It does not seem too much use being anything else."
> WINSTON CHURCHILL
> Politician, Historian, Writer, and Painter
> Prime Minister of the United Kingdom, 1940–1945 and 1951–1955
> Best Known for His Leadership during the Second World War
> (NOVEMBER 30, 1874–JANUARY 24, 1965)

---

2. No one is just one sign because everyone's chart is made up of different planets. Therefore, this section captures the Sagittarius archetype — the qualities of "Sagittarius-ness." Many other signs will have Sagittarius characteristics as well. Therefore, the discussion of one sign is not an exact description of that person; rather, it is a description of the qualities of that sign.

3. I borrowed from Fred Allen, who said, "You can take all the sincerity of Hollywood, place it in the navel of a firefly, and still have room enough for three caraway seeds and a producer's heart."

"I always like to look on the optimistic side of life,
but I'm realistic enough to know that life is a complex matter."
WALT DISNEY
American Film Producer, Director, Screenwriter, Voice Actor, Animator,
Innovator in Theme Park Design, and Philanthropist
Created and Produced Animated Pictures with Characters such as Mickey Mouse,
Donald Duck, Goofy, and Pluto
(DECEMBER 5, 1901–DECEMBER 15, 1966)

Size Does Matter

The huge size of Jupiter is your hot tip to understanding Sagittarius. You do everything in a *big* way. You're a big spender, and you're very generous to others. You're
always contemplating big ideas and dreaming up big schemes. You love money, and
you constantly look for ways to get rich quick. Incidentally, the reason you want
this money isn't just for the money itself. For you, money is your *ticket to ride*!

The expansive quality of Jupiter represents your desire for *freedom*. You are always
pushing outwards — pushing the boundaries in your life. You cannot be held back
or shackled. That would break you. For you, personal freedom is a survival issue.

Your need to expand your world began when you were a little child trying to go
as far as you could, literally and figuratively. You often wandered away from home
because you knew there was a big, exciting world out there waiting to be discovered!

She's Got a Ticket to Ride . . .

You are the globetrotter of the zodiac. You were born with wanderlust in your
blood. You mention the word "travel" to any astrologer and they will immediately
reply, "Sagittarius!"

Other signs take trips. They book five days in Vegas, or a week in Paris and a week
in Rome. But you pack your bags and go to Asia, or Europe, or North America. You
travel for the spring, or the winter, or the whole year. You're like a rolling tumble-
weed seeking adventure and knowledge.

Like your ruler, Jupiter, you want to *expand* your experience of life. You intend to
grow beyond your little test tube. You want more. You have always wanted more,
because it's out there!

But lo! There is another reason you love to travel. You want to *stay fresh*. You want
to see new places, new faces, new cities, and new cultures because it makes you feel
alive and alert! You have a horror of slipping into a somnolent ennui where you no
longer "see" your surroundings.

"It is I, Arthur, son of Uther Pendragon, from the castle of Camelot.
King of the Britons, defeater of the Saxons, sovereign of all England! —
and this is my trusty servant, Patsy. We have ridden the length and breadth of
the land in search of knights who will join me in my court at Camelot....
Go and tell your master that we have been charged by God with a sacred quest."

QUOTE FROM *MONTY PYTHON AND THE HOLY GRAIL*
(1975 Comedy Film Starring Graham Chapman, John Cleese,
Terry Gilliam, Eric Idle, Terry Jones, and Michael Palin)

Ah yes, the *sacred quest*!

Travel is vital for you because you are the quester. You seek the Grail. You want the answers to all the big questions. You want to know how life works. (Yes, we know Douglas Adams discovered the answer to the Ultimate Question of Life, the Universe, and Everything. It's 42.)

Actually, you know how to travel *beyond* the physical. Of course, you like to go somewhere by jet, train, bus, or car, or by walking or hitchhiking. (You love hiking.) But you also travel through ideas, concepts, philosophies, religions, cultures, and different experiences, including different careers and ways of living and loving. You want to go beyond what is *right here*.

"The only way to discover the limits of the possible is to go
beyond and into the impossible."

ARTHUR C. CLARKE
British Science Fiction Author, Inventor, and Futurist
2001: A Space Odyssey
(DECEMBER 17, 1917–MARCH 19, 2008)

The Domains of Jupiter

In addition to wealth and expansion, in astrology Jupiter also rules jurisprudence, universities, and institutions of higher learning, including museums, art galleries, and places where knowledge and art are stored.

Jupiter rules religion and the traditions that bind society, whether they are the laws of religion, or the laws of the land, or the laws of how society interacts.

Jupiter also rules healing and medicine as a profession.[4]

Publishing, libraries, and anything related to the storage of knowledge or the dissemination of knowledge are also under the domain of Jupiter. Naturally, this includes the media.[5] Teaching and spreading information through higher education, publishing, and libraries is what Jupiter is all about.

---

4. Pluto, the ruler of Scorpio, rules all things carnal and the medicine of surgery, whereas Jupiter rules the notions of healing and growth.
5. More specifically, Uranus is associated with the airwaves of radio, and Pluto is associated with how television reaches the masses.

This is pretty heady stuff! (You guys are smart.)

Just the appreciation of what Jupiter means in astrology gives you a good idea of Sagittarius. But so far this is simply about your ruling planet Jupiter. What about the symbol for Sagittarius, which is the centaur?

The Centaur

The Sagittarian centaur is half human and half horse. The human half carries a bow and arrow, representing the quality of shooting arrows into the sky, which, as you no doubt remember, is ruled by Jupiter.[6] These arrows represent your high ideals and desire to reach for further knowledge. You might say this is the part of you with "your head in the clouds."

However, the horse part of the centaur has four feet firmly planted on the ground. No matter how idealistic you are, or what a great visionary you are (and you are), you are also *practical*. In fact, not only are you practical, you love the earth! You embrace nature in all its elements and particularly the animal kingdom.

I ♥ Animals

All signs love animals, but Sagittarians are unusually passionate about animals and the care of animals.

True to your ruler — big Jupiter — you prefer larger animals like dogs and horses, although I once knew a Sadge who had a pet silverfish.

You are especially appalled at cruelty to animals. Of course, all signs can abhor cruelty to animals, and all signs can have compassion for animals. Nevertheless, Sagittarians are inexplicably closer to the animal kingdom than other signs. It's a curious truth.

The Podium

I believe the podium is an excellent symbol for Sagittarius. The variety of speakers at a podium aptly illustrates the wide range of manifestations of your sign.

At its highest expression, Sagittarius at the podium is the guru, the Saviour, the one who has all the answers for humankind.

At its next highest expression, we might have the religious leader, or the head of state, or someone to whom the country pays great respect. The level after that might be the judge, or the statesperson, or someone with the stature of elected office, or a military general. The next level at the podium might be a professor or a scientist. Then teachers, actors, and entertainers; then salespeople, promoters, and marketers.

But at the bottom there is always the Sagittarian con artist. Many of you are recoiling, because your sign is known for its honesty! But, hey — Sagittarians can sell anyone the Brooklyn Bridge! Then come back and pitch insurance for it as well.

---

6. There will be a test on this material next Wednesday.

The significance of the podium is this: you have the potential to be all these levels because one thing is certain — *you dazzle people with your words!*

"Life is a challenge, meet it! Life is a dream, realize it!
Life is a game, play it! Life is love, enjoy it!"
SRI SATHYA SAI BABA
South Indian Guru, Spiritual Figure, and Educator
(B. NOVEMBER 23, 1926)

Personal Freedom

Several signs need a lot of freedom, for example, Aries, Gemini, and Aquarius. However, for Sagittarius, freedom is different. The freedom you need is beyond just freedom of action and movement. You want freedom in *everything*.

For example, you express your freedom in how you dress. You flout the rules. You dress for comfort rather than style. You prefer casual clothes that "work" for you.

When others are dressed more formally, you show up in cut-offs and a T-shirt, just for the hell of it. Or you might wear hiking boots or gumboots or go barefoot. It satisfies your need to call attention to yourself, along with your need to remind the world that you don't take things too seriously. You're not an effete snob. You're in the moment, ready for life, and not constrained by sucking up to anyone to get their approval, or trying to "fit in" because of tradition or social mores. *Phfffft!*

"The more I like me, the less I want to pretend to be other people."
JAMIE LEE CURTIS
American Actress and Children's Author
Trading Places, A Fish Called Wanda, and *True Lies*
(B. NOVEMBER 22, 1958)

However, when it comes to traditional holidays, you're totally enthusiastic! In every workplace, the Sagittarian employee will do or wear something to acknowledge St. Patrick's Day, Valentine's Day, Halloween, or whatever holiday turns you on. It's an excuse to *party*!

As curious as this might sound, your love of freedom means you love to have a home — preferably, two homes — one in the country and one in the city. Why? Your home is your *base*. This means you can travel the globe and know you *belong* somewhere. You have a home to come back to. (Plus people are suspicious when you don't have a permanent address. You've learned this.)

You're wonderfully skilled at meeting people from all walks of life and staying in touch with them. You phone, write, email, and send appropriate cards to your pals around the globe reminding them of your warm bond (and making sure the next time you travel, you have lots of free places to stay).

"Friendship is one of the most tangible things in a world
which offers fewer and fewer supports."
KENNETH BRANAGH
Northern Irish Actor and Director
Much Ado About Nothing and *As You Like It*
(B. DECEMBER 10, 1960)

Four Sagittarius Personalities

There are four classic personalities to your sign. No Sagittarius is just one personality. More likely, you embrace some qualities of all four.

1. Pleasure-Loving Hedonist
2. Outdoors Enthusiast
3. Philosopher–Teacher
4. Businessperson–Financier

Pleasure-Loving Hedonist

"Decadence is wonderful."
JACK CHALKER
American Science Fiction Author
(DECEMBER 17, 1944–FEBRUARY 11, 2005)

Your approach to life is work hard, party hard. You love to entertain others, and Lord knows you're witty! (The word "jovial" actually comes from the god Jove.) You *love* to entertain at home, and you're a fabulous host who never stints on money. You really know how to show others a great time! (In fact, you're downright extravagant.) You're a natural crowd-pleaser who is thrilled by the presence of important people and VIPs.

But you don't always party at home. You party *everywhere*! This is because you're a thrill-seeking, risk-taking person who wants to be where the action is! At times, you're just plain reckless. (You know who you are.) You always buy someone a drink. People see you as happy-go-lucky and generous.

Small wonder others *want* to be in your presence because you are a promoter par excellence! You can enthuse people about anything. Above all, you can promote yourself. This self-promoting quality, combined with your breezy enthusiasm and optimistic take on life, magnetizes people to you. Everyone wants to have fun and ride on your coattails.

"I am not a heavy drinker. I can sometimes go for
hours without touching a drop."
NOËL COWARD
British Playwright, Composer, Director, Actor, and Singer
(DECEMBER 16, 1899–MARCH 26, 1973)

This is why so many of you overdo it on booze and drugs. You arrive at excess because you don't seem to notice when you're passing through satisfaction.

"I am a raging alcoholic and a raging addict,
and I didn't want to see my kids do the same thing."
OZZY OSBOURNE
British Singer-Songwriter, Lead Vocalist of Black Sabbath, and Reality TV Star
(B. DECEMBER 3, 1948)

Your love of freedom and your desire to have fun make you a gambler at heart. In part, this is because you are actually lucky! Sagittarians often win things. Plus you are the most optimistic sign in the zodiac! Every Sagittarius believes there's something better just around the next corner. This is why you're always game to play the next card, or put your money on the next roll of the dice.

Sagittarians swarm to Las Vegas and Reno, not only to gamble, but also to work as dealers and in other jobs in casinos. The reason you like to gamble is because this is *your approach to life*. You gamble on everything — where you live, where you work, whom you see. You are intrigued by the myriad possibilities the immediate future can hold for you — with a snap of your fingers!

If you went home and discovered your house was burned to the ground, no matter how upset you would be (and of course you would be upset), nevertheless one tiny part of you in the furthest recess of your mind would be excited, thinking, *What's next?*

"It's like gambling somehow. You go out for a night of drinking,
and you don't know where you're going to end up the next day. It could
work out good or it could be disastrous. It's like the throw of the dice."
JIM MORRISON
American Singer-Songwriter, Poet, and Lead Vocalist and Lyricist for The Doors
(DECEMBER 8, 1943–JULY 3, 1971)

This thrill of gambling runs through all four personalities. In other words, this is inherent in the Sagittarian psyche. The outdoors enthusiast might gamble on climbing K2 or tackling the West Coast Trail. The professional athlete is constantly taking a gamble with his life and reputation.

The scientist might gamble on a new theory. A judge or university professor might gamble on self-publishing a book or endorsing one side of a controversy. And the successful businessperson takes lots of gambles! Sagittarian billionaire J. Paul Getty's formula for success was: "Rise early, work hard, strike oil." Nothing is predictable.

> "How can they beat me? I've been struck by lightning,
> had two back operations, and been divorced twice."
> LEE TREVINO
> American Professional Golfer
> (B. DECEMBER 1, 1939)

Plus, you love money! You're extravagant, almost recklessly so. But you don't love money for its own sake. For you, money is your passport to freedom.

So here is someone who loves life and who definitely has a lucky streak, combined with a risk-taking temperament riding on top of an amazing attitude of optimism — naturally, you play the long shot. Who wouldn't?

It's your constant test of your belief in the power of positive thinking.

> "A champion is afraid of losing. Everyone else is afraid of winning."
> BILLIE JEAN KING
> American Women's Tennis Champion
> (B. NOVEMBER 22, 1943)

Outdoors Enthusiast

Above all else — sky.

Jupiter is the King of the Sky. No wonder that's what you want overhead. Every Sagittarius needs to be outdoors getting fresh air every day. In fact, your sign is slightly claustrophobic. You could never work in a tiny booth in an underground parking lot all day. Never!

I recall, on two separate occasions, two male clients (both Sagittarius) telling me they could never shop in malls. One of them said, "I have mall sickness." And the other said, "I have mall disease." They both said it with a completely straight face, convinced there was such a thing — and I guess, for Sagittarius, there is! Suffice to say, Sagittarians are not in big department stores on Christmas Eve. Oh no!

I repeat — what you want overhead is sky. You are an outdoors person! All Sagittarians have a functional wardrobe with shoes and boots for every kind of weather. You're a Gore-Tex go-to person.

Every astrological sign rules a particular body part. The part of the body Sagittarius rules is the thighs — the largest muscles in your body. This is why you like activities that use your thighs, such as walking, cycling, running, jogging, climbing, and hiking. Combine this with your love of gambling for the thrill of adventure and your need to travel and respond to new situations — it all fits! You're the one we all want to be with if we're stranded on a desert island. You'll figure out how to start the fire and make blankets out of leaves or whatever. ("I never leave home without my battery-operated Crock-Pot.") Like Capricorn, you are capable of withstanding hardship. Because many of you camp, hike, or go mountain climbing, you're prepared for a hardy existence, even though you *do* like the comforts of home.

(If you detect a jaded attitude, it's because, to me, outdoors is where the car is.)

Of course, we all have our contradictions. Yes, you are casual and comfortable about your clothing. But when you cycle — you're *serious*. Whenever I spot seventeen people sleekly cycling by, dressed in colourful, Italian-designed, body-hugging outfits, I think to myself, "Sagittarians." And when you climb — you're *serious*. When you do your outdoor thang — you have the *gear*. Smokin'!

Not only do you cycle, climb, jog, hike, row, and go horseback riding, but, when push comes to shove, you will also work out in the gym. But this is not your preference. I know a Sagittarius who loves to cycle, but he also has a special room for his stationary bike at home. Naturally, there's a TV set up in front of this bike, and a big fan that blows on him while he's working out. (But of course.)

Philosopher–Teacher

You come by your role of philosopher–teacher honestly, because you are by nature a seeker, one who constantly wants answers to the big questions of the universe. In addition, your ruler Jupiter is the planet that has domain over higher education, universities, and colleges, as well as publishing. In fact, Jupiter also rules jurisprudence and the theory and philosophy of lawmaking.

> "What's another word for thesaurus?"
> STEVEN WRIGHT, American Comedian, Actor, and Writer
> (B. DECEMBER 6, 1955)

Justice and honour are important to you. Many of you are in the legal profession, or academia, or publishing. Some of you are also in politics. You like to be noticed, but, more important, you want to be in a position where you can promote ideas you believe are valuable.

Many Sagittarians crusade against injustice. Many of you are whistle-blowers. You deeply value truth, and you are without question the most blunt — dare we say tactless? — sign in the zodiac. You don't wish to offend. You have a style of speaking frankly and off the cuff that comes out as shocking to the person who hears your words. Things like, "Buy the dark blue dress. You don't look so fat in it."

You love to learn, you love to travel, and you love the company of intellectual friends. You delight in discourse, and, since you are so articulate, people are eager to hear your opinions.

There is no aspect of life you're not keen to explore. For example, many of you are surprisingly diet-conscious and love to test different food fads. You might try being a vegetarian, especially because of your love of animals. I know some Sagittarians who not only avoid eating meat, they will not wear leather — including shoes!

Your broad-minded, tolerant views, combined with your humorous take on life, definitely make you an entertaining lecturer and author. You are the professor who cycles to campus to explore new theories in your ivory tower. You know the rules — publish or perish.

> "Never doubt that a small group of thoughtful, committed citizens can change the world; indeed, it's the only thing that ever has."
> MARGARET MEAD
> American Cultural Anthropologist
> (DECEMBER 16, 1901–NOVEMBER 15, 1978)

Businessperson–Financier

> "I like entrepreneurial people; I like people who take risks."
> BILLIE JEAN KING
> American Women's Tennis Champion
> (B. NOVEMBER 22, 1943)

The Sagittarian willingness to take a risk combined with your intuitive sense about money — which you love — propels many of you into business. No matter how sophisticated your education, you are always street-smart, with lots of savvy. Hey — you get around! You travel and you meet people from all walks of life!

Furthermore, you know you're lucky with money. When you combine this with your ability to promote yourself, you get a person who is lucky in business!

> "If you owe the bank one hundred dollars, that's your problem.
> If you owe the bank one hundred million, that's the bank's problem."
> J. PAUL GETTY
> American Industrialist and Founder of the Getty Oil Company
> (DECEMBER 15, 1892–JUNE 6, 1976)

I often make jokes about the Sagittarian penchant for get-rich-quick schemes. In truth, you have an uncanny ability to see many ways to make money. Your confidence in yourself and your faith in your ability, plus your inclination to be future-oriented, all promote your business success!

You understand that money is energy. You have to spend money to make money. J. Paul Getty said, "Money is like manure. You have to spread it around or it smells."

As in many other things, you are lucky in business. You attract money! In part, this could be your show of extravagance, but it's also due to your inner confidence and bravado. The word "failure" is simply not in the vocabulary of a Sagittarian.[7]

Another reason many of you are so successful in business is because Sagittarians are *doers*. You are future-oriented and you're a visionary. When you want to make a decision, you act! Not only that, you act *swiftly*. You are also well-organized, because you learned long ago that this gave you more freedom!

Business is a logical choice, considering that your ruling planet Jupiter is the planet of wealth, good luck, wisdom, confidence, and success.

Billionaire philanthropist Andrew Carnegie (November 25, 1835–August 11, 1919) was a Sagittarius who believed teamwork was the ability to work together toward a common vision. Nevertheless, his famous advice was, "Put all your eggs in one basket, then watch that basket."

Despite his well-known endorsement of teamwork, he also knew that the early bird gets the worm, or, as he put it, "The first one gets the oyster, the second gets the shell."

One of the richest men in the world, Carnegie spent the last twenty years of his life devoted to philanthropy. He donated vast amounts of money to universities and institutions of learning, but he is perhaps best known for establishing the Carnegie libraries in the United States, Canada, and Britain. Of course, a library is close to the heart of any Sagittarius, because it involves book publishing as well as higher learning, and it satisfies your impulse to teach and spread knowledge.

The personal dictum of Andrew Carnegie was:

- To spend the first third of one's life getting all of the education one can
- To spend the next third making all the money one can
- To spend the last third giving it all away to worthwhile causes

Of course, the fault with this plan is it assumes you will live a long life. If you believe in the benefit of helping those who are less fortunate or helping worthy causes, it's probably a good idea to begin to do this before your life is two-thirds over. (Ya think?)

---

7. One of the saddest examples of this kind of confidence was General Custer's defeat at the Battle of Little Big-horn in 1876. Custer had both Moon and Sun in Sagittarius.

Sagittarius in Love

"I believe that sex is a beautiful thing between two people.
Between five, it's fantastic."

WOODY ALLEN

American Filmmaker, Screenwriter, Actor, Comedian, Jazz Musician,
Author, and Playwright

Annie Hall, Manhattan, and *Vicky Cristina Barcelona*

(B. DECEMBER 1, 1935)

You're romantic when you want to be. You can do poetry, flowers, love letters, caring gestures — the works. In fact, to be wooed by a Sagittarian can be a thrilling experience because you're sooooo persuasive! Your greatest skill is making your loved ones feel very, very special! And because you have the ability to do this — they *adore* you.

You make your lover feel bigger than life — more attractive, more vivacious, and more desirable — simply by what *you* say and do. This is a pretty heady potion!

But your need for freedom can never be ignored. You are skittish about commitment. (If you think you have mall disease, wait till you try altar sickness!) You are a very leery customer! "Don't Fence Me In" is your theme song.

Nevertheless, because you love to party and have a good time, you develop good drinking buddies and chums to party with who soon become very clooooose friends.

Quite often, some of you are an innocent player in the classic Hollywood movie where one person is chasing the "love of their life," all the while confiding their hopes and dreams about this longed-for lover to their faithful, caring buddy (who is, of course, in love with them)! Shakespeare used this plot line a lot. It invariably involves the "ah ha!" moment of truth when you realize your best friend is the person you *really* want to be with. It's a classic Sagittarian scenario.

However, what is more likely is that you fall hard for the completely wrong person. (Ouch.) I think this is all tied up with your love of challenge and that big gamble in the sky. When you see something you can't have — you must have it. If someone is unattainable (for example, married to someone else) you just saunter on up to the bar and place your order.

You will even fall for somebody who is completely inappropriate. Perhaps this person has a very different educational background or comes from a different culture. This just turns you on! You have a blind faith that you can defy the odds and make anything work.

This reminds me of the end of that fabulous movie *Some Like It Hot*, where Jack Lemmon is dressed in drag pretending to be "Daphne," and Joe E. Brown, playing Osgood, is an oil magnate millionaire who has been oft married and divorced. Osgood is *convinced* he loves Daphne.

> Daphne: Osgood, I'm gonna level with you. We can't get married at all.
> Osgood: Why not?
> Daphne: Well, in the first place, I'm not a natural blond.
> Osgood: Doesn't matter.
> Daphne: I smoke. I smoke all the time.
> Osgood: I don't care.
> Daphne: Well, I have a terrible past. For three years now, I've been living with a saxophone player.
> Osgood: I forgive you.
> Daphne: I can never have children.
> Osgood (unperturbed): We can adopt some.
> Jerry-Daphne: But you don't understand, Osgood. [He whips off his wig, exasperated, and changes to a manly voice.] Uh, I'm a man.
> Osgood (unruffled, undaunted, and still in love): *Well, nobody's perfect.*

This is why many of you have a disastrous first marriage.

Nevertheless, you have no trouble meeting people, because you're charming, friendly, witty, and also quite aggressive about going after what you want. You're the classic person who plays the field and has fun in Las Vegas. (What happens in Vegas stays in Vegas.)

You might encounter romance running a marathon, or rowing a race, or on the side of a mountain, or playing tennis. You might be cheering your favourite team and suddenly — ta-dah! — there is your true love.

Obviously, many of you hook up with your lover when travelling. You will actually marry someone who does not speak the same language as you! Now *that's* a gamble. Others meet their partners through their professions or at university. Generally, friendship comes first with Sagittarius. You are often very casual in the beginning.

"By love, of course, I refer to romantic love —
the love between man and woman, rather than that between mother and child, or a boy and his dog, or two headwaiters."

WOODY ALLEN

American Filmmaker, Screenwriter, Actor, Comedian, Jazz Musician,
Author, and Playwright
Annie Hall, Manhattan, and *Vicky Cristina Barcelona*
(B. DECEMBER 1, 1935)

When you finally decide you need a partner for life, you will be loyal — but you'll be loyal *in your way*. Both sexes are inclined to slip up now and then because, hey — these things happen. ("It didn't mean anything.") Plus you're a very physical sign — and impulsive! Nevertheless, no matter what happens, from your point of view you're always loyal to your loved one because they are the only one in your heart. It's an idealistic loyalty. The other little incidents are just throwaway Chiclets or mere bonbons. What's the big deal?

Sex is passionate and very physical for you. However, once you lose your ardour for someone, you can't fake it. You'd rather have nothing than pretend. Sometimes you can live with this because, in the long run, despite your passionate nature, you regard your partner as your best friend.

"I was the best I ever had."
WOODY ALLEN
American Filmmaker, Screenwriter, Actor, Comedian, Jazz Musician,
Author, and Playwright
Annie Hall, Manhattan, and *Vicky Cristina Barcelona*
(B. DECEMBER 1, 1935)

But, hey — your partner needs to respect your freedom. You like to go out with your friends to do your thing, and you don't want to explain everything when you get home. That means you're going to have to find a partner who can handle this, because not everyone can. Obviously, another Sagittarius would be a likely candidate.

Ultimately, you will have to come to terms with the fact that both complete freedom and commitment to a partnership involve some kind of compromise. Either you're in or you're out. There are benefits and drawbacks to both. Eventually, you have to make a decision. Sometimes this is one of the toughest things a Sagittarius ever has to do. But the comment below by Margaret Mead is something worth pondering:

"One of the oldest human needs is having someone
to wonder where you are when you don't come home at night."
MARGARET MEAD
American Cultural Anthropologist
(DECEMBER 16, 1901–NOVEMBER 15, 1978)

The Sagittarius Boss

"Every revolutionary idea seems to evoke three stages of reaction.
They may be summed up by the phrases: (1) It's completely impossible.
(2) It's possible, but it's not worth doing. (3) I said it was a good idea all along."

ARTHUR C. CLARKE

British Science Fiction Author, Inventor, and Futurist

2001: A Space Odyssey

(DECEMBER 17, 1917–MARCH 19, 2008)

The Sagittarius boss is full of great ideas, and, yes, he or she wants credit for them! This is a boss who is friendly, easygoing, and enthusiastic. Nevertheless, don't let this fool you, because this boss also has standards. In fact, the Sagittarian boss is not too concerned about the working conditions of their employees, because they think people should be able to endure a little discomfort to get the job done. After all, nothing is easy. In all fairness, this boss is willing to be as stoic and to undergo the same kind of discomfort they expect their employees to endure. The Sagittarian boss is fair.

The most notable thing about any Sagittarian boss is that half the time they're not there! They love to travel, or get out of the office, or be away at meetings or conferences. You have to catch them on the fly!

The great talent of the Sagittarian boss is their ability to rally the troops and boost the morale of everyone. When the chips are down, this boss will give you something to believe in! Sagittarians have an incredible talent to inspire others. Everyone wants to play for their team!

One thing is important: Sagittarians value honesty and straightforward directness. If an employee is dishonest, especially by stealing or lying — it's game over. No discussion. There's the door. Never underestimate the smarts of your Sagittarius boss. This is a person who is very comfortable with study, and who will *delve deeply* into any field to understand it. And never forget that this boss *likes to be liked*! It would behoove you to laugh at their jokes. (Smart employees already do this.)

"I played the tour in 1967 and told jokes, and nobody laughed. Then I won the Open the next year, told the same jokes, and everybody laughed like hell."

LEE TREVINO

American Professional Golfer

(B. DECEMBER 1, 1939)

The Sagittarius Employee

"I've got a theory that if you give one hundred percent all of the time,
somehow things will work out in the end."

LARRY BIRD

American NBA Basketball Player and Longtime Member of the Boston Celtics
(B. DECEMBER 7, 1956)

The Sagittarius employee brings a marvellous quality to their job —
their positive state of mind. It's wonderful to work with these people! They're not a
drag. Quite the opposite — they boost the morale of the whole place.

Another bonus is that this is someone who is willing to work hard! Not only
that, but they rarely complain about hardship and discomfort. This is an extremely
adaptable person who is upbeat and friendly. A good person to be around.

However, this employee needs to be allowed to do their little shtick every holiday. They want to put up balloons, or posters, or streamers, or whatever for St.
Patrick's Day, Valentine's, and Halloween, and perhaps on staff birthdays and for
special sports events, as well. They love an *excuse to party* and celebrate! And why
not? It's all about having fun.

Listen carefully when this employee has some bright ideas, because they know
how to boost sales! I once had a fabulous Sagittarius woman working for me who
constantly made money-making suggestions. I invariably declined, partly because
making money is not what motivates me, and secretly I was afraid she might put
my face on coffee mugs or T-shirts. (In truth, she made suggestions about TV shows
or speaking on cruises and that sort of thing.) However, one suggestion she made
was excellent and I followed her advice. She told me to create my website. Thank
you, Bev! Your wonderful idea has benefitted many people.[8]

Always remember that Sagittarians are natural money-makers! They are also
marvellous communicators, and can sell, persuade, or promote any idea! And their
financial moxie is excellent.

---

8. All the money raised from my website goes to charitable causes.

Something you might want to keep in mind: this employee needs outdoor stimulation, fresh air, and exercise. The Sagittarius employee can't be cooped up. Give this person every opportunity to go outdoors to deliver something, or buy something, or stretch their legs. They hate to feel they're in prison!

"I'm really into my running workout. Running really helps me clear my head and makes me feel good, especially when I'm stressed."

KATIE HOLMES
American Film and Television Actress
Batman Begins and TV's *Dawson's Creek*
(B. DECEMBER 18, 1978)

The Sagittarius Parent

"Crowded classrooms and half-day sessions are a tragic waste
of our greatest national resource — the minds of our children."
WALT DISNEY
American Film Producer, Director, Screenwriter, Voice Actor, Animator,
Innovator in Theme Park Design, and Philanthropist
Created and Produced Animated Pictures with Characters such as Mickey Mouse,
Donald Duck, Goofy, and Pluto
(DECEMBER 5, 1901–DECEMBER 15, 1966)

The Sagittarius parent has so many wonderful qualities I hardly know where to begin. Perhaps what's most important is that, essentially, the Sagittarius parent is optimistic about life. This means there is a good likelihood the vibes in the household are positive and joyful.

The most important thing this parent teaches his or her child is to believe in a positive future, because Sagittarians always expect something better down the road. They are hopeful about their future, and, because of this, they are not inclined to be depressed for any length of time, or to be filled with self-pity. This positive attitude is a wonderful thing to model for children!

The Sagittarius parent will also put an extraordinary emphasis on education when raising their children. This is because the entire concept of "higher educa-tion" — universities, colleges, and advanced training, along with libraries and the entire publishing industry — all of this — is under the domain of Jupiter, the ruler of Sagittarius. Sagittarians are philosophical and take a classical approach to educa-tion. If they had their way their kids would study Latin. "*Et tu, Papa?*"

Naturally, this same strong emphasis will go for sports, because Sagittarians value outdoor activities, outdoor exercise, and most especially sports! These are the parents who get up at 4 a.m. for hockey ice time and faithfully show up to soccer and football games in the rain, or baseball games in the blazing hot sun. And they bring food and drink. Yay!

No one better than a Sagittarius parent appreciates how fresh air and daily exercise will energize, invigorate, and benefit their children. In fact, they will be frustrated if their children balk at sports and just want to play video games or watch TV. (Grrrr.)

Another big plus of the Sagittarius parent is their willingness to have pets. All children want pets! The trick is to get Mom and Dad to agree to having a pet, because they know who ends up feeding and walking this pet, or changing the tank, or cleaning the cage, or whatever. In this endeavour, the Sagittarian parent is more than willing, because Sagittarians love animals!

Incidentally, it's actually a good thing Sagittarius parents encourage pets for the children, because the Sagittarius parent is often absent, especially the father. This parent is constantly answering the call of business, travel, and adventure. The Sagittarius mother is a bit less inclined, but she, too, is out of the home frequently.

If possible, these parents will take their children travelling with them. They might consider a world cruise and home-school their children, but this is the exception rather than the rule.

A large number of Sagittarians are serious party animals because of the Sagittarian tendency to do everything over the top. (You know who you are.) But your kids will know how to socialize! The co-founder of Alcoholics Anonymous, Bill Wilson (November 26, 1895–January 24, 1971), was a Sagittarius.

"Getting sober just exploded my life. Now I have a much clearer sense of myself and what I can and can't do. I am more successful than I have ever been. I feel very positive where I never did before, and I think that's all a direct result of getting sober."
JAMIE LEE CURTIS
American Actress and Author
Trading Places, A Fish Called Wanda, and *True Lies*
(B. NOVEMBER 22, 1958)

Ethics, morality, and decency are values your children will learn because you have excellent values and will teach your children to be tolerant, broad-minded, and free of prejudice regarding race, religion, and culture. (Naturally, there are exceptions, because there are exceptions to everything.)

Your kids are lucky because you support them in school, you encourage them in sports, you let them have pets, and you give them excellent values so they grow up not being fearful of society, but instead looking forward to discovering more of the world.

You give your kids the courage to live with enthusiasm and greet the future!

"All our dreams can come true, if we have the courage to pursue them."
WALT DISNEY
American Film Producer, Director, Screenwriter, Voice Actor, Animator, Innovator in Theme Park Design, and Philanthropist
Created and Produced Animated Pictures with Characters such as Mickey Mouse, Donald Duck, Goofy, and Pluto
(DECEMBER 5, 1901–DECEMBER 15, 1966)

The Sagittarius Child

"Ever since I was a child I have had this instinctive urge for expansion and growth. To me, the function and duty of a quality human being is the sincere and honest development of one's potential."

BRUCE LEE

Chinese-American Actor, Martial Arts Instructor, Philosopher, Director, Producer, Screenwriter, and Founder of the Jeet Kune Do Martial Arts Philosophy

(NOVEMBER 27, 1940–JULY 20, 1973)

The Sagittarius child is a delight to raise because, essentially, this child is easygoing, upbeat, optimistic, and happy in a naive way. This child believes people are basically decent and life is basically good, and adults know everything and always do the right thing. This is a very trusting child.

Naturally, this trust is charming and appealing; however, your challenge as a parent is to help the Sagittarius child be realistic about the world without becoming fearful. Basically, this child *prefers* trusting people. They *want* to live in a world where they believe people are trustworthy. Well, so do we all!

Therefore, your challenge is to deal with the Pollyanna nature of your Sagittarius child. You want to educate this child in the realities of life and the disappointing conduct of some adults. Factoid.

You definitely have to keep an eye on this little one because Sagittarius kids love to "travel"! They're always seeking adventure. This child needs to go outdoors every day to play in a park or participate in sports. Sagittarius children love the freedom of the outdoors.

These kids are thrilled with their first bicycle ("I'm outta here!") but not as much as the joy they'll experience with their first pet! Sagittarius children *need* pets (plural). They'll adore a menagerie of birds, fish, cats, dogs, rabbits, and maybe a little guinea pig or an iguana thrown in for fun. Naturally, some lucky Sagittarians get a horse or a pony.

Be patient with the Sagittarius child when they begin school, because this child might appear to be not scholastic. What's happening is they're confined in a new environment, and it cramps their style! (And it's also kinda scary.) They're not too sure if they *like* school. However, once they begin to enjoy the camaraderie of playmates and school sports, in a year or two, when they begin to grab the concept of what learning at school is all about, they're fine. The six- or seven-year-old who you fear will be a slow student might graduate Phi Beta Kappa with a Ph.D. before the age of twenty-five. Never forget that Sagittarians love to learn. But they don't like to be *forced* to do anything — especially *indoors*.

The most important approach to take with the Sagittarius child is to reinforce their intrinsic belief that whatever you put into life is what you get out of it. Sagittarians are born with this attitude. And hey — life *does* work this way! *You plant daisies — you get daisies. You plant onions — you get onions.* These kids have a very positive faith in their future, and they believe that being decent and good will ultimately bring them the greatest happiness. And this is the truth!

The Sagittarius child is surprisingly wise.

"If you think a thing is impossible, you'll make it impossible . . .
As you think, so shall you become."
BRUCE LEE
Chinese-American Actor, Martial Arts Instructor, Philosopher, Director, Producer,
Screenwriter, and Founder of the Jeet Kune Do Martial Arts Philosophy
(NOVEMBER 27, 1940–JULY 20, 1973)

How to Be a
Happier Sagittarius

"Success consists of going from failure to failure without loss of enthusiasm."
WINSTON CHURCHILL
Prime Minister of United Kingdom, 1940–1945 and 1951–1955
Best Known for His Leadership during the Second World War
(NOVEMBER 30, 1874–JANUARY 24, 1965)

Almost all of you appear to be upbeat, breezy, and happy. However, it's almost as if you feel it's your duty to appear this way. Many of you cultivated this easygoing manner as a mask very early in life.

You have a deep drive within to be self-reliant, independent, and free to do your own thing. You were aware of this at a very early age, even if you could not articulate it. Therefore, when people started to give you the third degree about what was happening at school, or what you did — you learned to keep them at bay by giving them very little information. The more they knew — the more they wanted to know! Then, the more you had to tell them. Nosy parents! Nosy teachers!

Your defence against this was subtle and very smart. When people asked where you were going, you learned to say "Out." When they asked how things were going in school, you replied, "Fine." Somehow, instinctively, you learned at an early age that the less you divulge to others, the less troublesome they can become in your life. This left you with more freedom to make your own decisions, and go where you wanted to go, and do what you wanted to do. Yay!

You might not have consciously *decided* to do this. But this kind of defensive, noncommittal response to others developed into your persona.

There's absolutely nothing wrong with this. It's just your style. You adopted this game face to survive. ("What they don't know won't hurt them.")

The curious thing, however, is this has now become your habit in relating to everyone. (Yikes.) You *pretend* to the world that everything is just fine. That way people don't get "involved" and ask too many questions or pry into your life. If you meet a friend at a grocery store, you're upbeat and friendly. In fact, you'll probably suggest the two of you get together for lunch or a drink soon. If anyone asks how things are going, you'll grin and say, "Great!"

Then, after you leave the store and turn the corner, and no one can see you — you pull out the harpoon slooooowly.

You have learned to hide your pain under a mask of breezy humour. You started doing this as a kid. Some of you did this because you actually didn't want to burden your parents because they were too busy, or working too hard, or you thought they had too much on their plate. You had your reasons.

This means when it comes to dealing with your inner world, and your personal problems — not only do you hide your pain from *others*, in a way, you hide your pain from *yourself*! (It's sort of like thinking if you eat in the dark the calories don't count.)

There are pros and cons to this approach. The benefit of this is you are not wallowing in self-pity and making something worse by going over it again and again in your mind. (That never helps, although we all do it.) The downside is if you refuse to acknowledge something that has hurt you, it actually has *power* over you because you won't face it.

I don't have any answers for this. I'm just pointing out this is a common Sagittarius ploy. You can really avoid looking at what you don't want to see. "I'm Queen of Denial!"

Naturally, this is because you want things to be *positive* in life. But be careful you don't brush away the pain of those who are close to you, and your own pain, in an effort to pretend everything is fine.

Now I will contradict myself. I agree with you it is good to protect your positive attitude. This is why I think Sagittarians should take frequent news fasts. Don't read the papers or watch TV. For example, I don't have television. I gave it up decades ago. I raised my kids without TV, and for quite a few years after they left home, they didn't have TV.

In my own case, I wasn't objecting so much to the content of television, but rather, to the process. *Television gives you the illusion you have a life.* It feels like something is happening, but really you're just sitting there on your sofa. I mention this because I can tell right away when I'm talking to TV people — they're more fearful of society! They are so aware of murders, kidnappings, robberies, home invasions, and all kinds of things that happen to only a tiny percentage of the population. Obviously, if you really want to know what's happening — open your front door!

So in one way, you have to be careful you don't hide from the emotions of loved ones and your own emotions that might be painful. You have to acknowledge them and look at them because they're real. Ironically, once you acknowledge them, and taste them, they can more easily and safely be filed away to fade with time. To ignore important emotions creates discomfort and dis-ease.

But do continue to consciously avoid negative news from society. Physical activity, freedom, and your own belief in a better tomorrow are your saving graces. It's true *we become our thoughts.*

Your positive attitudes and beliefs actually attract positive energy to you. This is a divine blessing you were born with. Hold on to that. Don't let it go.

"Always be yourself, express yourself, have faith in yourself;
do not you go out and look for a successful personality and duplicate it."
BRUCE LEE
Chinese-American Actor, Martial Arts Instructor, Philosopher, Director, Producer,
Screenwriter, and Founder of the Jeet Kune Do Martial Arts Philosophy
(NOVEMBER 27, 1940–JULY 20, 1973)

SAGITTARIUS
YOUR 40-YEAR HOROSCOPE
1985 ~ 2025

Why Go into the Past?

I want you to believe and have faith in your predictions so you can derive benefit from them in guiding your future. The only way you can believe what I say is to test for yourself. This is why I start with brief highlights from the past twenty-five years. If anything in these past twenty-five years resonates with you, then what I say about your future will have the same validity. It is all one long timeline — your life.

The past predictions generally apply once you have left home or are "running your life" and making your own decisions. Prior to that, the major events in your life were dictated to you by other people, likely your parents.

1985 – 1990

Ever since 1983, you had been on a kick to streamline your life or get rid of what was no longer relevant. This meant saying goodbye to people, relationships, furniture, residences, jobs — practically anything. "Gone in sixty seconds!" This window of time existed roughly from 1982–83 until 1987.

Fortunately, by 1985–86, everything was looking much better in your domestic world in terms of family relationships and most definitely where you were living. That was also a great time for real estate. It was a good year to move to bigger and better digs. Many of you expanded your family at that time.

By 1987, romance, vacations, and kids were a positive boost. However, soon you could feel your life was changing dramatically. You were heading down a new road. Partnerships in 1989 and 1990 were beneficial to you. Some of you inherited money or benefitted through the wealth of partners. At this time, you started to give serious thought to what your real values in life were. *What really mattered?*

1991 ~ 1996

Here, you entered a window of several years when everything was in a state of flux. From 1991–95, many of you changed residences, or jobs, or both. This was also a great time for travel, especially long-distance travel — the kind you love. (After all, if you're going to go somewhere, make it worthwhile!) Around 1992–93, lovely opportunities to boost your reputation in the eyes of others came along. Some of you got a raise, a promotion, or a better job. People thought highly of you, especially important people.

By 1994, you had entered a window of time when you decided you had to solidify your home base. Some of you had just recently moved. If you were happy with this move, you stayed where you were. If you were unhappy with this move, you moved yet again. Those of you who stayed, improved where you lived by renovating, or making major changes, or repairing the roof or the basement — something considerably more substantial than buying new towels. You were starting to hatch some big plans!

The year 1995 was a groundbreaking year for your sign. To be more accurate, it was the beginning of fourteen years of mega-change for Sagittarius. Why? Big daddy Pluto entered Sagittarius in 1995, and stayed there until 2009. This was the first time this had happened in more than two centuries. Suffice to say it was a first in your life! And what did this mean?

For starters, this was a window of time when many partner-ships blew apart. The nature of Pluto is to get rid of what is no longer relevant in your life. Plutonian energy generally destroys something in order to rebuild it. The classic expression of this is how we strip down a piece of furniture to refinish or re-cover it, or take out kitchens and bathrooms and walls in order to renovate a house. The energy of Pluto intends to attain a *superior* result, but it does this by getting rid of the old to make room for the new. At this time, the people who were born in November and very early December most likely felt a drastic change.

Another way Plutonian change might have expressed itself was a sudden weight loss. In other words, Pluto takes away what you really don't need. If you're ready for this change, it doesn't have to be dramatic. If you resist this change, it's often difficult.

But what was very helpful to you during this window of time was that, from December 1994 until January 1996, lucky Jupiter was in your sign! What a relief! This greatly ameliorated the harsh effects of Pluto. You still were going through drastic, dramatic changes, but now Jupiter lifted your spirits, brought you new opportunities, attracted powerful, helpful people to you, and on the whole increased your happiness quotient. In the next few years, it moved on and boosted your income as well. *Sweet!*

1997 – 2000

In this window of time, those who were born in late November and up to December 2 felt these Plutonian changes the strongest. A Pluto transit can actually affect your personality! It certainly makes you much more controlling than usual. You want to control *everything* around you, including relationships as well as the environment.

Pluto also made you want to improve yourself. (Pluto makes you emotionally passionate and more inclined to see the world in black-and-white terms.) At this time, many of you were more attracted to the occult, the dark side, certainly the mysteries and secrets of life, and hidden knowledge. ("My precious!")

This is why those of you who were *dissatisfied* with a relationship either did everything to improve it or just moved on. ("So long, and thanks for all the fish.")

While Pluto in your sign continued to wreak havoc on partnerships and dictate changes in weight, personality, wardrobe, and how you related to your environment, 1997–99 saw a lovely improvement to your living situation. Many of you moved to larger digs or bought new furniture or perks for where you lived. Something made you feel richer and more affluent. This was also a time when many of you expanded your family through marriage, birth, or adoption. Of course, this was an excellent time for real-estate deals, and a good time to buy real estate for yourself personally, or to speculate in real estate.

By 1998–99, vacations, romance, love affairs, playful times with children, and anything to do with the arts, the entertainment world, show business, and sports — all these areas — got a lovely boost. (Yay!)

By 1999–2000, things were looking up on your employment scene. Many of you got a better job, better working conditions, a raise, or a promotion, or that impossible co-worker quit. (Thank gawd.) You were working hard then, so hard, in fact, that at times life was overwhelming!

I think it's interesting to note that Pluto takes 250 years to go through all twelve signs. This means it takes about 125 years to go through six signs. Obviously, many people live their entire lives and never have a Pluto transit like the one you were undergoing from 1995 until 2009. (Like, wow.)

2001 – 2005

This was another very pivotal time in your life. In the mid-1980s, you had embarked on an entirely new path, which (if you look back) you see was a time when you began to reinvent yourself. Certainly, by 1994–95, you were a different person entirely! Now you were entering a totally different window; you began to look out into the world and wonder how you could increase your power and influence and go after what you really wanted.

Because your focus was becoming more personally ambitious, partnerships were very stressed at this time. (Aaagggh!) Actually, many partnerships bit the dust, and the ones that survived had to undergo major changes and readjustments. (Which is not surprising, because a relationship is a living entity that grows and changes as the individuals who make up that partnership grow and change as well.)

In 2002, gifts, goodies, inheritances, money back from the government, insurance payouts, and indirect benefits through partners were helpful to you. (For some, this might have occurred in 2003.) Perhaps this financial advantage is why you were able to travel in 2003–4, or explore opportunities in further education.

Actually, this was an exciting time! By 2004, assistance from others had been cut off or diminished. However, you were looking good at work or in your community. People thought a lot of you in 2004–5, which is why you were able to create a fabulous impression on everyone.

Naturally, all of this great PR led to increased popularity for many of you. Clubs, groups, organizations, and friends all wanted you to be on their team.

2006 - 2010

At this stage in your life, you definitely had a strong sense of preparation. You knew you were getting ready for something. Many of you focused more intently on training, or getting more education, or travelling to broaden your experience of the world. (Gee, do you think any of those things would've appealed?) You knew something good was going to happen. And it did. In December 2006, lucky moneybags Jupiter entered your sign and stayed there until January 2008. (Sweeeet!)

The blessing of Jupiter comes once every twelve years. This means that 2007 was a year full of increased opportunities, increased popularity, and, essentially, increased good luck. When Jupiter is in your sign, it makes life easier except for one thing — it often creates a weight gain! Aagggh! (Time to let out another pleat in the shower curtain?) This is because it "attracts" so much goodness to you! (Like that yummy slice of New York cheesecake.)

By 2008, you were really starting to hit your stride. The next few years were a very telling time for you. Some of you graduated, others got new jobs, and some of you hit a real career peak. This was your time of harvest, when you could see clearly what was working and what was not. Increased earnings were a definite possibility at this time, and certainly major purchases as well.

By 2009–10, you were enjoying a wonderful window to explore real-estate opportunities for either your personal use or speculation. These were joyous times at home. Family reunions and domestic scenes were positive. Many of you expanded your family around this time through marriage, birth, or adoption.

On the heels of these warm times at home, many of you had a chance to take a great vacation. This was also when true love may have sparked your fire! Romance, sports, and all the arts were very promising then.

But the really good news during this window of time was that Pluto finally left Sagittarius! (Science has proved prayer works.)

All the insanity you underwent from 1995 to 2009 could now start to fade as a memory. Pluto will never visit your sign again in your lifetime. *Glory hallelujah!*

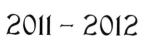

2011 ~ 2012

All these good opportunities brought you chances to improve your job scene. No question. That's why this is a year when wonderful job opportunities await you on the work scene. You can get a better job, or better duties, or a better boss, or nicer surroundings. Maybe all of the above! (Why not go for the whole enchilada?)

Not only will things improve in your job scene in 2011 (and for some in 2012), your health will also improve during this window of time. You will feel more vigorous! Quite likely, something will occur to create this feeling. You might start a regular exercise regime or spend more time outdoors, or you might join a club or a group that is active in sports. Whatever happens definitely benefits you!

Meanwhile, back in the VIP lounge, you are busy juggling so many balls in the air, your greatest challenge now is keeping everyone happy while, at the same time, making sure you also respect your own needs. After all, you can't sell out. You count, too! This is very important. (This is why you sometimes don't let others get too close.)

Nevertheless, while you're trying to protect your turf and not get too strung out socially, partnerships take a lovely turn for the better! New partnerships with the promise of commitment could be forming. These partnerships might be personal or professional. The year 2012 is an excellent time to consult experts about anything. That's because this year (and into 2013) you benefit from others.

2013 – 2015

Two big trends are starting to begin at this time. In a way, they might be considered opposite influences, and yet in another way they can be mutually supportive.

One influence lasts until 2016–17. During this period of about three years, you're going to start to let go of whatever is no longer relevant in your life. You will give up jobs, people, relationships, and certainly belongings. Either by choice or circumstance, you are going to downsize rather dramatically to lighten your load. Essentially, you are giving up what you no longer need. (Although, sometimes you don't think this at the time.) The last time you went through a process like this was in the mid-1980s. You are being urged to let go of things to create space for a whole new world, which begins around 2016.

The second influence is quite the opposite! It's all about receiving! In 2013–14, you will be the beneficiary of inheritances, gifts, goodies, scholarships, bursaries, loans, mortgages, and the indirect use of wealth through others. Perhaps others will let you use something they own? ("The cabin is yours for August. The keys to the [car, boat, Ski-Doo, motorcycle, _____ — fill in the blank] are in the cookie jar on top of the wine cooler.") Or your partner might get a raise or a bonus. This is certainly an excellent time to ask for a loan or get a mortgage. Ka-ching!

This means, on one hand, you're going through a three-year period of letting go, but while this is taking place, you have an eighteen-month window where you're on the gravy train! (Go figure.) Giving up your current residence and getting a mortgage to buy a new home would be a classic way to use this planetary combination. *It's very timely!*

(Generally, what the big print giveth, the small print taketh away — but not in this case. *You are such a lucky Sagittarius!*)

By 2015, travel opportunities look *mahvellous*, dahling! This is one of the best years to travel in more than a decade. (Do take note.) This is also a wonderful year to go back to school, or attend college or university, or begin any kind of higher education or

advanced training. You are preparing for a wonderful time in your career, and yet, at the same time, you are turning the corner in another way, because you're entering a whole new world by 2016.

"Honey, I'm home!"

2016 – 2017

We all have benchmark years. This is definitely a significant year for Sagittarians. I can't help being struck with how lucky you actually are as a sign. Naturally, astrological textbooks say this, but as I do this timeline for you it is so *obvious* to me.

This is a year where you are stepping into a completely new sandbox. You're in a whole new scene. In fact, it's so new, many of you will change your daily wardrobe. In the previous two or three years, you gave up a lot of things — people, relationships, jobs, residences, whatever. And, apparently, it was for this! This is the beginning of a new thirty-year journey for your sign, wherein you will reinvent yourself during the first seven years. It's major stuff.

Why do I say good fortune? Because just as you are stepping into this whole new world, lucky moneybags Jupiter is sailing across the top of your chart, bringing all kinds of opportunities and boosting your good name among your peers. You couldn't ask for better timing! It's like having an introduction to court. Here you are, on new turf, wearing new clothes, wondering what you're going to do, and you're receiving coveted invitations from important people.

This will likely mean a great new job opportunity for many of you. All of you will earn increased respect from others. The irony is that just as you are stepping into a whole new scene, you are enjoying a *culmination* of something. Another interpretation would be that you get a wonderful job offer that precipitates a residential move, or you are accepted by a marvellous school, or some event triggers a change of residence. It certainly looks good! Make the most of this opportunity. It's a time of progress for you. Many of you will expand whatever you're doing. This is a traditional time of "getting ahead," and yet it's also a completely new world for you in some way.

Expect promotions, public recognition, and the increased esteem of your colleagues. Some of you will change to a job in medicine, healing, the legal profession, or publishing and the media. You might possibly work in or with a foreign country.

By 2017, you are tremendously popular! Everyone wants to see your face. Groups, clubs, organizations, plus personal friendships will make demands on your time. This is also an excellent year to give serious thought to long-term goals. How can you make your dreams become a reality?

2018 – 2020

As this window of time begins, you are doing a lot of soul-searching about your job or the work you are doing. No matter what kind of success you enjoyed around 2016, for whatever reason you're starting to wonder what your values really are. *What matters in life?* You're not the kind of person who just takes the money and runs. (Oh, you can do this. After all, you love money. But you just want the money for other things — most especially to support your own freedom of choice.) You're quite philosophical about what you do.

In 2018, certain events will take place that stir your sense of compassion for others. Your sense of altruism will be heightened, either toward specific individuals or toward society as a whole.

"When we retire at night, we constructively review our day. Were we resentful, selfish, dishonest, or afraid? Do we owe an apology? Have we kept something to ourselves which should be discussed with another person at once? Were we kind and loving toward all? What could we have done better? Were we thinking of ourselves most of the time? Or were we thinking of what we could do for others, of what we could pack into the stream of life? But we must be careful not to drift into worry, remorse, or morbid reflection, for that would diminish our usefulness to others."

BILL WILSON
Co-founder of Alcoholics Anonymous
(NOVEMBER 26, 1895–JANUARY 24, 1971)

Sure enough, late in 2018, you will begin a new twelve-year cycle of growth. Essentially, you are trying to discover who you really are as an individual. You feel bolder about testing your talents in a more public way. You feel you can try things and you will not be laughed at or booed from the stage.

In fact, during the year 2019, all kinds of helpful people and re-sources are inexplicably drawn to you. Your recent soul-searching has deepened your inner world and your spiritual values. *You like yourself more.*

All these good things naturally promote your relationships with everyone. (Everybody likes a winner.)

This is also a time when many of you will come up with an entirely new job, or discover a new source of income, or perhaps even an extra source of income on the side. (That's definitely your style.)

By 2020, the money is rolling in! So, obviously, in 2019, your ideas about new sources of income paid off. (Money is so handy when you want to buy things, isn't it?) "We're iiiin the money . . ."

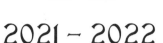

2021 – 2022

This is definitely a busy time in your life because you are experiencing a tremendous amount of flux and change. Some of you are undergoing residential moves, or job changes, or both. Make note of this, because often when this window of time begins, people are convinced that they are not going to move or change jobs — but they do!

Fortunately, 2021 is upbeat and positive for you. You're in a happy frame of mind. This is very important, because everything begins in your mind. *First comes the thought, then from the thought springs the word. From the word springs the deed, and the deed soon becomes habit. Habit eventually hardens into character — so watch your thoughts with care, and let them be loving and kind.*

This is a wonderful window for real-estate opportunities. You will either move to a larger home or spruce up where you live already. You'll buy lovely things for your home and family because, for some reason, you feel richer and more affluent where you live! Real-estate deals that you do now will be profitable for you in the future. These real-estate transactions could be for your own home or for speculation.

This sense of bounty and richness in your home scene translates into your family relationships as well. Family will be a source of joy for you! This is the classic time for an expansion of your family through birth, adoption, or marriage. Family reunions will be happy occasions.

This window of time has two strong, separate astrological influences: one that urges you to make a residential move, and the other that tells you almost any kind of real-estate deal will benefit you. (Hmmm. Quite a combo, and hard to ignore!) Some potential profits definitely exist now through home, real estate, and family businesses, as well.

By 2022, vacation plans look marvellous! You want to get away and have some fun. This is also a lovely window for romance, love affairs, and just schmoozing. Because the influence to change jobs

or residences is still at play now, perhaps the love of your life will appear and trigger a residential move?

This is also a good year for financial speculation, and anything to do with amateur or professional sports. Show business, the entertainment world, and the hospitality industry are also blessed.

Ah, yes. There's no time like the pleasant.

2023 – 2025

There are two major areas you are totally focused on at this time. One of them is about home, family, and real estate. (Still.) Although many of you might have moved in the past few years, believe it or not, many of you will move again! It's sort of a hippity-hop routine going on. Those of you who liked where you moved to recently will now start to renovate, or rebuild, or make major changes so you can solidify this home as your anchor in the world. Others will not be satisfied with a recent move, and will therefore move again. If possible, this is an excellent time to buy real estate because there's a good likelihood that wherever you move now, you will stay there for a long time.

Your focus on home, family, and your domestic scene is so strong, major changes within your family dynamic might also be taking place, especially those that affect parents. Some of you will have increased responsibility with parents or older relatives at this time.

Fortunately, the second area that is highlighted has to do with your job and your employment scene. This is your best chance in twelve years to improve your job! You might get a better job or better duties. Your evil boss might be transferred to Hell, Norway. Some of you might be happier with your job or improve your job simply because you have a different attitude. This new attitude will allow you to enjoy your work more or get along better with others. There are a number of ways your employment scene can improve, but one thing is certain — *it will improve.*

For those of you who are retired, this positive influence will still apply to the way you approach your daily tasks. You'll be happier doing them! You might get some kind of equipment or machinery that makes you more enthusiastic about what you do.

All Sagittarians will enjoy better health in 2023–24. Despite the increased responsibilities at home, you feel good about life right now.

By the end of 2024, many of you will enter into a committed partnership or marriage that is very rewarding. Your new partner

could be older and richer, more established, or more respected for some reason. Whatever the case, this relationship brings you increased benefits and probably wealth. (A rich partner is a wonderful labour-saving device.)

The window around 2024–25 is also an excellent time to enter into any kind of partnership, both personal and professional, because you benefit from others, even from experts or people who give you advice.

One of the things that makes you sure of yourself now is that the task of reinventing yourself is over. It began in 2015 and finished around 2024. This means you now have a far better idea of who you are. And you certainly know who you *aren't*! All you have to do is look back at what you were doing in 2013–14, and you can see how different your life is! (Holy cannoli!)

You are a future-oriented sign. You are not imprisoned by the past. You are forward thinking and you constantly plan different avenues to success and excitement down the road. This is why it's particularly good for your sign to be in touch with the possible avenues to explore that are in this book. Your choices will be easier. You won't be rowing against the tide. Instead, you'll be like a hot knife cutting through butter.

"If you love life, don't waste time,
for time is what life is made up of."
BRUCE LEE
Chinese-American Actor, Martial Arts Instructor, Philosopher,
Director, Producer, Screenwriter, and Founder of the Jeet Kune Do
Martial Arts Philosophy
(NOVEMBER 27, 1940–JULY 20, 1973)

Famous Sagittarius Personalities

Rodney Dangerfield	November 22, 1921–2004
Terry Gilliam	November 22, 1940
Billie Jean King	November 22, 1943
Jamie Lee Curtis	November 22, 1958
Mariel Hemingway	November 22, 1961
Scarlett Johansson	November 22, 1984
Boris Karloff	November 23, 1887–1969
Harpo Marx	November 23, 1888–1964
Erté	November 23, 1892–1990
Robert Barnard	November 23, 1936
Rick Bayless	November 23, 1953
Salli Richardson	November 23, 1967
Miley Cyrus	November 23, 1992
Baruch Spinoza	November 24, 1632–1677
Henri de Toulouse-Lautrec	November 24, 1864–1901
Eric Wilson	November 24, 1940
Spider Robinson	November 24, 1948
Arundhati Roy	November 24, 1961
Katherine Heigl	November 24, 1978
Andrew Carnegie	November 25, 1835–1919
Poul Anderson	November 25, 1926–2001
Amy Grant	November 25, 1960
John F. Kennedy, Jr.	November 25, 1960–1999
Holly Cole	November 25, 1963
Jill Hennessy	November 25, 1968
Christina Applegate	November 25, 1971
Bill Wilson	November 26, 1895–1971
Eugène Ionesco	November 26, 1909–1994
Robert Goulet	November 26, 1933–2007
Rich Little	November 26, 1938
Tina Turner	November 26, 1939
Natasha Bedingfield	November 26, 1981
Gail Sheehy	November 27, 1937
Bruce Lee	November 27, 1940–1973
Eddie Rabbitt	November 27, 1941–1998

Jimi Hendrix	November 27, 1942–1970
Kathryn Bigelow	November 27, 1951
Caroline Kennedy	November 27, 1957
Alberto Moravia	November 28, 1907–1990
Berry Gordy	November 28, 1929
Manolo Blahnik	November 28, 1942
Randy Newman	November 28, 1943
Rita Mae Brown	November 28, 1944
S. Epatha Merkerson	November 28, 1952
Jon Stewart	November 28, 1962
Anna Nicole Smith	November 28, 1967–2007
Louisa M. Alcott	November 29, 1832–1888
Edwin Hubble	November 29, 1889–1953
C. S. Lewis	November 29, 1898–1963
Madeleine L'Engle	November 29, 1918–2007
Diane Ladd	November 29, 1935
Joel Coen	November 29, 1954
Howie Mandel	November 29, 1955
Mark Twain	November 30, 1835–1910
Winston Churchill	November 30, 1874–1965
Lucy Maud Montgomery	November 30, 1874–1942
Dick Clark	November 30, 1929
Ridley Scott	November 30, 1937
Ben Stiller	November 30, 1965
Elisha Cuthbert	November 30, 1982
Mary Martin	December 1, 1913–1990
Lou Rawls	December 1, 1933–2006
Woody Allen	December 1, 1935
Lee Trevino	December 1, 1939
Bette Midler	December 1, 1945
Sarah Silverman	December 1, 1970
Georges Seurat	December 2, 1859–1891
Maria Callas	December 2, 1923–1977
Julie Harris	December 2, 1925
Gianni Versace	December 2, 1946–1997
Jim Cuddy	December 2, 1955
Lucy Liu	December 2, 1968
Monica Seles	December 2, 1973
Nelly Furtado	December 2, 1978
Joseph Conrad	December 3, 1857–1924
Ferlin Husky	December 3, 1925
Andy Williams	December 3, 1927

Ozzy Osbourne	December 3, 1948
Julianne Moore	December 3, 1960
Brendan Fraser	December 3, 1966
Bucky Lasek	December 3, 1972
Amanda Seyfried	December 3, 1985
Thomas Carlyle	December 4, 1795–1881
Edith Cavell	December 4, 1865–1915
Rainer Maria Rilke	December 4, 1875–1926
Anna McGarrigle	December 4, 1944
Roberta Bondar	December 4, 1945
Jeff Bridges	December 4, 1949
Patricia Wettig	December 4, 1951
Tyra Banks	December 4, 1973
Christina Rossetti	December 5, 1830–1894
Walt Disney	December 5, 1901–1966
Otto Preminger	December 5, 1906–1986
Little Richard	December 5, 1932
José Carreras	December 5, 1946
Margaret Cho	December 5, 1968
Frankie Muniz	December 5, 1985
Joyce Kilmer	December 6, 1886–1918
Ira Gershwin	December 6, 1896–1983
Agnes Moorehead	December 6, 1900–1974
Dave Brubeck	December 6, 1920
David Ossman	December 6, 1936
JoBeth Williams	December 6, 1948
Eli Wallach	December 7, 1915
Noam Chomsky	December 7, 1928
Ellen Burstyn	December 7, 1932
Harry Chapin	December 7, 1942–1981
Johnny Bench	December 7, 1947
Tom Waits	December 7, 1949
Larry Bird	December 7, 1956
Diego Rivera	December 8, 1886–1957
Sammy Davis, Jr.	December 8, 1925–1990
David Carradine	December 8, 1936–2009
Jim Morrison	December 8, 1943–1971
Gregg Allman	December 8, 1947
Kim Basinger	December 8, 1953
Teri Hatcher	December 8, 1964
Sinéad O'Connor	December 8, 1966
Grace Hopper	December 9, 1906–1992

Kirk Douglas	December 9, 1916
John Cassavetes	December 9, 1929–1989
Judi Dench	December 9, 1934
Joan Armatrading	December 9, 1950
John Malkovich	December 9, 1953
Donny Osmond	December 9, 1958
Eugene O'Keefe	December 10, 1827–1913
Emily Dickinson	December 10, 1830–1886
Dorothy Lamour	December 10, 1914–1996
Susan Dey	December 10, 1952
Kenneth Branagh	December 10, 1960
Bobby Flay	December 10, 1964
Emmanuelle Chriqui	December 10, 1977
John Labatt	December 11, 1838–1915
Naguib Mahfouz	December 11, 1911–2006
Carlo Ponti	December 11, 1912–2007
Aleksandr Solzhenitsyn	December 11, 1918–2008
Rita Moreno	December 11, 1931
Jim Harrison	December 11, 1937
Teri Garr	December 11, 1944
Viswanathan Anand	December 11, 1969
Gustave Flaubert	December 12, 1821–1880
Edvard Munch	December 12, 1863–1944
Edward G. Robinson	December 12, 1893–1973
Frank Sinatra	December 12, 1915–1998
Dionne Warwick	December 12, 1940
Jennifer Connelly	December 12, 1970
Mayim Bialik	December 12, 1975
Emily Carr	December 13, 1871–1945
Carlos Montoya	December 13, 1903–1993
Dick Van Dyke	December 13, 1925
Christopher Plummer	December 13, 1929
The Āgā Khān IV	December 13, 1936
Steve Buscemi	December 13, 1967
Jamie Foxx	December 13, 1967
Taylor Swift	December 13, 1989
Tycho Brahe	December 14, 1546–1601
Spike Jones	December 14, 1911–1965
Charlie Rich	December 14, 1932–1995
Patty Duke	December 14, 1946
Natascha McElhone	December 14, 1969
Kim St-Pierre	December 14, 1978

Michael Owen	December 14, 1979
Gustave Eiffel	December 15, 1832–1923
J. Paul Getty	December 15, 1892–1975
Tim Conway	December 15, 1933
Don Johnson	December 15, 1949
Michael Shanks	December 15, 1970
Adam Brody	December 15, 1979
Ludwig van Beethoven	December 16, 1770–1827
Jane Austen	December 16, 1775–1817
Noël Coward	December 16, 1899–1973
Margaret Mead	December 16, 1901–1978
Arthur C. Clarke	December 16, 1917–2008
Liv Ullmann	December 16, 1938
Ben Cross	December 16, 1947
Benjamin Bratt	December 16, 1963
Donovan Bailey	December 16, 1967
Thomas Chandler Haliburton	December 17, 1796–1865
William Lyon Mackenzie King	December 17, 1874–1950
Jack L. Chalker	December 17, 1944–2005
Eugene Levy	December 17, 1946
Bill Pullman	December 17, 1953
Giovanni Ribisi	December 17, 1974
Milla Jovovich	December 17, 1975
Craig Kielburger	December 17, 1982
Betty Grable	December 18, 1916–1973
Jacques Pépin	December 18, 1935
Keith Richards	December 18, 1943
Steven Spielberg	December 18, 1946
Leonard Maltin	December 18, 1950
Brian Orser	December 18, 1961
Brad Pitt	December 18, 1963
Rachel Griffiths	December 18, 1968
Christina Aguilera	December 18, 1980
Édith Piaf	December 19, 1915–1963
Cicely Tyson	December 19, 1933
Robert Urich	December 19, 1946–2002
Jennifer Beals	December 19, 1963
Alyssa Milano	December 19, 1972
Jake Gyllenhaal	December 19, 1980

CAPRICORN

DECEMBER 22 – JANUARY 19

CAPRICORN THE MOUNTAIN GOAT
(DECEMBER 22 – JANUARY 19)

"I USE."

"March on. Do not tarry. To go forward is to move toward perfection.
March on, and fear not the thorns, or the sharp stones on life's path."
KHALIL GIBRAN
Lebanese-American Artist, Poet, and Writer
The Prophet
(JANUARY 6, 1883–APRIL 10, 1931)

"Everyone wants to be Cary Grant. Even I want to be Cary Grant."
CARY GRANT
British-American Actor
To Catch a Thief and *An Affair to Remember*
(JANUARY 18, 1904–NOVEMBER 29, 1986)

Element: Earth
Ruling Planet: Saturn
Quality: Cardinal
Opposite Sign: Cancer
Symbols: The Mountain Goat or the Mythical Half-Goat, Half-Fish Creature
Glyph: Goat Above, Fish Below
Lucky Gems: Turquoise, Onyx, and Green Tourmaline[1]
Flower: Poppy
Colours: Dark Greens and Browns
Parts of the Body: Bones and Teeth

You Like: Tradition, reading, painting, music, punctuality, good manners, money in the bank, a solid family life, having influence and power, facts, and familiar things. You like designer labels, prestige cars, big corner offices, and big bouquets of flowers delivered to your workplace, accompanied by cards extolling your virtues for all to see!

You Don't Like: Emotional scenes, broken promises, wanton waste, public displays of affection, feeling rushed, being ridiculed, laziness, and unruly conduct. And public failure! (The worst.)

Where You Shine: Industrious, determined, entertaining, profound, responsible, disciplined, patient, loyal, and high-minded. You always look great — you fit in. Not too flamboyant, yet current. We can take you anywhere.

So Who's Perfect? Austere, withdrawn, avaricious, narrow-minded, pessimistic, forbidding, and gloomy. You worry too much and are always thinking, "What will others think?"

---

1. Different texts will name different gems for different signs. Everything in life needs to be double-checked!

What Is Capricorn-ness?[2]

The quickest way to understand your sign is to understand your ruling planet. The planet Saturn is the ruler of Capricorn, so let's take a look at Saturn, and what Saturn means in astrology.

Since the time of the Mesopotamian empires, Saturn was the outermost planet. (Uranus was not discovered until 1781.) As such, Saturn represented the ultimate boundary of our solar system.

This is why Saturn rules everything that defines, confines, limits, and restricts. Saturn is all about demarcation points — where something ends and something else begins. Saturn rules dimensions, structures, and forms. It's not the final frontier — it's the final barrier! It *contains*.

Therefore, in astrology, Saturn rules our skin, because our skin confines and holds us in. Saturn also rules our bones and our skeletal structure, which defines our shape: two arms, two legs, one head. Without Saturn, we would not be upright — we would be a big mushy mess on the floor!

So this is the first thing to get hold of — the notion that Saturn defines shape, form, and structure.

It should be no surprise, therefore, that Saturn, the ruler of structure, rules the government, law courts, and all pyramidal organizations in society, including multi-national corporations, the military, the police, firefighters, and even the Boy Scouts.

Oops — time out! Let's be very clear here and not get confused. Mars rules war and Mars rules Aries. Therefore, Mars and Aries are the military. But the kind of military that is associated with Aries is the actual fighting — i.e., the warriors, their battles, and their losses or victories. "No prisoners!" But the *organization* of these warriors — from the general at the top down to the private at the bottom — this is the domain of Saturn. Do you see the difference? Saturn rules the *structure* of every organization.

Similarly, Pluto, the ruler of Scorpio, rules manufacturing. But the *organization* that is necessary to successfully manufacture anything — this organization is Saturn. There is always a boss or CEO, then the people who report to this boss, then the people who report to this next person, and so on down the line. This *structure of reporting order* is Saturn.

---

2. No one is just one sign. That is impossible. Therefore, this is a discussion about the Capricorn archetype — the qualities of "Capricorn-ness." Many other signs will have Capricorn qualities as well. Therefore, the discussion of one sign is not an exact description of that person, but rather, it is a description of the qualities of that sign.

Saturn (the ruler of Capricorn) relates to the structure of our physical bodies, the structure of governing bodies, and all structures and buildings in the world.

Wow!

Who's on First? Who's on Top?

Imagine that you have a hundred people who are stranded on an island. Naturally, they are going to start scrambling for food and shelter. However, within a matter of hours, days, weeks, or months, this group will establish a leader. It's inevitable. Even chickens have a pecking order. But, on this island of a hundred people, what will be the factors that determine who the leader is?

Simple.

The leader is going to be the person with *the most* of something. The leader might have the most guns, or the most boats, or the most soldiers, or the most food, or the most years of experience, or the most influence, or the most important title, or the most money, or, if it's a democracy, they might have the most votes — but the leader is definitely the one with the most.

This notion of *counting something to determine who has the most* is Capricorn. Who's on top?

This is why no sign is more aware of who is exactly in charge. (You know on which side your bread is buttered!) Where Leo is quick to see the big picture, you are quick to see the power echelons in any social paradigm. You know who's running the show, who's calling the shots, and who's on gofer duty. This way you know whom to defer to, and who should defer to you!

> "His huff arrived and he departed in it."
> ALEXANDER WOOLLCOTT
> American Critic and Commentator for *The New Yorker* and
> Member of the Algonquin Round Table
> (JANUARY 19, 1887–JANUARY 23, 1943)

Life Is Tough and Then You Die

Saturn rules boundaries and demarcation points, which means Saturn rules death. Saturn is Father Time, that hooded figure in a shroud holding a scythe. (We're not talking Teletubbies here.)

Because Saturn marks the passage of time and, certainly, death, Capricorns are the only sign with a quirky relationship to time!

1. It is not unusual for Capricorns to have friendships, love affairs, and marriages with people who are significantly older or younger than they are. Your lover or best friend could be the age of your parents or your kids.

2. Capricorns are the most long-lived of all the signs.

3. Capricorns can fool the world about their age. Capricorn babies and little children are "old" and serious or solemn. By the time they're in their early teens, they definitely look older! (You were the one who bought the beer.) Then, a curious flip occurs around age thirty-five, when Capricorns start to look younger than their age! And by the time Capricorn is eighty-plus, this person can easily pass for twenty years younger.
You are old when you're young, and young when you're old.
This is why you should never talk about your age — some day, you could pass for being twenty-five years younger! (Of course, you can't fool a flight of stairs.)

Because Saturn rules all pyramidal structures, including the government, the military, and the police, it represents obligations and duties. Oy vey! Saturn is about shoulds, not wants.

I think of Saturn as that stern prairie grandfather: "Go to your room and go to bed. Get up in the morning and chop that wood before six." Nobody calls Saturn "Chuckles." When a sweet little six-year-old says, "I want to be a ballerina!" Saturn scoffs, "Learn to type."

Because Saturn has a hair-shirt mentality, Capricorn is a no-nonsense sign. Not only do you understand what is serious in life, you believe in "no pain, no gain." You know the hard knocks of experience are character building.

> "Out of suffering have emerged the strongest souls;
> the most massive characters are seared with scars."
> KHALIL GIBRAN
> Lebanese-American Artist, Poet, and Writer
> *The Prophet*
> (JANUARY 6, 1883–APRIL 10, 1931)

However, let's be very careful. Yes, Capricorn is serious. But, hey — every sign can be serious! Leos are serious. In turn, Capricorns can be goofy, lighthearted, and gay! (Look at Diane Keaton.) This serious aspect of Capricorn does not mean that Capricorn people themselves have to be particularly serious — but, rather, it means that Capricorns understand what is serious in life. They are not naive or foolish. They know life is full of hard challenges. Before we walk, we fall down a lot.

"Take chances, make mistakes. That's how you grow. Pain nourishes your courage. You have to fail in order to practice being brave."
MARY TYLER MOORE
American Actress
The Mary Tyler Moore Show
(B. DECEMBER 29, 1936)

One of the reasons you have a realistic point of view about life is you often have a difficult childhood. Something in your early years introduces you to solitude, increased responsibilities, or the sober realization that life is not a bowl of cherries, it's a bowl of pits! This could be due to hardship, poverty, taking care of siblings, taking care of relatives, or starting to work at a young age. Sir John A. Macdonald (January 11, 1815–June 6, 1891), the first prime minister of Canada, once said, "I had no boyhood."

Because you instinctively have a respect for the harsh realities of life, you will save money for that proverbial rainy day. You will also save money for your old age. Capricorns have well-planned endings, which is a good thing, since they are so long-lived!

"A penny saved is a penny earned."
BENJAMIN FRANKLIN
American Politician, Inventor, Author,
and a Founding Father of the United States of America
(JANUARY 17, 1706–APRIL 17, 1790)

A penny saved? I should say so! Capricorn hates waste. You save leftovers and you *eat* them!

The planet that is associated with planning for the future is Saturn. Whenever Saturn enters the picture, everybody gets serious and practical. If you're shopping, you will buy items that will last a long time. Saturn is not frivolous. Saturn saves, and faithfully prepares for a precarious, fickle future. ("I don't want to end up being a bag lady!")

We All Have Our Contradictions

Perhaps as proof that the cosmos has a sense of humour, Capricorn natives embrace a curious contradiction. They are conservative, respectable, law-abiding (although Al Capone was a Capricorn), and rather proper people, yet they do the most inexplicable, bizarre things!

I have a dear Capricorn friend who is wonderfully gracious and socially polished. (She could have advised Amy Vanderbilt and Emily Post.) She lived for a while near the University of British Columbia in Vancouver and, one spring, she decided to rent her home to Russian scientists for the summer, while she visited friends on Salt Spring Island, Cortes Island, and Denman Island. She had planned an adventurous summer that would also help her financially. However, her island-hopping plans fell through, and, by July, she had nowhere to go. She was homeless! (A Capricorn's greatest fear.) Because "those damned Russians" were living at her place!

Capricorn people are not necessarily dramatic; they're just goofy or inexplicable. But they always pretend everything is normal and just fine, thank you.

I know someone who rented a basement suite from a woman who was Capricorn. She was renovating her house, and had borrowed a Ford pickup truck for the weekend from the renter's friend Roy. My friend said he came home at 2 a.m. on a heavily raining Saturday night to discover the truck parked at a crazy angle on a huge mound of sand in the middle of the front lawn, with its headlights pointing up into the sky. The engine was running and both doors were wide open! Alarmed, he ran into the house, but no one was home. He went back outside, turned the engine off, cut the lights, closed the doors, put the keys on the kitchen counter, and went to bed. The next day the truck was gone. His Capricorn landlady said nothing. Even Roy was none the wiser.

Every Capricorn occasionally stuns everyone with their bizarre behaviour.

Three Big Clues about Capricorn

To further understand Capricorn, in addition to the description of Saturn, here are also three broad traits that describe your sign:

1. Respect for the Status Quo
2. Fixation on Achieving Goals
3. Need to Be Useful

Respect for the Status Quo[3]

Saturn represents the government; therefore, Capricorn represents the suits. Most Capricorns are conservative people who play it straight. You dress like everyone else because you don't want to call unwanted attention to yourself. *You like to fit in.* (Scandal horrifies you.)

You represent the navy blue pinstripe suit, or the uniform of the blue-collar worker, or whatever the prevailing dress is in your social set. Unlike Aquarius or Leo, you don't want to stand out in a crowd.

I recall a Capricorn Rising client who came to see me in Victoria. She was wearing a double-breasted tweed jacket with wool pants (with cuffs, no less) and beautiful brogue shoes, and she had a smart brown leather handbag with a long strap worn diagonally across her front. She looked like she had just stepped out of a cab on the High Street in Oxford.

As I did her reading, I discovered that prior to living in Canada, she had lived in Taos, New Mexico, for five years. When I mentioned to her that, as Capricorn Rising, she had a desire to "fit in" and dress the way the locals did, she told me that when she was in Taos, she always wore denim skirts with lots of turquoise jewellery. However, she said that her longest job was working as a bush pilot in the Bahamas, where she always wore khakis and a military vest.

Classic Capricorn.

Although you want to fit in, you don't want to be *invisible*! You want respect and admiration. This is why your wardrobe is the best example of whatever is going down in your scene. If you wear a suit to work, it will be smashing and well cut. Your winter coat will be a camel hair coat or a pea jacket. (Or a Burberry, if you can afford one.)

---

3. The staus quo is the way things normally are. Therefore, the status quo changes dramatically with geography and different cultures. An illustration of this is in the movie *Local Hero* (1983), where a punk girl with a green mohawk, leather jacket, ripped net stockings — the whole bit — keeps making a play for a shy young man who is conservatively dressed in a brown suit. She says, "I like you! You're *different!*"

You value tradition, plus you never want to hear criticism. You agonize over the possibility that others might think you have bad taste, or that you've made a terrible gaffe or faux pas. You're extremely sensitive to the opinions of others.

This is why you like designer labels. It's safe to wear what is considered to be *la crème de la crème*. Who could criticize you? You're bulletproof! (This is also why you can spot a Louis Vuitton at ten paces.)

You want to look like you pay your taxes, you wear deodorant, and you floss twice a day. You are a law-abiding citizen who always makes your bed.[4]

Capricorns are courteous. ("Step away from the car.") You obey rules and regulations. You are punctual, and like to be perceived as being correct. You also give the impression that you are well-informed about whatever is important at the moment. (What is important is whatever everybody is talking about.) *You want respect.*

> "It takes many good deeds to build a good reputation,
> and only one bad one to lose it."
> BENJAMIN FRANKLIN
> American Politician, Inventor, Author,
> and a Founding Father of the United States of America
> (JANUARY 17, 1706–APRIL 17, 1790)

Your need for prestige and respect should come as no surprise when you consider that your symbol is the Mountain Goat. This is why many of you are social climbers. You love to rub shoulders with the rich and famous. Not only do you have the thrill of the moment, but what a story to tell!

Perhaps this is why from an early age you always intended to *be* somebody. It's a destiny factor.

All Capricorns have an interest in politics. Many Capricorns go *into* politics. If they don't go into politics in a formal sense, they are politically involved with groups and organizations in their own community. It's what they do for a hobby. They get "involved." Most Capricorns think hobbies that are just for pleasure are a trivial waste of time. They prefer to use their spare time to create organizations to help their community — and they *love* doing this!

Your fabulous skill in establishing organizational structures is also how you establish your popularity and heighten your social standing in your group. You might do this through your church, your kids' schools, sporting events, or for any cause you wish to endorse. You're the person who *makes things happen!*

---

4. It's a big deal to Capricorns to have their bed made. For starters, many of you actually *do* make your bed every day. But if a surprise visitor witnesses your unmade bed, you will apologize for this with a swift explanation. My mother is Capricorn Rising, and I have always suspected she makes her bed before she gets out of it. (It even looks made when she's in it!)

Fixation on Achieving Goals

"The goal wasn't to be a millionaire or to be a Hollywood star. That was not the goal. The goal was something about — the goal was to find the goal."

JAMES EARL JONES
American Stage and Screen Actor
The Voice of Darth Vader in *Star Wars*
(B. JANUARY 17, 1931)

I once read an article about a study done to determine the *one single astrological factor* that contributed to high achievement. They studied many charts and concluded — it was Moon in Capricorn! When you have your Moon in Capricorn you have a *need* for success. It's not just a want or desire. Overachieving is your knee-jerk reaction to life! George Washington and Napoleon Bonaparte had Moon in Capricorn, as does Arnold Schwarzenegger.

"I always had a repulsive need to be something more than human."

DAVID BOWIE
British Musician, Actor, and Record Producer
The Rise and Fall of Ziggy Stardust and the Spiders from Mars
(B. JANUARY 8, 1947)

All Capricorns are high achievers, which is why you're such a perfectionist. Your sense of destiny, your desire to be somebody, and your need to be useful all combine to make you driven to achieve your goals. Because you're always focused on your goals, everything else is secondary.

You have marvellous discipline. The words "Saturn" and "discipline" are synonymous in astrology. You deny yourself the pleasures of today for the achievements of tomorrow. You're a workaholic. Nothing is too much trouble for you. You pay your dues. You do your homework. You're prepared.

"It does not do to leave a live dragon out of your calculations
if you live near him."

J. R. R. TOLKIEN
British Writer and Poet
The Lord of the Rings Trilogy
(JANUARY 3, 1892–SEPTEMBER 2, 1973)

I find it interesting that your dedicated focus makes you *compartmentalize* your life. The people you have fun with are over there. Family members are over here. The people you work with are at your job. You rarely mix these groups! It would not be unusual for a Capricorn to work somewhere for twenty-five years and his co-workers never meet his family and vice versa. (Unless their father was the mayor.)

Part of this is your need for prestige. You save your money for designer labels to impress people at work. But what if your situation at home is surprisingly modest? This is one of the reasons you keep everything separate. Or you might have a home with a swanky address, but no furniture inside. *Appearances are everything!*

> "I live in a kind of controlled awareness. I wouldn't call it fear, but it's an awareness. I know I have a responsibility to behave in a certain way. I'm able to do that."
> MARY TYLER MOORE
> American Actress
> *The Mary Tyler Moore Show*
> (B. DECEMBER 29, 1936)

Please understand this: you are not any more shallow or superficial than any other sign. You just want your life to *count* for something! You intend to achieve things and make your contribution to the world. This is why you have your Master Plan.

You're loyal, hard-working, and faithful. No one has more perseverance than you. Your preoccupation with status, prestige, and appearances is all tied in with your need for success and your need to achieve what you want to do.

My Uncle Jack, who was an Aries, naturally joined the Mounties and fought in the navy during World War II, and later became a policeman for the Canadian Pacific Railway. These were all Aries choices. But because he was Capricorn Rising, he stayed at that job for more than thirty years. I still remember that every day before he went to work — without exception — he polished his shoes and every button and bit of brass on his uniform. Perfectionist! Attention to detail! Respect for tradition! Awareness of the image of power and prestige.

Because you focus on achieving your goals, you see life's obligations and duties as par for the course. ("Suck it up, princess.")

This is why you are one of the great achievers and doers in the zodiac.

"I have been ambitious to be a somebody from the time I was five years old."
ETHEL MERMAN
American Actress and Singer Known as the First Lady of the Musical Comedy Stage
"Everything's Coming Up Roses" and "There's No Business Like Show Business"
(JANUARY 16, 1908–FEBRUARY 15, 1984)

Need to Be Useful

All Earth signs are concerned with tangible results. Furthermore, all Earth signs are willing to work hard. But you are the most *evolved* of the Earth signs (the others are Taurus, Virgo, and Capricorn). Taurus can get caught up in the pleasures of life, and Virgo is a magpie for facts and can be easily sidetracked. But you are like Sisyphus, who pushed a huge boulder up a hill for eternity. You give effort relentlessly.

"The proper function of man is to live, not to exist.
I shall not waste my days in trying to prolong them. I shall use my time."
JACK LONDON
American Author
The Call of the Wild, White Fang, and *The Sea-Wolf*
(JANUARY 12, 1876–NOVEMBER 22, 1916)

You're also extremely self-sufficient. My mother, who is Capricorn Rising, painted her living room and stripped the wallpaper in her bathroom when she was ninety-one. ("Well, I didn't do the top six inches or so," she said, almost apologetically.)

Naturally, with their respect for tradition and conservatism, Capricorns like to be *married, and have a house with a white picket fence and 2.5 kids*. They work hard to keep their homes in order, especially the *outside* that everyone can see!

They work equally as hard at their job, especially if it is mentally stimulating, because Capricorns hate to be bored!

You want to make a difference by having lived. You know there's more to life than putting food on the table and keeping a roof over your head. You're extremely loyal to family. You support your family, and will take care of an ailing family member or aging parents. You never shirk your responsibilities, even if they are gargantuan.

"Do not squander time, for that is the stuff life is made of."
BENJAMIN FRANKLIN
American Politician, Inventor, Author,
and a Founding Father of the United States of America
(JANUARY 17, 1706–APRIL 17, 1790)

Just as you are loyal and supportive to your family, you are loyal, supportive, and useful to your community. Many Capricorns have an influence that extends beyond their own community. Consider these fellow Capricorns who shared their efforts with the world: Howard Hughes, Lady Byrd Johnson, Louis Pasteur, Woodrow Wilson, General James Longstreet, William Gladstone, Barry Goldwater, Sir John A. Macdonald, Alexander Mackenzie, David Lloyd George, Alexander Hamilton, Daniel Webster, General Robert E. Lee, Sir Isaac Newton, Louis Braille, Charles Babbage, Albert Schweitzer, Joan of Arc, Konrad Adenauer, Richard Nixon, Aristotle Onassis, Martin Luther King, Jr., and Benjamin Franklin.

You plan ahead, you prepare for what you want, and you have the patience of Job to wait until opportunities ripen.

The life of Sir John A. Macdonald is almost textbook Capricorn. Macdonald once admitted to his private secretary and biographer, Joseph Pope, that he regretted leaving school, for he might have become a writer. In his memoir, Pope sums up what applies to all Capricorns who explore their full potential:

"[Macdonald] did not add, as he might have done, that the successful government
of millions of men, the strengthening of an empire, the creation of a great
dominion, call for the possession and exercise of rarer qualities than are
necessary to the achievement of literary fame."[5]

"The strengthening of an empire." "The successful government of millions." These are lofty Capricorn achievements! There is no question that every Capricorn gets the job done.

You are the most reliable, hard-working, disciplined, stoic sign in the zodiac. You display fortitude in the face of adversity. Your willingness to face life shows a realism that is bravery. You accept your fate as eternally established. It is what it is.

---

5. Joseph Pope, *Memoirs of the Right Honourable Sir John Alexander Macdonald*, vol. 1 (Ottawa: J. Durie and Son, 1894).

Capricorn in Love

Your ruler, Saturn, rules time, and this seems to be the reason you have a unique relationship to time. Your approach to time is almost a defiance of the norm, which is pretty curious, considering you are the sign that so highly values the status quo. But when it comes to love, you often partner with someone who is the age of your parent or your child. (It happens.)

You're a very earthy, passionate sign! You like sex. And you like to have it frequently!

Because you are so aware of respectability, the status quo, your reputation, and "what will the neighbours say" — the sexual act is often where you explore the freedom to rebel! Now nobody can see you. The lights are off and the door is locked. "Yippee!"

Remember how much you care about what others think of you? Remember how much you want to look successful, pulled together, independent, and respectable? This is why you have a cool, aloof demeanour. You send a message to the world that says, "I'm fine. I'm in control." It actually projects an air of mystery about you.

Privately, nothing could be further from the truth. You hugely desire intimacy! But you can never show this side of yourself to others because your fear of rejection outweighs your desire for love and intimacy! Aaaghhh.

This is one of the reasons you rarely demonstrate your affections in public. It's just too bloody risky! You don't want to look like a fool. You don't want to do or say anything you might later regret. Plus you like to keep your most personal feelings *very* private.

You can be painfully shy, although you try very hard to never show this. Instead, you invariably bail. You refuse invitations, or you just don't show up, or you don't make that call because you can't take the pressure, especially the fear of ridicule or rejection!

One thing that others should know about you is that you have a bean-counter mentality. (Remember? You add things up to see who has the most.) Therefore, if a lover gives you a gift, it had better be expensive! You think if someone spends more money on you, it means they care more. And, conversely, you will buy your loved one whatever you can afford as a way of showing how much *you* care.

Despite your goody-two-shoes public persona, you can be very promiscuous! Capricorn is definitely not above paying for sex. It's quick, it's easy, and there are no strings attached. The downside is getting caught. (Horrors!)

Be careful not to be too impressed with fame and money, because you could end up in a relationship that is not fulfilling, even though your partner is a great accessory. (This is easy for you to fall into.)

In the same vein (other arm), sometimes Capricorn is tempted to marry for money. Caution: *you'll earn every penny*!

You're a wonderful host. You care about your home. You make a fabulous impression on others. Obviously, anyone in love with you will realize you need lots of strokes! Like Leo, you need to be told daily how wonderful you are. Your partner will soon learn that it pays to do this. But they have to be clever — no false flattery! Your lovers have to observe you carefully so that their praise has validity. Then you'll snuggle up to them with pleasure, delight, and promise.

You want the emotional security of love. You also like to be needed by others, because then, of course, you can be *useful*. In fact, you want to be so useful that you become indispensable. Your lover can't live without you! This gives you a double blessing: you feel supremely accomplished and, at the same time, you feel secure because this person needs you so much. (This would scare the hell out of many other signs, but you're not a sign who is afraid of responsibility.)

Just be careful you don't develop a martyr syndrome. Your need to feel useful can do this. What's worse, it makes you lay guilt trips. ("After all I've done for you!") Don't even go there, because it only drives others away, and you don't want that. You want them in the palm of your hand, begging for more.

Incidentally, the knees are one of the body parts associated with Capricorn. Skirts and shorts with boots or knee socks that "frame" the knees appeal to you and also make you feel great. (Works both ways.) Net stockings, garter belts, stiletto heels, and eye-catching apparel that focuses on the knees and the legs are sexy Capricorn ploys. This surely brings to mind the old pub song "Knees up, Mother Brown." The saying "knees-up" is a Cockney expression meaning "party"! (Saucy you.)

You have the most rapacious sexual appetite in the zodiac, although few would guess this unless they knew you personally (ahem), because you somehow don't look the part. It's your navy blue cover. But, wow — when the door is locked and the lights are out — you're a different animal!

The Capricorn Boss

A Capricorn boss is a curious phenomenon. Most Capricorns love being the boss. However, some definitely do not. It's a toss-up which Capricorn you are.

Capricorn bosses are often stern taskmasters. They are extremely hard-working and prepared to suffer for the results they want ("no pain, no gain"). Unfortunately, they also expect this high standard from anyone who works for them! (Oops.) However, even if they are stern, they are fair.

Capricorns are excellent at organization. As a perfectionist, the Capricorn boss is a stickler for details and adherence to routine, especially punctuality. (Yup. Watch that clock!)

The Capricorn boss hates to be wrong, so don't call attention to their errors. (Baaad move.) On the other hand, the Capricorn boss loves a successful project. (Kudos all around!)

One of the great strengths of Capricorn bosses is that they're not afraid to hire people who are better than them. (Believe me, many people are, especially mediocre managers.) Capricorns, however, are out to get praise, prestige, and an enviable reputation from a job well done. They know the fastest route to success is to have great people working for them.

Capricorns are unsurpassed at bringing in projects on time and under budget. However, their greatest strength is being able to establish an organizational structure that works like a well-oiled machine. After all, organization is what their ruler Saturn is all about!

You also understand the importance of respect for authority. No matter how casual or friendly you are with "the guys," you never let them forget who is boss.

Because you're such a hard worker, you set the pace and the example for others to follow. No matter what you demand of others, you are always more demanding of yourself.

People who work for you know this, and they respect your prodigious efforts and huge capacity for work. You are also capable of making tough decisions. It's because you just accept the responsibility, which is often not an easy thing to do. You never shirk your duties or anything you have to face. You've got guts!

The Capricorn Employee

The Capricorn employee is an ideal hire, because here is a person who likes to be punctual, who is courteous, and who shows respect for authority. Furthermore, the Capricorn employee has a natural inclination to be organized and work hard. Capricorns love to be part of a well-oiled system!

Capricorns will work very hard for the right kind of carrot. They love titles, salary raises, prestigious offices, and any kind of perk that shows they are important.

They are extremely loyal and hard-working. They don't rock the boat. They support the status quo and they obey rules. (At least, they give the appearance of doing so.) They are probably the easiest of all employees to supervise because they understand where they fit in.

However, another reason they are easy to supervise is that Capricorns want to be viewed as obedient, proper, and good at their job. They take pride in being the Employee of the Month. ("That's me up there on the wall.")

If they are working in a disorganized environment, they will quickly and quietly create order out of chaos. It's their nature to do this, and they have the savvy and know-how to make it happen. (And they generally do it without putting too many noses out of joint.) It's a fact that all of the Earth signs are great employees, but Capricorn is the best.

Needless to say (but I'm going to say it), not only is your hard-working Capricorn a great hire — this employee will stay fooooreeeeever. Capricorns get thirty-five-year watches. (Or they used to. Our modern world rewards this kind of loyalty less and less.) Like their opposite sign, Cancer, Capricorns often end up sitting in the boardrooms of big corporations. You can spot them because they're wearing Escada, Hugo Boss, and Prada.[6] They have Montblanc pens, Cartier watches, and Hermès briefcases. (Let's not forget the Italian shoes.)

Capricorns like to look respectable in a successful way.

---

6. One exception is Dolly Parton (b. January 19, 1946), who said, "You'd be surprised how much it costs to look this cheap!"

The Capricorn Parent

The Capricorn parent wants to be a successful parent. Why? Because Capricorn wants to be successful in *everything*! We're talking perfectionism. You want the respect of your peers.

Every Capricorn parent at some point has said, "Did you go out looking like that?" (Read: Did you go to school looking like that? Did you go to church looking like that? Did you go to work looking like that?) The Capricorn parent believes their children represent them in the community. If their children are well-behaved, well-dressed, and getting good grades, naturally the Capricorn parent has done his job well!

Always remember that Capricorn wants respect. (And is horrified by public criticism.) In fact, this need for prestige and respect often triggers a situation where the Capricorn parent lives vicariously through their children. This is why they want their children to succeed in the way they believe is proper.

> "My mother's passion for something more, to write a different destiny
> for a dirt-poor farmer's daughter, was to shape my entire life."
> FAYE DUNAWAY
> American Actress
> *Network, Bonnie and Clyde,* and *Chinatown*
> (B. JANUARY 14, 1941)

The average Capricorn parent thinks that "starving artist" is a hyphenated word. Because they want security and happiness for their children, they're afraid their kids will entertain ideas that will lead to decades of failure, and perhaps worse: sex, drugs, and rock 'n' roll!

This might sound like the Capricorn parent is superficial. This is not the case at all! Capricorns make conservative choices (remember the mantra?): married, in a house with a white picket fence, and 2.5 kids. No sign more than Capricorn represents traditional family values.

Capricorn parents work extremely hard to make their family life work in a successful way. They want to raise kids who are responsible citizens, who know how to take care of themselves, who know how to fit into society, and who are well-mannered and law-abiding.

The Capricorn parent stresses the values of planning ahead, saving for a rainy day, taking care of tools and possessions, and avoiding waste. All excellent qualities to encourage!

Capricorns will help their children study, send them to good schools (especially private schools), take them to sports practice, encourage them to get music lessons, gym time, or rink time, or do whatever is necessary to help their children excel.

Capricorn parents will also deny themselves so that their children can have a better education, or even a better wardrobe. Because Capricorns have a long-range view of things, they are less likely to indulge the child of the moment and more likely to focus on shaping the citizen of tomorrow.

I suspect that if all the parents in the world were Capricorn, our society would be a much safer place!

Every Capricorn parent reads their children the story of *The Little Engine That Could*.

The Capricorn Child

"Often and often afterwards, the beloved Aunt would ask me why I had never told anyone how I was being treated. Children tell little more than animals, for what comes to them they accept as eternally established."

RUDYARD KIPLING
British Author and Poet
The Jungle Book and "Gunga Din"
(DECEMBER 30, 1865–JANUARY 18, 1936)

Life is not always easy for the Capricorn child. This child tries to be obedient, because being good is generally the best way to fit in. However, this child not only wants to fit in with their own family, they wants to fit in with their classmates, their neighbourhood, and their community. If for any reason (an alcoholic mother, an unemployed father, conditions of poverty, or poor performance at school or in sports) this acceptance is threatened, then this child will suffer excruciatingly.

It is very important for the Capricorn child to be respected in a genuine way, and to have a sense of feeling worthwhile. It is not unusual for Capricorn children to feel that they don't quite identify with their own families. For different reasons, they often feel full of self-doubt.

Nevertheless, Capricorn children are surprisingly stoic. They appear to be independent and even aloof, but, actually, this is a protective facade. These children need enormous amounts of affection and cuddling! And praise! However, the praise must be well placed. The Capricorn child is no fool. You can get away with false flattery with a Leo kid, but Capricorn children will be insulted by false flattery! In fact, this will actually backfire. They will think to themselves that they are so desperately wanting and inadequate, others are willing to do anything to "buck them up." Aaaaggghh.

Capricorn rules the knees, so be careful about this part of the body with your Capricorn child. When it comes to sports, protect those knees!

The Capricorn child is happy being useful. This doesn't mean just putting away their own toys. This child would rather help you put away what *you* need to put away, or help you dry the dishes, or load the dishwasher, or help you rake leaves. Praise for good work is what makes this little Capricorn heart pump for joy.

Pride in a job well done!

How to Be a Happier Capricorn

You want the respect of your peers and a chance to show others how well you can do something, especially if it makes a difference in the world. These things are important to you.

Naturally, to achieve your ambitions, you need confidence. However, from the moment you were born, almost like a destiny factor (and, indeed, Saturn is the planet of karmic destiny), life sometimes conspires to make you undergo experiences that erode your self-confidence.

The first thing that happened for many of you (not all) was that you were born into a family with which you couldn't really identify. You might not have said this to yourself in so many words, but you felt separate and apart from your family. This doesn't means you were walking around muttering "I see dead people," but there's a good chance you asked your parents if you were adopted.

At a deep, unconscious level, this can only mean that somehow you were born wrong! You opened the door, you stepped in, you let the door close behind you, and *bam*! You're in the wrong family! *You goofed!* Of course, none of this occurs to you in an articulate, conscious way. It's just a general feeling of uneasiness and questioning.

Sure enough, because you subconsciously feel that the first door you ever opened was the wrong door, for the rest of your life, you are very cautious about opening new doors.

You might remember that, as a child, when you visited other homes and then returned to your own home — you might have had the feeling you weren't in the right family, which in turn planted the seed that you had failed to get born right. Therefore, from a young age, through no fault of your own, you had a sense of *failure*. You couldn't even get born right!

And now, here you are — stuck with *this* family. Naturally, your next move is you decide you have to *save* your family! (Make them stop drinking, or earn more money, or get a home, or whatever you perceive to be the solution.) But, of course, you can't possibly do this, because you are just a little child. And here we have your second big failure.

This means that by the age of ten you had two strikes against you. You couldn't get born right (and what is more axiomatic than that?) and you couldn't save your family!

This is the beginning of an underlying fear and lack of confidence that is crippling for all Capricorns. Later, it expresses itself as a fear of success, a fear of failure, a fear of discovery: "Wait till they find out I don't know!" Capricorn is constantly seeking the security of acceptance and respect in society, in friendships, in family relationships, and at work.

The truth is that we are all born into imperfect families![7] Your self-doubt has no basis in fact, other than that you are a frail mortal *like every other person on the planet*. I think the best way to turn this around is by having minor successes. It's like learning to walk.

One way to get in touch with your own minor successes is to start a little diary. When you go to bed at night, write down what you did that day. *Nothing is too inconsequential.* I remember one time after a major operation a doctor told me that, at the beginning of the recovery process, I could only do two things a day. He said, "If you shower, that's one thing." (I was shocked.)

Give yourself credit for *everything* you do. You get out of bed, you bathe, you get dressed, you feed yourself, and, perhaps, you go to work, and so on. Every night, write down what you actually did. These are your accomplishments.

Depending on who you are or what you do, your list might be modest or impressive. Either way, your Capricorn soul needs to see in black and white how much you actually accomplish each day. You need to take credit for this. You need to own what you do. And you do a lot! As the weeks go by, if you keep this journal, your self-respect will increase. I guarantee it.

Now, you might think this is a corny, lame-o exercise. Especially if you are relatively successful at what you're doing. But, hey — you secretly know you lack confidence.

So, try it. It's just a gimmick. But everything is a gimmick. A gimmick is what you use to make something work! What you're trying to do is to reduce feelings of self-doubt and increase your sense of self-worth and self-confidence. You can't *kid* yourself into this. And the praise of others is only momentary. You still have to lie in bed in the dark.

The act of writing down every night everything you accomplished every day, will swing your mind 180 degrees from focusing on what you *didn't* achieve to focusing on what you *did* achieve. This takes you from the negative to the positive.

Little by little, you will train yourself to become aware of your achievements, which, believe me, because you're such a hard worker, are considerable! As you observe what you do each day (and everything you do is an accomplishment), your mind will slowly start to feel less scattered and more focused on what you might do tomorrow. And this focus slowly replaces anxiety. Why?

Because we are creatures of habit and whatever we do grows. Whatever you did today increases the odds you will do it tomorrow. Whatever you did not do today increases the odds that you will not do it tomorrow.

By focusing on your accomplishments — no matter how small — you will start to diminish your anxiety that there is not enough time. Unless you disarm bombs

7. Horatio Alger (January 13, 1832–July 18, 1899) was a Capricorn who wrote "rags to riches" stories of people who achieved respectability against great odds.

for a living, this "time" thing is a big illusion. We each have twenty-four hours every day. The rich do not have more than twenty-four hours, and the poor do not have less. When you get down to it, all we ever have is the present moment. Everything else is a hope or a memory. (Einstein said, "I never think of the future — it comes soon enough.")

There is great satisfaction in seeing improvement in your life. This is where you have an advantage over all the other signs. You are surprisingly willing to accept responsibility. You're happy to do your duty.

Do you realize that acting responsibly involves an element of caring? It means you care about the results, or you *care* about other people. Certainly the reverse is also true! Irresponsibility is certainly not caring.

Give yourself credit for your strong sense of responsibility and caring.

If you try this, your self-respect will grow, your awareness of your willingness to accept duty and responsibility will grow, and, as a result of this, you will become a more confident and caring person.

"Hide not your talents. They for use were made.
What's a sundial in the shade?"
BENJAMIN FRANKLIN
American Politician, Inventor, Author,
and a Founding Father of the United States of America
(JANUARY 17, 1706–APRIL 17, 1790)

CAPRICORN
YOUR 40-YEAR HOROSCOPE
1985 – 2025

Why Go into the Past?

I want you to believe and have faith in your predictions so you can derive benefit from them in guiding your future. The only way you can believe what I say is to test it for yourself. This is why I start with brief highlights from the past twenty-five years. If anything in these past twenty-five years resonates with you, then what I say about your future will have the same validity. It is all one long timeline — your life.

The past predictions generally apply once you have left home or are "running your life" and making your own decisions. Prior to that, the major events in your life were dictated by other people, likely your parents.

1985 ~ 1990

For those of you who are old enough to remember, if you look back you will see that you were really on top of your game in the early eighties. By 1985, your spending power was greater. However, for different reasons according to the details of your life, you entered a window of time in the mid-eighties to late eighties when you had to let go of things. Relationships ended. Many of you moved or changed jobs. Some of you lost loved ones.

The year 1987 was an opportunity to regroup at home and enjoy warm relationships with family. In fact, 1987–88 probably saw an expansion in your family in terms of birth, adoption, or marriage. This was also a very good time for real-estate deals or purchases.

By 1989, many of you had improved your job and your health. For some of you, especially early Capricorns, this job improvement could have been the beginning of a whole new cycle for you. One thing is certain: by 1990, all of you had begun a new thirty-year journey in which you would completely redefine who you were in the world. Yikes!

Fortunately, as you set off in this completely new direction (so new that many of you actually changed your daily wardrobe), one lovely perk offered you support, namely that relationships and partnerships in 1990 were swell! In fact, 1990 was a great year to enter new partnerships. Even your relations with the general public were improved at that time, despite the fact that you personally might have felt unsure of yourself because you were on new turf. Hey — sometimes you've got to fake it till you make it.

1991 – 1996

A strange combination of circumstances came into play now. Just when your own earnings might have been restricted, or you began to question how you should earn money and even what your basic values were — at this very time, around 1991, you received wonderful favours, cash, perks, help, inheritances, money back from the government, scholarships, bursaries, loans, mortgages, or practical and financial assistance from others. Talk about timing! So, just when you needed it most, the resources of others opened up to you.

No doubt this is why you had wonderful opportunities in 1992, and also why many of you could explore further education, going back to school, or taking needed training. Actually, this was also an excellent time to explore avenues in publishing, the media, medicine, and the law.

By 1993, things were looking good! At this time, lucky Jupiter was crossing the top of your chart, bringing all kinds of opportunities to you and boosting your good name. This was the year when your reputation could shine! Many of you got a promotion or some kind of public recognition. You increased the esteem your contemporaries had for you. In a way, your name was up in lights!

Once again, perhaps this success forced changes in residence and jobs, which followed shortly afterwards. Finally, after a time of uncertainty and change, you became determined to establish a home base for yourself by 1996. You wanted some stability.

1997 – 2000

At this time in your life, you were determined to establish an anchor for yourself in the world in terms of your home, by buying a home, or fixing up where you were, or doing major repairs. It was fortunate that your earnings probably got a boost in 1997. (You were certainly spending more then.)

In fact, your entire frame of mind was pretty positive at that time, despite your responsibilities at home. This led to a much happier year around 1999 in your private life and with your family. This was a time (approximately) when many of you expanded your family through birth, marriage, or adoption. This was also a wonderful time at home because family relationships were warmer. Entertaining at home was more fun. It was a good time for family reunions.

Around 1999, your private and domestic life improved. This was also a great time for real-estate purchases. You might have done something to expand where you live, or, at least, you felt richer about where you lived. This feeling of increased wealth and optimism probably led to a fabulous vacation sometime around the millennium. You decided to do it up big!

This was a wonderful time to expand your family and to enjoy children, as well as to participate or delight in sports, the arts, and any opportunity to express your creative talent.

The turn of the millennium was also a juicy time for romance and love affairs. You were turning heads!

Although this was an enjoyable stage, privately, you were wondering what you wanted to do with the rest of your life. You felt you needed more fulfillment, or a greater sense of accomplishment from your efforts.

2001 – 2005

This is when you really started to bust your buns! You were working hard! You believe in the "no pain, no gain" approach to life, and you're right. Just when you began to put your shoulder behind the proverbial wheel, you had all kinds of opportunities to either get a better job or improve the job you had. That was reassuring!

In fact, rewards did follow, because in the next few years, partnerships, close friends, and the wealth and resources of others came to your aid. Some of you got inheritances, or money back from the government, or the use of things that other people owned. But, whatever happened, it was as if the universe was looking out for you.

However, at this time, relationships and partnerships were seriously challenged. Those that were not going to make it bit the dust. Other relationships had to undergo major readjustments if they were going to endure. (You know who you are.)

In 2004, travel opportunities came your way. Many of you had schooling opportunities then as well. Some explored new avenues in publishing, the media, medicine, or the law. You felt an increasing sense of personal power, that's for sure.

Around 2005 was a very fortunate time for you. You were able to increase your personal power, or perhaps you boosted your charisma within your inner circle of friends. Something occurred that put you in a much more favourable light in terms of your reputation and how others viewed you.

This was good because you were entering a time when the support from others would soon be withdrawn. (Yikes!)

2006 – 2010

Let's take a moment to talk about a major change that starts to enter your life. We're talking about big daddy Pluto. Actually, Pluto is rather small — it's just that its influence is so big.

At this time, the planet Pluto entered Capricorn for the first time in your life. To be more precise, it was the first time in the lives of everyone on the planet! That's because the last time Pluto was in Capricorn was from 1763 to 1778.

Now, more than two centuries later, Pluto returned to Capricorn in November 2008, and it will stay there until 2024. Naturally, the question is, *What does this mean for me?*

For starters, it means you are undergoing a Pluto transit you have never experienced before in your life, because nobody alive has ever felt Pluto in Capricorn. Pluto is intent on brutal reformation! It represents the tearing down of things so that they can be rebuilt in a better way. Because Pluto rules garbage and everything that is extraneous or no longer necessary — Pluto will urge you to get rid of what is no longer necessary *in your life.*

Therefore, from 2009 to 2024, depending on where Pluto lines up with your birthday, you will be busy going through cupboards, lockers, storage areas, closets, basements, and garages, getting rid of stuff you don't need. You will give it away, recycle it, sell it, whatever. This is the easy part.

Some of you will experience a more dramatic change by giving up countries, residences, and jobs because it's time to move on. To stay in this place or position is just marking time.

At a more subtle level, some will leave relationships and friendships because they, too, are no longer relevant in your life.

At the most subtle level, you will give up prejudices, ideas, false notions, and beliefs that are no longer appropriate because they don't serve your best interests anymore. During 2009–11, all Capricorns might feel this; however, the Capricorns who were born in December will feel this the strongest.

One lovely piece of news is that in January 2008, lucky money-bags Jupiter entered your sign, giving you excellent opportunities to travel or explore opportunities in publishing, the media, medicine, or the law. It attracted positive situations to you because *that was your year to shine*!

Those of you who exploited the opportunities that came your way probably increased your earnings and your spending power in 2009. In fact, by this time, you could sense you were heading somewhere that was going to pay off. Finally! You had been working for this ever since around 1994.

2011 ~ 2013

For the next fourteen years, I will make references to the Capricorn birthdays that are most likely to feel the effects of Pluto. Between 2011 and 2013 people born in the first three days of January will likely feel Pluto's impact most strongly and undergo a time of great change.

It's important to know that when you're dealing with Pluto, even though you are getting rid of outmoded structures or that which is no longer relevant in your life — *whatever changes you make should benefit others as well as yourself.* If you can do this, your benefits will be considerable, and they will be long-lasting. If the changes you make benefit yourself only, your benefits will be lesser, and briefer in duration.

Certainly 2010–11 is a good time for real-estate deals, or seeking ways to expand your home, or making it feel richer and more comfortable. Family life will also wonderfully improve! In fact, your family might expand now (in 2011 or 2012) through the birth of babies, marriage, adoption, whatever.

Despite whatever is going on, there's no question that this is a time of achievement in your life. We're talking notable achievement! Yes, the kind of achievement that makes *you feel proud.*

Your accomplishment might be a graduation, a job promotion, marriage, the birth of a child, or a move to self-employment — whatever it is, it's a dream come true! This is something you want to happen. For some, it could be considerable success!

Perhaps this is why vacations, parties, romance, love affairs, sports, and all kinds of fun events are on the agenda for 2012. Yee-haw! Time to party hard! After all, you deserve it. And then, appropriately, after you've had your fun, in 2013 marvellous opportunities come along to improve your job and your health. It doesn't get much better than this.

Ah yes. Time to alphabetize your blessings.

2014 – 2015

In 2014, your closest friendships and partnerships (both intimate and professional) will improve dramatically. Casual relationships might become committed. This is a wonderful time to enter into new partnerships or to get married.

In fact, some of you will dramatically change partners at this time, because Pluto is strongly affecting those who were born in the first six days of January. Nevertheless, it's important to know that Pluto can be affecting all Capricorns as well.

For example, many of you are changing your daily wardrobe. You might switch from tailored clothes to casual wear, or vice versa. This could be due to a job change or a residential move to a different climate. Hey — this might be exciting!

Many of you feel a strong drive for power. However, please don't let this make you ruthless. You will regret it if you do.

"A loving person lives in a loving world. A hostile person lives in a hostile world. Everyone you meet is your mirror."

KEN KEYES, JR.
Inspirational Author and Lecturer
(JANUARY 19, 1921–DECEMBER 20, 1995)

At the same time, you're facing another challenge: because of recent successes, more demands are being made on your time by other people. How can you keep everybody happy, and yet at the same time maintain your own integrity and sense of independence? After all, you're not a doormat. You still have your personal life that requires your respect and allegiance. This is a tricky juggling act!

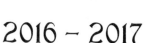

2016 ~ 2017

Pluto now strongly affects people born January 4 to January 9. But once again, I repeat, it can affect all Capricorns.

In fact, in this two-year interval, all Capricorns are facing decisions regarding giving up people, places, and possessions. You're entering a time in your life when you're dismantling much of what you have created since 2003. It's a bit like deciding who stays and who goes. This also applies to your possessions.

The best way to approach this is to plan for this and do it willingly. I say this because there is an inevitability about all this. If you try to resist it, circumstances might wrench it away from you, which is always messier and tougher to handle.

Therefore, if it is time to move on — and it certainly is in some areas — then *accept this* and go with the flow gracefully, under your own terms.

The year 2016 is marvellous for travel opportunities! In addition, opportunities for higher education look fabulous as well. Many of you will explore excellent chances in publishing, the media, medicine, and the law. Quite possibly, these opportunities, or what you learn through travel, will trigger your decision to make a move, or leave a job, or end a relationship. (All of this is interrelated and tied together in some way.)

A wonderful boon comes to you in 2017! Just when you are letting go of so much, fabulous career opportunities are at hand. The last time things were this good was in 2004–5, and before that in 1992–93.

Great stuff is coming out of the woodwork! Some of you might change your career to a new area related to the law, healing, dealing with foreign countries, or something to do with publishing, the media, or higher education.

Looking swell, kiddo!

2018 – 2020

In this particular time interval, those who were born between January 7 and January 16 will undergo the most dramatic changes.

Nevertheless, this is the beginning of a new thirty-year cycle for all of you. All of you have survived the past few years of loss — letting go of things, giving up possessions, saying goodbye to people, and streamlining your life — to prepare for this exciting new journey!

Why is it exciting? Because, between 2018 and 2026, you are going to reinvent yourself!

It begins in 2018, which is an unusually popular year for you. Many of you will join groups, clubs, and organizations. Others will be involved in classes where you meet new people. All of you will schmooze much more than usual. This is a good time to begin new partnerships and friendships. This is also a year when others will benefit you with their helpful feedback. Therefore, talk to people about your dreams and wishes for the future. After all, you're setting off on an entirely new journey, which is unknown and therefore a bit unsettling. Get feedback from others that will help you!

In December 2019, moneybags Jupiter enters Capricorn for the first time in twelve years, bringing you wonderful opportunities along with increased joy and happiness. *Jupiter will stay in your sign for a year.* Whenever this happens, your happiness quotient increases, good opportunities and powerful people are attracted to you, travel is easy, and you just feel lighter! The last time you felt a lovely boost like this was in 2008. It's a feel-good, confidence-building experience.

Everybody loves Jupiter in their sign!

"You must be passionate, you must dedicate yourself,
and you must be relentless in the pursuit of your goals.
If you do, you will be successful."
STEVE GARVEY
American Businessman, Motivational Speaker,
and Former Major League Baseball Player
(B. DECEMBER 22, 1948)

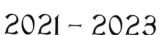

2021 – 2023

This two-year window is the time when Capricorns born after January 14 to the end of the sign will feel the strongest hit of Pluto touching their sign. Pluto is trying to introduce a revolutionary change for the better, generally by removing something that you are "finished" with. This could be an indication of the ending of a partnership, or a time of giving up other aspects of your life that are really no longer beneficial to you. Incidentally, this includes losing weight. In the past ten years, many Capricorns will have suddenly just dropped extra pounds with relatively little effort.

Oh, how the money rolls in! The year 2021 is a particularly powerful time for you because you have the benefit of having had Jupiter in your sign in the previous year. This means you now have more self-confidence and poise than you've had in more than a decade! *You're in the zone, and you know what to do!*

Employment will have a strong emphasis this year. And, lucky you, just as you are seriously looking for new kinds of work, money-bags Jupiter hits one of your Money Houses, specifically, your House of Earnings. Ta-dah!

This definitely attracts well-paying jobs or a raise. It's also an indication that many of you are spending a lot of money this year. You're buying beautiful things for yourself and your loved ones. (Well, seems to me if you are blowing a lot of money, you must be earning it. Something looks good.)

The period 2022–23 is an excellent time for buying real estate as well as improving your home and where you live. For some reason, you feel richer in your private life. You will move to a bigger home, or buy bigger digs, or do something to where you live so that it feels richer, more expansive, and more luxurious.

Other things might occur that encourage meetings and groups to gather at your home to learn something new. (Groups of people meeting at your home might well be one reason you're buying goodies for where you live. We must keep up appearances!) In fact, in 2022–23, many of you will expand not only your home but

also your family, through marriage, birth, adoption, or something like that. It appears that your family becomes larger in a joyful way. (This rules out the possibility of your deadbeat brother-in-law staying on your sofa.)

By 2023, your romantic scene looks excellent! New love affairs can begin and existing love affairs will heat up! This is also a great year for sports, whether you participate or watch. By all means, *plan on a vacation this year.* All the arts are beautifully favoured now because you're in touch with your muse! Playful activities with children are delightful. This is the classic year to expand your family through marriage or birth. The bottom line is that 2023 is all about fun, pleasure, and having a good time!

Let the festivities begin!

2024 – 2025

Well, the really good news is that Pluto finally leaves your sign in February 2024. You never have to worry about Pluto again, because it won't pass through Capricorn for another 250 years. If you look back at your life since 2009, you will see what dramatic changes have taken place. A Pluto transit is relentless. Now it's a thing of the past.

In many ways, 2024 continues to be a fun-loving year full of pleasure, romance, vacations, and exciting outings connected with sports, the theatre, and the arts.

However, other influences dictate the likelihood of a residential move or a job change between 2024 and 2026. It might be one or the other, or both. Fortunately, your job scene will improve beautifully at some point in 2024, and this could be because of a job *change*. Or it could be the reason for your residential move. There's no question that something looks extremely good here in terms of employment.

The other thing that looks good is your health. The period 2024–25 is a window of time that nicely blesses your health, with the only downside being possible weight gain. Even then, it would primarily be from too many sweets and too many seconds of desserts. A lot of Capricorns have a sweet tooth,[8] which is kind of curious when you consider that your ruler, Saturn, rules the teeth.

Make the most of this opportunity in 2024–25 to improve your job, because you *really can do it*. You can either get a better job, or better duties at your current job, or a promotion. Something will work out in your favour — big time! Milk this for all it's worth!

---

8. My mother, who is Capricorn Rising, loves her sweets. I grew up in a small town, and we had three meals a day at the kitchen table. (The streets were empty at dinnertime.) And, yes — we had two desserts a day! A dessert at lunch and another at dinner as well. I thought everyone lived this way. There were always several cookie tins with home-baked cookies, and, generally, a cake around as well. I particularly loved her cakes! It was great to come home after school and have a glass of milk and a piece of fresh banana cake with buttery brown-sugar icing on it. On top of all this, my mother hid candies in the kitchen drawer where she kept the tea towels. She thought we didn't know. We all knew. Nevertheless, she was smart to choose big white peppermints or those brown striped humbugs, which nobody liked. (Maybe she did it on purpose.)

"I made a commitment to completely cut out drinking and anything that might hamper me from getting my mind and body together. And the floodgates of goodness have opened upon me — spiritually and financially."

DENZEL WASHINGTON

American Actor, Screenwriter, Director, and Producer

Glory, Malcolm X, The Hurricane, and *Training Day*

(B. DECEMBER 28, 1954)

Famous Capricorn Personalities

Giacomo Puccini	December 22, 1858–1924
Barbara Billingsley	December 22, 1915
Héctor Elizondo	December 22, 1936
Diane Sawyer	December 22, 1945
Ralph Fiennes	December 22, 1962
Vanessa Paradis	December 22, 1972
Yousuf Karsh	December 23, 1908–2002
José Greco	December 23, 1918–2000
Robert Bly	December 23, 1926
Chet Baker	December 23, 1929–1988
Susan Lucci	December 23, 1946
Eddie Vedder	December 23, 1964
Carla Bruni-Sarkozy	December 23, 1967
Catriona Le May Doan	December 23, 1970
Matthew Arnold	December 24, 1822–1888
Juan Ramón Jiménez	December 24, 1881–1958
Howard Hughes	December 24, 1905–1976
Ava Gardner	December 24, 1922–1990
Mary Higgins Clark	December 24, 1927
Ricky Martin	December 24, 1971
Stephanie Meyer	December 24, 1973
Clara Barton	December 25, 1821–1912
Helena Rubenstein	December 25, 1870–1965
Humphrey Bogart	December 25, 1899–1957
Cab Calloway	December 25, 1907–1994
Anwar Sadat	December 25, 1918–1981
Rod Serling	December 25, 1924–1975
Carlos Castaneda	December 25, 1925–1998
Ismail Merchant	December 25, 1936–2005
Jimmy Buffett	December 25, 1946
Sissy Spacek	December 25, 1949
Annie Lennox	December 25, 1954
Henry Miller	December 26, 1891–1980
Mao Zedong	December 26, 1893–1976
Steve Allen	December 26, 1921–2000

Alan King	December 26, 1924–2004
Carlton Fisk	December 26, 1947
Candy Crowley	December 26, 1948
Elizabeth Kostova	December 26, 1964
Jared Leto	December 26, 1971
Johannes Kepler	December 27, 1571–1630
Louis Pasteur	December 27, 1822–1895
Marlene Dietrich	December 27, 1901–1992
Mike Pinder	December 27, 1941
Gérard Depardieu	December 27, 1948
Emilie de Ravin	December 27, 1981
John Molson	December 28, 1763–1836
Calixa Lavallée	December 28, 1842–1891
Stan Lee	December 28, 1922
Moe Koffman	December 28, 1928–2001
Maggie Smith	December 28, 1934
Richard Clayderman	December 28, 1953
Gayle King	December 28, 1954
Denzel Washington	December 28, 1954
Sienna Miller	December 28, 1981
Pablo Casals	December 29, 1876–1973
Mary Tyler Moore	December 29, 1936
Jon Voight	December 29, 1938
Marianne Faithfull	December 29, 1946
Ted Danson	December 29, 1947
Gelsey Kirkland	December 29, 1952
Jude Law	December 29, 1972
Rudyard Kipling	December 30, 1865–1936
Stephen Leacock	December 30, 1869–1944
Jack Lord	December 30, 1920–1998
Bo Diddley	December 30, 1928–2008
Skeeter Davis	December 30, 1931–2004
Meredith Vieira	December 30, 1953
Tracy Ullman	December 30, 1959
Douglas Coupland	December 30, 1961
Tiger Woods	December 30, 1975
Eliza Dushku	December 30, 1980
Henri Matisse	December 31, 1869–1954
Elizabeth Arden	December 31, 1878–1966
Anthony Hopkins	December 31, 1937
John Denver	December 31, 1943–1997
Ben Kingsley	December 31, 1943

Donna Summer	December 31, 1948
Bebe Neuwirth	December 31, 1958
Patrick Chan	December 31, 1990
Alfred Stieglitz	January 1, 1864–1946
J. Edgar Hoover	January 1, 1895–1972
Xavier Cugat	January 1, 1900–1990
J. D. Salinger	January 1, 1919–2010
Deepa Mehta	January 1, 1950
John O'Donohue	January 1, 1956–2008
James Wolfe	January 2, 1727–1759
Thérèse de Lisieux	January 2, 1873–1897
Isaac Asimov	January 2, 1920–1992
Jack Hanna	January 2, 1947
Tia Carrere	January 2, 1967
Cuba Gooding, Jr.	January 2, 1968
Kate Bosworth	January 2, 1983
J. R. R. Tolkien	January 3, 1892–1973
Ray Milland	January 3, 1907–1986
Victor Borge	January 3, 1909–2000
Dabney Coleman	January 3, 1932
Bobby Hull	January 3, 1939
Mel Gibson	January 3, 1956
Isaac Newton	January 4, 1643–1727
Louis Braille	January 4, 1809–1852
Floyd Patterson	January 4, 1935–2006
Dyan Cannon	January 4, 1937
John McLaughlin	January 4, 1942
Patty Loveless	January 4, 1957
Michael Stipe	January 4, 1960
Julia Ormond	January 4, 1965
Jane Wyman	January 5, 1917–2007
Robert Duvall	January 5, 1931
Umberto Eco	January 5, 1932
Charlie Rose	January 5, 1942
Diane Keaton	January 5, 1946
Joe Flanigan	January 5, 1967
Carl Sandburg	January 6, 1878–1967
Khalil Gibran	January 6, 1883–1931
Earl Scruggs	January 6, 1924
E. L. Doctorow	January 6, 1931
Rowan Atkinson	January 6, 1955
Nigella Lawson	January 6, 1960

John Kavelin	January 7, 1944–2009
Jann Wenner	January 7, 1946
Kenny Loggins	January 7, 1948
David Caruso	January 7, 1956
Katie Couric	January 7, 1957
Nicolas Cage	January 7, 1964
Gypsy Rose Lee	January 8, 1911–1970
Elvis Presley	January 8, 1935–1977
Stephen Hawking	January 8, 1942
Terry Brooks	January 8, 1944
David Bowie	January 8, 1947
Sarah Polley	January 8, 1979
Gracie Fields	January 9, 1898–1979
Simone de Beauvoir	January 9, 1908–1986
Richard Nixon	January 9, 1913–1994
Judith Krantz	January 9, 1928
Wilbur Smith	January 9, 1933
Joan Baez	January 9, 1941
Dave Matthews	January 9, 1967
Ray Bolger	January 10, 1904–1987
Gisèle MacKenzie	January 10, 1927–2003
Jim Croce	January 10, 1943–1973
Rod Stewart	January 10, 1945
George Foreman	January 10, 1949
Pat Benatar	January 10, 1953
Alice Paul	January 11, 1885–1977
Alan Paton	January 11, 1903–1988
Naomi Judd	January 11, 1946
Diana Gabaldon	January 11, 1952
Mary J. Blige	January 11, 1971
Amanda Peet	January 11, 1972
Bill Reid	January 12, 1920–1998
Tim Horton	January 12, 1930–1974
Long John Baldry	January 12, 1941–2005
Joe Frazier	January 12, 1944
Kirstie Alley	January 12, 1951
Howard Stern	January 12, 1954
Melanie Chisholm	January 12, 1974
Robert Stack	January 13, 1919–2003
Frances Sternhagen	January 13, 1930
Julia Louis-Dreyfus	January 13, 1961
Patrick Dempsey	January 13, 1966

Orlando Bloom	January 13, 1977
Joannie Rochette	January 13, 1986
Marcus Antonius	January 14, 83 B.C.–30 B.C.
Albert Schweitzer	January 14, 1875–1965
Nina Ricci	January 14, 1883–1970
Cecil Beaton	January 14, 1904–1980
Faye Dunaway	January 14, 1941
Maureen Dowd	January 14, 1952
Jason Bateman	January 14, 1969
Mazo de la Roche	January 15, 1879–1961
Aristotle Onassis	January 15, 1906–1975
Lloyd Bridges	January 15, 1913–1998
Martin Luther King, Jr.	January 15, 1929–1968
Andrea Martin	January 15, 1947
Chad Lowe	January 15, 1968
Robert W. Service	January 16, 1874–1958
Dian Fossey	January 16, 1932–1985
Ronnie Milsap	January 16, 1943
Sade	January 16, 1959
Kate Moss	January 16, 1974
Brenden Morrow	January 16, 1979
Nevil Shute	January 17, 1899–1960
Betty White	January 17, 1922
James Earl Jones	January 17, 1931
Muhammad Ali	January 17, 1942
Jim Carrey	January 17, 1962
Michelle Obama	January 17, 1964
A. A. Milne	January 18, 1882–1956
Oliver Hardy	January 18, 1892–1957
Cary Grant	January 18, 1904–1986
Kevin Costner	January 18, 1955
Mark Messier	January 18, 1961
Jane Horrocks	January 18, 1964
Edgar Allen Poe	January 19, 1809–1849
Paul Cézanne	January 19, 1839–1906
Jean Stapleton	January 19, 1923
Janis Joplin	January 19, 1943–1970
Dolly Parton	January 19, 1946
Paula Deen	January 19, 1947
Katey Sagal	January 19, 1954

AQUARIUS

JANUARY 20 – FEBRUARY 18

AQUARIUS THE WATER CARRIER
(JANUARY 20 – FEBRUARY 18)

"I KNOW."

"My country is the world, and my religion is to do good."
THOMAS PAINE
Author, Inventor, and Revolutionary
(JANUARY 29, 1736–JUNE 8, 1809)

"If you're playing a poker game and you look around the
table and can't tell who the sucker is, it's you."
PAUL NEWMAN
American Actor, Film Director, Humanitarian,
and Co-founder of "Newman's Own" Food Products
The Hustler, Cool Hand Luke, and *Butch Cassidy and the Sundance Kid*
(JANUARY 26, 1925–SEPTEMBER 26, 2008)

Element: Air
Ruling Planet: Uranus
Quality: Fixed
Opposite Sign: Leo
Symbol: The Water Carrier
Glyph: Waves of Air, Electricity, or Sound
Lucky Gems: Amethyst, Turquoise, and Quartz Crystal[1]
Flowers: Daffodil and Violet
Colours: Electric Blue, Glow-in-the-Dark Shades, and Plaids
Parts of the Body: Ankles

You Like: Gadgets, planes, new inventions, books, experiments, travelling, prizes, equal rights, groups co-operating together, liberty, and truth. You value your independence. You take a smug pleasure in being eccentric. You know people like you and admire your fine mind.

You Don't Like: Corruption, quarrels, personal remarks, patronizing behaviour, exploitation, feeling bullied or cornered, and injustice. You hate to be rushed. You're impatient with stupidity.

Where You Shine: Fair-minded, intellectual, philanthropic, inventive, refreshing, perceptive, truthful, progressive, and friendly.

So Who's Perfect? Stubborn, perverse, remote, reclusive, overly sensitive, absent-minded, distrustful, long-winded, and rebellious.

---

1. Different texts will name different gems for different signs.

What Is Aquarius-ness?[2]

To Infinity, and Beyond![3]

I love to write for Aquarius because the sign Aquarius rules astrology. To be more specific, Aquarius rules everything to do with the heavens — the infinite universe, astronomy, astrology, aviation, rocket technology, space travel, and, of course, *Star Trek*. ("Live long and prosper!")

But, hey — you are more than one sign. The fact that you're an Aquarius is just one part of you (specifically, your ankles). Since I don't know the rest of your chart (which is based on your time and location of birth), let's look at your Sun in Aquarius, which you have if you were born between January 20 and February 18.[4]

The quickest way to get a handle on what Aquarius is all about is to study your ruling planet, which is Uranus. Incidentally, I use the British pronunciation of this planet, which puts the emphasis on the first syllable — URanus — as opposed to the North American pronunciation, which puts the emphasis on the second syllable — UrANus. (And so would you, if you had to say it as often as I do.)

First, let's clear up a common confusion about Aquarius the Water Bearer — Aquarius is an Air Sign, *not* a Water Sign! The water reference goes back to the time of the Babylonians. Remember Hammurabi and his gang? Very bright bunch, especially with mathematics. (On the other hand, there was very little competition back then. I mean, hey — you could wake up one morning and say, "Eureka! I just thought of the number seven!" And you were famous.)[5]

While it is true that the Water Bearer is an ancient symbol from the time of the Babylonians, there are different and conflicting theories as to its origin. I don't think this is important. What *is* important is that you lose this water fixation. Begone! You are an Air Sign, and as such you use intellectual reasoning to make your decisions. You are a thinker. You are one of the most intelligent and brilliant signs of the zodiac! In fact, you are so far ahead of the pack, you might be intellectually lonely. ("Sigh. Nobody to talk to. Everyone's so dumb.")

2. No one is just one sign. That is impossible. Therefore, this is a discussion about the Aquarius archetype — the qualities of "Aquarius-ness." Many other signs will have Aquarius qualities as well. Therefore, the discussion of one sign is not an exact description of that person, but rather it is a description of the qualities of that sign.
3. Buzz Lightyear is sooooooo Aquarian!
4. These dates, as with the dates in horoscope columns, are average dates. The true dates vary depending on the year. So if you're born at the beginning or end of a sign (i.e., on the cusp), you need to check that particular year to know your sign. How? You need to get hold of a good astrologer — like me.
5. The Babylonians had bread but they did not have pi. Although they were very, very close. Their pi was more like a *tourtière*.

The Big Picture

For centuries, astrology and astronomy had an accepted notion of the heavens — and the outermost planet was Saturn. Then, in 1781, British astronomer William Herschel discovered a planet beyond Saturn. (Whaaat?) This upheaval to traditional astronomy broke the mould! (Which is what Uranus always does.)

It's a curious thing, but when a planet is discovered, whatever it "rules" gets a spike of attention on planet Earth. In astrology, Uranus is associated with revolution, rebellion against authority and the status quo, and advocating change for the better.

Sure enough, at the time of the discovery of Uranus, the crowned heads of Europe were toppling! The discovery of this new planet coincided with the American Revolution, the French Revolution, and the Industrial Revolution. Nothing could be more fitting.

Aquarians are humanistic social reformers. They're in their element when it comes to uniting like minds to fight for a cause that makes the world a better place. Imagine the streets of Paris in 1789 — "Liberty! Equality! Fraternity!"

Uranus is the energy behind Greenpeace, Amnesty International, and all labour unions. In fact, Samuel Gompers, founder of the American Federation of Labor (AFL), was an Aquarius.

> "Show me a country in which there are no strikes
> and I'll show you that country in which there is no liberty."
> SAMUEL GOMPERS
> Founder of the American Federation of Labor
> (JANUARY 27, 1850–DECEMBER 13, 1924)

Another famous Aquarian was U.S. President Franklin Delano Roosevelt.

> "If I went to work in a factory, the first thing I'd do is join a union."
> FRANKLIN DELANO ROOSEVELT
> Thirty-Second President of the United States of America (1933–1945)
> (JANUARY 30, 1882–APRIL 12, 1945)

American trade union leader Jimmy Hoffa (February 14, 1913–disappeared July 30, 1975) was the president of the Teamsters Union. He was actually a double Aquarius, which means he had Sun in Aquarius and was also Aquarius Rising.[6]

The planet Uranus rules earthquakes, volcanoes, dynamite, and anything that is unpredictable and surprising. It represents a rebellious break for freedom against oppression. ("To the gates!")

---

6. For those who did their homework and read Chapter One.

Because of its unpredictable, explosive nature, Uranus also rules inventions. It is the "eureka!" principle. Consider the famous equation from the theory of relativity, $E=mc^2$. Sure enough, Albert Einstein had his Mercury (thinking process) in Aquarius.

Uranus also rules electricity, science, electronics, and computers, plus the telegraph, telephone, radio, anything to do with airwaves, and, of course, anything to do with space travel and aviation. In fact, to my way of thinking, the glyph for Aquarius represents two airwaves, one above the other — not two water waves.

"We will make electricity so cheap that only the rich will burn candles."
THOMAS EDISON
American Inventor
Developed the Electric Light Bulb
(FEBRUARY 11, 1847–OCTOBER 18, 1931)

By extrapolation, this quality of breaking out means Uranus is the planet of social rebellion. It's all about being unconventional or unorthodox, or going up against the status quo. It is likewise the symbol of originality and individualism. (You unique types are all alike.)

This is why you have all these bold, exciting qualities!

Aquarius is also the sign of friendship and, by extension, collective bargaining. Aquarians are always getting people to sign petitions. You people are the most excellent networkers in the zodiac![7] Because of your networking ability, you, more than any other sign, see the planet as a global village.

Uranus in Its Own Sign, 1995–2004

Your ruling planet, Uranus, takes eighty-four years to go through all twelve signs. This means it travels though Aquarius roughly once a century.

Since Aquarius is about networking, electricity, technology, computers, and whistle-blowing, as well as gathering people together to make the world a better place — look at what happened between 1995 and 2004, when Uranus was finally in its own sign.

The planet became wired!

Prior to 1995, the use of email and the Internet was minimal. Check it out in 2004! The inventive, exploratory energy of Uranus exploded in wireless and electronic technology, creating a network of shared information, education, and a vehicle to expose the abuses of human rights. Liberty! Equality! Fraternity!

---

7. How telling that Aquarian Ashton Kutcher (b. February 7, 1978) was the first to get a million followers on Twitter.

The Shocking Part

There is an interesting little foible about your sign. (Actually, you have lots of interesting little foibles. Aquarians are eccentric oddballs. You are the square peg in the round hole. That's why I refer to you as "wild and wacky.")

Your ruling planet Uranus rules electricity. Anyone who works in acupuncture, or reiki, or any one of a number of subtle healing disciplines, will agree that we have electrical systems in our bodies. You might say *we are all sort of buzzing.*

Aquarians, however, *buzz big*! Because your sign is the sign that rules electricity, you embody erratic zaps of electrical energy. This is why you can put out street lights! (Not a word of exaggeration.) Many of you can never wear a wristwatch for more than a year. Also, your small appliances, like hair dryers, often break down within six months.

This affinity you have with electricity is also why you are so intuitive. It's as if messages come to you through the air. Who knows? Maybe they do. (Been picking up acid rock through your mercury fillings?)

> "What is the answer? In that case, what is the question?"
>
> GERTRUDE STEIN
> American Writer
> *The Autobiography of Alice B. Toklas*
> (FEBRUARY 3, 1874–JULY 27, 1946)

The Fame Thang

You have a curious relationship with fame. Many signs, especially Leo and Capricorn, eagerly seek fame and celebrity status. The unusual thing about Aquarius is that your sign is actually associated with fame. (Not a word of a lie.[8]) You are actually the "sign of fame." This is why many of you encounter overnight success through a discovery or a sudden event in your life.

---

8. Kapow! The overnight twenty-year success story. (Sometimes you are close to someone famous.)

Here is a bit of trivia that intrigued me:

The British poet Lord Byron (January 22, 1788–April 19, 1824) was a classic Aquarian. He is considered to be the first "star" celebrity (like the rock stars we have today). The success of his published work, plus his heroic exploits abroad and his numerous love affairs (with both sexes), enthralled the public. (Ya think?) He is said to have remarked, "I awoke one morning and found myself famous."

His wife called it "Byronmania."

He was one of the leaders of the Carbonari (not a pasta), a secret revolutionary society founded in Italy. He later fought with the Greeks in their war of independence, for which he became a beloved hero. It is said that some believe had he lived, he would have been made king of Greece. Who knew?

Another reason for your propensity for fame is that Aquarius is strongly associated with genius. (You guys are smart.) Your ability to think outside the box promotes brilliant, original ideas — not all of the time, but definitely sometimes.

Therefore, whether because of an invention, or your ingenious ideas, or just the fact that your sign is associated with fame — Aquarians often become famous!

"Better pass boldly into that other world, in the full
glory of some passion, than fade and wither dismally with age."
JAMES JOYCE
Irish Writer and Poet
Ulysses and *A Portrait of the Artist as a Young Man*
(FEBRUARY 2, 1882–JANUARY 13, 1941)

Planes, Planes, and Planes

Aquarius rules the heavens, and that's where you love to be! As children, most of you wanted to be an astronaut or fly a helicopter. Here are a few Aquarians who acted on this urge: American astronauts "Buzz" Aldrin, Alfred Warden, and Joseph P. Kerwin; American aviators Charles Lindbergh and Douglas "Wrong Way" Corrigan, who mistakenly flew to Ireland instead of California; U.S. Marine Corps aviation pioneer Brigadier General Norman J. Anderson; U.S. Air Force Major General Chuck Yeager; actors Paul Newman and John Travolta; television personality and media mogul Oprah Winfrey; and country-and-western singer Garth Brooks.

Naturally, not all Aquarians can fly a plane, nor do all Aquarians own one — but they *love* the idea of air travel!

They also deplore the fact that early pioneers didn't build cities closer to the airports.

Three Big Clues about Aquarius

In addition to the insights into your sign that your ruler, Uranus, offers, these three traits also describe Aquarius:

1. Need for Freedom of Individual Expression
2. Drive for Social Reform
3. Friendly Co-operation in Life

Need for Freedom of Individual Expression

All Aquarians are born fifty years ahead of their time. You're a maverick. You are modern-thinking and visionary in your grasp of how society and humankind are evolving. You see the planet as a global village.[9]

> "True originality consists not in a new manner but in a new vision."
> **EDITH WHARTON**
> American Novelist and Short Story Writer
> *The Age of Innocence*
> (JANUARY 24, 1862–AUGUST 11, 1937)

Of course, all signs are intelligent. (That's why we have the phrase "signs of intelligent life in the universe.") But some signs *do* have an edge. Like, look at all those Virgos sitting around sipping banana smoothies and analyzing everything. They are so cerebral!

You are smart in a different way. Uranus rules explosions. This is why all Aquarians think *out of the box*. Your ideas and thoughts burst beyond the accepted parameters of reality. You're *beyond* beyond! You verge on crazy genius, and, for some — just plain crazy!

Aquarius Wolfgang Amadeus Mozart (b. January 27, 1756–December 5, 1791) was a child genius who was composing music by the age of five and performing for the crowned heads of Europe when he was nine. (And that was before television.)

Small wonder that Aquarius Matt Groening (b. February 15, 1954), creator of *The Simpsons*, is so mind-bendingly original!

---

9. The term "global village" is traditionally associated with Marshall McLuhan, who had his Sun in Leo, directly opposite Uranus by only half a degree. No wonder *Wired* magazine chose him as their "patron saint."

"But Marge, what if we chose the wrong religion?
Each week we just make God madder and madder." — Homer Simpson

"If you really want something in life, you have to work for it. Now, quiet,
they're about to announce the lottery numbers." — Homer Simpson

"Here's to alcohol: the cause of, and answer to,
all of life's problems." — Homer Simpson

MATT GROENING
Creator of *The Simpsons*
(B. FEBRUARY 15, 1954)

You will always have a strong need for personal freedom. It's not just that you want to do your own thing. Your need for freedom is more mature and less self-serving than that. You have high ideals and are concerned about your neighbour-hood, your city, your country, your planet. "Think globally. Act locally." These are important issues. If you're going to fight the good fight, you have to be *free* to do so! To you, the security that others so faithfully seek or long for is just an illusion.

"There is no security on this earth; there is only opportunity."
GENERAL DOUGLAS MACARTHUR
Chief of Staff of the United States Army during the Second World War
(JANUARY 26, 1880–APRIL 5, 1964)

"Security is when everything is settled. When nothing can happen to you.
Security is the denial of life."
GERMAINE GREER
Australian Writer, Academic, Journalist, and Feminist
The Female Eunuch
(B. JANUARY 29, 1939)

Naturally, highly individualistic types appear eccentric. (Let's face it — you don't do normal.) In fact, you are often a bit clumsy in an absent-minded way. You bump into things. The so-called absent-minded professor in mismatched socks is an Aquarian archetype. Gorgeous Marilyn Monroe with her Moon in Aquarius had attractively, knock-kneed, slightly clumsy moves.

In addition, your mom dresses you funny. Most Aquarians look quirky and individu-alistic. For example, if everyone else is wearing a straight tie, you'll wear a bow tie. Hock-ey pundit Don Cherry (b. February 5, 1934) totally exploits his kooky wardrobe. But I think Aquarians just don't care. They wear what's fun, easy to grab, and comfortable.

One thing is certain — you love plaids.

If I meet anyone who is tall, slightly eccentric, magnetic in a friendly, easygoing way, and wearing a checked shirt, I know I have a wild, crazy Aquarian in sight. When he gets out of his hybrid car (or off his bicycle) and approaches me to sign a petition or make a monthly contribution to Save the Children, he is *so busted* — Aquarius!

"I don't think life is absurd. I think we are all here for a huge purpose."
NORMAN MAILER
American Novelist, Journalist, Essayist, and Screenwriter
The Naked and the Dead and *The Executioner's Song*
(JANUARY 31, 1923–NOVEMBER 10, 2007)

Drive for Social Reform

Always hearken back to the characteristics of your ruler to get the best clues for your sign. The discovery of Uranus forced science to go beyond Saturn, and Saturn rules the status quo and the government. Connect the dots. You fight the accepted way of doing things that no longer fits the current paradigms.

"We have had our last chance. If we do not devise some greater and more equitable system, Armageddon will be at our door."
GENERAL DOUGLAS MACARTHUR
Chief of Staff of the United States Army during the Second World War
(JANUARY 26, 1880–APRIL 5, 1964)

Your impulse is to network, and, because your sign rules computers, the Internet is the perfect Aquarian tool! Networking in cyberspace is the classic way to interface with your world. Consider the Aquarians who didn't have computers. They had to be resourceful in exploiting every opportunity to go public about their causes.

For example, in 1977, actress Vanessa Redgrave (b. January 30, 1937) won the Oscar for Best Actress in a Supporting Role and shocked the audience when she used her acceptance speech as an opportunity to make a political statement about the Israeli-Palestinian conflict. She left the stage with the full support of fellow Aquarian John Travolta (b. February 18, 1954).

Aquarian women are activists and feminists:

Edith Wharton	January 24, 1862–August 11, 1937
Virginia Woolf	January 25, 1882–March 28, 1941
Angela Davis	January 26, 1944
Colette	January 28, 1873–August 3, 1954
Germaine Greer	January 29, 1939
Oprah Winfrey	January 29, 1954
Vanessa Redgrave	January 30, 1937
Gertrude Stein	February 3, 1874–July 27, 1946
Alice Walker	February 9, 1944
Mia Farrow	February 9, 1945
Frances Moore Lappé	February 10, 1944
Susan B. Anthony	February 15, 1820–March 13, 1906
Toni Morrison	February 18, 1931
Yoko Ono	February 18, 1933

In March 1969, after her marriage to John Lennon (who had Moon in Aquarius), Yoko Ono (b. February 18, 1933) used their honeymoon to stage a "bed-in" for world peace in the presidential suite of the Amsterdam Hilton Hotel to protest the Vietnam War.[10]

On December 1, 1955, Rosa Parks (February 4, 1913–October 24, 2005) refused to go to the back of the bus, sparking the Montgomery Bus Boycott. The U.S. Congress later referred to her as the "mother of the modern-day civil rights movement."

10. Lennon's "The Ballad of John and Yoko" chronicles that week: "Drove from Paris to the Amsterdam Hilton / Talking in our bed for a week / The news people said / 'Hey, what you doin' in bed?' / I said, 'We're only tryin' to get us some peace!'"

Born on the same day, activist and feminist Betty Friedan (February 4, 1921– February 4, 2006) shocked the world in 1963 with her book *The Feminine Mystique*. In 1969, she organized the Women's Strike for Equality.

Reggae singer Bob Marley (b. February 6, 1945–May 11, 1981) was wounded by gunshots two days before a political concert. He performed anyway. When asked why, Marley responded, "The people who are trying to make this world worse aren't taking a day off. How can I?"

Actress Mia Farrow (b. February 9, 1945) is a UNICEF Goodwill Ambassador who constantly speaks out about the plight of civilians in Darfur, Chad, and the Central African Republic. In 2008, *TIME* magazine named her one of the most influential people in the world.

A strong advocate of social reform, author Charles Dickens (February 7, 1812– June 9, 1870) called attention to child labour and poverty in London.

Country-and-western singer Garth Brooks (b. February 7, 1962) began the Teammates for Kids Foundation. He performs at benefit concerts for many charities and good causes.

Hockey commentator Don Cherry (b. February 5, 1934) raises awareness about organ donation. He organized Rose Cherry's Home for Kids, and has worked to promote many good causes.

Anywhere on the planet, wherever there is social injustice, Aquarians will be protesting and fighting to make the world a better place. Liberty! Equality! Fraternity!

Friendly Co-operation in Life

Aquarius is the sign of friendship. But why? Every sign has friends, and friends are important to every sign. Does this mean Aquarians make the best friends? Not really. Some Aquarians are fabulous friends, and some aren't — just like every other sign. The reason Aquarius is associated with friendship is because it is part of their value system.

Basically, you run in packs.

You can work a room with finesse, then jump up on a chair and make everyone vote the way you want. Think for a minute of hockey legend Wayne Gretzky (b. January 26, 1961) rallying people for a cause. How many will go along with him?

It's unanimous!

You're an idealist, and you care about the human condition. And, because you care, others respond to you![11] This is why your sign rules clubs, organizations, associations, and all gatherings of people. People who meet you are thrilled to bask in your charm and friendly manner. However, later, they're chagrined to see you pay the *same friendly attention* to everyone else! (Whaaat?)

---

11. I read about George Clooney's concern for the extras on set when making the movie *Three Kings*, and how he fought with director David O'Russell on their behalf. I immediately thought, "Ah ha! An Aquarius!" I checked his birthday and saw he was a Taurus. Then I did his chart and saw he had his Jupiter in Aquarius. Mystery solved.

In one way, your "same taste" approach to everyone is admirable. But, let's face it, for those who really want to feel special, you're perplexing!

"I'm not concerned with your liking or disliking me . . .
all I ask is that you respect me as a human being."
JACKIE ROBINSON
First Black Major League Baseball Player
(JANUARY 31, 1919–OCTOBER 24, 1972)

Very few discoveries are made in isolation. (Even though thesis advisers take the credit.) You're democratic about sharing knowledge to boost scientific discoveries. Many scientists are Aquarians, or they have Mercury in Aquarius (like Einstein), or they are Aquarius Rising (like Thomas Jefferson, Benjamin Spock, and Tycho Brahe). You're comfortable in the field of science because you're an original thinker. In fact, many Aquarians invent things! You see possibilities others miss.[12]

All those wizards and computer geeks from the early days of *Dungeons & Dragons* to the current, state-of-the-art gamers are hard-core Aquarians. And they're very willing to exchange information with each other before they disappear again into their monitors.

"We never stop investigating. We are never satisfied that we know enough to get by. Every question we answer leads on to another question. This has become the greatest survival trick of our species."
DESMOND MORRIS
British Zoologist, Ethologist, Surrealist Painter, and Popular Author
(B. JANUARY 24, 1928)

12. I still recall watching my Aquarius nephew (a total geek) play as a child. I said to his mother, "Oh my god! He's a baby scientist." I meant it.

Aquarius in Love

When it comes to romance, the first thing you have to remember is that your middle name is freedom and your theme song is "Don't Fence Me In." You're an individualist of the highest order! You will not be captured and pinned to a wall like a butterfly.

Because you are an Air Sign, and very intelligent, the first link you want to make with someone is a meeting of the minds. Not only must the other person have a thinking process that intrigues you, they must be intellectually independent! You want them to have a mind of their own. You want them to have opinions, principles, ideals, and preferably a passionate cause that excites you as well. Now they're interesting!

You're attracted to characters — people who are bizarre or unconventional. You love people who have the courage to be different or make an individual statement.

> "Human beings have an inalienable right to invent themselves;
> when that right is pre-empted it is called brain-washing."
> GERMAINE GREER
> Australian Writer, Academic, Journalist, and Feminist
> *The Female Eunuch*
> (B. JANUARY 29, 1939)

I know a charming Aquarian who likes to tell the story of his first acid trip. He was riding on the back of a camel in Morocco wearing a purple velveteen monk's robe. (He later had a brief stay in a mental hospital in Casablanca and had to be rescued by his mother, but that's another story.) His tales are always punctuated with a forced, phony (but funny) "Bwa-ha-ha!" He is highly amusing and incredibly articulate. He dazzles people with his psychobabble.

But back to you. Once you have determined that someone has an interesting mind, you must next discover how many boundaries this other person is willing to test. You love to breakthrough limitations and taboos.

Aquarian women often have non-traditional jobs. They work as plumbers, light-house keepers, helicopter pilots, snowcat groomers, painters, or carpenters. I recall an evening appointment with a client who was Aquarius Rising. It was in the winter, and I was visiting my mother in Victoria, British Columbia. As I went to open the door to greet this client, I was well aware that I was about to encounter an independent

Aquarius. When the door opened, my first impression was "bag lady." Although she was young (perhaps around twenty-eight), she had a man's dark peaked woollen cap pulled low over her forehead, and she was wearing one of those big red plaid lumberjackets. She appeared quite large and masculine, like a tough character out of a Paul Bunyan story.

She stepped in, and once she had removed her plaid lumberjacket I saw that she was not a "big" woman at all — she was just enormously curvaceous, with bodacious ta-tas.[13] When she whipped off her hat, a breathtaking pile of gorgeous blond hair cascaded down her back. In an instant, her image changed from invisible bag lady to stunning, gorgeous, and impossibly sexy! I was slack-jawed.

She was delightful, and I later learned she worked for the Coast Guard. She was torn between training to be a helicopter pilot and saving money to go to medical school. I recall her telling me that she had an extremely active sex life. (Hello? Gorgeous babe. Working in the Coast Guard. Ya think?) But she said she was always faithful to her man. She flashed a wonderful smile and said, "I'm a serial monogamist — I'm with only one man at a time, even if it's just for a weekend."

Aquarian lovers are dynamite! They're unconventional in a freedom-loving way, and they have a track record that would raise anyone's eyebrows. French actress Jeanne Moreau (b. January 23, 1928) was married twice, and she was also involved with three men who directed her in movies: François Truffaut, Louis Malle (who married actress Candice Bergen), and Tony Richardson (who left the gorgeous Vanessa Redgrave to take up with Moreau). She was also involved with Pierre Cardin and playboy Theodoros Roubanis. Her close friends were Henry Miller, Jean Cocteau, Jean Genet, and Marguerite Duras. She now counts Sharon Stone as one of her close pals. Classic Aquarian!

But beware! Beautiful Aquarian people can love you and leave you! Nevertheless, it's always worth the wild ride.

Because Uranus represents rebellion against the status quo, it often figures prominently in the charts of people who are bisexual, homosexual, or lesbian. Aquarians love to experiment, and they love to be a friend to all! Even in so-called traditional relationships, Aquarians often have unorthodox arrangements.

---

13. Who can forget that reference by David Keith in *An Officer and a Gentleman?*

Naturally, you love to experiment. (I recommend buying C batteries at a discount.) I have an Aquarian friend who was dating a Scorpio man with Moon in Aquarius, so they had a double-Aquarius thing going. One weekend he showed up at her place with some electrical apparatus — all wires and suction cups(!). He said it was used by people who suffered from arthritis; apparently they hooked themselves up to this gadget to give themselves little jolts to mask the pain.

He suggested she attach some of the wires to some strategic spots on her body, and he did likewise. The idea was that when they touched each other, they would complete the current and create an electrical connection. (This is so Aquarian it boggles the mind.)

I said to her, "So did you do it?"

She said, "Oh yes."

"Were you afraid?"

"I was a bit nervous," she admitted. "But he said we couldn't hurt ourselves. We both wanted to know what would happen."

"So what happened?" I asked. (You can imagine my prurient curiosity.)

She sighed. "It didn't work like we thought it would. When we came together and kissed, our teeth kept chattering wildly against each other's. It was a failed experiment."

But a classic Aquarian experiment!

"I've tried several varieties of sex. The conventional position makes me claustrophobic, and the others give me a stiff neck or lockjaw."

TALLULAH BANKHEAD

American Film, Television, and Stage Actress

(JANUARY 31, 1902–DECEMBER 12, 1968)

A little warning: because Uranus is impulsive, you can fall in love in a heartbeat and fall out of love just as quickly. Therefore, you are well advised to have a long engagement or live with somebody before you commit to marriage. Plus, Aquarians often have sex with friends. Or they confuse having friends with benefits with being in love. (It's complicated.) This warning is so you don't wake up one day and realize you're married to your roommate!

Anybody who has been involved with you will know the baffling frustration you invariably present when you split up and say, "I hope we can still be friends." And you mean it!

Please take note: not everyone wants to stay friends after a devastating love affair has gone sour, especially if you were the person who needed "space" and strayed off to yonder pastures. Get real. Wake up and smell the coffee. (Yeah, yeah — you hate smelling the coffee.)

I know another Aquarian who split from her husband when she was living in Toronto. (She also had an affair with the husband of her best friend when she was married.) After her marriage ended, she took out an ad in the *Toronto Star* along the lines of "Woman in her 30s, seeks relationship but is having gender questions. Please call, etc."

She told me that more than a hundred women responded to her ad!

I asked, "What did you do?"

She replied nonchalantly, "I invited them all to my house for a wine-and-cheese party."

"My God! You invited them all together at the same time?"

"Yes," she smiled impishly.

"Well, what happened? Just a great wine-and-cheese party?"

"Oh no," she smiled. "One of them stayed for the night. In fact, it was rather humorous because about ten years later I was giving a talk and I noticed a woman in the third row, looking at me. After the talk, several people came up to me and she was one of them. When I looked into her eyes, I recognized her as the woman who had stayed behind! What a small world."

Small world? You believe it's a global village!

The Aquarius Boss

The Aquarian boss is democratic. To position this, the opposite sign of Aquarius is Leo — the sign of royalty and noblesse oblige. Aquarius is the antithesis of royalty. Aquarius is all about the common man and woman. We're talking togetherness, equality — you get the picture.

The Aquarian boss will be fair — truth, justice, equality for everyone, and equitable pay. Naturally, there are exceptions to every rule. You might have an Aquarian boss who is a tyrant, but this is not at all typical.

Aquarian bosses hold meetings, establish committees, and do surveys. They welcome employee feedback and strive for two-way communication, not just a downward flow of information. They're liberal and progressive.

They want the latest high-tech equipment for everyone. However, they don't necessarily want to be the role model for their employees. They like the freedom to work the hours they want to work. They might like to come in late or early, or leave late or early. Aquarians are unpredictable.

The big thing they have going for them is their sense of fair play, plus their intelligence. Think of Abraham Lincoln (February 12, 1809–April 15, 1865). What an enlightened leader! During the Civil War, when detractors of General Grant told Lincoln that Grant was always drunk, Lincoln's response was, "Tell me what brand of whisky Grant drinks. I would like to send a barrel of it to my other generals!" You gotta love that chutzpah.

The secret to the success of Aquarian bosses is that they really don't care what others think about them. *This is enormously empowering!* They just want results. In fact, they even get a perverse pleasure out of doing things differently or flouting management tradition.

"Hell, there are no rules here — we're trying to accomplish something."
THOMAS EDISON
American Inventor
Developed the Electric Light Bulb
(FEBRUARY 11, 1847–OCTOBER 18, 1931)

I would welcome an opportunity to work for an Aquarius boss, because you can't beat enlightened management. The only reason we need unions is to protect workers from bad management, which unfortunately is everywhere.

The Aquarius Employee

There's good news and bad news when it comes to the Aquarius employee. The good news is, who better than an Aquarius can get along with everyone? People love you! You style-flex and schmooze with all walks of life. You can work with the people at the bottom or the people at the top. After all, it's your nature to co-operate. You're happy in group settings. You don't mind meetings and discussions (within reason).

Furthermore, as an Air Sign, you're an idea person. You're intelligent, which makes you quick to grasp what needs to be done and skilled in communicating this to others. Like your opposite sign, Leo, you are swift to see the big picture.

So what's the bad news? You can be stubborn and rebellious! Although you're a hard worker when you're doing something you like to do, you're essentially a shit-disturber. A union organizer. Just imagine what an Aquarian employee is like working for a jerk boss — hmm, let's go one further — a stupid jerk boss. (Grrr.) Not only will the Aquarius employee rebel, this person will feel obligated to rescue the rest of the crew. We're talking mutiny!

It's curious that Taurus has a reputation for being stubborn. Let me say unequiv-ocally, any Aquarius can give a Taurus a run for their money. It's a different kind of stubbornness with a different kind of motivation, but it looks like, smells like, and feels like stubbornness! Of course, this kind of stubborness, with a little rhetoric and idealism thrown in, is the perfect recipe for a saucy rebellion!

> "All growth is a leap in the dark, a spontaneous
> unpremeditated act without benefit of experience."
> HENRY MILLER
> American Novelist and Painter
> *Tropic of Cancer*
> (DECEMBER 26, 1891–JUNE 7, 1980)

The Aquarius Parent

My Aquarian sister told me she was taken aback when one day her Aquarian three-year-old son looked up at her and said, "Why are you yelling at me? I don't like it."

Invariably, the Aquarian parent will often rebel against the kind of parenting he or she received as a child. It is the natural impulse of Aquarian parents to be liberal and freethinking, and to give their children a lot of rope. Basically, they believe that their duty is to raise a child to be independent in society. They don't want their children to be sheep and just follow the herd. They instill in their children the need to think for themselves and make their own decisions.

This impulse to step back in order to allow children to find their own way can sometimes result in the child feeling a lack of leadership. And what if the child needs boundaries? After all, the Aquarian parent might not necessarily have Aquarian children. (Although the likelihood of there being Aquarius influences in these children is high.)

Aquarius parents are classic for letting kids "fight it out among themselves." They are loath to interfere. This approach has its pros and cons, because children need rules, regulations, guidelines, and leadership. (But, mostly, they just need to be loved and kept safe. If they have a good role model to follow, it all generally works out.)

One of the great strengths of Aquarian parents is they know how to be friends with their children. They're not afraid to relate to their kids on their level. They're not afraid of losing authority, because, down deep, they don't really respect authority anyhow.

Without question, Aquarian parents will teach their children fair play, kindness, and a respect for all walks of life, races, and nationalities. They will also buy them the latest high-tech equipment.

Bonus!

The Aquarius Child

There is something you need to know about the Aquarius child. (All parents and teachers should know this.) Aquarius is the sign that "rules" electricity, and I don't know why, but Aquarius people can put out street lights. Small appliances and wristwatches often break down around them.

This electrical energy seems to stay in check if Aquarian people can live naturally according to their own unique biorhythms. As adults, many Aquarians can do this. However, Aquarian children do not have this luxury. They have to fit in to schedules that adults prescribe for them. When this happens, their inner electrical system starts to build up and "comes out" as skin rashes, eczema, or headaches.

Obviously, you cannot take Aquarian children out of school. So what can you do to treat rashes or headaches? Don't ask me why, but singing seems to help. It has nothing to do with carrying a tune or knowing the words to a song. It's all about the breath. So if you encourage encourage children to sing to themselves, in an aimless manner or even energetically — who cares? *Singing can help them.*

Another activity that can help ground this electrical buildup is to play with electronic objects. To use the computer, or play with tape recorders, CD players, iPods, MP3 devices, and, of course, video games! — will help ground the Aquarian child.

The other thing to remember is this child's independence is fragile! It's important for Aquarian children to know they can express their individuality. They need to feel empowered. They need to feel they have some power over what they eat and even when they sleep. Be flexible about bedtimes! Don't be a tyrant at the table.

It's also important to know how valuable *friendships* are to Aquarian children. If they don't have friends as neighbours, then you have to arrange play dates. They need to interact with friends and participate in extracurricular activities, groups, and clubs. After all, this is going to be their lifestyle! They need to learn these skills as soon as possible.

Since Aquarius rules all form of aviation, take your Aquarius child to the airport! Buy them toy planes. Help them to explore an interest in astronomy, astrology, or space travel.

Very soon, even at a young age, your Aquarian child will be able to persuade you to go along with something they're passionate about. (They're like tiny little union leaders!) These children are also rebellious. Help them to express this quality in a positive way. Respect their individuality. (You don't own your children — they are people with rights.)

The Aquarian child needs the confidence of knowing he or she can have differing opinions. These kids are growing up to be independent people — not sheep. You can either delay this natural process or nurture it. To delay it is to flirt with danger. If you arouse their rebellious nature, they might rebel against valuable traditions and the laws of society. Let them rebel in little ways.

> "It is not a bad thing that children should occasionally,
> and politely, put parents in their place."
>
> COLETTE
> French Novelist
> *Gigi*
> (JANUARY 28, 1873–AUGUST 3, 1954)

Aquarian children love computers! Nowadays, most Aquarian kids learn to write their name with a keyboard. Their only frustration is that they want to play video games but they don't know how to read yet! Aquarian children love technology. Give them every opportunity to learn as much as they can.

Make sure they learn to type.

How to Be a Happier Aquarius

Your ruling planet, Uranus, is the planet that is all about explosions and unpredictable events. Therefore, it's associated with celebrity and sudden success.[14] This means no sign more than you has a built-in factor to suddenly make it big. But here's the cute part: no sign more than you has such ambivalence (if not even dread) of this actually happening! It's the cosmic joke. The sign most likely to achieve sudden success is also the sign that wants desperately to avoid it.

It's not that you're trying to hide. ("Pay no attention to that man behind the curtain.") You're not afraid of fanfare, kudos, or admiration. What you fear is a loss of personal freedom and independence. As long as you have a lot of latitude to run your life the way you want, this is never an issue. But once circumstances change around you and people begin making demands and having expectations of you, your teeth start to itch!

You might not be consciously aware of this. For example, how aware are you of your need for freedom and independence? You might take these things for granted *until they are threatened.*

The reason it's important to be aware of this dynamic is that, if you're not aware of it, you won't understand why you demonstrate behaviour that others say is self-destructive. In other words, you sabotage yourself.

The classic Aquarius scenario is to enjoy your job and enjoy whatever you do, and then, as you near success or promotion, you decide to go off in a new direction because you feel it's "time for a change." Friends ask you accusingly, "Are you crazy?" Of course, this challenge only fortifies your choice. You're going to stick to your guns! You're captain of your ship, master of your fate, and you're running your life!

Your decision to move on to something new is cloaked in the guise of spirited (perhaps even foolhardy) adventure. ("To go where no man has gone before.")

This is where you need to look at yourself honestly. Are you afraid of success? Do you fear success will come at too high a price?

If you don't want success because it's really not all that it's cracked up to be, that's fine. Many would agree with you (especially a bunch of other Aquarians). So whether you choose to go for this particular success or you choose to leave to do something else is not the issue. The issue is — do you *know* what you're doing? Are you *aware* of why you're making this decision? Do know what you're avoiding?

---

14. Sometimes you achieve fame on your own, and sometimes you receive it through a connection (perhaps a family member).

Aquarians often delude themselves about what they want or don't want because they're trying to ward off anything that restricts their freedom.

Recently, there has been much discussion in the medical community about the harmful effects of kidding ourselves. I recall talking to Dr. Don Grant, a professional in Burnaby, B.C., whom I very much admire and respect. He talked to me about lying to your body.

"Lying to your body?" I said. "What does that mean?"

He said, "Have you ever been in a situation where someone asks you to do something and you agree, but you really don't want to do it?"

Gulp. I immediately knew what he meant.

"That's lying to your body?"

"Yes," he said. "When you agree to do something you really don't want to do, your body knows you're lying."

So, do I care? ("I confess! I lied! I fooled you all! The kidneys, the lungs, and most pointedly the spleen. I did it and I have no remorse!")

According to Dr. Grant, when you lie to your body, you introduce incongruities that force your body to adapt in some way in an attempt to restore balance. When these incongruities are too many for the body to handle, the body will react by starting to shut down things. (Hmmm, not good.)

In your gut, you know this is true. Any of us can recall a character in a movie who slowly becomes more shrill and neurotic through living in denial of something that the audience can clearly see. *We know that scenario.*

This is what can happen when you agree to pursue a success you really don't want. Or, vice versa, when you decide to avoid success (because of your fears) but you really *do* want it.

Either way, you are lying to your body, which is not healthy! And you are more likely to do this than any other sign. Ironically, this is partly because of your belief in the greatest good for the greatest number. Sometimes you get involved in an idea that is bigger than yourself, and this makes you believe you're required to make sacrifices.

Far better to remind yourself that without your body you are useless! You need your health, your vitality, and your energy to do the work you aspire to do, which essentially is to make the world a better place.

Fortunately, there is one area where you do understand success. You know you enjoy networking with others. You know you need friendship. An article by David Brooks in the *New York Times* (April 1, 2010) states, "According to one study, joining a group that meets even just once a month produces the same happiness gain as doubling your income."

Now, that sounds successful!

I recall once hearing a teacher I respect answer a woman who asked, "I live alone and I don't like it. How can I make friends?"

He looked at her and said, "Be friendly."

AQUARIUS
YOUR 40-YEAR HOROSCOPE
1985 - 2025

Why Go into the Past?

I want you to have faith in your predictions. The only way you can believe what I say is to test for yourself. This is why I start with brief highlights from the past twenty-five years. If anything in these past twenty-five years resonates with you, then what I say about your future will have the same validity. It is all one long timeline — your life.

The past predictions generally apply once you have left home or are "running your life" and making your own decisions. Prior to that, the major events in your life were dictated by other people, likely your parents.

1985 – 1990

The mid-1980s were a time of achievement for you. You were looking swell! Some of you might have graduated, or got your first job, or got married. Something happened around 1985 that made you feel proud. You felt fortunate with your achievements, and by 1986 you were even more confident. (Yay!) Soon, you started to earn more money or boost your assets in some way. Your home and family scene improved around 1988. But big changes were on the horizon by 1989, because that's when you started to let go of people, places, and possessions. This was a time of giving up things and saying goodbye. (Oh yeah, all that.)

1991 – 1996

One of the biggest reasons you were letting go and saying good-bye in the late 1980s was because, whether you knew it or not, you had to create space for a new cycle in your life. This is why around 1991 you were in an entirely new sandbox! In fact, things might have changed so dramatically that some of you even changed your daily wardrobe. (But life was *fresh!*)

Fortunately, new romance, love affairs, vacations, and big changes with respect to children were taking place. Soon your job improved and relationships were great. By 1992–93, gifts, goodies, and favours from others allowed you to travel, or go back to school, or explore opportunities in publishing, the media, medicine, or the law.

By 1994, many of you got a promotion, a better job, accolades, or praise, or in some way you managed to boost your reputation in the eyes of others. Naturally, this led to increased popularity, new friendships, and perhaps meaningful memberships in clubs, groups, or organizations. (You like to run with the pack, remember?)

1997 ~ 2000

The year 1997 was lovely, because lucky moneybags Jupiter was in your sign. (More yay!) Jupiter attracted opportunities to you and increased your confidence in yourself. It was also the beginning of a new twelve-year cycle of growth. This was a time of good health and happy feelings. But, mainly, you were able to attract resources that were *useful* to you! It is always fortunate when Jupiter enters your sign, even though it happens only once every twelve years.

On the heels of this good fortune, many of you changed residences or jobs, or both, in the next few years. Fortunately, increased earnings probably helped. By the turn of the millennium, your main purpose in life was to establish a solid home base for yourself. You were tired of footloose instability. You wanted to enter the new millennium with a firm home base — something you could count on.

2001 – 2005

By 2001–2, love affairs, romance, joyful times with children, vacations, sports, and ways to expand your world through show business, the entertainment world, or the hospitality industry were areas of opportunities that opened up for you. This was a fun time! Very soon, you improved your job. Children became an increased responsibility, and relationships became joyful and also more serious.

The good news is that, in 2004, gifts, goodies, and help from others made a difference in your life. This was a great time to get a loan or a mortgage. In fact, 2005 was a fabulous year to travel, or explore higher education, or opportunities in publishing, the media, medicine, and the law. Although you were keen to learn new things and discover adventure, you were also busy busting your buns. No question. Whew! "Let's sing the 'Song of the Volga Boatmen.' The Red Army Chorus will join in. Everyone ready?"

2006 ~ 2010

Even though this was a time of hard work for you, many of you did whatever you could to become self-employed. That's because your ruler, Uranus, was starting to shake up how you earned your money. This is also why your source of earnings may have been shaky, unstable, and constantly changing. (Yikes.)

Fortunately, by 2006, lucky Jupiter was at the top of your chart, making you look good. Promotions, increased earnings, kudos, and opportunities from others gave you a real boost. Whatever happened definitely increased your recognition and the esteem you received from your contemporaries. (Your bathroom mirror was covered in kisses.)

Some, however, instead of getting promotions and increased recognition, acted on an opportunity to change their work to one that involved medicine, healing, the law, or something to do with higher education, publishing, or perhaps even travel.

Naturally, there is often trouble in paradise. This was also a time when partnerships were sorely tested. (Groan.) Those that were not going to make it bit the dust. But even those that endured underwent a very tough time from 2006 to 2008. (Ouch.) Fortunately, 2007 was a popular year for you, so you had a chance to escape to your friends for sympathy and fun diversions. ("Fresh horses and whisky for my men!")

By 2009, you were back in the saddle again because lucky Jupiter was in Aquarius. This couldn't have happened at a better time. (Whew!) Good fortune was smiling on you, bringing you increased opportunities and increased confidence, and putting you in touch with important people — just at the time when you had lost practical support or input from partners and other people or sources. (But this lack of support from others threw you back on your own two feet, forcing you to rely on yourself.)

It's interesting to note how lucky you were, because just when resources were withdrawn from you in one area, Lady Luck smiled

on you in another area. (Quite the balancing act you were able to pull off.)

No doubt, this is why many of you had an opportunity to boost your salary, or secure a better job, or otherwise solidify your money scene in 2010. Ka-ching! (Money is so handy when you want to buy things.)

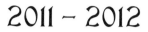

2011 – 2012

Without question, the keyword for your sign in 2011 is "hope." For various reasons (that differ according to the details of your life), you are more hopeful and optimistic about your future than you have been in ages. And all this is for a good reason. Not only have some of you recently improved your earnings (and many will continue to do so), but you also sense it is a time of preparation.

Since 2005, you have slowly been assuming more and more power and taking greater responsibility for what you believe is actually possible for you to achieve. Most recently, you have had to give up things and get along with less. But, according to Nietzsche's cheery observation, "What doesn't kill you only makes you stronger." And this has been very much the case with you. Now you are either travelling or getting further training or more education, because you actually can see your distant goal. You see what it is you want to achieve! It's no longer a blurry hope. And what is quite lovely is that just at this time when your goals are in sight, you have hope, not discouragement.

By 2012, things will improve even more, especially in your personal life. Everything to do with home, family, and your private life will become a source of joy, pleasure, and expansion. In fact, many of you will expand your family through marriage, birth, or adoption. Others will expand your home. Do take note: 2012 is a wonderful year for real-estate investment or for improving your property in any way. This is a good time to buy personal property or real estate for financial speculation. You will also not regret any money that you put into your home, because it will prove to be profitable or valuable in the future. (Certainly, something you will be glad you did!)

This is also a wonderful year to entertain at home or to have a family reunion where you live. One of the reasons you want to reach out and solidify your personal bonds with family members is that you are about to enter a very successful time in your life. Why not rally the troops now? So often we come together at times of loss. Why not *celebrate times of joy*?

2013 – 2014

Glory hallelujah! Finally, you are really hitting your stride. This is a banner year in many respects! Where to begin? Let's go for the fun stuff first. You couldn't pick a better year for a vacation. One of your themes this year (and there are several) is simply to have fun and experience pleasure! This is why it's a great time for a holiday. It's also a wonderful time to explore the arts and to take advantage of opportunities in show business, the entertainment world, and anything to do with the hospitality industry.

You are very much in touch with your muse this year. Therefore, many of you will take delight in any chance to express your creative talents, whether you are a so-called professional or not. After all, you are a verb, not a noun. It is in the *doing* that you get your pleasure and your sense of accomplishment. (However, it's entirely possible to make money for the first time, or to make *more* money, from your creative output this year.)

Children will be a great source of joy this year! Quite literally, if you did not expand your family last year through the addition of children to your tribe, then that might happen this year.

This is also a wonderful time for love affairs and romance. New love can begin for many of you. These new relationships will be characterized by feelings of joy and increased well-being. Your partner might be older, richer, or more established than you. You have a sense of learning something from this new love. The relationship somehow broadens your appreciation of life. (Sounds to me like someone might pick up the tab for your vacation!) Very often, with this kind of celestial timing, your new love could be someone who comes from a different background or a different culture. *It's exciting and stimulating!*

Existing relationships will also be rekindled in a lovely way. A mutual joy will be stronger. It's all good.

"When people are laughing, they're generally
not killing one another."
ALAN ALDA
American Actor, Director, and Screenwriter
TV's *M*A*S*H*
(B. JANUARY 28, 1936)

Because you are enjoying a wider range of freedom of self-expression, you are growing! You don't have to hide your light under a bush anymore. You're not afraid to take credit for what you do and who you are. You like who you are! (Is that Sally Field across the room?)

Small wonder, therefore, that this is the beginning of a run of marvellous achievements for you. Ever since 2005, you've been gearing up for success. This year *that moment has arrived!* To be more precise, it is not so much a career peak (although it might very well be), but, rather, a time of *harvest* for you. Furthermore, it's a time of harvest after completing a thirty-year cycle. (Big!)

As such, like any time of harvest, you see very quickly what is working and what is not. For most people, this will be a career peak or a time of increased success, adulation, popularity, prestige, promotions, earnings, and the like. For some, it will be a time of graduation. For others, it will be a marriage or a first child. In other words, you are achieving something you have been striving for — *a cherished dream.*

But, in a few cases, the harvest simply shows where you planted the wrong seeds. (I hate that part.)

Something else is also taking place that begins around now. For the next six years, you are going to undergo sudden and major changes. Quite likely, these changes will be reflected in your everyday encounters with relatives, siblings, and neighbours. It's as if you will be encountering different people. Or they will see you in a different light. Certainly, your everyday mental attitude will change.

In addition, in the next six to seven years, your daily tempo will increase for some reason. Obviously, the addition of children for the first time in your life could be one factor. You will have to be lighter on your feet, flexible, and ready to go with the flow. This is because you're entering a seven-year window when your every-day life is much more stimulating and exciting! Dare we say full of wonder? (We dare.)

And finally! (So much good news.) In 2014, your job can improve wonderfully! You will either get a better job or different and better duties in your existing job, or your evil boss will be transferred to Vladivostok. In fact, this is one of the most opportune times in more than a decade for you to improve your employment scene.

For those of you who are retired (and naturally, this applies to everyone as well), your health may improve in 2014. You feel stronger, more robust, and have a greater joie de vivre!

Mom always liked you best.

2015 ~ 2017

Now we see all your partnerships — professional, as well as intimate partnerships and marriage — improving beautifully. In fact, you are so much happier because your closest relationships are going so well — even your dealings with the general public will improve.

This year, lucky Jupiter is directly opposite your sign, which in some respects indicates a culmination of sorts. Jupiter revs your ambition! You're eager to reach out for big things. You are emboldened by your recent successes and feel that you can do anything! And why not?

> "Excess on occasion is exhilarating. It prevents moderation from acquiring the deadening effect of habit."
>
> **W. SOMERSET MAUGHAM**
> British Playwright, Novelist, and Short Story Writer
> *Of Human Bondage* and *The Razor's Edge*
> (JANUARY 25, 1874–DECEMBER 16, 1965)

This is also an excellent year to seek out any kind of professional help or assistance. If you have to consult an expert, now is the time to do it. Those of you who now commit to a relationship or get married will probably hook up with someone who is older, richer, and more established. In many ways, you are surrounded by good fortune! In fact, in 2016, inheritances, gifts from others, increased wealth through your partner, or money back from the government, plus other perks and goodies, will come your way.

This is also a time when your sex drive is strong! Ah yes, a healthy libido makes life interesting this year. Let's just say *your sex life is richer*. (And by that, I don't mean you'll start to charge money for it.)

Some of you will find this is a time of spiritual regeneration. You might find religion. (I didn't know it was lost.)

Exciting travel opportunities appear in 2017. Many of you will take to the skies. You will travel for business, pleasure, education,

or adventure. Some of you will travel because you're going to explore religious experiences — like perhaps the Way of St. James in Spain or along with the Highlands of Scotland. Classic Aquarian trips! (You know who you are.)

This is also a wonderful year for writers who want to explore publishing opportunities. In fact, anything connected with higher education, publishing, the media, medicine, and the law will all get a marvellous boost.

Basically, you are reaching out with enthusiasm to grab more of the world for yourself. You'll do it either by learning more or travelling more, or both. You're hungry for adventure and knowledge, and your recent successes have made you confident about your ability to get what you want.

2018 – 2020

A delightful year! For the first time since 2006, lucky moneybags Jupiter is slowly travelling across the top of your chart, attracting all kinds of opportunities to you, in addition to making you high-viz in the eyes of powerful people.

The big difference is that this time you are in a far better position to maximize the opportunities available to you. In 2006, partnerships and relationships were very stressed. Furthermore, you were still testing the waters with your new-found freedom. But in 2018 you have much more confidence in your abilities. And as that old proverb goes, "Success has many friends." (Success is relative: the more successful you are, the more relatives you seem to have.)

However, something else is starting to come into play. In many respects, you are entering a two- to three-year window similar to the one in the late 1980s. In other words, having achieved your recent successes, many of you will now start to dismantle much of what you have created since 2005. This means you will start to let go of people, places, and possessions.

The first thing you'll notice will be that you're downsizing and streamlining your life by going through closets, garages, lockers, and cupboards. You might have garage sales or recycle possessions and clothing, as well as give things away.

But soon, you will see that you are starting to wear out friendships and relationships. (Whaaat?) This is not something you normally do! After all, friendships are important to you. Nevertheless, let's face it, at times we do outgrow some relationships, and this will start to happen now. Furthermore, some of you will let go of jobs or residences and contemplate a complete life change.

No worries! You don't have to do anything drastic. But this is definitely a time of letting go for you. The key is this: *you only have to let go of what is no longer relevant in your life.* You're getting rid of excess baggage. Whatever is truly meaningful and valuable will remain.

While this streamlining process is going on, 2019 will be an unusually popular year for you. You love to be in the thick of things! This is a great year to join clubs, classes, organizations, and groups. New friendships will form. The people you meet now will plant ideas in your mind that will grow — and, ultimately, these will change your long-term goals. In fact, this could be one of the reasons you are letting go of other things. (Ya think?)

You feel unusually idealistic in 2019. Friends will benefit you now. Expect to be actively working with others to promote your ideas. It's definitely a year of new acquaintances, new friendships, and new associations. ("Let's have lunch at my club.")

In 2020, your ruler, Uranus, changes signs and starts to slowly travel through the bottom of your chart. It will stay there until 2026. You will recall that Uranus is unpredictable, explosive, and keen to introduce greater freedom and new discoveries.

This particular sojourn of Uranus means many of you will change your residence or undergo a big shift in your family dynamic. Some of you will break ties with family members. (Hot tip: wherever you have settled into a rut will probably be the area that will undergo some upheaval.) It's as if your home and family scene are *being tested* so that you will get a fresh grasp on your reality and discover what is *really important* to you. Uranus is all about vitality, youth, and fresh, vibrant ways of doing things. It always attacks whatever is rigid, stodgy, and stagnant.

On the other hand, you should never take a fence down until you know why it was put up in the first place. *Capisce?*

2021 – 2022

This year Lady Luck visits you big time! I say this because the year 2021 (within twelve months either way) is a hugely pivotal time in your life. In fact, it's so major, many of you will be in a completely new situation. You might even be in a new country. This new sandbox is so different, it will probably force you to change your daily wardrobe. ("Are all the straitjackets in white?")

Essentially, what is happening now is that you're entering a new thirty-year cycle. The first seven years or so are going to be about completely reinventing yourself. (Cool!) This happens about twice (and maybe three times if you are long-lived) in your lifetime.

This process of reinventing yourself last happened around 1991– 95. In fact, all you have to do is look back to see how much your life has changed since then! Not only that, but the early 1990s were a time when you also changed in a *personal* way, so that the person you had changed into by the millennium was very different! (You probably weighed more, too. Time to let out another pleat in the shower curtain?)

So here you are again, starting off on a completely new journey. And just when you probably need it most, *lucky Jupiter is in your sign*! How cool is that? Jupiter will be in Aquarius from December 2020 until January 2022. *Yee-haw!* (It slips into Pisces for two months during the summer, which, trust me, is totally excellent for you as well, because it could boost your earnings.)

This means that just at a time when you are entering a whole new world, Jupiter will lift your self-confidence, attract opportunities and important people to you, and instill you with increased charm and poise. (Omigawd.) By the summer of 2021, you are *hot*!

Naturally, following this hit of good fortune, you can expect increased earnings in 2021–22. Look for ways to boost your income, or get a better job, or possibly even make extra money on the side. All of these options are a distinct possibility.

In many ways, this is a time of fulfillment. Around 2007, you had to face challenges that weren't easy, but this was also a time of new beginnings for you. Now you are seeing how those decisions are panning out. This is still a time of perseverance and hard work, which means you want to concentrate your energy, not scatter it.

2023 – 2025

A fair number of changes are taking place now because you are in the middle of this journey in which your own ruler, Uranus, is stirring things up at home and in your private life (from July 2018 until July 2025). This particular influence is entirely new for you because it can occur only once every eighty-four years. (You can run but you can't hide.)

It's important to keep in mind that Uranus wants to enliven things, to keep them fresh, dynamic, and real. Naturally, a dramatic change of residence is classic.[15]

In this window of time (2018–25), family changes will be taking place as well. One of your parents might come out of the closet. Relationships with family members will undergo surprising shifts. It could be anything! But, essentially, both your relationship to your residence and your relationship with family members will somehow change so that you ultimately feel freer, more current with the times, and more true to your inner being and who you really are. Uranus has no time for phonies. (Hey, Uranus is your ruler; you know whereof I speak.) Furthermore, Uranus tends to force you to make changes or let go of things that have imprisoned you.

The year 2023 is upbeat, positive, busy with short trips, and a wonderful year for writing, teaching, acting, and promoting your ideas. You're very enthusiastic about something. In fact, you're downright optimistic! Perhaps that injection of money or boost to your earnings in 2022–23 did the trick. (It's nice to wrap yourself in cash.)

Once again, in the year 2024, you have a fabulous chance to make money through real estate. This is definitely the year to buy or sell homes, or speculate in real estate, or renovate or fix up where you live. Any kind of money that you pour into real estate or your own home will turn out to be profitable in the long run.

In the same vein (but a different arm), everything to do with your home life and your family scene will be happier and more

---

15. There's an old army saying that three moves are worth a fire. (I think it's true.)

joyful, and will feel more expansive. In fact, quite literally, your family might expand! This is the classic time to have children, grandchildren, or some kind of family expansion through marriage, birth, or adoption. This family expansion could also occur in 2025, when, no matter what, children are a source of joy. Count on this.

The year 2025 is also a wonderful time to take a vacation. Do plan ahead for this because this is your year to kick up your heels and enjoy yourself. You want to have fun!

Similarly, 2025 is a great year to express your creative talents. You can make money through your creative expression, or through the entertainment world, the hospitality industry, or anything to do with show business. It's also a great year for sports!

Last but certainly not least, 2025 is a fabulous year for love, romance, flirtations, and new relationships. New love that begins now will likely be with someone older, or more established, or more worldly, and probably richer. (Could this mean a cruise?)

How sweet it is!

"We travel together, passengers on a little spaceship, dependent on its vulnerable reserves of air and soil, all committed for our safety to its security and peace. Preserved from annihilation only by the care, the work, and the love we give our fragile craft."
ADLAI STEVENSON
American Politician and U. S. Ambassador to the United Nations
(FEBRUARY 5, 1900–JULY 14, 1965)

Famous Aquarius Personalities

George Burns	January 20, 1896–1996
Federico Fellini	January 20, 1920–1993
DeForest Kelley	January 20, 1920–1999
Edwin "Buzz" Aldrin	January 20, 1930
Edward Hirsch	January 20, 1950
Bill Maher	January 20, 1956
Apa Sherpa	January 20, 1960
Will Wright	January 20, 1960
James Denton	January 20, 1963
Rainn Wilson	January 20, 1966
Christian Dior	January 21, 1905–1957
Jack Nicklaus	January 21, 1940
Plácido Domingo	January 21, 1941
Richie Havens	January 21, 1941
Mac Davis	January 21, 1942
Jill Eikenberry	January 21, 1947
Billy Ocean	January 21, 1950
Paul Allen	January 21, 1953
Geena Davis	January 21, 1957
Emma Bunton	January 21, 1976
Dany Heatley	January 21, 1981
Sam Cooke	January 22, 1931–1964
Joseph Wambaugh	January 22, 1937
John Hurt	January 22, 1940
Linda Blair	January 22, 1959
Diane Lane	January 22, 1965
Olivia d'Abo	January 22, 1969
Stendhal	January 23, 1783–1842
Django Reinhardt	January 23, 1910–1953
Chita Rivera	January 23, 1933
Rutger Hauer	January 23, 1944
Richard Dean Anderson	January 23, 1950
Mariska Hargitay	January 23, 1964
Tiffani Thiessen	January 23, 1974
Doug Kershaw	January 24, 1936

Neil Diamond	January 24, 1941
John Belushi	January 24, 1949–1982
Mary Lou Retton	January 24, 1968
Shae-Lynn Bourne	January 24, 1976
Mischa Barton	January 24, 1986
Robert Burns	January 25, 1759–1796
Virginia Woolf	January 25, 1882–1941
Etta James	January 25, 1938
Mia Kirshner	January 25, 1975
Alicia Keys	January 25, 1981
Douglas MacArthur	January 26, 1880–1964
Paul Newman	January 26, 1925–2008
Angela Davis	January 26, 1944
Eddie Van Halen	January 26, 1955
Ellen DeGeneres	January 26, 1958
Wayne Gretzky	January 26, 1961
Gustavo Dudamel	January 26, 1981
Wolfgang Amadeus Mozart	January 27, 1756–1791
Lewis Carroll	January 27, 1832–1898
Mordecai Richler	January 27, 1931–2001
Máiread Corrigan	January 27, 1944
Keith Olbermann	January 27, 1959
Bridget Fonda	January 27, 1964
Colette	January 28, 1873–1954
Jackson Pollock	January 28, 1912–1956
Alan Alda	January 28, 1936
Carlos Slim Helú	January 28, 1940
Mikhail Baryshnikov	January 28, 1948
Sarah McLachlan	January 28, 1968
Elijah Wood	January 28, 1981
Germaine Greer	January 29, 1939
Tom Selleck	January 29, 1945
Oprah Winfrey	January 29, 1954
Edward Burns	January 29, 1968
Heather Graham	January 29, 1970
Adam Lambert	January 29, 1982
Franklin D. Roosevelt	January 30, 1882–1945
Dick Martin	January 30, 1922–2008
Gene Hackman	January 30, 1930
Vanessa Redgrave	January 30, 1937
Boris Spassky	January 30, 1937
Phil Collins	January 30, 1951

Christian Bale	January 30, 1974
Wilmer Valderrama	January 30, 1980
Tallulah Bankhead	January 31, 1902–1968
Thomas Merton	January 31, 1915–1968
Jackie Robinson	January 31, 1919–1972
Carol Channing	January 31, 1921
Norman Mailer	January 31, 1923–2007
Suzanne Pleshette	January 31, 1937–2008
Anthony LaPaglia	January 31, 1959
Minnie Driver	January 31, 1970
Justin Timberlake	January 31, 1981
Clark Gable	February 1, 1901–1960
Langston Hughes	February 1, 1902–1967
Don Everly	February 1, 1937
Brandon Lee	February 1, 1965–1993
Michael C. Hall	February 1, 1971
Ayn Rand	February 2, 1905–1982
Tom Smothers	February 2, 1937
Farrah Fawcett	February 2, 1947–2009
Christie Brinkley	February 2, 1954
Shakira	February 2, 1977
Gertrude Stein	February 3, 1874–1946
Norman Rockwell	February 3, 1894–1978
James Michener	February 3, 1907–1997
Blythe Danner	February 3, 1943
Stephen McHattie	February 3, 1947
Nathan Lane	February 3, 1956
Maura Tierney	February 3, 1965
Isla Fisher	February 3, 1976
Rosa Parks	February 4, 1913–2005
Betty Friedan	February 4, 1921–2006
Alice Cooper	February 4, 1948
Denis Savard	February 4, 1961
Hank Aaron	February 5, 1934
Don Cherry	February 5, 1934
Barbara Hershey	February 5, 1948
Jennifer Jason Leigh	February 5, 1962
Laura Linney	February 5, 1964
Babe Ruth	February 6, 1895–1948
Ronald Reagan	February 6, 1911–2004
Rip Torn	February 6, 1931
Tom Brokaw	February 6, 1940

Bob Marley	February 6, 1945–1981
Kate McGarrigle	February 6, 1946–2010
Natalie Cole	February 6, 1950
Kathy Najimy	February 6, 1957
Charles Dickens	February 7, 1812–1870
Sinclair Lewis	February 7, 1885–1951
Buster Crabbe	February 7, 1908–1983
Miguel Ferrer	February 7, 1955
Garth Brooks	February 7, 1962
Steve Nash	February 7, 1974
Ashton Kutcher	February 7, 1978
Jules Verne	February 8, 1828–1905
Audrey Meadows	February 8, 1922–1996
Jack Lemmon	February 8, 1925–2001
Neal Cassady	February 8, 1926–1968
James Dean	February 8, 1931–1955
Nick Nolte	February 8, 1941
Mary Steenburgen	February 8, 1953
John Grisham	February 8, 1955
Seth Green	February 8, 1974
Ronald Coleman	February 9, 1891–1958
Carole King	February 9, 1942
Joe Pesci	February 9, 1943
Alice Walker	February 9, 1944
Mia Farrow	February 9, 1945
Travis Tritt	February 9, 1963
Ziyi Zhang	February 9, 1979
Bertolt Brecht	February 10, 1898–1956
Leontyne Price	February 10, 1927
Robert Wagner	February 10, 1930
Roberta Flack	February 10, 1937
Adrienne Clarkson	February 10, 1939
Frances Moore Lappé	February 10, 1944
Laura Dern	February 10, 1967
Leslie Nielsen	February 11, 1926
Mary Quant	February 11, 1934
Burt Reynolds	February 11, 1936
Sheryl Crow	February 11, 1962
Jennifer Aniston	February 11, 1969
Charles Darwin	February 12, 1809–1882
Abraham Lincoln	February 12, 1809–1865
Franco Zeffirelli	February 12, 1923

Michael Ironside	February 12, 1950
Josh Brolin	February 12, 1968
Christina Ricci	February 12, 1980
Chuck Yeager	February 13, 1923
Kim Novak	February 13, 1933
George Segal	February 13, 1934
Stockard Channing	February 13, 1944
Peter Gabriel	February 13, 1950
Mats Sundin	February 13, 1971
Robbie Williams	February 13, 1974
Jack Benny	February 14, 1894–1974
Hugh Downs	February 14, 1921
Carl Bernstein	February 14, 1944
Meg Tilly	February 14, 1960
Harvey Korman	February 15, 1927–2008
Jane Seymour	February 15, 1951
Matt Groening	February 15, 1954
The Twelfth Tai Situpa	February 15, 1954
Renée O'Connor	February 15, 1971
Sonny Bono	February 16, 1935–1998
Iain Banks	February 16, 1954
James Ingram	February 16, 1956
LeVar Burton	February 16, 1957
John McEnroe	February 16, 1959
Sarah Clarke	February 16, 1972
Hal Holbrook	February 17, 1925
Rene Russo	February 17, 1954
Loreena McKennitt	February 17, 1957
Michael Jordan	February 17, 1963
Denise Richards	February 17, 1971
Jerry O'Connell	February 17, 1974
Jack Palance	February 18, 1919–2006
Helen Gurley Brown	February 18, 1922
Len Deighton	February 18, 1929
Toni Morrison	February 18, 1931
Yoko Ono	February 18, 1933
Cybill Shepherd	February 18, 1950
John Travolta	February 18, 1954
Greta Scacchi	February 18, 1960

PISCES

FEBRUARY 19 – MARCH 20

PISCES THE FISH
(FEBRUARY 19 – MARCH 20)

"I BELIEVE."

"There are only two ways to live your life. One is as though nothing
is a miracle. The other is as though everything is a miracle."
ALBERT EINSTEIN
Physicist, Philosopher, Author, and Winner of the Nobel Prize in Physics (1921)
(MARCH 4, 1879–APRIL 18, 1955)

"I'm every bourgeois nightmare —
a Cockney with intelligence and a million dollars."
MICHAEL CAINE
British Actor
Alfie, The Italian Job, and *The Cider House Rules*
(B. MARCH 14, 1933)

Element: Water
Ruling Planet: Neptune
Quality: Mutable
Opposite Sign: Virgo
Symbol: The Fish
Glyph: Two Fish Tied Together, Representing Co-operation and Opposition
Lucky Gems: Bloodstone, Moonstone, Aquamarine, Amethyst, and Pearl[1]
Flowers: Lotus and Mimosa
Colours: Turquoise, Sea Green, and Lavender
Part of the Body: Feet

You Like: Shoes, dancing, fantasy, make-believe, meditation, yoga, pleasant places near water, dreams, cultural pastimes, film, and photography. You're a great dresser and you present well. You often wear "costumes."

You Don't Like: Hostility, cruelty, drabness, routine tasks, refusing someone, hurting anyone, and feeling rejected. You weep easily.

Where You Shine: Open-minded, soothing, comforting, sympathetic, imaginative, charitable, loving, spiritual, wise, and romantic.

So Who's Perfect? Helpless, playing the victim, over-emotional, too talkative, impractical, and self-pitying. You have too many shoes.

---

1. Different texts will name different gems for different signs.

What Is Pisces-ness?[2]

The quickest way to explore the mystery of your sign is to understand what your ruling planet means in astrology. The ruling planet of Pisces is Neptune, the Roman god of the sea. To be sure, Pisces rules the ocean, but Neptune is also the planet of smoke and mirrors. *Neptune is illusion!* Wooooooo. (*Twilight Zone* riff here.)

This is why Pisces is the stuff of dreams, fantasies, and the perfection of whatever you could possibly imagine! But, my dear Pisces, *perfection is an illusion*, is it not?

Therefore, your ruling planet Neptune is the muse — the inspiration of all art and beauty. However, whatever your muse conjures up can never really be achieved, can it? I mean, not *really*. This is because the perfection of the inspiration in your mind is unattainable. You visualize a piece of music, or a perfect love, or an idyllic situation, but it is never like that in real life. Real life is imperfect. Perfection is only an ideal, an ideal that cannot be attained in reality. (I hate that part.)

One could say Neptune is the music Beethoven *heard*, but Venus is what he *wrote*. The painting you visualize is never what actually appears on canvas. Venus is the actual form and expression of art, but the inspiration for this art is Neptune.

Sounds exotic, doesn't it? And it is!

You yearn for perfection and beauty in your world. Not just beauty in your surroundings, but also beautiful people in beautiful shoes in beautiful places with beautiful thoughts and beautiful values. A beautiful utopia!

"My ambition is to have beautiful encounters, not to make money."
JULIETTE BINOCHE
French Actress
The English Patient and *Chocolat*
(B. MARCH 9, 1964)

Let's kick it up a notch. This allure is even more appealing if it is cloaked in mist. Imagine a naked body standing before you, then imagine that same body covered with chiffon fabric wafting gently in a sunset breeze — well, we might as well put this body standing on a beach, with white sand and turquoise waters shimmering in the background. Now, consider this — the body that is covered in sheer fabric is

---

2. No one is just one sign, because everyone's chart is made up of different planets. Therefore, this section captures the Pisces archetype — the qualities of "Pisces-ness." Many other signs will have Pisces characteristics as well. Therefore, the description of one sign is not an exact description of that person; rather, it is a description of the qualities of that sign.

infinitely more enticing than the naked body — no? And it's not just because the cellulite is obscured, it's because that which is suggested or implied — a hint of promise (be still, my beating heart) — has more allure and enticement! This is why Neptune is the sign of glamour! And all glamour is illusion. (As any good makeup artist knows.)

> "A picture is the expression of an impression.
> If the beautiful were not in us, how would we ever recognize it?"
>
> ERNST HAAS
> Austrian Artist and Photographer
> (MARCH 2, 1921–SEPTEMBER 12, 1986)

Hey, before you get carried away humming the lost chord — in the same way that Neptune rules illusion, it also rules deceit. (Oh dear.) More smoke and mirrors! Not only is Neptune the ruler of confusion and delusion, Neptune rules gas, oil, paint, chemicals, chemistry, alcohol, everything that dissolves in water, pharmaceuticals, prescription drugs, recreational drugs — *your whole medicine cabinet*!

Neptune is all about being able to alter one's reality, whether by ingesting something or fantasizing. It's a very *tricky* influence!

> "Reality is merely an illusion, albeit a very persistent one."
>
> ALBERT EINSTEIN
> Physicist, Philosopher, Author, and Winner of the Nobel Prize in Physics (1921)
> (MARCH 4, 1879–APRIL 18, 1955)

We all know that drugs and pharmaceuticals are a mega-business, but another big use of illusion is film. We're talking movies! Although show business and the entertainment world fall under the domain of Leo, the process of moving film, which is an illusion, is Neptune.

Think about it for a moment. We file into a big room and we sit in rows and rows of chairs all facing in one direction. We look at a screen and, suddenly, we are moved to tears or horror. We cackle with laughter, weep, or shriek with fear! But if someone suddenly turned the lights on, we would look up sheepishly, because, hey — we're all looking at a blank wall. What was that all about? Who was that masked man?

This is Neptune. This is Pisces. This is you.

You are the most imaginative, playful, exotic, fascinating, mesmerizing sign. *People adore you!* You entertain them with your wit, your charm, and most definitely your fluid, graceful movements. I remember years ago watching Bruce Willis in *Die Hard*.[3]

---

3. "Come out to the coast; we'll get together, have a few laughs." (The words of John McClane, huddled bleeding in an air duct.)

During the scene where Bruce is running around on the roof of the Nakatomi Plaza building in his bare feet, with a body-hugging athletic undershirt (this guy has such a bod), I suddenly sat up and looked more closely. "Waaaait a minute. He moves like a dancer! This guy has to be Pisces." Sure enough, I checked later and discovered that Bruce was born March 19, 1955. He has his Sun in Pisces and his Mercury in Pisces, and his Mercury has a lovely fit with Neptune in his chart. Willis must be a very entertaining man at dinner! (Probably in a few other rooms as well.)

Why did I twig to Pisces when I saw Willis's graceful movements? Because Pisces rules the feet. All great dancers have Pisces somewhere in their chart. This also explains why you have so many shoes in your closet, even though you don't think so (in fact, you intend to buy a pair this month, right?). Your feet are your strength and your weakness. But you move so well! And you *love* to dance![4]

Your mind is full of fantasies and daydreams! In your fantasies, you achieve prizes, honours, wealth, fame, and the love of your life. You rescue the downtrodden. You tell off bullies. You actually have imaginary conversations in which you address the jury, or the judge, or a teacher, or a father-in-law, or a jerk boss. It varies, depending on who you feel like *talking* to today. You right the wrongs of the world, and others adore you! And, of course, what you really want — down deep — is to make your dreams come true!

"We have the capacity for infinite creativity; at least while dreaming,
we partake of the power of the Spirit,
the infinite Godhead that creates the cosmos."
JACKIE GLEASON
American Comedian, Actor, and Musician
The Honeymooners
(FEBRUARY 26, 1916–JUNE 24, 1987)

Those who hang out with you know you have a way of upping the ante. If you're sitting with your lover, you think, "This is wonderful. But, hey, wouldn't it be better if we turned the lights down low?" Now you and your lover are sitting with the lights low, and you think, "This is wonderful, sitting here with the lights low, but, hey — wouldn't it be better if we had some wonderful music playing?" Now you and your lover are sitting with the lights low, and the music is playing, and you think, "This is wonderful. The lights are low, the music is playing, but, hey — wouldn't it be better if we had some wine?" Now you and your lover are sitting with the lights low, and the music is playing, and you're sipping wine, and you think, "This is wonderful. The lights are low, the music is playing, and we're sipping wine, but, hey — wouldn't it be better if we had some brie and havarti, and fresh

---

4. Raúl Juliá (March 9, 1940–October 24, 1994) was one of my all-time favourite actors. Although not a dancer, he was wonderful in *Tango Bar*. (Sigh.) And what about Cyd Charisse (March 8, 1922–June 17, 2008) in *Singin' in the Rain*? Omigawd.

strawberries, and pâté and a baguette, and some mood-enhancing additives (which of course, we won't inhale), and, and, and, and, and . . ." and the list never ends. *You are always going for that perfect moment.* Sound familiar?

This is why people have so much fun with you! Plus — hands down — you are the most polite sign in the zodiac. It's just who you are.

> "Now, it's a very difficult job and the only way to get
> through it is if we all work together as a team, and that means you do
> everything I say." — Charlie Croker, *The Italian Job*
> MICHAEL CAINE
> British Actor
> *Alfie, The Italian Job*, and *The Cider House Rules*
> (B. MARCH 14, 1933)

Not only are you polite, you're unusually engaging in a charming, sweet, almost angelic way. You look too good to be true! You might be incredibly hungover, but you somehow look "pure." Think of Rob Lowe (b. March 17, 1964) or Glenn Close (b. March 19, 1947) or Ron Howard (b. March 1, 1954) or Billy Crystal (b. March 14, 1948) or Elizabeth Taylor (b. February 27, 1932). Such sweet faces! So beautiful, so innocent.

Always remember that murky, inspirational, ephemeral, seductive, illusory Neptune is your ruler. This puts you in a class all by yourself.

> "People hate me because I am a multifaceted, talented,
> wealthy, internationally famous genius."
> JERRY LEWIS
> American Comedian, Film Producer, Writer, and Singer
> *The Nutty Professor*
> (B. MARCH 16, 1926)

Three Big Clues about Pisces

Three other categories will throw more light on the secrets of your Piscean soul. For greater self-understanding, be aware of these qualities:

1. Compassion
2. Dreams
3. Projection

Compassion

> "Let your heart feel for the afflictions and distress of everyone, and let your hand give in proportion to your purse."
> GEORGE WASHINGTON
> First President of the United States of America (1789–1797)
> (FEBRUARY 22, 1731–DECEMBER 14, 1799)

Compassion is perhaps the most important quality for a person to have. I say this because anyone without compassion is a sad example of a human being. (On the other hand, is any sane person without compassion? I think not.)

Eastern thought makes a distinction between compassion and kindness. They define kindness as the desire to make others happy, whereas compassion is the desire to relieve suffering. Therefore, an aspect of compassion most definitely is awareness of the suffering of others.

Because Pisces is perhaps the most sensitive sign in the zodiac, you are obviously extremely aware of the suffering of others. (You're sensitive to everything!) This sensitivity is why you show compassion for others. You are the most caring, kind, gentle, and thoughtful of all the signs in the zodiac. There's no question about this. (Why else do you think I have a Pisces dentist?)

The Pisces impulse is to save the world before bedtime. You want to save your friends, your loved ones, and your family. Surprisingly, you are quick and willing to give the shirt off your back to someone you don't even know if they are sick or suffering. You truly want to help.

In addition to having strong feelings of compassion for others, you are a patient listener as well. This is why Neptune is the planet that is always associated with therapy and counselling. Pisces people do extremely well in this field. (Ya think?)

"It always amazes me to think that every house on every street
is full of so many stories, so many triumphs and tragedies;
and all we see are yards and driveways."

GLENN CLOSE
American Film and Television Actress
Fatal Attraction and *Dangerous Liaisons*
(B. MARCH 19, 1947)

THE SPONGE EFFECT

However, I have to make a distinction here. I think Pisces people should *avoid working in areas where there is extreme pain* — for example, with burn victims in a hospital. Not only do you observe the suffering of others, and not only are you aware of the suffering of others, you seem to almost take it on. You sort of suck it up into your own system, which is not a good thing. Ideally, you should avoid areas of extreme pain. But, if you do work in a situation like this, you have to learn techniques to "clean" the heavy vibes of others that you absorb like a sponge into your own psyche.

I talked to one doctor who moved quickly from patient to patient, and he told me a visualization technique that he used. He said that after doing it many times, he could do this visualization almost instantly. What he did was visualize a huge tree growing from the top of his head high, high, high up into the sky. And, from his feet, he visualized deep roots going down, down, down into the earth. He said by doing this quickly between patients, he seemed to "clean" his own aura or psyche (call it what you will) so that he felt fresh and strong enough to deal with the next patient.

Many Pisces people have natural healing qualities. (To some, this will sound pretty corny.) But there's no question, I think, that certain Pisces people, or people with a very strong Neptune in their chart, can actually heal others by their mere presence.

Princess Diana has two astrological charts according to different astrologers. This is because one birth time is according to Buckingham Palace, and the other birth time is according to her mother. The chart I endorse shows that Princess Diana had the planet Neptune right on her Rising Sign. Although she was not a Pisces, because Neptune (the ruler of Pisces) was right on her Rising Sign she was "like" a Pisces. *Capisce?*

Anyone who has read some of the media about Princess Diana knows of the countless instances when people she visited in hospitals and in troubled areas claimed her presence seemed to heal them or make them feel better. I don't doubt this.

Ironically, this same rather blurred quality (which is so empathetic) makes you highly suggestible! Pisces people can be easily swayed by others. Therefore, it's important to be discriminating. You have to be careful whom you hang out with. Negative people will bring you down. They will suck the life out of you! Furthermore, negative or harmful people can easily lead you astray. (We all know that birds of a feather flock to freshly washed cars.)

Choose your friends carefully. You have to live your life as if you were on an acid trip.

"ALL THINGS ARE CAUSE FOR EITHER LAUGHTER OR WEEPING"[5]

Two things are almost a sure guarantee for any Pisces. You have more shoes than anyone else in the family, and you weep easily. Admittedly, I know a few Pisces who are not that crazy about shoes. They're like everybody else in the world. (I'm not sure what's wrong with them.)

Similarly, there are a few Pisces who do not weep easily. (What's with that?)

You might notice I'm not using the term *cry*. Pisces people don't cry. *They weep!* They fling themselves on the bed and really get into it. They sometimes say, "I just needed a good cry." (I'm thinking, Whaaat?)

So what's with all this weeping? It's simple, really. The sign of Pisces rules the lachrymal glands, which is a fancy name for your tear ducts. That's why it's easy for you to suddenly cry — your tears are almost waiting to fall.

Yes, you are the most sensitive, caring, compassionate sign of the zodiac. Yes, you weep very easily. But does this mean you're a wuss? Not at all! Just a glance at some famous Pisces listed on pages 600–4 is ample testimony to the fearless grit and courage of your sign. In addition to which, intelligence is definitely an important component of compassion. No question. And Pisces is *an intelligent sign*! Einstein? Schopenhauer? Dr. Seuss? I rest my handbag.

Dreams

Everyone dreams. However, most people don't remember their dreams. In fact, some people say they don't dream, but, of course, they do — they just can't remember dreaming.

However, almost all Pisces people remember dreaming. In fact, your dream world is a very big part of your life. To me, people who can remember their dreams have "more life." I say this because if you can remember your dreams, then the next day, you not only remember the previous day and the previous evening, you also remember the previous nighttime. Considering that time is the stuff life is made of, this means you have *more to remember* than other people do. Your dream time gives you more of life! Most people lose that time. Therefore, I think Pisces people have richer lives, because you have your dreams to ponder and remember, in addition to your waking moments.[6]

The fact that Neptune is the ruler of dreams affects you 24/7, not just while you're sleeping. When you are awake, you still have dreams and fantasies. In fact, you think in pictures. If you remember something, it comes back to you like a picture.

5. This quote is from Seneca (*c.* 4 B.C.–A.D. 65), a Roman philosopher, statesman, and dramatist.
6. I enjoyed reading a book called *Creative Dreaming* by Patricia Garfield, Ph. D. She says our dreams comprise about six years of our lives!

You remember what part of the room you were in, or which chair you sat in, or on which side of you someone was when they said something. You might think everyone else does this, but they don't.

Your dreams affect your life because they are very much a part of your thought process. This is huge. Why? Because your thoughts are the beginning of everything. *Your thoughts create your world.*

> *In the beginning is the thought.*
> *From the thought springs the word.*
> *From the word springs the deed.*
> *And soon the deed becomes habit;*
> *Habit eventually hardens into character.*
> *Therefore, watch your thoughts with care,*
> *and let them be loving and kind.*
> **EASTERN PROVERB**

Roger Bannister (b. March 23, 1929) was the first man in recorded history to run a mile in less than four minutes. This historic event took place on May 6, 1954, in Oxford, U.K. What intrigues me is that once this barrier had been broken and others knew it was humanly possible to break this barrier, by the end of 1957 sixteen other runners had also broken the four-minute mile (including Roger Bannister, who did it again several times). They broke through the wall! *The wall was in their minds.*

Roger Bannister was a competitive Aries, but he had his Mercury in Pisces, and Mercury ruled his thought process and his perceptions of life.

This is why your dreams are important. They are like *test runs* for you. You try on ideas, hopes, and possible future scenarios in your dreams — be they daydreams or night dreams. Your dreams are like the boot camp for life.

DREAMS AND IMAGINATION

Because you have the ability to daydream and fantasize during your waking moments, and to dream so vividly at night, your visualization skills are extraordinary. To put it another way, you have a *fantastic imagination*! This is one of the reasons so many Pisces people are unusually creative. You are very much in touch with your muse. You easily visualize and imagine what it is you want to create in terms of performance art, artistic ideas, projects, and works of art.

However, this same creative imagination can apply to any field. Albert Einstein — probably the most famous Pisces of all — said, "Imagination is more important than knowledge." This shocks many people! He also said, "Logic will get you from A to B. *Imagination* will take you everywhere." Of course, this is true. If you look around you — every piece of furniture, every building, every car, bicycle, item of clothing, cooking utensil, including the food you eat — all of it was first an imagined idea in somebody's mind.

You are so very fortunate to have this fabulous talent at your fingertips. Your ability to imagine creatively can yield solutions, inventions, and life-changing discoveries for humanity. That's kinda cool.

DREAMS AND ESCAPE

One of the reasons you like to daydream and fantasize is because it's a form of escapism. What you want is a perfect world. You certainly want a pleasant one! You don't like poo-poo caca.

Therefore, when you encounter unpleasant situations, sadness, or strife, or any kind of bummer scene — you want to escape. ("Run away! Run away!") In fact, some of you will physically escape a situation by leaving town or travelling somewhere else, hoping for a geographic cure.

Unfortunately, your Pisces proclivity to seek escape often draws you into drugs and alcohol. Rather than face what is unpleasant, you check out by drinking or getting high. Small wonder your ruler, Neptune, rules all forms of drugs — pharmaceutical and recreational. Hmmmm.

Projection

This is a tricky thing to discuss, but you will know right away what I'm talking about. The planet Neptune is your ruler. We know this. Neptune rules illusion, smoke and mirrors, Vaseline on the lens. This is why many Pisces people are chameleon-like.

You guys are shape-shifters!

It's easy for you to project a particular image, and you do so without even trying. For example, if I hand a top hat and a cane to just anyone, they will look like they're standing there holding a cane and wearing a top hat. But if I hand a top hat and a cane to a Pisces — voila! — this person immediately brings to mind Fred Astaire!

You need only a few props to suddenly blossom into a caricature or a particular image. It's as if the *image you project to the world is highly malleable.* Most Pisces people know this. This is also one of the reasons you are the most fabulous, imaginative dressers.

I used to be a movie critic. The newspaper I worked for was so small I covered both movies and stage plays. For those who go to plays a lot, there's a "look" to a theatre crowd. Sure, there are a lot of posers, but mostly this crowd looks like they are trying to underplay who they really are. Sort of the "I'm so famous I'm wearing sunglasses and downplaying my status" kinda thing. There's a lot of brown, and black, and leather. Don't get me wrong there's also a lot of average, everyday types as well.

One evening, my editor asked me to cover a dance performance. I told him I wasn't qualified to do this, but he sent me off to do it anyway. During intermission, as I surveyed the crowd, I was stunned. *This was a very different crowd!* (And it was not until I saw that crowd that I realized there even *was* a "look" to the theatre crowd.) This dance crowd was spectacular! And exciting! All this Pisces stuff! For starters, there probably *were* a lot of dancers in the crowd. These people were *far more imaginative and daring in their dress*. They wore feathers, sequins, and rather revealing, skin-showing numbers. The men were equally turned out in a stylish, almost costume-like way.

In fact, I am reminded now of a well-dressed Pisces man with Virgo rising who came to see me. He was an actor. He leaned across the table and said, with vehement passion, "I just got back from Italy, and I realize I dress like a boy. I looked like this in high school. But in Italy, the men are *dressing*! And they're not *apologizing*!"

This projection aspect works both ways. Not only are you able to quickly project any kind of image (if you choose to do so), but others will easily project an image onto you! It's as if they see you with Vaseline on *their* lens. Once they have decided you are a certain type, then they freeze you in that mould or that image. Because of this, countless *Pisces people feel misunderstood by others*. Or people will say they don't "get" you. In other words, there's a confusion about your image — both how you project your image in the world and also how you are perceived by others.

Again, I will hearken back to the image of Princess Diana, who had Neptune right on her Rising Sign. We all know the media were stunned at the extent to which the world reacted to her death. But when I saw her chart, I was not surprised. Because of this Neptune factor, when Princess Diana died, one woman didn't die — millions of women died. Everyone had their own personal Diana. Some people saw her as a fairy princess with a sparkly halo. Others saw her as a fashion icon. Some saw her as the royal princess. Some saw her as a mother and a caring, sensitive individual. Some saw her as a neurotic bulimic. In other words, everyone had their own personal projection of who Princess Diana was, which is why *so many Dianas died that day*.

Marilyn Monroe is another person who had Neptune on her Rising Sign. Even to this day, twelve-year-old girls have pictures of Marilyn Monroe on their bedroom walls. Surely this is not because she's a sex symbol. What made Monroe a legend? There were many blond, buxom actresses in Hollywood then. The secret of her fame was that everyone had *their own* Marilyn Monroe.

Deep inside Marilyn knew this Neptunian illusion was at work. She said, "I've never fooled anyone. I've let people fool themselves. They didn't bother to find out who and what I was. Instead they would invent a character for me. I wouldn't argue with them. They were obviously loving somebody I wasn't."

To a greater or lesser degree, depending on how Neptune is operating in your chart, and depending on how strong a Pisces you are (some people have more Pisces in them than others), you, too, will project a quality where others see you as they *think* you are, which might have shockingly little to do with who you *really* are. This is bloody weird! But many of you know whereof I speak.

Pisces in Love

"What a grand thing, to be loved! What a grander thing still, to love!"
VICTOR HUGO
French Poet, Playwright, Novelist, and Eassyist
Les Misérables and *The Hunchback of Notre-Dame*
(FEBRUARY 26, 1802–MAY 22, 1885)

The romantic idealism of the Pisces lover is mind-boggling. Nothing is beyond the realm of possibility! *You believe in magic.*

I think it's because you have a fabulous imagination, hope, and the expectation of the ideal. Remember what Einstein said: "Logic will get you from A to B. *Imagination* will take you everywhere."

A Pisces in love entertains every possible notion of every possible fantasy and believes it really could be a reality. Ironically, even though the rest of us pooh-pooh this pie-in-the-sky thinking, Pisces people actually *make their dreams come true!*

Take, for example, Michael Caine, who is a Pisces (b. March 14, 1933). The story of how he met his wife is a classic fairytale. One day, while watching television, he saw this incredibly beautiful face in a Maxwell House coffee commercial. He immediately became obsessed with finding this face — "the most beautiful woman" he had ever seen. He made plans to go to Brazil to track her down but then suddenly discovered she was living in London. He found her, married her, and they are married to this day. Incidentally, Michael Caine's wife, Shakira, is also a Pisces (b. February 23, 1947).

Now, you may be thinking, well, this can happen to Michael Caine, because he is rich and famous, and has the resources and influence to make this kind of magic happen. This is true. Nevertheless, it doesn't stop every Pisces from still dreaming and hoping for the same kind of thing to happen in *their* lives. What they secretly hope for is just as fantastic.

I recall a dear, sweet Pisces friend whom I shall call K. (she will read this book). When K. was twenty years old, she was devastated to learn that Gary Oldman, on whom she had a passionate crush, had married Uma Thurman. She actually cried upon learning the news. Her long-standing friend Trinity consoled her. Two years later, when the split between Thurman and Oldman made the news, Trinity immediately phoned K. to tell her the good news! Together they rejoiced. Gary Oldman was free and available!

Hello? How can someone who is intelligent and living in the real world (and K. is both) be devastated, and then relieved, at the marriage and divorce of a celebrity she will never likely meet? I think this true story positions the romantic longing every Pisces soul earnestly entertains.

The Pisces lover is wonderfully romantic. This person will never forget an important day like your birthday or your anniversary or even a not-so-important day. *Pisces is extremely thoughtful.* The Pisces lover completely spoils the object of their affection with gifts, favours, coffee every morning in bed, and delightful little indulgences, because all these things support the belief Pisces has about *what constitutes the romantic ideal.*

Above all, the Pisces lover is thoughtful, gentle, considerate, fun-loving, and full of whimsy. But do not mistake this gentleness for weakness. *Au contraire!* Pisces people have enormous mettle. (I make jokes about them being wusses only because they can be so sensitive and weepy at times.) In truth, Pisces has *enormous inner strength.*

However, the true weakness of the Pisces lover is their ability to delude themselves. They are always looking at their lover through rose-coloured glasses. They want to be in love with someone perfect; therefore, they quickly put this person on a pedestal and see them in the most positive light possible.

You will know if you're doing this because your friends will tell you that you're nuts. They will implore you to stop seeing this person because your lover weighs three hundred pounds, never bathes, and shoots heroin all the time. But you cannot see this. Instead, you reply that the poetry you share with each other is transcendent. You know that you're soulmates. In fact, at times, you have the exact same heartbeat!

But one day you will get out of bed so quickly you won't have time to slip on your rose-coloured glasses, and you'll look over and see someone in your bed who weighs three hundred pounds, never bathes, and is shooting up heroin! At this moment, you will feel *utterly disillusioned.* You'll be devastated. You'll say things like, "How could they do this to me?"

What you have to remind yourself is that this person really never did anything to you. *This person is the same person* that you met on day one. The only difference is that you have taken off your rose-coloured glasses.

So this is your Achilles heel when you are in love. It isn't that you forgive the bad behaviour of your partner; it's that *you don't even see it.* You are so desirous of being in love with someone who is perfect, you project this onto the other person. Please take note: if more than two friends are telling you that you are in the wrong relationship, you have to listen to them. And if you think back to times in your life when you thought, "How could this person do this to me?" your incredulity is testimony to your refusal to see who this person was right at the beginning.

In all fairness, we all have Neptune in our charts somewhere. We all kid ourselves about relationships. But Pisces people can do this tenfold over the rest of the population.

Would I advise you to throw away your rose-coloured glasses? Definitely not. Your ability to see life in your own particular way is wonderful and magical. Why would you ever want to change that? Just be aware of your penchant to put someone on a pedestal.

Keep your rose-coloured glasses with you at all times, because Einstein was right — "There are only two ways to live your life. One is as though nothing is a miracle. The other is as though everything is a miracle."

The Pisces Boss

You're definitely an interesting boss to work for, and you're certainly nice. I know that *nice* is one of those mushy, overused words, but it aptly applies to Pisces. *You guys are just nice.*

You are a thoughtful boss, and very aware of whatever is going on in the lives of your employees or your co-workers. If someone is going through a tough time, you are sympathetic about what they have to deal with. You might encourage them to take time off, or you might send flowers. You will definitely not ignore them. Instead, you will extend a gesture of sympathy and understanding to them.

In this way, you might be considered to be a bit too lenient at times. And perhaps you are. It's a given that you don't like to say no to others, because you're polite and, hey — you're nice!

Financially, you are inclined to go over budget. You spend impulsively! You love to spend when a good idea occurs to you, especially if it's on something beautiful. You also love to travel.

Your great strength is as a problem solver. Not only do you think out of the box as an Aquarius would, you can transcend the universe! Your imagination helps you see things and suggest solutions that others could never fathom.

You're also not afraid to try for the impossible. Those who work for you know you have this spirit, and they love you for it. It's inspiring! It's also exciting, and sometimes it's downright funny.

Most Pisces bosses are popular because of the sympathy and empathy they share with their co-workers and employees. Your people are willing to go the extra nine yards for you because they know you've got their back.

The Pisces Employee

"The dream was always running ahead of me. To catch up,
to live for a moment with it, that was the miracle."
ANAÏS NIN
French Author and Writer of Female Erotica
The Diary of Anaïs Nin
(FEBRUARY 21, 1903–JANUARY 14, 1977)

You're an extremely pleasant person to work with. You are easygoing, playful, polite, and gentle in a civilized way. People know they can instinctively trust you. You're not going to hurt them. Your ability to easily get along with others is a major plus wherever you work.

However, you go one step further. You tend to be the resident counsellor and therapist wherever you are. People come to you with their problems. Not only are you sympathetic but you're also a natural, instinctive amateur shrink, and, in many cases, a *healer*! This is why people are so glad to work with you.

Your main challenge is finding a job that you really care about. You have a lot of fantasies and daydreams and what-ifs. It's not easy for you to discover what you really want to do. When you find it, of course, you are hard-working! In fact, you are relentless in pursuing your dreams! The trick is to find what turns you on, which is quite another matter.

Quite often, you will work in a field that is related to your sign, like therapy, counselling, pharmaceuticals, movies and film, alcohol or wine, teaching, or anything related to fisheries and oceans. You might even work in the realm of shoes, boots, or stockings. You most definitely can work in the fashion industry or any field that has to do with makeup, cosmetics, and glamour. Dance, of course, is your primary choice. If not dance itself, then anything related to dance performances.

Essentially, no one is better than you at understanding how to create the illusion of glamour, or the illusion of anything! Pisces people are great at event planning, throwing parties, and *encouraging others to believe in themselves*.

Pisces people are inspiring actors, entertainers, and artists. They might also work behind the scenes in set design, makeup, writing, directing, whatever.

You can explore almost any vocation because you are so flexible, chameleon-like, and imaginative.

The Pisces Parent

Pisces people make marvellous parents because they are kind, sympathetic, and, above all, empathetic. You are keenly aware of the sufferings and insecurities of your child. This makes you a caring, loving parent, which, of course, is the most important quality any parent can have.

I believe essentially children need to be loved and kept safe. One can provide children with all sorts of role models, lessons, equipment, and opportunities to learn and expand in many directions. Nevertheless, the world has known little geniuses who grew up with none of this. The key to the happiness of any child is that they were loved.

Naturally, your propensity to place a loved one on a pedestal applies to your parenting style as well. When you're in the hospital and all the little newborns are in their rows of nursery baskets, you're almost embarrassed because it's *so obvious* that your baby is *by far* the most beautiful!

The Pisces parent might be too indulgent, too lenient, and too vague with boundaries and rules. It's important to remember that children *like* boundaries and rules to make them feel safe. It also helps them have a better understanding of how the world works.

You are certainly a parent who will understand dress-up, playtime, and the need to fantasize and daydream. You will be quick to provide your children with art supplies and to applaud their love of music and dance. As someone who appreciates the arts, you naturally encourage artistic expression in your children.

At times, your vulnerability (and perhaps the weeping) might alarm your children, who want you to be strong and always right. Ironically, to display your vulnerability is a valuable lesson to children. They have to learn that adults don't know it all. In fact, that adults can be horribly fallible! The children of Pisces parents will have fewer illusions in this respect.

You are very forgiving and tolerant, for which children are always grateful. You are polite, thoughtful, kind, considerate, and compassionate — what better role model could anyone offer?

The Pisces Child

"I see my purpose in life as making the world a happier place to be in."
DAVID NIVEN
British Actor and Novelist
Around the World in 80 Days and *The Pink Panther*
(MARCH 1, 1910–JULY 29, 1983)

I think it's incredible how many Pisces children look like little angels! These children can be so beautiful, so innocent, so angelic, it's positively endearing. Naturally, they can be little imps, but they don't *look* like it. Oh no! The Pisces child is a very winning child.

Here we have intelligence, creativity, and enormous sensitivity. Needless to say, the Pisces child will weep easily. Please, please remember that this is simply because the sign of Pisces rules the tear ducts, which means they are easily activated for Pisces people, and especially Pisces children. It does not mean they are crybabies. I cannot emphasize this enough. *They are not being crybabies.* This single aspect alone can make many Pisces children very misunderstood, especially by a tougher, more severe parent.

Naturally, Pisces children live in a dream world. They can fantasize and daydream for hours. Because Pisces children sometimes have trouble making friends when they're younger, they are often lonely. This is why they invent imaginary friends. (And you would, too, if you had their imagination!)

Pisces children are natural actors. They will act like everything is fine, except for those moments when their tears just overflow because they can't help it. Nevertheless, it's important to know that the Pisces child has trouble developing self-confidence. This child needs praise and encouragement — and lots of love.

It might take a while for young Pisces to find the right niche in life. However, as this child gets older, their popularity is likely to increase, because people sense how compassionate and caring this person truly is. Unfortunately, these wonderful qualities are often overlooked when the child is very young, because they can be construed as weaknesses.

Quite often, young Pisces children are drawn to spiritual disciplines. They instinctively understand any methodology or belief system that endorses compassion. The older Pisces child will always be popular with younger kids because the younger kids will immediately sense how kind and compassionate the older child is.

I recall seeing a nine-year-old Pisces boy playing with his two-year-old brother in a playground area on a ferry. Within minutes, the older boy was completely swarmed by other children. It was funny to watch! The younger children adored this boy because of the gentle and patient way he played with his younger brother.

Would that we could all be so fortunate in life as to have a Pisces older brother.

How to Be a Happier Pisces

Life has blessed you with a particular talent, because, more than any other sign, you have a fabulous ability to fantasize and visualize. It's not just that you have great imaginary powers, which you do; it's that you can picture things quite clearly in your mind. For example, right now, if you wanted to see a picture of the Eiffel Tower in your mind, you can do this. Or perhaps the Space Needle in Seattle. You can see it in your mind. Therefore, you have a greater ability than any other sign to practise the law of attraction.

I have not read the book *The Secret*, which I understand is based on the law of attraction, but I wasn't surprised to learn that the author is a Pisces (Rhonda Byrne was born March 12, 1951). Pisces people have the ability to put purchase orders out into the universe, or requests for what they want, and *magically* these things *materialize* in their life! (Not too shabby.)

In theory, anyone can do this. But, in actuality, it's not so easy for most people. However, Pisces people have the *power to manifest what they believe in*. To put it another way, whatever their core beliefs are about themselves and the world around them are what soon becomes a reality for them.

Now, this ability of yours is both good news and bad news. The bad news is that, when you believe you cannot do something, that you are inadequate to the task, that you are doomed to fail, that nobody will ever love you, that you can never earn much money, that you will not succeed at your job, that you can't have a happy family — whatever it is that you feel apprehensive about — *this is what you manifest!* Your core beliefs become a reality.

This means that this special skill you have — to visualize something and make it a reality — is both dangerous and yet at the same time a wonderfully positive potential.

Therefore, the first thing you have to know is that this is what you are doing, every day, every week, every month, every year. All the time! Whatever you believe about yourself, whatever you believe is probably going to happen, happens. This means you are your own worst enemy — but, hey, you can also be your own best friend. In fact, it is entirely *within your own power to be your own saviour*.

You have to become constantly aware of your own negativity and the silent conversations that are always going on in your mind. "I'm always late. I never finish anything on time. I'll never be rich. Relationships never turn out well for me. I could never do that. I'm not smart enough. I don't have enough time. I'm not as sharp as others. I don't have what it takes. Nothing ever goes my way. I always get the short end of the stick. I never get the breaks." These are the requests you are constantly putting out into the universe! Horrors! *They will manifest!*

This is why you must be mindful and aware of what you are telling yourself, because what you tell yourself will become a reality in your world. As corny as it sounds, you have to start to replace some of those negative tapes that play in your head. "I am punctual. I finish things on time. I can be rich. I can enjoy a happy relationship. I can do that because I'm smart enough. I have just as much time as everybody else — we all have twenty-four hours every day. I am as sharp as others. I don't always get the short end of the stick. I get lots of breaks."

It's slow work to change the habits of a lifetime, but it can be done. "I can change my self-sabotaging thinking. I can catch myself feeling sorry for myself. I can turn this around!"

Remember: *you are already doing this.* You have been sending out requests to the universe all your life. You are only going to change *the content*, not the process. You *know* how to do this. The trick is to be aware of *what* you are telling yourself and flip it into a positive version.

You've got to ac-cent-tchu-ate the positive and ee-lim-in-ate the negative.

As an example of how you might change your thinking, take a look at your earnings. Let's say you earn $45,000 a year. This means you earn $173 a day. This also means you earn $86.50 for half a day. So here you are, earning $86 for half a day's work. If, somehow, in your mind you can truly believe, truly convince yourself, that *you are worth $100* for half a day's work instead of $86 — your earnings will increase.

Now, you can't just say this to yourself. (This is the bummer part.) You have to think about it enough until you finally *believe* it! You believe it in your bones, in the cells in your body, you believe, "Hey, I'm worth a hundred bucks for half a day's work!" When you finally, really believe that you're worth $100 for half a day's work, before you know it, you'll be earning $52,000 a year. That's $7,000 more a year!

Wanna try that exercise again with a higher figure? Let's say you're earning $60,000 a year. (Lucky you!) Based on a five-day week, this means you're earning $230.77 a day, which is $115 for half a day's work. Hmmmm; $115 for half a day for what you do? You can blow that any Friday night with friends. You are certainly worth more than that. Is it too much to expect $150 for half a day's work at what you do? I think not. (It's a stretch, but Lord knows you're worth it.)

Now, once you finally decide that you *deserve* $150 for half a day's work, that *you are worth* $150 for half a day's work — once you *really have this belief* and *expectation* in your bones — you will be making $78,000 a year. Surprised? Yeah, I bet you are. That's $18,000 more a year. You are "freezing" yourself at your present earnings level. Don't do this.

The trick is to put what you think you're worth into terms that you can finally believe. If you just say to yourself, "I think I'm worth seven thousand dollars more

a year," I don't think this will work. You have to bring it down to some smaller figure that is blatantly apparent to you *that it is possible*. You can do it. You are worth
this. The reason you have to play a trick like this on yourself is because whatever
you manifest is what you *truly believe you're worth*. It's what you truly believe is
going to happen to you. If you think you don't deserve something — you won't get
it. Or, if you do get it, it will slip away very soon.

Therefore, use this great advantage that you have simply because you are a Pisces.
Your beliefs manifest in your world. Don't ask how. Don't ask why. It just works
that way.

> "If you have it and you know you have it, then you have it.
> If you have it and don't know you have it, you don't have it.
> If you don't have it but you think you have it, then you have it."
> JACKIE GLEASON
> American Comedian, Actor, and Musician
> *The Honeymooners* and *The Hustler*
> (FEBRUARY 26, 1916–JUNE 24, 1987)

Dreams

Dreams are extremely powerful, and nobody dreams more powerfully than you.
There are many books written about dreams. Furthermore, in sophisticated systems
of Eastern thought and meditation, there are techniques for working with your
dreams. I don't know enough about this to offer any advice here, except to tell you
that they exist.

I recall reading a true story somewhere; for the life of me, I have tried to remember where I read this, and I can't recall. Therefore, this is my mixed-up recollection
about a man who is helping a woman overcome her fears. (Or perhaps overcome
her nightmares?) In order to make headway with her, they discuss her dreams. Sure
enough, in her dreams, there are these monsters she is always trying to run from,
but she can never get away. He suggests that she fly or jump in a car or catch a train.
But she is not able to dream this kind of helpful escape. Finally, one night she is able
to give herself a bicycle to outrun her demons. Yay! Success. But then one day she
says the bicycle in her dreams is broken. She can no longer escape her demons. He
tells her she can fix it. She tries to fix it in her dreams, but can't. So, to help her, he
gets a real bicycle, and, in her waking state, he teaches her how to fix this bicycle.
*After she learns how to fix her bicycle in the waking world, she is then able to fix
her bicycle in her dreams* and get away from her demons! Now, I do believe I have
horribly mangled this story, and some of you will recognize it because it is based
on a true story. (I think the man was a professional counsellor and perhaps even
the woman's husband.) Nevertheless, the gist of the story is simply this: she did

something in her waking state that was empowering, and she was able to transfer this power into her dreams.

Of course, *this is a two-way street*! If you learn to empower yourself in your dreams, you can transfer this power, strength, and confidence into your waking state. Many books have been written about this. Carlos Castaneda explores this idea in his books *Journey to Ixtlan* and *Tales of Power*. (Those books I *did* read because they were required reading for any self-respecting hippie.)

Compassion

In the same way that you can use your Pisces strengths (the power of visualization and the power to dream), you also have enormous compassion to work with. You can use this quality to become happier! *(Quelle surprise.)*

How does this work? Actually, practising kindness and compassion is the quickest way to be happy! Nobody can doubt this. All great writings will attest to this. If you are having a bummer day, all you have to do is look for an opportunity to practise a kindness for somebody else. You might give them a gift. You might give them flowers, a compliment, a thank-you card. You might assist them in a task they have to do. You might run an errand for them. It can be very small, and in some cases it can be large.

The minute you start to help somebody else, I guarantee you'll feel better. There's a lot of reasons why this works, but one of the obvious reasons is that you immediately feel increased self-respect and self-love, which triggers a happier state of mind. In other words, you feel happier being in your own skin.

I recall reading a story in a newsletter by Dr. Ben Kim, a chiropractor I very much respect in Barrie, Ontario. You can go to his website and read the same story, which essentially describes a day when he got very frustrated dealing with a bank (now why would that ever happen?) and he became grouchy with himself and others. Later, when driving home, he realized his negative state of mind, and made a conscious decision to change it. He decided to do something nice for someone. He bought a card for a librarian who had done his son a favour. When he dropped the card off for this person, *he immediately felt happier*!

It's curious, because doing this is essentially selfish. You're trying to help yourself. You know that by helping someone else, you are going to feel better. *It's a selfish/wise approach to life.* It certainly doesn't lessen the goodness of the act, though, does it?

One extra tip here to really get some bang for your buck.

True generosity is giving what is needed.

If you want to get a quick booster charge of happiness right now, go to my website (www.georgianicols.com) and, for ten dollars, you can buy a mosquito net that will save the life of a child in Africa. Like, wow! These mosquito nets last for about three years. You'll probably save the lives of several children, and, at the same time, give enormous piece of mind to their mothers. Can you think of a better way to spend ten bucks?

And you'll love yourself for doing it.

"Compassion is the basis of all morality."
ARTHUR SCHOPENHAUER
German Philosopher
(FEBRUARY 22, 1788–SEPTEMBER 21, 1860)

"Only a life lived for others is worth living."
ALBERT EINSTEIN
Physicist, Philosopher, Author, and Winner of the Nobel Prize in Physics (1921)
(MARCH 4, 1879–APRIL 18, 1955)

PISCES
YOUR 40~YEAR HOROSCOPE
1985 ~ 2025

Why Go into the Past?

I want you to have faith in your predictions so you can derive benefit from them in guiding your future. The only way you can believe what I say is to test things for yourself. This is why I start with brief highlights from the past. If anything in your past resonates with you, then what I say about your future will have the same validity. It is all one long timeline — your life.

The past predictions generally apply only once you have left home or are "running your life" and making your own decisions. Prior to that, the major events in your life were dictated by other people, generally your parents.

1985 – 1990

This was a good time. The year 1985 was very much a year of preparation for 1986, when you somehow stepped out into the world, by graduating, getting a job, or getting recognition in some way for your achievements. That was the year Jupiter was in your sign, bringing you bonuses, popularity, and increased confidence. ("I love me!") However, many sudden changes were taking place that either threatened your stability or created greater freedom for you, or both. Very soon, you felt on top of your game, even though you had increased responsibilities. This was a time of hard work, but at least you got recognition for your accomplishments.

By 1989, real estate was blessed! Family relationships greatly improved, and, quite likely, something related to home and family expanded your view of the world. In fact, some of you literally expanded your family this year or the next through adoption, birth, or marriage.

Vacations, smoochy love affairs, exciting travel, and playful times with children brought a lovely boost to your life in 1990. Many of you encountered sizzling romance! You had lots of fun choices, especially related to sports, the arts, show business, the entertainment world, and even the hospitality industry. *It's fun to have fun!*

1991 ~ 1996

Finally, job opportunities were looking better! This was a good time to get a better job, or improve where you were working, or get out from under the clutches of an evil boss. However, other influences encouraged you to let go of things and to streamline your life. This is why many of you began to give up and say good-bye to people, places, and possessions. You were lightening your load as you prepared for 1994, which, without question, opened up a whole new world for you!

By that time, gifts, goodies, and the benefits of others were coming your way. In fact, 1993–94 was a great time for getting a mortgage or a loan or benefits from others such as inheritances, scholarships, and insurance monies. Soon afterwards, you wanted to hit the road and travel! This was also a great time for higher education and anything to do with the media, publishing, and the law.

Essentially, 1994 was a major turning point. You entered a completely new sandbox that ultimately changed your identity in the world. In fact, everything was so different, many of you even changed your daily wardrobe.

The year 1995 was particularly sweet because lucky moneybags Jupiter was sailing across the top of your chart, bringing you opportunities to promote your good name, which, of course, you did. Everybody thought *you were the cat's meow*.

1997 – 2000

Initially, this was a time of struggle for you, because important changes were taking place. Essentially, your life direction began to undergo a huge change. This change was very apparent to others as well, because they saw your image in the world changing as well.

Fortunately, 1998 was a sweet year! Lucky Jupiter was in your sign for the first time in twelve years. ("Bring it on!") This boosted your earnings by 1999, which, in turn, began to trigger job changes, residential moves, and lots of upheaval. You probably got rid of a lot of shoes and books then. "It all has to go! I'm starting over."

The turn of the millennium was a mixed bag. In one way, you were optimistic, excited, and very active. However, the instability of job changes and residential moves was nerve-racking. You're pretty good at being light on your feet, but eventually enough is enough!

2001 – 2005

Thank heavens, by 2001 you felt more settled where you lived. Some of you moved to larger digs, or bought a condo, apartment, or house. Without question, you developed a serious focus on your home scene during 2001–2. You wanted something you could rely on — something that gave you a warm feeling in your tummy. You needed to create a safe haven for yourself and your loved ones.

This was an enriching time for family relationships. In fact, many of you actually expanded your family through birth, adoption, or marriage in 2002–3. Opportunities abounded to enrich your world through real-estate purchases, family relationships, and renovations and changes that improved your home. By 2002, children became a strong focus. This was also a fabulous time to meet a new love. Romance, love affairs, vacations, sports, and playful times with children were all fun stuff.

Nevertheless, many of you were still focused on home repairs and working to fix up where you lived so that you had a solid anchor in the world.

Your health and job definitely improved in 2003. Lovely job opportunities came your way then. At the very least, you improved the way you did your job. By 2004, increased responsibilities with children were something you had to juggle. By now, you also had an increasing desire within you to gain greater independence. This is because Uranus, that wild, wacky planet that causes us to strike a blow for freedom, was *now in your sign*. Uh-oh, look out world!

Partnerships were warm and supportive in 2004–5. Later, in 2005–6, you benefitted from the wealth of others through inheritances, gifts, goodies, or indirectly through your partner. This was also a good time to go for a mortgage or get a loan.

2006 – 2009

Travel looked sweet in 2006! (I hope you managed to get away then.) This was also a great year for higher education, universities, and colleges. Ditto for publishing and the media. You had many opportunities to broaden your horizons and increase your experience of life. However, work was still hard. Many of you were virtually in the salt mines at this time. But, in 2007, when lucky Jupiter started to cross the top of your chart, bringing you all kinds of opportunities plus increased recognition from others, you didn't care! Life was suddenly promising! This was also a good time to get your name up in lights. People *noticed* you in a positive way.

By 2008, relationships and partnerships were in the toilet. This was a challenging time because stern Saturn now opposed you. In fact, life was challenging, discouraging, and a real test for you. (I hate tests!) Fortunately, your friends were there to support you and your popularity was strong. (*"I am loved!"*)

2010 – 2012

This continues to be a pivotal time with respect to relationships. Let's just say, most of them are in the toilet or on the rim of the bowl. *It's a challenging time for partnerships and close friendships.* But it's a mixed bag. All is not lost, because lucky Jupiter is in your sign this year for the first time since 1998. (Thank gawd.) You could say this is a time of mixed blessings. Jupiter will increase your self-confidence and poise. (You'll notice this by 2011, and so will others.)

Another aspect of the mixed bag is that one of the reasons you're having difficulty with committed relationships and partnerships is that you are getting stronger. *You are taking your powah!* This upsets the status quo of existing partnerships. In the past year or so, you were no longer willing to take a back seat to certain situations. Ever since 1994, you've been redefining who you were in the world, and, since 2001, your drive and motivation to discover what you can do have been growing. Now you're finally looking over the fence and seeing what is possible. Hey, it's a big world out there!

As your ambition and hopes for your future grow, you're changing the rules in your closest relationships. This is one of the reasons you're undergoing stress and tension with others.

Fortunately, by 2011, you can earn more money. How sweet it is! It's a good thing too, because the practical support from others — partners, rent support, scholarships, bursaries, assistance — will diminish or disappear. Fear not; this actually *strengthens you*. It makes you realize that you can stand on your own two feet. (Especially if they're well shod. Puh-leeze! Are those Christian Louboutins?)

Naturally, all this leads to an increased positive and more joyful attitude in 2011–12. Short trips are fun. Relations with siblings improve beautifully. There's a light at the end of the tunnel — *and it's not a train!*

2013 ~ 2015

This is a fabulous year for real estate! If you buy, sell, or speculate in real estate you will gain a profit in the future. (Please note that this is your best shot at real-estate deals in twelve years.) In fact, anything to do with home, family, and your domestic life can get a lovely positive boost this year.

You will definitely do something to increase the value of where you live or expand where you live. You might move to bigger digs. You might buy something for your home that makes you feel richer. This positive domestic vibe will also improve family relationships. In fact, there's a good chance that your family will expand this year or in 2014 through marriage, birth, or adoption.

Plan on a fun vacation during 2014. Yippee! Get serious about this, because this is your year to kick up your heels and have a great time. (Bermuda is a wonderful place for Pisces.) The arts, the entertainment world, show business, and even the hospitality industry are beautifully favoured this year as well. Romance, love affairs, and new romantic encounters will be thrilling. Some of you will meet the love of your life. Buff your bod. Make sure you love how you look this year. ("My bathroom mirror is covered in kisses!")

Children can also be a source of joy for you this year. On top of all this, it's a fabulous year for sports. *Looking swell!*

One of the reasons you're celebrating and feeling so joyful about life is that, finally, you now see some important goals. They are still beyond your grasp, but at least you can see what you want to go for, and this energizes you tremendously. Small wonder that in 2015 you have many opportunities to *improve your job*. You might get a better job, or better working conditions, or a better boss. Or all of the above! ("I've got hotels on Broadway and Park Place.")

Your health improves nicely this year as well, except do guard against overdoing it partying, drinking, and eating sweets and desserts. (A minute on the lips is a decade on the hips.)

2016 ~ 2017

Now we approach a wonderful turning point in your life. In fact, two major celestial events are taking place that make you the big winner! For starters, relationships are improving this year in a fabulous way. (About time!) Perhaps the recent romance you encountered is now settling into a serious commitment. Existing partnerships will certainly improve as well. It's as if you're starting to appreciate that a successful relationship means you have to be as good for your partner as he or she is for you.

This is an excellent year to not only improve existing partnerships but also to enter into new ones, both intimate and professional.

The reason this year is a big turning point, however, is because finally you will start to get the recognition you deserve. *It is your time of harvest!* You are entering a five- to seven-year window when you are really on top of your game. Something will happen that makes you feel proud. Naturally, this will depend on where you are in your life and your career path, and how old you are. It might mean that you graduate, and you feel very proud about this. It could mean a first job that is stellar in your eyes. It could mean a promotion, or your first chance to be self-employed. And, for some, it will be a political win, or a major promotion, or an ultimate career peak. It depends. What is certain is that you are on a roll! ("Look, Ma, no hands!")

At this stage (2017–18) you also stand to benefit from the wealth of others. Many of you will receive inheritances, money back from the government or insurance payouts, or you will benefit indirectly through partners who get bonuses and increased wealth. Naturally, this is the perfect time to ask for a loan or to get a mortgage. The universe is pouring gravy in your direction. (We like!)

2018 – 2020

The year 2018 is wonderful for travel, especially long-distance travel to foreign countries. It's also a great year for anything to do with publishing, medicine, the law, or dealing and working with the media. Higher education is also beautifully blessed, so this is a great time to go back to school or to get a job working at a college or university.

Romance with someone from a different background, or another culture, or a different country, is also very likely. (What a fun way to learn a new language.)

By 2019, you're laughing! Lucky moneybags Jupiter is sailing across the top of your chart for the first time since 2007. However, this time you are in a far better position to exploit this boost to your reputation. You have more confidence and more influence, and you're probably in a much better job. Make the most of this time! Whenever Jupiter is at the top of your chart (once every twelve years), the public perception is that you are enjoying success. (Nothing succeeds like the appearance of success!)

At this time, you can definitely expect a promotion at work, and certainly recognition for things you've accomplished. You will have increased respect and esteem from your peers. You'll feel more confident. Many of you will have work-related travel opportunities. Some, however, will use this so-called good-luck time to change fields to something related to medicine, healing, the law, higher education, or publishing. If this latter shift occurs, you will likely not get a promotion. Instead, you have the opportunity to switch to a field you want to explore.

In 2020, your accomplishments push you into the limelight to the extent that you are more popular than usual. In fact, this popularity could be a bit of a problem. Suddenly, you feel demands being made on you from every direction, which is overwhelming. Now your challenge is to protect your own interests and yet, at the same time, satisfy the demands of others. You want to keep everyone happy, but you also have to respect your own integrity, your own independence, and your right to do your own thing! *You can't let others own you.*

2021 – 2022

This is a pivotal time. You're slipping into an entirely new phase in your life. Essentially, on one hand, you're beginning a new twelve-year cycle when you will learn many things, not the least of which will be discovering who you really are as an individual. *This is a fortunate time for you.* VIPs and people who have power and influence are attracted to you. Your casual relationships are fun, and yet somehow more meaningful. You feel lucky, successful, and grateful to be who you are.

Meanwhile, in another part of the forest, something entirely different is taking place! While all this good stuff is going on, another part of you is going through cupboards, garages, closets, attics, and storage spaces, cleaning out what you think you no longer need. You're on a serious kick to streamline your life.

In fact, over the next few years, you will start to get rid of whatever is no longer relevant in your life. Excess baggage will go! This will include jobs, places where you live, and, certainly, relationships. What's happening is that, between 2021 and 2024, you are going to divest yourself of anything that is holding you back from entering a whole new world in 2024.

This is a huge turning point! The last time anything like this happened was around 1994. Fortunately, while you undergo this, good fortune comes to you in 2021, and by 2022–23 you are earning more money! (Whew!) Perhaps the pull of increased earnings is one of the reasons some of you are moving?

In the bigger picture, however, 2023 is when you begin a journey wherein you will *completely reinvent yourself*. This process will probably take about seven years. At the end of that time, you will look back at this time and say, "Wow! Has my life ever changed! (And I weigh more, too.)"

2023 ~ 2025

This is the beginning of the new thirty-year journey that I just mentioned. You're setting off on a new path by taking a new job, or quitting a job, or teaming up with someone, or moving to an entirely new area, or having children, or saying goodbye to children who leave home — it's one of those major, pivotal times in your life.

Fortunately, while this is happening, lucky Jupiter is going through the part of your chart that affects your thinking and your everyday activities. This makes you enthusiastic, optimistic, and excited about life on an everyday basis. It boosts relationships with relatives and siblings. It also increases your opportunities in reading, writing, and studying. The year 2023 is a great time for writers, teachers, and actors.

In large measure, one of the reasons you are so excited about life is that you know *you're at the threshold of something completely new*. You're entering a whole new sandbox, which is so different that you will even change your daily wardrobe. Cool! What better excuse to buy new clothes and new shoes, and cultivate a new image? (You're so good at this.)

"I like nonsense — it wakes up the brain cells. Fantasy is a necessary ingredient in living. It's a way of looking at life through the wrong end of a telescope . . . and that enables you to laugh at all of life's realities."
DR. SEUSS (PEN NAME OF THEODOR SEUSS GEISEL)
American Children's Author and Illustrator
Green Eggs and Ham, The Cat in the Hat,
and *How the Grinch Stole Christmas*
(MARCH 2, 1904–SEPTEMBER 24, 1991)

Famous Pisces Personalities

Smokey Robinson	February 19, 1940
Karen Silkwood	February 19, 1946–1974
Amy Tan	February 19, 1952
Andrew, Duke of York	February 19, 1960
Seal Samuel	February 19, 1963
Justine Bateman	February 19, 1966
Benicio del Toro	February 19, 1967
Robert Altman	February 20, 1925–2006
Sidney Poitier	February 20, 1927
Buffy Sainte-Marie	February 20, 1941
Phil Esposito	February 20, 1942
Ivana Trump	February 20, 1949
Kenn Nesbitt	February 20, 1962
Cindy Crawford	February 20, 1966
Rachel Griffiths	February 20, 1968
Rihanna	February 20, 1988
Andrés Segovia	February 21, 1893–1987
Anaïs Nin	February 21, 1903–1977
Tyne Daly	February 21, 1946
Alan Rickman	February 21, 1946
Jennifer Love Hewitt	February 21, 1979
Ellen Page	February 21, 1987
Robert Baden-Powell	February 22, 1857–1941
Edward Kennedy	February 22, 1932–2009
Steve Irwin	February 22, 1962–2006
Jeri Ryan	February 22, 1968
Clinton Kelly	February 22, 1969
Drew Barrymore	February 22, 1975
Samuel Pepys	February 23, 1633–1703
Majel Barrett-Roddenberry	February 23, 1932–2008
Marc Garneau	February 23, 1949
Patricia Richardson	February 23, 1951
Kristin Davis	February 23, 1965
Emily Blunt	February 23, 1983
Dakota Fanning	February 23, 1994

Barry Bostwick	February 24, 1945
George Thorogood	February 24, 1950
Jane Hirshfield	February 24, 1953
Steve Jobs	February 24, 1955
Paula Zahn	February 24, 1956
Michelle Shocked	February 24, 1962
Billy Zane	February 24, 1966
Ashley MacIsaac	February 24, 1975
Pierre-Auguste Renoir	February 25, 1841–1919
Enrico Caruso	February 25, 1873–1921
Adelle Davis	February 25, 1904–1974
Anthony Burgess	February 25, 1917–1993
George Harrison	February 25, 1943–2001
Téa Leoni	February 25, 1966
David Powter	February 25, 1971
Victor Hugo	February 26, 1802–1885
Jackie Gleason	February 26, 1916–1987
Tony Randall	February 26, 1920–2004
Fats Domino	February 26, 1928
Johnny Cash	February 26, 1932–2003
Elizabeth George	February 26, 1949
Michael Bolton	February 26, 1953
Corinne Bailey Rae	February 26, 1979
Henry Wadsworth Longfellow	February 27, 1807–1882
John Steinbeck	February 27, 1902–1968
Lawrence Durrell	February 27, 1912–1990
Joanne Woodward	February 27, 1930
Elizabeth Taylor	February 27, 1932
Ralph Nader	February 27, 1934
Josh Groban	February 27, 1981
Linus Pauling	February 28, 1901–1994
Frank Gehry	February 28, 1929
Mario Andretti	February 28, 1940
Bernadette Peters	February 28, 1948
John Turturro	February 28, 1957
Daniel Handler (Lemony Snicket)	February 28, 1970
Eric Lindros	February 28, 1973
Dinah Shore	February 29, 1916–1994
Henri Richard	February 29, 1936
Dennis Farina	February 29, 1944
Tony Robbins	February 29, 1960
Antonio Sabàto, Jr.	February 29, 1972

David Niven	March 1, 1910–1983
Harry Belafonte	March 1, 1927
Roger Daltrey	March 1, 1944
Ron Howard	March 1, 1954
Javier Bardem	March 1, 1969
Ana Hickmann	March 1, 1981
Dr. Seuss	March 2, 1904–1991
Desi Arnaz	March 2, 1917–1986
Tom Wolfe	March 2, 1931
John Irving	March 2, 1942
Jon Bon Jovi	March 2, 1962
Daniel Craig	March 2, 1968
Madeleine de Verchères	March 3, 1678–1747
Alexander Graham Bell	March 3, 1847–1922
Norman Bethune	March 3, 1890–1939
Jean Harlow	March 3, 1911–1937
Tyler Florence	March 3, 1971
Jessica Biel	March 3, 1982
Charles Goren	March 4, 1901–1991
Miriam Makeba	March 4, 1932–2008
Richard B. Wright	March 4, 1937
Catherine O'Hara	March 4, 1954
Patricia Heaton	March 4, 1958
Chaz Bono	March 4, 1969
Rex Harrison	March 5, 1908–1990
Dean Stockwell	March 5, 1936
Mike Resnick	March 5, 1942
Penn Jillette	March 5, 1955
Eva Mendes	March 5, 1974
Niki Taylor	March 5, 1975
Elizabeth Barrett Browning	March 6, 1806–1861
Alan Greenspan	March 6, 1926
Gabriel García Márquez	March 6, 1927
David Gilmour	March 6, 1946
Rob Reiner	March 6, 1947
Moira Kelly	March 6, 1968
Piet Mondrian	March 7, 1872–1944
Maurice Ravel	March 7, 1875–1937
Ivan Lendl	March 7, 1960
Wanda Sykes	March 7, 1964
Rachel Weisz	March 7, 1970
Jenna Fischer	March 7, 1974

Anne Bonny	March 8, 1702–1782
Oliver Wendell Holmes	March 8, 1841–1935
Cyd Charisse	March 8, 1922–2008
Lynn Redgrave	March 8, 1943–2010
Richard Ouzounian	March 8, 1950
Camryn Manheim	March 8, 1961
Mickey Spillane	March 9, 1918–2006
Yuri Gagarin	March 9, 1934–1968
Raúl Juliá	March 9, 1940–1994
Juliette Binoche	March 9, 1964
Ben Mulroney	March 9, 1976
Matthew Gray Gubler	March 9, 1980
E. Pauline Johnson	March 10, 1861–1913
Chuck Norris	March 10, 1940
Kim Campbell	March 10, 1947
Sharon Stone	March 10, 1958
Edward, Earl of Wessex	March 10, 1964
Carrie Underwood	March 10, 1983
Lawrence Welk	March 11, 1903–1992
Rupert Murdoch	March 11, 1931
Sam Donaldson	March 11, 1934
Douglas Adams	March 11, 1952–2001
Didier Drogba	March 11, 1978
Christopher Rice	March 11, 1978
Thora Birch	March 11, 1982
Irving Layton	March 12, 1912–2006
Jack Kerouac	March 12, 1922–1969
Liza Minnelli	March 12, 1946
James Taylor	March 12, 1948
Aaron Eckhart	March 12, 1968
W. O. Mitchell	March 13, 1914–1998
Neil Sedaka	March 13, 1939
Dana Delany	March 13, 1956
Annabeth Gish	March 13, 1971
Danny Masterson	March 13, 1976
Emile Hirsch	March 13, 1985
Albert Einstein	March 14, 1879–1955
Michael Caine	March 14, 1933
Quincy Jones	March 14, 1933
Michael Martin Murphey	March 14, 1945
Billy Crystal	March 14, 1948
Megan Follows	March 14, 1968

Punch Imlach	March 15, 1918–1987
Judd Hirsch	March 15, 1935
David Cronenberg	March 15, 1943
Ry Cooder	March 15, 1947
Eva Longoria	March 15, 1975
Jerry Lewis	March 16, 1926
Margaret Weis	March 16, 1948
Kate Nelligan	March 16, 1951
Duane Sutter	March 16, 1960
Lauren Graham	March 16, 1967
Sienna Guillory	March 16, 1975
Nat King Cole	March 17, 1919–1965
Rudolf Nureyev	March 17, 1938–1993
William Gibson	March 17, 1948
Daniel Lavoie	March 17, 1949
Kurt Russell	March 17, 1951
Gary Sinise	March 17, 1955
Rob Lowe	March 17, 1964
Mia Hamm	March 17, 1972
Peter Graves	March 18, 1926–2010
John Updike	March 18, 1932–2009
Wilson Pickett	March 18, 1941–2006
Joy Fielding	March 18, 1945
Ben Cohen	March 18, 1951
Vanessa L. Williams	March 18, 1963
Queen Latifah	March 18, 1970
Philip Roth	March 19, 1933
Ursula Andress	March 19, 1936
Glenn Close	March 19, 1947
Jeanne Beker	March 19, 1952
Bruce Willis	March 19, 1955
Rachel Blanchard	March 19, 1976
Carl Reiner	March 20, 1922
Fred Rogers	March 20, 1928–2003
Jay Ingram	March 20, 1945
Bobby Orr	March 20, 1948
William Hurt	March 20, 1950
Spike Lee	March 20, 1957
Holly Hunter	March 20, 1958

Acknowledgements

After twenty years of writing newspaper and magazine columns, I have finally written a book. So there is no question in my mind that my first acknowledgement is to you — my loyal readers. I love you all. Your positive feedback and loving responses have inspired and encouraged me all these years and have been a touchstone for me. I was always flattered and delighted (and amazed) to get inquiries from all over the world asking where to find my books. (Plural, no less!) This motivated me to finally write this book and so — thank you, thank you, thank you.

The next acknowledgement of gratitude is to my son, Scott Benson, who opened my eyes to the possibility of writing a daily horoscope in the first place. (I initially rejected this offer when I was first approached with the idea.) Scott has been, and continues to be, a source of wisdom and guidance in my life. (I know he is modestly shaking his head.)

Rae Bilash, Malcolm and Heather Kirk, Coralie Mackie, Michael Cooke, Vivienne Sosnowski, Rita Silvan, and others too numerous to mention were instrumental in making my daily and weekly columns a reality for everyone. (A special nod to Diane Smith and Glen Mott.) Thank you, all.

Aside from letters to newspapers, the main way I hear from my readers is through my website, which has been made possible by my genius geek nephew, Graham Ter-Marsch. "Gooch" (as I call him) has donated his time and expertise generously for years to make it possible for you, the reader, to read my work online, and, in turn, for me to communicate with you. In addition, his efforts have raised much-needed money for a Tibetan school in Nepal.

On that note, I thank Beverly Wood (promoter par excellence) for suggesting this website in the first place, and also for her swift and clever assistance in promoting this book. Thank you, Bev!

Without question, this book got off the ground with the generous encouragement of Margaret Atwood and, shortly thereafter, my agent, Rick Broadhead. This was the nuts and bolts of the beginning of this adventure. It would not have happened *now* without Margaret.

Right from the start, always cheering from the stands, Tricia Barker increased my confidence in what I was doing. This was invaluable to someone who needs daily flattery. When I really needed "help!" (surely every writer has moments of panic, discouragement, or both), Renee Doruyter, who for years edited my copy at the *Vancouver Province*, gave me enormous, generous, practical support. She saved me when I needed it.

My sister Bette Kosmolak (and mother of genius geek "Gooch") never hesitated to offer her research skills, for which I am grateful. Thank you also to Linda Davis for her ongoing research assistance.

I cannot imagine working in an environment without support and love. My mother, Eileen, always encouraged me to write this book ("It will walk right off the shelves!"). Her enthusiasm was warmly echoed by her sister Betty (my favourite aunt). I am also grateful to my ever-supportive daughter, Kelly Verchere, and her two wonderful sons, Chase and Emmett, who have been a precious source of joy to me. Kelly is the only one in the family with whom I can really "talk astrology."

Every book is also a major production, and for this seamless process I thank House of Anansi Press, and in particular, the always cheerful, encouraging support of Janie Yoon, who was extremely helpful and who also had the daunting task of dealing with a Leo diva!

You and Your Future is the end result of many experiences I have had and people I have met. I have been lucky enough to hear many great teachers, and their influence is, both indirectly and directly, on these pages. Good friends and casual acquaintances have also contributed to this process. My sincere apologies to names not mentioned who should be here.

Once again, to my most devoted fan, Pat, thank you for patiently helping me in every way possible. You understood, you believed, and you cared.

About the Author

Author photograph: Bayne Stanley

GEORGIA NICOLS is Canada's most popular astrologer. Her wisdom and wit have made her an international columnist, and her horoscopes appear in the *National Post, Vancouver Province, Calgary Herald, Winnipeg Free Press, Chicago Sun-Times, Press Democratic* (California), and *China Daily* (Beijing). She is a regular columnist for *Elle Canada, San Francisco Examiner, Washington Examiner* (D.C.), and *The Examiner* (Baltimore), among others. She makes regular appearances on television and radio, and has a popular web site, www.georgianicols.com, which has more than a million annual readers. Born in Winnipeg, Manitoba, she lives in Vancouver, British Columbia.